"Since the invasion in 2003, Reidar Visser's stature as one of the world's leading experts on Iraq has continued to grow. Visser's reputation is based on his superb language skills, a historian's commitment to detail and accuracy and a powerful ability to subject the day-to-day politics of Iraq to precise analysis based on many years of expert knowledge.

"Visser has shared his expertise through his copious writings and detailed blogs. These have now been gathered together for the first time in one book, *A Responsible End? The United States and the Iraqi Transition, 2005-2010*. This book provides an invaluable resource for anyone seeking to understand Iraqi politics from 2005 to the present. Visser examines the major events shaping post-invasion Iraqi politics, explaining their significance in a clear and very readable way. The result is a book that should be required reading for anyone seeking to understand the terrible costs of regime change in Iraq and what the future holds for that country beyond occupation and civil war."

—TOBY DODGE
International Institute for Strategic Studies

"Visser offers a trenchant critique of US entanglement in Iraq and points to avenues of positive engagement on the part of the international community… His analysis of the promise and pitfalls of federalism is the best I have read."

—DINA RIZK KHOURY
George Washington University

Just World Books
"Timely Books for Changing Times"

This title, like most of our titles, is being published first in paperback, and will later be released as a hardcover, in two or more e-book versions, and in several overseas editions.

Please check our website for updates on the publishing plans and to buy the books:

 www.justworldbooks.com

Our fall 2010 schedule includes initial publication of the following additional titles:

America's Misadventures in the Middle East
Chas W. Freeman Jr.
(October 2010)

Afghanistan Journal: Selections from Registan.net
Joshua Foust
(November 2010)

Gaza Mom: Palestine, Politics, Parenting, and Everything In Between
Laila El-Haddad
(November 2010)

JUST WORLD BOOKS
In early 2011, we will publish titles on Pakistan (by Manan Ahmed); on food policy, especially in the Middle East (by Rami Zurayk); on China (by Chas W. Freeman Jr.); on issues in Christian nonviolence (by Ron Mock)—as well as a family memoir by the Israeli peace activist Miko Peled and an atlas of the Palestine Question.
Visit the website for more news and to sign up for updates.
Also, follow us on Facebook and Twitter.
www.justworldbooks.com

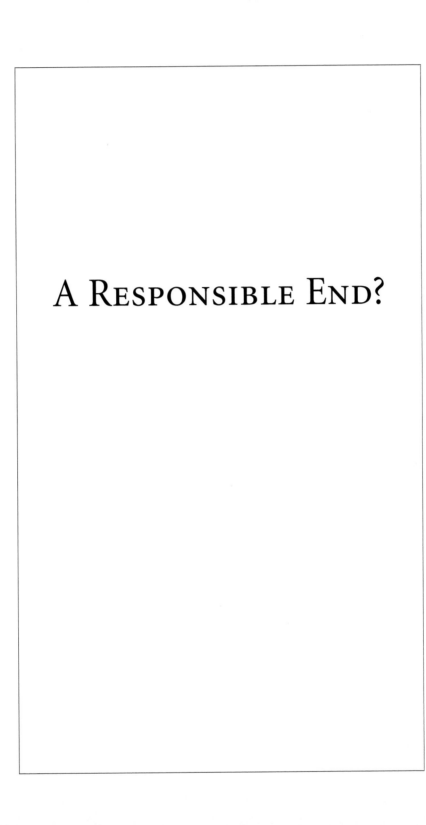

A RESPONSIBLE END?

Other books by
Reidar Visser

Basra, the Failed Gulf State:
Separatism and Nationalism in Southern Iraq
 (2005)

An Iraq of Its Regions: Cornerstones of a Federal Democracy?
(co-edited with Gareth Stansfield, 2007)

A Responsible End?

The United States and the Iraqi Transition, 2005–2010

Reidar Visser

JUST WORLD
PUBLISHING LLC

CHARLOTTESVILLE, VIRGINIA

**Publisher's Cataloging-in-Publication
(Provided by Quality Books, Inc.)**

Visser, Reidar.
    A responsible end? : the United States and the Iraqi
transition, 2005-2010 / Reidar Visser.
    p. cm.
    Includes bibliographical references.
    LCCN 2010937127
    ISBN-13: 978-1-935982-03-6
    ISBN-10: 1-935982-03-6

    1. Postwar reconstruction--Iraq. 2. Iraq--History--
2003- 3. Iraq--Politics and government--2003- 4. Iraq
--Foreign relations--United States. 5. United States--
Foreign relations--Iraq. I. Title.

DS79.769.V57 2010   956.7044'31
                    QBI10-600210

This book is dedicated to Tim Berners-Lee,
inventor of the World Wide Web.

Contents

Preface

"As a candidate for president, I pledged to bring the war in Iraq to a responsible end," President Barack Obama told a gathering of U.S. Army veterans on August 2, 2010. He went on to cite what he saw as the achievements of the U.S. military in Iraq since the beginning of the Iraq War in 2003: "When terrorists and militias plunged Iraq into sectarian war, our troops adapted and adjusted—restoring order and effectively defeating al Qaeda in Iraq on the battlefield." It was a simple but compelling narrative: U.S. soldiers came, fought, and went home after having completed their mission.

This book features a radically different interpretation of recent Iraqi history. Some progress did indeed take place in Iraq after 2003, but it was fragile, developed largely independently of or even despite the policies of the Bush administration, and was finally reversed again on the watch of the Obama administration. When the U.S. combat mission ended on August 31, 2010, Iraq seemed more internally divided, ungovernable and prone to regional influences than at any point since the end of the Gulf War in 1991. Today, it looks as if a miracle is needed for the next Iraqi government to be strong and capable of satisfying the needs of its citizens instead of catering for its own narrow interests and those of predatory neighboring states.

While agreeing with the overall direction toward the complete disengagement of U.S. military forces in Iraq, the narrative in this book focuses on weaknesses in the story of an American triumph in Iraq in the period covered, from the adoption of the Iraqi constitution in 2005 to the end of the first elected parliament in 2010. Many of those weaknesses are quite easy to identify, such as the obvious survival of elements capable of staging spectacular and lethal terrorist attacks and the steadily growing influence of neighboring states and Iran in particular. But the greatest flaw of them all is one which has so far failed to receive attention: the U.S. failure to exploit a real window of hopefulness in Iraq between July 2008 and January 2010, thanks above all to the combined illiteracy of the Bush and Obama administrations in terms of reading and analyzing domestic Iraqi politics. In that critical period, there were in fact tendencies in Iraqi politics supportive of the process of democratization outlined in the constitution adopted in 2005, where the first parliamentary cycle from 2005 to 2010 period is defined as a "transitional" period featuring certain temporary power-sharing arrangements that were supposed to come to an end in 2010 with the emergence of a strong, nationally oriented prime minister. But even though Prime Minister Nuri al-Maliki in 2009 seemed eager to follow the constitutional path of moving from ethno-sectarian power-sharing to an issue-based government of a "political majority", the United States generally discouraged such steps and instead, directly and indirectly, sought a perpetuation of the Lebanon-like power-sharing arrangements that were supposed to be transitional only. The transition period did come to a formal end on November 11, 2010, when the election of Jalal Talabani as president signaled the demise of the transitional and powerful tripartite presidency council. But the ambiguous political deal that accompanied that event introduced new, ill-defined power-sharing elements into the mix, including—with U.S. backing—the creation of a national council for strategic policies for which there was no provision at all in the Iraqi constitution.

Let me highlight some of the crossroads at which Washington could have acted differently. Of course some of the gravest U.S. mistakes in Iraq actually stem from the fateful decision to go to war and the early days of the wartime administration of Iraq, during the Coalition Provisional Authority. In particular, the attempt by Paul Bremer to enshrine ethno-sectarian identities in the governing structure of the Iraqi state through the creation of the so-called governing council back in 2003 set the tone for the politics and the constitutional regime that emerged during the two first years of the occupation: The subnational identities (or "subidentities") of the Iraqis were given greater weight than their shared sense of being a nation. Direct American input was probably greater in the Transitional Administrative Law of 2004 than in the constitution adopted in 2005, but the point is that the subidentity spokesmen that created these documents—primarily the Kurds as well as the most pro-Iranian of the many Shiite parties, the Supreme Council for the Islamic Revolution in Iraq (SCIRI, later known as the Islamic Supreme Council for Iraq, ISCI)—had been systematically empowered by the Americans ever since 2003.

Once the constitution with its excessive concessions to the centrifugal forces in Iraqi politics had been adopted in a confused referendum in October 2005 where few Iraqis knew what they were voting for, the key mistake of the Bush administration between 2005 and 2008 was to continue to back up these elites and spin them as "moderates"—when in fact much of the progressive input in the period, including the demand for fresh local elections and a revision of the constitution that would bring back the center, actually came from the opposition. Crucially, when Prime Minister Nuri al-Maliki finally discovered this and turned nationalist in late 2008 and early 2009, the last remaining officials of the Bush administration in Baghdad still remained more focused on supporting their old "moderate" partners among the Kurds and ISCI against Maliki, who was now all of a sudden seen as too strong and nationalist—incidentally a view also shared by Iran at the time. Key junctures at which different signals from Washington could have produced a different climate for the 2010 parliamentary elections included the election of a new parliamentary speaker in April 2009 (Washington lobbied heavily in favor of the candidate supported by the Kurds and ISCI), the debate on the elections law in the autumn of 2009 (the new Obama administration insisted that the Kirkuk issue be kept off the table in a context where its inclusion might in fact have helped produce an alliance between Maliki and some of the secular and Sunni forces), and finally the de-Baathification debacle in early 2010 (where a clearer U.S. response might have prevented the situation from escalating to the point where the tone of the election became a lot more sectarian than it had been during the local elections just a year earlier.)

Even in those areas where a certain degree of U.S. leverage survived after the drawdown to 50,000 troops on August 31, 2010—forming the new government, plus settling issues between the central government and the Kurds, as well as between Iraq and Kuwait—one could get the impression that Washington did not quite know how to exploit it or what sort of end scenario constituted a reasonable goal. For example, instead of encouraging the formation of a small, governance-oriented cabinet based on the two biggest winning lists emerging from the March 7, 2010, parliamentary elections, Washington seemed to insist on the inclusion of at least the four biggest entities, thereby discouraging the Iraqis from seeking simpler and arguably more viable non-sectarian solutions. In fact, the four-party formula is precisely the Shiite-dominated solution for Iraq that Tehran has pursued ever since 2003; as such it highlights the empowerment of Iran in post-2003 Iraq at the expense of more indigenous forces and casts considerable doubt on the degree of "responsibility" in the Obama administration's end game in Iraq. Iran can live with any Iraqi government that is either defined by a dominant Shiite coalition or weakened by convoluted ethno-sectarian power-sharing arrangements; the U.S. government has encouraged both.

Ultimately, then, counterfactual musings about what the U.S. could have done differently seem somewhat futile because the analytical problems involved in U.S. policy are so deep. The Bush administration seemed to believe in Iraqi national-ism, but did not possess the skills to figure out which forces in Iraqi politics would be most likely to restore a strong government in Baghdad—and were apparently also always distracted by wild ideas of a second war with Iran that could correct policy contradictions in Iraq. The Obama administration, for its part, did not really seem to believe in Iraqi nationalism and rarely moved beyond the outdated cliché of an Iraq subdivided into Sunnis, Shiites and Kurds. Different arms of the U.S. bureaucracy and military, in turn, created variations on this theme: The Democratic skepticism towards Iraqi nationalism and the concomitant predilec-tion for Kurds, minorities and détente with Iran could be seen among some in the State Department already under Bush; conversely, in the military, a genuine belief in the possibility of an Iraqi nation seemed to survive even under Obama and Biden, even it was often confused with unrealistic ideas about an assumed Iraqi desire for continued U.S. military assistance well into the 2020s. However, what all of these representatives of the U.S. government continued to do irrespective of their political views was to support the centrifugal forces in Iraqi society instead of the centripetal ones, by glorifying such politicians as Masud Barzani, Ammar al-Hakim and Ayad al-Samarraie.

How can I make such sweeping claims about supposed American incompetence? Two reasons stand out to me as plausible explanations of why the account of developments in Iraq that follows should differ so significantly with the official U.S. government version. Firstly, I take a longer view of the situation in Iraq. Unlike many of those who have studied Iraq mainly since the beginning of the Iraq War in 2003, I have worked with Iraqi politics on a daily basis since the early 1990s and have also done historical studies reaching back to periods of Iraqi history that were characterized by relatively peaceful conditions and coexistence—like the monarchy and even the late Ottoman period. Above all, I think that kind of bird's eye perspective may provide a better basis for assessing the relative weight of internal and external forces and thereby differentiating between ephemeral phenomena and long-term drivers in the chaos that is post-2003 Iraq. What, for example, is really the historical basis of the "natural role of Iran in Iraq" that so many Americans keep talking about? Second, for the past five years I have had the privilege of interacting with numerous U.S. officials and Iraq experts without having to share the burden of creating U.S. policy. I think this may provide a good vantage point for appreciating the surprising amount of "analysis" that actually has as its main purpose to serve as political spin as events in Iraq unfold largely outside the control of the American forces and diplomats there.

What follows are mostly blog posts from the period from 2005 to 2010. My blogging career started rather abruptly in 2005 when in order to get my first Iraq book onto the market in a timely fashion I opted to place it with a small German publisher and soon realized I needed some extra public-relations effort. I created a small website with a focus on my main research interests—in particular the politics of Basra and southern Iraq, as well as the broader debate relating to state structure and constitutional issues in post-2003 Iraq (www.historiae.org). I also added a subscription feature that enabled readers to sign up for email alerts whenever I uploaded new articles to the site, which for the first three years was no more than once a month. The response was beyond my wildest expectations, thanks not least to the intense interest in Iraq issues at the time. With the kind help of other, more established bloggers who generously linked to and discussed my pieces at their own sites, the number of subscribers grew exponentially until it hit the 3,000 mark in 2010, with website statistics consistently showing visitors from the United States, the United Kingdom, and Iraq at the top of the list. In August 2009, with the revived interest in Iraq because of the upcoming 2010 parliamentary elections, I also launched a parallel blog with interactive features and shorter pieces (gulfanalysis.wordpress.com).

In many ways, academic blogging has been a positive experience. Not least, the internet has removed barriers that used to be there in terms of getting a point of view across, especially for a semi-introvert researcher who preferred to spend as much time as possible delving into obscure mysteries such as those of the Shaykhi and Akhbari Shiite sub-sects of Basra and their regional entanglements. Quite soon, I realized that my subscribers included numerous members of policymaking communities devoted to Iraq issues in Washington as well as in many European capitals. Thanks to the internet, after having been a completely unknown researcher based in the sub-Arctic European periphery in 2005, over the next five years I became sufficiently established in the field to get invited to Iraq conferences across the globe, including some 35 trips to the United States—mostly to Washington, including four consecutive appearances at the biggest inter-departmental annual conference for government Iraq experts. I had always been rather sharp in my criticism of Joe Biden's Iraq policies and had thought those visits would come to an abrupt end when the Obama administration assumed power in 2009, but if anything interest actually grew stronger during the run-up to Iraq's March 7, 2010, parliamentary elections and the de-Baathification controversy on the eve of the polls. The international media, too, discovered my website, generating interviews with publications I had never dreamt of talking to, like *The New York Times, The Washington Post,* and *The Wall Street Journal.* It was a far cry from the situation ahead of the Iraq War in 2003 when no one had the slightest idea that I was working on Iraq and all my angry letters to the editors of various British newspapers protesting the war had been summarily rejected. (I had naively assumed the UK parliament was the last institution with a degree of power in the Western world where reason might still prevail). Today, cyberspace makes it possible to reach a global, exclusive and Iraq-interested audience at the touch of a button.

And yet on the other hand, with this very modest success in terms of an increased readership in mind, I think it is equally important to reflect on the limits of the experience of academic blogging, not least in terms of actual influence and ability to change anything. It is easy to become Google-centric and lull oneself into the belief that everything that appears on a website is actually being read. Not only that; perhaps even more sobering is the realization that some of the people who may be most complimentary in their comments have not always really understood the intended message. Or they may show a great interest in the empirical detail (after all, few others wrote in English about such themes as the sub-divisions of the Tanzim al-Iraq branch of the Daawa party) and yet still end up dismissing the overall conclusions. For example, I would frequently get invited to prestigious events because of my blogging, where a central theme was my challenge to the standard Western narrative of Iraqi politics in which everything is supposedly about ethno-religious groups vying for power (Sunnis versus Shiites versus Kurds and so forth, on which much more follows in chapter 1). And yet at the end of the day, I would often still get questions from these highbrow audiences about what "Sunnis want" or what the "red lines of the Shiites" were, suggesting I had in fact not been able to get my message across at all. Essentially, despite posh hotels, stately conference venues and polite dinner conversation, my most important mission remained unaccomplished.

Enough about blogging. This is a book and an attempt at a synthesis of posts related to political developments in Iraq between 2005 and 2010. Chapter 1 features some discussion about basic assumptions—and potential fallacies—in the way we Westerners tend to discuss Iraq. It is followed by Part I of the book, with six chapters focusing on a chronological description of key events in Iraqi politics from the constitutional referendum in 2005 and the subsequent election of the first parliament proper to the end of the term of that parliament in 2010, the March 7 elections and the ensuing government-formation process. Part II of the book consists of four chapters on selected themes of Iraqi politics: Questions pertaining to state structure (chapter 8), constitutional issues (chapter 9), soft partition (chapter 10) and finally the role of external players and the United States in particular (chapter 11). As far as sources are concerned, most of the text has not been footnoted except for references to the original posts, but a bibliography of my relevant academic work—which forms the main source base for most of my writings, and where extensive source references to primary materials can be found—has been enclosed at the end. Additionally many of the original online postings also include various supporting materials such as extracts of relevant Arabic texts and images of key documents.

Reidar Visser
Oslo, Norway
November 12, 2010

Chapter 1

Talking about Iraq: Paradigmatic Issues

"Visser is a nationalist," a critic once wrote. "And by that, I mean that his attachment to the idea of Iraqi national unity goes beyond the academic." "Visser offers Iraqi nationalism," said another, "but that's not a whole lot of potatoes." One fellow panelist some years ago cheerfully suggested that I was on the payroll of the Saudis because of my vehement defense of Iraq's territorial integrity.

These are serious charges, so I want to address them here at the very outset of the book, not least since several of the chapters that follow are indeed supportive of the idea of a unified Iraq with no decentralization except for the Kurdish areas. And above all, I would like to deal with the charge that I defend Iraqi nationalism for certain political reasons. In fact, nothing could be further from the truth: I have no affiliation with any Iraqi political party nor with any regional state; indeed I spend much of my time criticizing some of those Iraqi and regional players that are nominally committed to the idea of Iraqi unity for being insincere when it comes to practical politics. Rather, my sometimes passionate and robust defense of the idea of Iraqi national unity is based on academic experiences and an epistemological orientation shaped mainly in the pre-2003 era; when I express a preference for this or that in Iraqi politics it is mostly based on a judgment of which players I see as being truthful to the long lines of Iraqi history and which ones are simply pursuing selfish motives.

I began working on Iraqi history in 1993 after a visit to Syria and Lebanon and numerous failed attempts at getting a visa to Iraq. Of course the first thing I learned was the then-prevalent, trite thesis that Iraq was a completely artificial country randomly assembled after the First World War from three very disparate Ottoman provinces (one Shiite, one Sunni, and one Kurdish, it was claimed). This argument held that Iraq was the brainchild of cunning British imperialists; because of assumed chronic conflict between the three ethno-religious components, only an iron-fisted ruler could control the country. At first, this trichotomy appealed a lot to me. It was easy to remember and yet it sounded quite sophisticated: Iraq and its problems, all explained in a nutshell. I remember developing a habit of always underlining this aspect when I came across it in introductory texts on Iraq, as in a note to myself to quote this important point copiously.

My heresy started developing around 1996 when I accidentally came across references in British archives to something called the Basra separatist movement, which had unfolded in the south of Iraq in the 1920s. It occurred to me then that the thesis of an artificial, tripartite Iraq had in fact never been tested empirically: What was this separatist movement, and why had we never heard about it in books on Iraqi history? Surely its fate in the turbulent 1920s—when the modern "invented" kingdom of Iraq had just been inaugurated and borders across the Gulf region were changing rapidly—could speak volumes about the relative strength of separatist and nationalist aspirations in the Iraqi people at the time? Or to put it more bluntly, if the "artificial Iraq" thesis could not make sense of the Basra separatist movement of the 1920s and its fate, then it was probably invalid.

And so it was that I began studying Basra separatism, and I continued to do so for the next seven years. I have been called an "Iraq expert" in many different contexts and mostly feel rather uncomfortable with this appellation; the only area where I am reasonably confident about my doctoral title and the positivistic, medical-white associations that sometimes go with it is when it comes to questions about Iraq's territorial structure. This is where I have done the relevant experiments, checked all the sources and considered every conceivable and inconceivable variable. And this is also the yardstick I employ to evaluate to what extent Iraqi politicians in the post-2003 are being loyal to the traditions of their own country or are propagating agendas that are essentially foreign and have been imported from abroad.

To begin with, I was on the side of the Basra separatists. I have no idea why I was so attracted to separatist movements at the time, but I think it may have had to do with the fact that I like studying things that no one else has been looking at before—an attitude that easily fosters a passion for the obscure and the marginal. For several years, I tried to study developments in Basra from the angle of the separatists, looking at the potential for the movement to thrive and the resources at its disposal. In many ways, the separatist movement seemed to me destined for success: Its proponents were enormously rich, and it is possible to read certain aspects of Basra's history in a particularistic light if one wishes to do so. I meticulously studied possible historical precedents like the 17th-century Afrasiyab Emirate, the Zanj Rebellion in the 9th century, and even the somewhat tenuous link to the ancient civilizations of Sumeria; in short, there was no lack of interest in Basra separatism on my part in that period.

However, my passion for the Basra separatist cause abated gradually. The first reversal came in winter 2000, when I lived in Richmond outside London and would go every weekday to what was then called the Public Record Office at Kew to work with documents on Iraq from the late Ottoman and early British Mandate period. In those documents, the Basra separatist movement came across as a rather unimpressive undertaking—basically the enterprise of a clique of wealthy merchants who wanted to emulate the Kuwaiti model of a British protectorate on the strategic Gulf coast. The British attitude was somewhat negative but not unambiguously so: Another interesting discovery was the extent to which many leading British politicians and policy-makers at the time were in fact prepared to withdraw to Basra, leaving Baghdad and its political problems behind. What really shocked me, though, were the constant references to "Iraq" and "nationalists" in these British documents, much of it intelligence reports. This uniform chorus of references to Iraq by both the local people and the British diplomats even during the First World War was not how it was supposed to be according to the artificiality thesis that I had been taught since I was an undergraduate.

I later added to my source materials newspaper archives that provided a fascinating window on popular opinion in Basra at the time—and yet more ammunition against the artificiality thesis. In the first explorative steps of the local press in Basra in the 1920s there was not much in the way of support for the Basra separatist undertaking. Instead, young writers of various ethnic and sectarian backgrounds—Christians, Jews, Sunnis and Shiites; Arabs and Turkmens—were writing agitated letters in defense of Iraqi unity. Perhaps most striking in all of this was the pronounced socioeconomic contrast between the rich separatist elite, often Sunni, Christian and Jewish, and the more middle-class and lower-class group of nationalists, who belonged to all ethno-religious groups, including the Shiite Arabs. Clearly the nationalists were not doing this at the behest of the British mandatory power, which they often criticized and whose number-one enemy at the time—Mustafa Kemal Atatürk of the young Turkish Republic—they would often applaud. Nor were they doing it, obviously, as a result of pressures from "the state" in Baghdad, which was still in its infancy institutionally speaking and in terms of its ability to enforce particular policies. They did it because they subscribed to an organic notion of Iraqi nationalism even at this early stage of the history of the modern state.

When I finished my dissertation in 2003, I concluded that the Basra separatist movement had died because it failed to thrive. By way of contrast, the supposedly artificial Iraq concept had seemed to resonate among the public of Basra as early as the 1920s, suggesting that its roots were in fact better established than many scholars claimed. As I revised my thesis for publication in 2004, I made several trips to Istanbul to work with Ottoman materials in the archives there, and to my astonishment I was able to trace the Iraq concept back well into the 19th century, when it was used in an administrative sense by the Ottomans and as a category of identity by many local writers. I also worked with Arab journals from the late Ottoman era which were also full of references to Iraq. One of them in particular seemed to me to encapsulate a rejection of the "artificiality thesis" and its connotations of chronic division among Iraqis: An article in Lughat al-Arab *by Kazim al-Dujayli, a Shiite poet, which highlighted the "history of Iraq in the nineteenth* century" and celebrated a number of historians from that period—including both Sunnis and Shiites. The article was dated 1911, several years before the arrival of the British and their supposed creation of Iraq!

In short, my conviction about the durability of the territorial and conceptual framework of Iraq even in times of extreme external pressure does not stem from contacts with Baathists or Arab nationalists; it is based on nothing other than a collection of hidden old documents that have a story of their own to tell, independently of later historiography and textbook versions of Iraq's creation as a modern state. Since this revised version of Iraqi history is particularly challenging to impress on an American audience, I find it somewhat ironic that one of the best sources for comprehending it is actually situated on U.S. territory, in a warehouse in a small place called Landover outside Washington, D.C. I learned about this by chance, in 2001, as I was ceaselessly browsing the internet for untapped sources on Basra and suddenly came across a reference in the newspaper catalogue of the Library of Congress to Times of Mesopotamia (Basra). I had seen odd copies of this English-language newspaper in the UK before, but never a complete run. The Library of Congress had years 1920–1931, which to the best of my knowledge is a more complete collection than any Iraqi library possesses. But that was not all: Times of Mesopotamia, as the title suggests, was a British expatriate publication with only limited space devoted to domestic Iraqi issues. What triggered my interest, though, was an intriguing additional note in the catalogue entry: "Incorporating Iraq Times in Arabic." That was the big find—complete holdings of a local, Arabic-language newspaper from Basra from the British Mandate period that had never previously been exploited by researchers (it is called Al-Awqat al-Iraqiyya in Arabic). Thanks to the liberal opening hours of the Library of Congress, I was able to work my way through most of this material through a couple of weeklong visits in 2001 and 2002. I made reference to this newspaper in my book on Basra when it was published in 2005, but the only query that I have since received about the whereabouts of this formidable source was from a German doctoral student some years ago. In contrast, American scholars on the Middle East do not seem to be in a hurry when it comes to exploiting this magnificent mine of easily accessible information to revise their own ideas about Iraq's history as an "artificial" state, despite the fact that those ideas played a key role in designing a new system of government in the country after the invasion in 2003.

For my part, I have tried to use my examination of the centrifugal versus the centripetal forces in Iraqi history at that critical moment of the collapse of the Ottoman Empire to make some sense of the myriad political projects that mushroomed in the post-2003 period, and not least to try to distinguish the truly enduring Iraqi schemes from the novel and often foreign concoctions. Naturally, I became suspicious about any project that advocated decentralization south of Kurdistan since my own studies had shown so clearly that no precedent existed in history whatsoever. How could a new federal arrangement that so clearly ran against centuries of history offer *stability in the turbulent post-2003 period? This axiom made me deeply skeptical about Kurdish attempts to stimulate the emergence of some kind of Shiite region in the south to mirror that of Kurdistan. It is also the reason why I have wondered how anyone can take seriously Shiite politicians like Ammar and Abd al-Aziz al-Hakim of the Supreme Council for the Islamic revolution in Iraq (SCIRI, later the Islamic Supreme Council of Iraq, ISCI). These people spent more than two years between 2005 and 2007 propagating a vision of a federal Shiite region that is taken completely out of the air, and yet prominent officials in the U.S. government and leading intellectuals in American public opinion continued to take them seriously even long after the Iraqi people signaled a rejection of their schemes.*

A separate book could have been written about just how pervasive and widespread the fallacious, tripartite version of Iraq's genesis as a modern state is. Let me just highlight a few anecdotes. Back in 1998, at Oxford, I had the opportunity to discuss my doctoral thesis with several extremely competent scholars of the modern Middle East. One of them expressed surprise that my work on the Basra separatist movement would not go into developments in the Shiite holy cities of Karbala and Najaf, since they "were also part of the Ottoman province of Basra." I pointed out that in fact they belonged to Baghdad rather than to Basra, and hence did not back up the standard image of Basra as "Shiite" and Baghdad as "Sunni." My interlocutor reached for one of the standard works on modern Iraqi history on his shelf and I was about to say something rather undiplomatic about its coverage of the Ottoman era when we were saved by the telephone. Pretty much the same thing repeated itself almost a decade later when, armed with my published book, I had the audacity to suggest to an American-dominated listserv on Gulf affairs that no serious work based on Ottoman and Arabic sources could defend the "artificiality thesis" of Iraq's origins. I hadn't considered that my ultimatum might actually prompt a response, since no such empirically founded work exists. Nonetheless, another list member identified a general study on Iraq by a very big name in U.S. Middle Eastern studies, rhetorically asking whether this distinguished scholar could conceivably have made a mistake in reiterating the "Iraq was cobbled together" thesis. My reply to the effect that the book in question used no Ottoman primary sources—it deals mainly with the latter half of the 20th century, where the source base is much better—prompted a minor diplomatic crisis, and the listserv editor hesitated to publish it for a while.

More generally, a review of primary-source studies of Iraq in the late Ottoman and early monarchical period reveals an astounding number of lacunas and suggests that our Western knowledge base for Iraqi history is often informed by scholars speaking from fake ivory towers. The mainstream media constitutes another main arena for the replication of the fallacious artificiality thesis. The BBC, for example, is often seen as progressive by American viewers who consider it comparatively unadulterated by the commercial forces that dominate U.S. television. However, as far as Iraq is concerned, the BBC's coverage over the past seven years has been as substandard as that of the others, if not worse. I remember losing my faith in them already during the run-up to the Iraq War when the host of the BBC program HARDtalk, Tim Sebastian, whom I once admired, was interrogating an Iraqi guest and in reviewing various problems on the Iraqi political scene proclaimed, "The Kurds want to separate, the Shiites want to separate!" Had Sebastian done any research on the subject, he would have known that no substantial "Shiite separatist" movement existed in Iraqi history. To use plain English, he was making it up. Much later, in 2007, at the height of the "soft partition" debate, I criticized a BBC spokesperson who had misrepresented a poll commissioned by BBC themselves on federalism in Iraq by saying that one of the questions concerned the partition of Iraq into "three" separate states. The actual question in the poll had simply dealt with "partition of Iraq into separate states" with no number specified and hence was quite consonant with the most frequent scenario of Kurdistan separating but the Sunnis and the Shiites staying within the joint Iraqi framework. I pointed out that the number three had been invented by the BBC on their own, something which was actually acknowledged by the BBC spokesperson who nonetheless complained about "overreaction" on my part.

I could give numerous other examples of this phenomenon, but they would add little further to the picture I have painted. The real culprit that I want to identify here are all those little partitions—the small, innocuous, often unconscious reiterations of the false tripartite paradigm of Iraq's history and origins that take place in casual conversations among Western intellectuals. Today, most people in the West think that it was wrong to go to war with Iraq, but few seem to realize how many of us contribute to destroying Iraq on a daily basis simply by talking the country to pieces.

Divide and Rejoice: The Myth of the Artificial Iraq[1]
August 2006

The main message in Peter Galbraith's recently published *The End of Iraq* is that Iraq is a non-viable polity well on its way to predestined disintegration. U.S. policy in Iraq, Galbraith maintains, should be adjusted accordingly.

Galbraith is not the first author to write along such lines, but he may be one of the more important ones to do so. He has sympathizers in liberal and Democratic Party circles in the United States, and has written extensively on Iraq in such prestigious publications as the *New York Review of Books*. Galbraith's latest offering runs to 260 pages and is thus the most voluminous contribution yet to a growing corpus of texts by partition-keen American intellectuals. On the back cover, Galbraith is touted as "the smartest and most devastating" of the critics of President George W. Bush's Iraq policies.

Chapter 8, "Kurdistan", is by far the most interesting part of the book—not primarily for what it says about that area, but for its blunt and autobiographical account of how a U.S. intellectual became deeply engaged in fuelling Kurdish ideas about breaking ranks with the rest of Iraq. In considerable detail Galbraith explains how he personally fostered many of the specific Kurdish demands for federalism, including principles which in one form or another would later find their way into the current Iraqi constitution: Residual powers of the regions in the federal system, the idea of the supremacy of local law over federal law, and the right of local authorities to manage future oilfields—all apparently drafted by Galbraith as far back as in the period August 2003–February 2004. Galbraith provides an amazingly frank account of how he himself played a central role in framing the Kurdish elites' demands on the center, even impelling them at certain junctures when he found them to have "conceptual problems" (p. 160). He sounds distinctly satisfied about the severe restrictions placed on the central government in the final constitution (p. 169, sarcastically declaring it the exclusive prerogative of the central government to ensure that "a meter in Basra is the same length as one in Arbil") and cheerfully recounts how he himself contributed to upholding the restraints on the center during the tense final stages of the charter negotiations (by warning off British officials who seemingly intended to raise alarms about the limited tax powers of the central government, p. 199, footnote).

It is on the basis of the pro-Kurdish, pro-partition views expressed in chapter 8 that Galbraith's general reading of Iraqi history and society as well as some of the oddities in the book must be understood. Galbraith is at pains to render Iraq as an "artificial" and highly fissile construct. Indeed, he accuses his political opponents of "a misreading of Iraq's modern history" (p. 206). But as soon as he moves beyond his particular area of expertise—the Kurdish north—the narrative becomes less convincing and the arguments more strained. For instance, Galbraith on two occasions reiterates the now widespread but highly erroneous notion that current ethno-religious divisions in Iraq strongly correlate to the old administrative organization of the Ottoman Empire: Mosul was supposedly "Kurdish", Baghdad "Sunni", and Basra "Shiite" (p. 7, and in a footnote on p. 100 where he repeats this image even while admitting the existence of what he portrays as enclave-like minorities of Sunni Arabs in Mosul and Shiite Arabs in the holy cities of Baghdad province). In reality, however, Mosul was essentially a mixed-race province, whereas Baghdad, though home to a large Sunni community, was probably the largest Shiite province of the Ottoman Empire—with its borders extending as far south as today's Muthanna governorate and with all the rural territory surrounding the holy cities of Najaf and Karbala solidly Shiite, Baghdad was actually far more of a Shiite point of gravity than was Basra (which politically was Sunni-dominated). This in turn means that there was never any such close fit between ethno-religious and administrative maps as that suggested by Galbraith, and that Iraq has in fact a far longer record of ethno-religious coexistence than he seems prepared to admit.

Galbraith's "Iraq was just cobbled together" thesis is similarly trite and equally misleading: It is true that for some thirty years between the 1880s and 1914 there was administrative separation between Basra, Baghdad and Mosul, but before that there had been frequent intervals of administrative unity between some or all of these areas (especially Basra and Baghdad)—as was the case under the Ottomans and Georgian Mameluke rule in the early nineteenth and eighteenth century as well as during long periods of the classical Islamic age (and even under a succession of Mongol rulers after 1258, if more flimsily so). Finally, on a more exotic note, on p. 219 Galbraith devotes a line to the long-overlooked Basra separatist movement of the 1920s—but his interpretation of the movement is misleading. In Galbraith's view, the historical emergence of a Basra separatist movement proves that Shiite ambitions for separate statehood are a "natural" and "historical" thing; the snag here, however, is that the Basra bid for separation in the 1920s had nothing whatsoever to do with Shiism—it was ideologically non-sectarian and in terms of the background of its participants overwhelmingly dominated by Sunni merchants (many of Arabian origin), along with Christians and Jews. Only a few rich Shiite traders joined the project, and then at a late stage.

Galbraith similarly seems to read the contemporary Iraq situation with lenses not admitting more than three colors. An important subtext throughout the book is the charge that the Bush administration has inadvertently handed power in Iraq over to the Iranians; to buttress this argument Galbraith stereotypes the entire Shiite community as "pro-Iranian". While there can be no doubt that Iran's influence in Iraq was greatly augmented after 2003 and that Galbraith's interpretation may hold true for at least some adherents of the Supreme Council for the Islamic Revolution of Iraq (SCIRI), there is great diversity among Iraqi Shiites, not to mention the strong anti-Iranian leanings in large parts of the community. In particular, he disregards the rift between exiles and non-exiles, which has grown into a formidable cleavage within the all-Shiite United Iraqi Alliance (UIA). In fact, inside the UIA supporters of such home-grown forces as Muqtada al-Sadr, the Fadila Party and various Daawa factions have traditionally been skeptical of close ties to Iran—and indeed to any linkage between sect and territory of the kind that Galbraith variously propagates as a confederal or outright three-state solution. On one occasion (p. 174) Galbraith quotes the widespread but as of August 2006 unsubstantiated media cliché that "elements of the Iranian regime have close ties to the firebrand cleric Muqtada al-Sadr", but generally he resorts to the even more hackneyed claim that SCIRI is the "most influential Shiite party in Iraq" (p. 3, p. 17 footnote). That claim is however imprecise with regard to levels of parliamentary representation and provincial power: In parliament, the Sadrists (including the two-person Sadrist Risaliyun bloc) have 30 deputies just like SCIRI; at the local level, SCIRI do not control eight out of nine Shiite provinces, as Galbraith maintains (p. 198)—they are in fact out of office in the two most oil-rich provinces of the south (Basra and Maysan), and their nominal hold on several other provinces south of Baghdad is based on rather tenuous coalitions.

Galbraith's biases with regard to this intra-Shiite pluralism are particularly important, because they lead the reader to uncritically accept another problematic standard phrase about the Shiites, namely that they monolithically support a bid for a federal unit that would be made up of all majority-Shiite provinces in Iraq (this would have tallied with Galbraith's ideas). Again, a closer look at the situation on the ground reveals competition between different visions—especially between proponents of a small-scale federal entity limited to three oil-rich Shiite provinces in the far south (this is the most enduring federal project by Shiites and it is regionalist rather than sectarian), and the more recent scheme to create a nine-governorate explicitly Shiite super-unit from Basra to Baghdad as a fence against Sunni terrorism (an idea which received a boost after the Samarra blast in February 2006, but whose core support still seems to come mainly from SCIRI politicians and their network of preachers and media outlets). This crucial distinction goes unrecognized in many journalistic reports out of Iraq, where increasing Shiite enthusiasm for the general principle of federalism almost automatically tends to get portrayed as support for the particular plan of a single large Shiite entity, and where considerable remaining Shiite skepticism towards federalism in all its forms (especially among independents and Sadrists) is often overlooked completely.

On such empirical foundations rests Galbraith's analysis of Iraq. With the exception of the author's claim that, in their inner conscience, leading Kurdish politicians are not in favor of Iraqi unity (p. 99), much of the remainder of his argument for partition is either based on the increasing levels of political violence more generally, or not related to Iraq at all. The idea of coexistence in Iraq is "absurd" charges Galbraith on pp. 100–101. The decisive proof? Yugoslavia and Czechoslovakia and the Soviet Union all fell apart. But what about other possible comparisons, such as Lebanon—which descended into ethno-religious mayhem and saw extensive internal displacement of its population from 1975 to 1990, only to rise again as a unitary "mosaic"-like state? Today's sectarian violence in Baghdad is certainly reminiscent of Beirut during the Lebanese civil war, where talk of partition and confederations materialized in some circles at particularly gloomy junctures, only to dissipate later on. And what is Galbraith's position on the large numbers of other "artificial", post-colonial, multi-ethnic states worldwide that somehow continue to function?

Galbraith seems to have scant interest in such examples of ethno-religious coexistence and reconciliation; instead he mocks anyone who shows interest in keeping Iraq unified. He roundly condemns the Bush administration for the heinous crime of trying to secure a "non-ethnic Iraq" (p. 166) and castigates them for speaking of an "Iraqi people, as if there were a single people akin to the French or even the American people" (p. 83). But he fails to provide any historically convincing justification for his own quantum leap from diagnosing a state of civil strife to prescribing territorial, segregationist solutions. That lack of historical perspective is a serious problem, because it precludes the writer from distinguishing between societies that are chronically unstable and those that experience a serious but reversible flare-up of civic violence. It should serve as a reminder to Galbraith that his claims about Kurdish leaders' anti-Iraq attitudes cannot possibly be repeated with regard to Sunni and Shiite elites, and that, despite the ongoing horrific violence, large masses of Iraqis, certainly in the Arab areas, continue to demand a "national Iraqi" army, a "national Iraqi" oil distribution policy, and a meaningful role for Baghdad as capital.

But Galbraith has already made up his mind. His "solution"—the "three state solution"—is covered in chapters 10 and 11 and may be what many readers of this book are really interested in. Such a territorial solution of separating Kurds, Sunni Arabs, and Shiite Arabs may appear superficially attractive to Democratic and liberal audiences in the United States, simply by offering a clear-cut alternative to Bush's Iraq policy. Instead of semantic fidgeting with "timetables for withdrawals", "threats of withdrawal" or "deadlines for withdrawal", partition may come across as an innovative, hands-on approach that can mark a clear alternative to the line of the current administration. (If implemented it could also be trumpeted as ultimate evidence that everything the Republicans ever did in Iraq was profoundly misguided.) In short, after years of Democratic discomfiture over an Iraq situation where criticism of U.S. policy always risked being deemed unpatriotic, partition schemes may now give the impression of being deliciously refreshing. That is also why they are particularly worrying, first and foremost for the Iraqi people who would experience an exacerbation of ethno-religious conflict instead of its reversal, but also as precedents that could lead to the dismantling of multi-ethnic polities elsewhere in the world. What a sad prospect it would be to have a twenty-first century agenda in international politics dominated by an uninspired revival of First World War ideas about ethno-religious self-determination—all as the result of the opposition's scrabbling around for a vote-winning U.S. foreign policy.

One concludes this book with the impression of an author who may well end up serving in a T.E. Lawrence–like capacity for the Kurds, but who lacks a solidly cast policy proposal for all the territory of modern Iraq. At its best, Galbraith's book offers interesting insights into the mind of an influential U.S. intellectual. At its worst it seems a pre-written obituary that has long been languishing in a desk drawer. The country it describes stubbornly refuses to lie down and die; hence, the author has turned sour and through increasingly heated ad hoc addendums to the text does his utmost to accelerate the final exit. *The End of Iraq* is in itself far from lethal, but the possibility that other Western intellectuals may try to surpass Galbraith remains.

The Historical Endurance of the Iraq Concept[2]

September 10, 2007

A steady stream of U.S. commentators keep expressing support for the idea of some kind of ethnic partition, be it "soft" or "hard", of Iraq. Despite the repeated warnings against division by military advisors and experts in humanitarian aid, the partition theme simply refuses to fade away from the American debate. One possible explanation for the strong attraction of the partitionist propaganda is its claim to resurrect what are taken to be "the long lines of history"; according to the partitionist canon, the Iraqis cannot live together because they have never done so in the past—at least not of their "free will". Iraq is seen as "artificial", a tripartite division is what is "natural".

No appeal to history could have been more ironic. Had these proponents of partition bothered to check the facts they would have found that the long-term trends in Iraqi history point in exactly the opposite direction of what they advocate. Those who take the trouble to examine the weak links in the partitionist argument (Iraq's monarchical era from 1921 to 1958, and pretty much everything prior to 1914) will find that not only does the country have a long history of coexistence, it also has considerable pre-modern roots as a proto-region—centralized under Baghdad, and associated with the name "Iraq".

Perhaps the most serious error in the partitionist take on Iraqi history is precisely the idea that the name of the country was somehow "invented" in 1920, or "borrowed" from some far-distant past. This is another contention found exclusively among armchair historians who have never seen actual documents from the period they talk about. The reason why no serious area specialist subscribes to this view is that it is impossible to maintain once one looks into written materials from before 1914. The word "Iraq" is simply all over the place. It can be found in the writings of British consuls like J.G. Lorimer; in the works of Persian diplomats such as Muhammad Hasan Khan Badi; and in the journal articles of many local intellectuals, including for example Anastas Mari al-Karmili. How can partitionists explain that already in 1923—a mere two years after Iraq had supposedly been "invented"—a Shiite activist from Hilla, Muhammad Mahdi al-Basir, would write passionately about the strength of "Iraqi" nationalism among the people of Mosul? Was that the result of indoctrination by the British (whom Basir hated), or by King Faysal (who hardly had made any impact on the institutions of state yet) or perhaps the Baath party (which did not exist)? For the duration of the monarchy, sectarian relations in Iraq would remain overwhelmingly peaceable, if not entirely frictionless; only the gradual advance of Kurdish nationalism shows any convincing correlation with the plans being proposed by U.S. partitionists today.

When confronted with these facts, partitionists tend to react in one of two ways. Most ignore the information altogether, preferring to cling to the idea of an "artificial" Iraq simply because that provides them with peace of mind. In predictable fashion, despite the overwhelming evidence, they go on ranting: "Iraq was cobbled together. . . ." The more sophisticated partitionist response is to accept the facts but to dismiss history as irrelevant in view of the horrific scale of the sectarian killings being perpetrated in today's Iraq. The problem with that sort of approach is that, once the historical perspective is abandoned, the specter of myopia emerges. It becomes impossible to distinguish between long-term trends and more ephemeral (albeit horribly violent) eruptions. Those who choose to reduce Iraqi politics to the hysteria unleashed by the Samarra bombings in February 2006 risk making assumptions and policy decisions with wide-ranging implications based on a bout of temporary xenophobia instead of the true basic drivers of Iraqi politics. After all, when the false historical argument in favor of partition is subtracted, there really is not much left. Very few Iraqis south of Kurdistan are asking for sectarian division, none of the regional powers want it (except possibly Iran and Kuwait), and the wider Arab and Islamic worlds generally are against it (apart from al-Qaida, which would finally obtain its long-coveted manifest evidence of a Western conspiracy against the Muslim world).

Perhaps the greatest irony of the partitionist propaganda is the idea that what we are seeing today is somehow "natural" and an echo of past experiences in Iraqi politics. Any serious empirical historical investigation will show that it is the concept of three ethnic statelets—not the idea of a unified Iraq state with its capital in Baghdad—that lacks historical resonance. In a context when so many critical questions are being asked about the "short-lived" unitary state in Iraq, it is absolutely mind-boggling that no one has thought of shifting the burden of proof to the partitionists. Two out of three of their proposed statelets have never existed, and their targeted audiences have never asked for them. Why then should anyone expect such a thoroughly artificial system to become more successful, resistant against external and internal challenges, and politically stable than the existing one?

"They Have Been Fighting Each Other for Centuries"[3]
September 27, 2008

Senator Barack Obama to Senator John McCain, during yesterday's presidential debate: "You said that there was no history of violence between Shiite and Sunni. And you were wrong".

Since this is forceful claim about Iraqi history was presented during a contest for the position as the world's most powerful leader, it is worth examining in some further detail: Let's take a closer look at that "history of violence between Shiite and Sunni" in Iraq. Shiites and Sunnis have coexisted in Iraq since they crystallized as two distinctive religious communities in Baghdad in the tenth century, when the struggle for power between various factions of the Islamic caliphate that had been going on since the seventh century became transformed into a theological one with the (Shiite) doctrine of the imamate. In the subsequent centuries, there was certainly tension between these two communities at times (not least because the rival ruling elements of the caliphates chose to cultivate links with particular communities to further their own power struggles), but outbreaks of violence on a large scale were extremely rare. In fact, not more than three cases stand out before the late twentieth century, and these were all related to invasion by foreign forces rather than to internal sectarian struggles between the Iraqis.

The first major case of extensive Shiite–Sunni violence was in 1508: A massacre by invading Persian Safavids that hit Sunnis and Christians in Baghdad. The Safavids returned a little more than one hundred years later, in 1623, and once more went ahead with a massacre of Sunnis in Baghdad. Later, in the nineteenth century, extremist Sunni Wahhabis from the Arabian Peninsula would regularly overrun the settled areas of Iraq; on one occasion, in 1801, this took on a clearly sectarian nature as Bedouin warriors massacred Shiites in the holy city of Karbala. The list can be completed down to 2003 and the U.S. invasion with a series of ugly episodes that took place in the late twentieth century: Between 1969 and 1971, the Sunni-dominated Baathist regime performed mass expulsions of Shiites (including a high number of Fayli Kurds); in 1980 there was another wave of mass deportations of Shiites in the wake of the Iranian revolution; finally, in 1991 there were massacres of Shiites after the failed *intifada* that followed the Gulf War. (Conversely, some of the other historical episodes that are occasionally described as instances of "sectarian violence" simply do not fit this label. For example, the conflict between the government and the mostly Shiite tribes on the Euphrates in the 1935 was interwoven with questions relating to agrarian issues and conscription; Sunni politicians had ties to both the government and the opposition camps.)

On the one hand, there can be no doubt that this is a grim record: it involved thousands of innocent people who were massacred simply because they belonged to the wrong sect. On the other hand, however, it is important to keep things in perspective. These six cases of widespread sectarian violence took place in a time span of more than 1,000 years. Moreover, they were mostly instigated by foreign invaders. The Iraqis themselves repeatedly closed ranks against these aggressions, uniting Shiites and Sunnis against the foreign forces. For example, in 1623 when the Safavid army was about to massacre the Sunni population of Baghdad, Shiites of Karbala intervened to save Sunnis from Shiite aggression. Similarly, in 1801, when Sunni Wahhabis sacked Karbala, the Sunni pasha of Baghdad punished the Sunni governor of Karbala for having failed to prevent the attack on the Shiites. Also, in none of these cases did the victims propose separatist solutions. Never in Iraqi history has there been any call for a small Sunni state. And with the exception of feeble and short-lived attempt by some low-ranking clerics and notables of Baghdad in 1927, the Shiites have also consistently shied away from a call for a small Shiite breakaway state. Neither of the major upheavals of twentieth-century Iraqi history—1920 and 1958—featured sectarian conflict as the main mode of political action.

The accumulation of cases of sectarian violence during the decades of Baathist rule calls for special comment. True, the measures taken against the Shiites in the early 1980s and in 1991 were extremely repressive, and in an episode in the immediate wake of the 1991 uprising they turned into fully-fledged explicit sectarianism through a series of chauvinist Sunni editorials in the *Thawra* newspaper in which the Arabness of the Shiites was questioned. However, subsequent developments in Iraqi politics show that the "Sunni" character of the Baathist regime was not its real core and that it was first and foremost an authoritarian regime built on relations between patrons and clients: In the mid-1990s the dominant political trend in Iraq was intra-Sunni struggles, as tribe after tribe challenged Saddam Hussein, who ended up executing people from his hometown Tikrit and his own family. When the defector Hussein Kamil Hasan al-Majid returned from Jordan in 1996, he was put to death just like many Shiite rebels had been after the 1991 uprising.

Perhaps most importantly in the context of the U.S. elections, this record needs to be compared with that of the country Barack Obama represents himself. Did not the Civil War cause some 600,000 deaths between 1861 and 1865? How many thousands of African Americans have been killed in KKK violence? What about the Native Americans? The numbers here are clearly higher than the number of deaths caused by sectarian violence in Iraq, and yet few are prepared to question the viability of the United States as a political project. So where did Senator Obama really want to go with those comments?

It seems reasonable to criticize the Iraq War on several grounds: there were no weapons of mass destruction, no al-Qaida link and no 9/11 relationship, and the unilateral action without a UN mandate created yet another dangerous precedent in international affairs. But Democrats sometimes go further than this in ways that just do not fit the empirical record: They frequently claim that the sectarian problems seen in Iraq since 2003 and especially in the wake of the Samarra bombing in 2006 were a "natural" expression of Iraqi politics, and that the high degree of Iranian influence seen in today's Iraq is somehow a "natural" phenomenon in a country with a large Shiite population. The argument is that the Bush administration should have known that any tampering with the authoritarian structures of Baathist Iraq would automatically have prompted a civil war with a strong Iranian role among the Shiites. It is also a way of ultimately blaming the Iraqis themselves for all the problems they are currently going through.

This is to ignore the historical record of coexistence between Shiites and Sunnis in Iraq and the fervent anti-Iranian attitudes among large sections of Iraq's Shiites. Of course, on the latter point, John McCain is off the mark just like Obama: By suggesting that "the consequences of defeat would have been increased Iranian influence" he overlooks the fact that some of America's best friends in the Maliki government such as the Islamic Supreme Council of Iraq have extremely close ties to Iran and that Iran's interests so far have been well served by the Republican "victory" project and Washington's peculiar choice of alliance partners among Iraq's Shiites. But on the whole, Republicans, to a greater degree than Democrats, at least seem to recognize the historical roots of Iraqi national unity. From the Iraqi point of view it could be even more dangerous to have a U.S. president who based on some extremely superficial reading pretends to know something about the divide between Sunnis and Shiites than the present situation, in which the president reportedly is completely ignorant about the subject.

The bottom line is that there is nothing in Iraq's history that should prevent the country from reverting to its natural role as one of the world's great nations. Those who try to suggest otherwise either ignore the empirical record or do not care for the well-being of the Iraqi people. It is said that Obama has several top-notch, progressive and knowledgeable advisors who know about all these things, and who are unlikely to look to soft partitionist Joe Biden when it comes to actual policymaking. But unless these voices can have a real impact on what their candidate says in front of millions of Americans in prime-time televised debates, their usefulness seems unclear. If yesterday's unfounded attack on Iraq's record of coexistence is the most inspirational thing Obama can come up with on Iraq then it is hard for a non-American observer to see any fundamental difference between his candidacy and that of all the others before him. Obama's remarks were yet another example of how American politicians can be careless in dealing with other sovereign nations and their histories, and they also go in exactly the wrong direction at a time when politics in Iraq is once more becoming more cross-sectarian.

The Futile Search for an Ethno-Sectarian Concord[4]
July 6, 2009

On 27 February of this year, President Barack Obama made one of the best speeches on Iraq delivered by a U.S. senior official for a long time. Obama congratulated the Iraqis for having resisted the forces of partition, and while he noted the need for political reconciliation, he pretty much refrained from imposing his own interpretation of what the relevant problems were and how they should be solved. As such, the statement was in harmony with the better parts of his speech in Cairo in June, in which he went out of his way to make it clear that he had no intentions of framing America's relationship with the Muslim world as a monologue where only the values of one side receive attention.

However, after the reappearance of Joe Biden on the Iraqi stage this weekend—this time as vice-president of the United States and special envoy charged with facilitating national reconciliation in Iraq—there is considerable danger that both the optimism among Iraqis from Obama's first speech as well as the substantial progress towards a more mature form of politics seen during the January local elections may be reversed. Biden's brief public remarks as well as those offered by high-level U.S. officials in conjunction with the visit all suggest that while Iraq itself may be maturing, U.S. policy in Iraq is not. Conceptually, Washington seems stuck in language dating from 2007, and it consistently adheres to a public discourse on Iraq that features old and stale categories of analysis. At worst, the choice of words by U.S. leaders could help resuscitate the very sectarian forces that are cited by Washington as its main concern.

Perhaps this development should not come as too much of a surprise. After all, for Obama, the Camp Lejeune speech in February represented something of an exception to his general approach to Iraq. In other contexts, his comments relating to national reconciliation in Iraq have been surprisingly off the mark, and often framed in such outdated language that they have been directly at odds with his declared ambition to be on talking terms with the Middle East.

For example, just weeks after the promising speech at LeJeune, in remarks to CBS News on 29 March, Obama commented that "there's still work to be done on the political side to resolve differences between the various sectarian groups around issues like oil, around issues like provincial elections". Whereas this statement may seem innocent and even bland at first, in reality it contains a grave error concerning the relationship between oil and ethno-sectarian identity. Frequently misconstrued in the West as a problem of revenue-sharing between three ethno-sectarian groups, the oil issue in Iraq is in fact not so much about revenue distribution but rather about the right to sign contracts with foreign companies—where the two biggest Kurdish parties are facing off against everyone else. Most Iraqis south or Kurdistan would in fact probably balk at notions such as a "Shiite quota" or a "Sunni quota" for oil, and seem to agree that Iraq's oil revenues should be distributed according to a strict per-capita formula, equally across the entire country. Both Sunnis and Shiites stand to benefit from this, because almost all the oil is located in the far south in Basra, which in the past has shown itself to be equally skeptical to domination by outsiders from central Iraq, be they Shiites or Sunnis. In other words, oil in Iraq is not an issue that needs agreement *between* "sectarian groups" as per Obama's suggestion.

More recently, Obama has reiterated similar ideas. At a press conference in June he complained, "I haven't seen as much political progress in Iraq, negotiations between the Sunni, the Shia, and the Kurds, as I would like to see". He went on to suggest "the bigger challenge is going to be, can the Shia, the Sunni, and the Kurds resolve some of these major political issues having to do with federalism, having to do with boundaries, having to do with how oil revenues are shared". Again, many of these observations are empirically problematic. Yes, there are boundary issues between the Kurds and the Arabs, but Sunnis and Shiites, on top of their consensus as regards oil-revenue sharing, are now mostly in agreement on federalism. The main cleavage during the last local elections was between centralists (including Sunni Islamists, Shiite Islamists, secularists) and decentralists (Kurds and a very small number of Shiite Islamists). The decentralists lost badly, and it is generally expected that in the future—absent any foreign intervention—there will be widespread support among both Sunnis and Shiites for a more centralized state structure in Iraq south of Kurdistan. (The one big issue that does have a certain sectarian component, the integration of the largely Sunni "Sons of Iraq" militias into the Iraqi security forces, was not mentioned by Obama in this context. However, its overall significance diminishes dramatically as soon as one realizes that the main cleavage is not between Sunnis and Shiites and that the Sunnis of Iraq at any rate are more than "Sons of Iraq" militia members and often have other, non-sectarian, priorities.)

Re-enter Joe Biden. Before he was elected vice-president, Biden had been among the foremost American exponents of the theory that the key to peace in Iraq is some kind of grand compromise between its assumed key components—the three main ethno-sectarian communities. Back then, he had developed this argument to a territorial solution in which federalism was supposed to be the key instrument for structuring the new Iraqi political system. His plan to territorialize the process of national reconciliation in this way was roundly condemned in Iraq south of Kurdistan, and gradually met with criticism in Washington too. But whereas little has been heard about the first iteration of the "Biden plan" since Obama was elected president, Biden himself has gradually reverted to the spotlight on Iraq issues. This time, he appears to be promoting a non-territorial variant of his same old theory of a tripartite grand compromise.

During Obama's visit to Iraq in April, Biden commented, "One of the things the president has said from the beginning is in addition to us drawing down troops, it was necessary for there to be further political accommodation between the Sunnis, Shia, and the Kurds". This weekend, as Biden himself visited Iraq, he declared that his goal was to "re-establish contact with each of the leaders among the Kurds and the Sunnis and the Shiites". As if to underline the idea that this effort of diplomacy was a benevolent act on the part of the United States designed to rescue a country otherwise doomed to disintegration, high-level U.S. officials (some say Biden himself) evoked Humpty Dumpty to describe the current state of affairs: "There also wasn't any appetite to put Humpty Dumpty back together again if, by the action of people in Iraq, it fell apart", a clear analogy between the country of Iraq and the clumsy, fragile and egg-like character of the old rhyme:

> Humpty Dumpty sat on a wall,
> Humpty Dumpty had a great fall
> All the king's horses,
> And all the king's men,
> Couldn't put Humpty together again.

Is this how the U.S. views Iraq?

The modified and non-territorial version of the Biden plan has an impact on the situation in Iraq in several ways. Firstly, it serves to reiterate the misleading idea that the problem in Iraq is basically between three mutually hostile and internally monolithic groups (who but for the "help" of the United States would have parted ways long time ago). This approach is so sociologically problematic that few academics bother to take it seriously anymore (intra-communal divisions, intersectarian alliances, mixed social backgrounds, endurance of Iraqi nationalism). But when Washington keeps repeating it, it could easily feed back into the Iraqi conflict. When Obama wants to enhance national reconciliation "between" three groups, and when Biden wants to talk to "each of the leaders" of the three, American diplomacy becomes structured in such a way that it will eventually bring to the fore again those very tripartite structures it supposedly is designed to combat.

For example, with this paradigm, secularism becomes virtually impossible in Iraq, because America only wants to conduct serious talks with those leaders that appeal to ethnic and sectarian sentiments, and will craft a "grand bargain" on this basis. Also, ethno-sectarian cleavages, which Iraqi leaders sought to transcend during the 2009 local elections, are once more reified and get back on the agenda simply because Iraqis are reminded about them in a powerful way. In fact, each time Biden and Obama keep repeating these ideas about the need for political compromise "between Sunnis and Shiites and Kurds" on issues like "oil revenue-sharing", they make it more and more likely that the 2010 parliamentary elections will become a rerun of 2005, with sectarian loyalties center stage. Conversely, those "new forces" that bravely emerged during the recent local elections will feel discouraged. And certainly if any reconciliation is forced on the Iraqis now, prior to the 2010 elections, and with the current dysfunctional and unrepresentative parliament as a framework, the net effect will be to divest the non-sectarian forces of Iraq of powerful arguments in the upcoming elections campaign. Those forces want to give the Iraqi public a unique chance to openly discuss the fundamental features of the Iraqi political system—in other words, the opposite of some kind of backroom compromise between sectarian leaders under American chairmanship.

The non-territorial variant of the Biden plan has a name in Arabic: *muhasasa*, or the sharing of quotas—in this case between ethno-sectarian groups. According to this logic, Iraqi politics is structured on the basis of the relationships between the three biggest ethno-sectarian groups, and a sharing formula is used as point of departure for a grand political compromise. What Biden and Obama don't seem to understand is that most Iraqis detest this psychological sort of partition just as much as they hated the territorial variant that was advocated in the name of ethno-sectarian federalism in 2007. This hatred is abundantly clear from the discourse of Iraqis who are critical of the political system adopted in 2005. Here *muhasasa* is portrayed as a weakness of Iraqi politics which was introduced by returning Iraqi exiles and Paul Bremer in 2003, and which has since festered and grown into a fundamental problem that prevents professionalism and *esprit de corps* from taking root in the Iraqi state. But while American observers applaud Iraqi intellectuals (including many Shiites) who warn about increasing authoritarianism in the Iraqi state as well as growing Iranian influences, they seem to turn a blind eye to those same intellectuals when they criticize the concept of *muhasasa*. On this subject there is simply a total breakdown of communication between Iraqis and Americans.

There is a regional dimension to this too. Lately, there had been positive signs that Iraqis were in the process of overcoming *muhasasa*. Maliki's performance in the January local elections was generally ascribed to his vocal defense of national and centralist values, with a promise to work for constitutional reform in the future. The Iraqi constitution itself opens for a more majoritarian political system from 2010 onwards, because the tripartite presidency—the clearest expression of formal *muhasasa* within the 2005 constitution and one of the greatest obstacles towards the formation of viable cabinets—simply expires at the end of the first parliamentary cycle. But despite these positive tendencies, there are also unfortunate pushes in the opposite direction, from those who attempt to remind the Iraqis about their sub-identities as Kurds, Shiites and Sunnis. The first and very predictable move came from the East, from Iran. Having witnessed Maliki's success and the failure of the Islamic Supreme Council of Iraq (ISCI) in the local elections, Tehran is now busy trying to rebrand the all-Shiite United Iraqi Alliance (UIA) as a supposedly nationalist alliance; however even people in the Daawa party have publicly declared that this is an attempt by Iran to once more unify the Shiite parties on a single sectarian platform. Even more surprising, then, is this latest push from the West, probably with different intentions, but with exactly the same impact: Just like Iran, Biden came to Baghdad to talk about "Kurds, Shiites and Sunnis" at a time Iraqis were struggling to transcend these categories.

If Obama wishes to be sincere to his own promise of greater respect for the Arab and the Muslim worlds, he needs to understand that Iraqis will reject both territorial and psychological variants of a partition approach. The best thing he and his administration can do is probably to talk as little as possible about "Shiites, Sunnis and Kurds" in the future. Rather than trying to force some kind of grand compromise using ideas that clearly belong to the past and leverage Washington no longer possesses (Maliki has already rejected Biden's offer twice), the U.S. should simply spend its energies helping the Iraqis facilitate the required compromises themselves. The next parliamentary elections in 2010 could become the transformative moment which Iraq did not get back in 2005; the U.S. could do its part simply by trying to make those elections free and fair in the widest possible sense, and by generally refraining from reproducing notions of tripartite reconciliation that only play into the hands of the sectarian forces of the past.

Beyond Power-Sharing?[5]

July 6, 2010

The contradiction in the Obama administration's public diplomacy in Iraq is encapsulated in a recent letter to Prime Minister Nuri al-Maliki from Congressman Bill Delahunt and signed by some 30 other members of the U.S. Congress, mostly Democrats. In it, they congratulate the Iraqi electorate for having voted en masse on 7 March 2010 for what is described as the two "cross-community" lists in Iraq, Iraqiyya led by Ayad Allawi and State of Law (SLA) headed by Nuri al-Maliki. That is just about right: Both Iraqiyya and SLA started out as non-sectarian projects, and although thanks to de-Baathification they both ended up looking more sectarian (leaning Sunni and Shiite respectively), there was no doubt that the pressures towards sectarian repolarization came from the other parties. Those other, sub-identity-oriented parties, in turn, did a lot worse: The Iraqi National Alliance and the Kurdistan Alliance could manage only around 115 seats altogether, which is markedly less than the 180 seats shared by Iraqiyya and State of Law.

So, having correctly taken note of this important distinction, the congressmen presumably go on to recommend that the two cross-community lists join each other in a strong alliance? Alas, this is where the logic stops. The letter from Delahunt goes on to talk about a "national unity" government and while in theory this could have meant just Allawi and Maliki, the accompanying press release makes it perfectly clear that the U.S. politicians want Maliki to include all the "winning coalitions". In other words, they want to add the "retrograde" sectarian lists (their implicit judgment) to the "progressive" cross-sectarian ones in government! What a remarkable way of reasoning this is: "Even though you brave Iraqis clearly prefer a non-sectarian government, we, fat-cat congressmen in Washington feel a little uneasy about that prospect. You see, certain highbrow think tank types over here who just recently did a terrific crash course on Iraq keep telling us that in order to avoid a complete unravelling of the situation we must also include the straw men of Masud Barzani and Ammar al-Hakim in the government. Oh, yes, we know those two are the authors of many of the problems in Iraq over the past five years including the silly idea of a Shiite sectarian region and the purge of most competent bureaucrats from the machinery of the state in the name of de-Baathification but you see these men are very important, and if they feel ever so slightly unhappy things could go seriously wrong. So it does not really matter what the electorate said about cross-community dreams; unfortunately you will just have to put up with another dysfunctional, incompetent and weak government in Iraq for the next five years. We really do hope you may understand our concerns".

And unfortunately, this is precisely the message Biden has been pushing publicly in Iraq during the weekend. After having held his cards tight to his chest on his first day, some worrisome signs were beginning to emerge after the visit to Ammar al-Hakim early Monday. According to an ISCI statement, Biden had "conveyed the respect of President Barack Obama to Ammar al-Hakim and his praise for ISCI's role in bringing about rapprochement between the Iraqi parties [!] in order to form a government of real partnership of all Iraqi factions. . . ." Of course, this was an ISCI press release and it could have been suspected of perhaps bending the message a little to fit the party's own agenda. But shortly afterwards, Biden himself spoke to the media, and there it was: "In my humble opinion, in order for you to achieve your goals you must have all communities' voices represented in this new government, proportionately. . . . Iraqiyya, State of Law, Iraqi National Alliance, the Kurdistan Alliance, all are going to have to play a meaningful role in this new government for it to work". In fact, the basic idea of including "all the winning lists" was also conveyed during the meeting with Maliki on Sunday according to his spokesman Ali al-Dabbagh.

This is the Paul Bremer fallacy repeated. It just seems America will never pass ontological puberty in Iraq: Even as they celebrate non-sectarian tendencies they still want to make sure all the sectarian parties are in there, disregarding that the Kurds have actually already been empowered locally through federalism and the fact that Shiites and Sunnis clearly dislike the idea of enshrining sectarian identity at the level of the state. The element of proportionality, in turn, is of course a veritable cave-in to the Iranian agenda in Iraq—Tehran has openly argued in favor of a "strong Shiite-led government" of the kind Biden's formula will produce if it succeeds. No one should be surprised though, since Biden previously spoke glowingly about the idea of "bringing in the region" in Iraq, and has been unable to move beyond the paradigm of "Shiites, Sunnis and Kurds" ever since he was charged with the Iraq portfolio by Obama.

Even more worryingly, with respect to the practical aspect Biden repeated his own past mistake of not reading the Iraqi constitution properly. For a long time back in 2007 he thought there were constitutional mechanisms in place that could easily produce his preferred vision of a tripartite Iraq of three ethno-sectarian regions. Only gradually did he realize that the federalization law passed in October 2006 is a lot more complex and if activated can produce countless scenarios, with the tripartite one being one of the least probable. And so this time, he wants four parties in government. But in 2010, does he realize that if the constitution is followed, the chances of getting his four preferred ones into government are actually quite small? And that if it does succeed, it is likely to take a lot more time than most other scenarios? What Biden does not appear to understand is that Iraqiyya will disintegrate in an oversized government where they are not given the premiership and that Maliki is unlikely to go quietly if there are attempts by other Shiites to use his votes while at the same time marginalizing him as premier candidate. Absent any rewriting of the constitution, the particular four-way alliance preferred by Biden is actually a rather unlikely outcome, no matter how much some Iraqi politicians may pay lip service to the idea.

Operation Iraqi Partition[6]
September 1, 2010

"Iraq is free to chart its own course". The message from the Obama administration as Operation Iraqi Freedom came to an end sounded wonderful, like the release from captivity of a beautiful bird.

Alas, Iraq today is anything but a beautiful bird. Rather it is a wounded prisoner, incarcerated for the past seven years in a mental prison. True, things were not great before 2003 either: Back then, Iraq was ruled by a brutal regime whose excesses would at times assume sectarian or racist forms. Nonetheless, equally problematic, in a different way, are the acts of the motley crew of members of the "international community" whose task it was to rehabilitate the victims of the Iraq War after 2003 and put the country on the right path to true freedom. Instead, through their blind insistence on a discourse of ethnic and sectarian division they gave political opportunists returning from exile a head start and charted the way for a constitution and a political system that resonate poorly with Iraq's historical past.

To truly appreciate the immensity of this crime and the degree of complicity in it among Western intellectuals more generally, let's not focus here on the big, famous or powerful, whose agendas and intellectual parameters are well known. They include of course people like Paul Bremer, Peter Galbraith, Joe Biden, Chris Hill and Ad Melkert who in their various ways have all insisted on dividing the Iraqis territorially and conceptually, as if ethno-religious communities somehow constituted distinct branches of humanity. And let's not go so much into what journalists have done in this regard, except mentioning that probably the most consistent offender is the elusive "Qassim Abdul-Zahra" of AFP/AP (probably a pen name) as well as pretty much every Baghdad correspondent that has worked for the BBC over the past seven years (yesterday, the BBC simply subtitled an interview with Ala Makki of Iraqiyya with "Sunni MP". How would they describe [the Shiite] Ayad Allawi of the same secular party?) No, let's instead look at the writings of a less known, bright young American professor at Harvard who in many ways has tried to engage in constructive dialogue with the Islamic world and at one point in 2004 also had a role as a consultant on the Transitional Administrative Law that governed Iraq from 2004 to 2005. Even he cannot get Iraqi history right.

In a recent op-ed in *The Wall Street Journal*, Noah Feldman made the case for a prolonged U.S. presence in Iraq beyond 2011. Feldman writes, "Iraqis' primary identities are still of religious denomination or ethnicity, not of Iraqi nationhood—and that may remain the case indefinitely. Iraqi national identity under Saddam Hussein never truly incorporated Shiites or Kurds. Sunnis, who identified most closely with the Iraqi nation, remain in some ways disenfranchised relative to the other groups, or at least they perceive themselves that way".

So Feldman claims Iraqi Shiites are less identified with the Iraqi nation than the Sunnis! The only problem with that bold assertion is that it totally lacks an empirical basis. Had the Harvard professor bothered to read Iraqi newspapers from the 1920s, he would have been astonished by the countless contributions by prominent Shiite intellectuals who celebrated Iraqi nationalism and their alliance with the (mainly Sunni) population in the northern areas of Iraq in opposing the British presence at the time. Muhammad Mahdi al-Basir from Hilla and Jaafar Abu Timman from Baghdad are but a few examples that come to mind. As for Feldman's assertion elsewhere in the article that Iraq was somehow "born" as a result of British machinations, why doesn't he turn to the *Lughat al-Arab* journal that was published in Baghdad in the Young Turk era (1908–1914)? It is in fact littered with patriotic references to Iraq as a *watan* (homeland) in articles by writers like Anastas al-Karmili (a Christian) and Kazim al-Dujayli (a Shiite).

There has been much talk about conspiracies by hostile powers to divide Iraq into separate statelets, and most of it is probably unfounded. This partition conspiracy, however, is real and since it mostly goes undiagnosed it represents arguably the far most dangerous aspect of the Iraq War: Brilliant Western academics who may have the best possible intentions towards Iraq and its people but who in an attempt at sounding sophisticated perpetuate the toxic paradigm of a tripartite Iraq—be it territorially or sociologically—simply because they have failed to study the country's history properly through primary sources. The suggestion is not that sectarian and ethnic issues are non-existent in Iraqi history. But if Western academics had stopped reproducing what are outright lies about the origins of the modern Iraqi state, the whole climate of the discourse on Iraq would have looked vastly different. Rewrite that Feldman op-ed, delete everything that is empirically incorrect about Iraq's history, and check to see how much is left of the original argument.

Operation Iraqi Freedom may be over, but Operation Iraqi Partition lives on, regardless of Security Council resolutions or status of forces agreements. Unfortunately, there is no anti-war movement against it in the Western world because most of the academics there are in fact its loyal soldiers.

CHAPTER NOTES

1 The original version of this text was published on History News Network. See http://hnn.us/roundup/entries/29297.html.

2 See http://hnn.us/articles/42598.html.

3 See http://historiae.org/obama-mccain.asp.

4 See http://www.historiae.org/muhasasa.asp.

5 See http://gulfanalysis.wordpress.com/2010/07/06/delahunt-biden-and-obamas-contradictive-public-diplomacy-in-iraq/.

6 See http://gulfanalysis.wordpress.com/2010/09/01/operation-iraqi-partition/.

PART I

Key Political Developments, 2005–2010

Iraq's cities

Cartography by Ross Bradley and © 2010 Just World Publishing, LLC

Iraq's governorates and the Kurdistan federal region

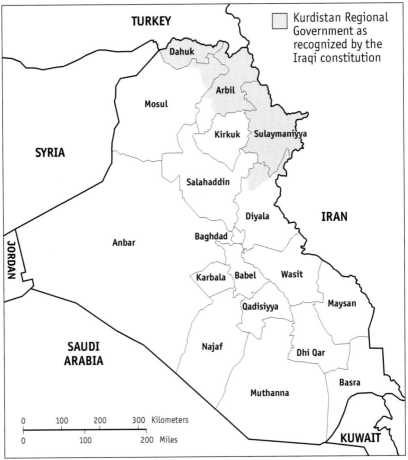

Cartography by Ross Bradley and © 2010 Just World Publishing, LLC

Chapter 2

The Collapse of the UIA and the Disintegration of Sectarian Politics, 2005–2007

My writings between 2005 and 2007 focused on two main topics: The diversity of the Iraqi Shiites generally (as a contrast to the monolithic image often conveyed in the Western press), and the overall marginality among the Shiites of the Supreme Council for the Islamic Revolution in Iraq (SCIRI/ISCI) and its pet project of establishing a single Shiite federal region comprising the nine Shiite-majority governorates south of Baghdad (both often described in the Western media as very significant factors). Beyond the Shiite areas, I concentrated on how a strategic alliance with the Kurds plus the increasingly fragmented Tawafuq bloc as some kind of symbolic "Sunni" ornament enabled SCIRI/ISCI to hold on to influential positions despite its faltering support base among the Shiites themselves.

Referring to history—or more correctly, to the complete lack of historical precedents for a purely sectarian polity in Iraq—it was pretty easy to predict that SCIRI/ISCI's Shiite federal region would never fly. Gradually, even the politicians who had concocted the scheme must have realized this, even though it took quite some time before the outside world understood what was happening. I highlighted an apparent decline of interest in the Shiite region on the part of ISCI already in summer 2007, but the Western media kept reporting the scheme as a dominant theme throughout 2008. What happened in reality was that ISCI gave up the specific idea of creating a nine-governorate Shiite region and transformed itself into a party favoring broad decentralization and a weakening of Baghdad more generally—if need be by strengthening the powers of the existing governorates in what seemed to be a "light" version of the more openly predatory approach pursued by their Kurdish partners. The failure of ISCI's attempts to give their projected region a name—first they called it the "Region of the Center and the South," before they proceeded to rename it "The South of Baghdad Region"—stood out as a particularly apt reflection of their inability to drum up popular support for what most Iraqis saw as a novel and strange scheme.

It was a tougher job to convince readers that the Shiites of Iraq were more than SCIRI/ISCI and its then-leader Abd al-Aziz al-Hakim. At the time, the U.S. government used Hakim and his friends as their almost exclusive point of contact with the Shiites of Iraq, and the mainstream media would invariably refer to Hakim as a "cleric" heading "the most powerful" or the "biggest" Shiite political party in Iraq. (A more accurate profile of Hakim would have referred to him as an ex-student of religion of no distinction in the Shiite hierarchy of learning who had gone on to become a militia boss based in Iran from the early 1980s to 2003.) The key theme in my analyses of the elections of December 15, 2005, was to deconstruct the idea of SCIRI's assumed mightiness, with an emphasis on showing how the followers of Muqtada al-Sadr were almost equally strong numerically and that most parties within the diverse, all-Shiite United Iraqi Alliance (UIA) actually disagreed quite strongly with SCIRI's ideas about federalism. That tension came to the fore as Ibrahim al-Jaafari, a supporter of a strong central government, sidelined SCIRI's Adil Abd al-Mahdi in the UIA's internal contest to name a premier in March 2006. Jaafari, in turn, was sidelined by Nuri al-Maliki—who just like Jaafari surrounded himself with people who preferred a strong center instead of devolution.

Even the destruction of the Samarra shrine by terrorists in February 2006—an act that was so clearly aimed at rousing sectarian hatreds in Iraq—did nothing to instill sectarian unity among the Iraqi Shiite parliamentarians. Perhaps the first significant manifestation of this intra-Shiite disunity in the national arena was the joint Shiite–Sunni resistance to the federal legislation project in October 2006, which clearly foreshadowed the nationalist tendencies that would dominate Iraq in 2008 and early 2009. Equally telling was the fact that, as the soft partition debate got going in earnest in the United States in autumn 2007 (on which more follows in chapter 10), this debate met with deafening silence from Iraq's Shiites and the expected Shiite bid for a federal entity simply failed to materialize—though many U.S. senators continued to make elaborate references to the assumed vitality of Shiite-led regionalism!

I did not write much about U.S. policy beyond making a general recommendation that Washington might diversify its contacts beyond SCIRI and establish dialogue with a greater array of political forces among the Shiites. Since SCIRI's force and appeal to the Iraqi electorate was exaggerated, I argued, Washington was performing a great disservice to itself by perpetuating SCIRI's privileged status as the main Shiite interlocutor with the outside world. In particular, I tried to emphasize that there were a wide range of parties inside the UIA—such as Daawa, the Sadrists, and Fadila—that had historically been less inclined than SCIRI to cooperate with Tehran and that the failure of the U.S. to engage with such parties would inevitably push them into Iranian arms, the historical record of mutual antagonisms notwithstanding.

The point about Shiite diversity was generally well taken by analysts in Washington, it seemed. In particular, the fiction of SCIRI as the "most important

Shiite party" in Iraq was relatively easy to dismiss empirically. Nonetheless, the seemingly contradictory U.S. alliance with this the most pro-Iranian of all the Iraqi Shiite parties appeared to have its vocal defenders even among intelligence analysts who had a good grasp of the situation as a whole. One of them once explained to me that the idea was that gradually SCIRI would develop a sense of Iraqiness and cut its ties to Iran, with "mid-level commanders of the Badr forces" supposedly forming a particularly important force in the process of conversion. However, I could still not get a good answer as to why Washington remained uninterested in talking to the 75 percent of the UIA that had far looser ties to Iran at the time. As a result, when the "surge" started in early 2007 there really was no point in trying to reach out to someone like Muqtada al-Sadr anymore. After several years of having been erroneously labeled as a "pro-Iranian firebrand cleric" in Western newspapers and the Bush administration, Sadr finally got to the point where his fear of arrest or death became such that he actually fled to his old arch-enemies in Tehran and ironically became an asset to them at long last.

In The Gamble *Tom Ricks* writes that my essays were being read by advisors to General David Petraeus during this period, but my own American contacts at the time were mostly limited to analysts. As for the way that high-ranking U.S. policy-makers viewed SCIRI/ISCI, one academic friend who had discussed the subject with Vice-President Dick Cheney described how Cheney had flatly rejected a proposal to integrate a larger number of competent former officers of the old regime into the new Iraqi army by saying: "Abd al-Aziz al-Hakim [SCIRI's pro-Iranian leader] does not want that." One is left with the choice of interpreting U.S. policy in Iraq during Cheney's time in office as either flawed to the point where it verged on the ridiculous in terms of empowering Iranian clients in Iraq, or as having been premised on a belief in some kind of very dramatic rupture, i.e., a second war in the region, with Iran.

One final interesting realization in this period was that even as I had started as some kind of "Basra expert," I was soon expected in U.S. government circles and the international media to play the role of a "Shiite expert." At first, I resisted this rather abrupt expansion of my newfound authority; gradually, however, I concluded that this was probably the way things operated in Washington and the mainstream media. By April 2006 I had written a paper on the political philosophy of the leading Shiite cleric of Najaf, Ali al-Sistani, which met with a much more favorable reception than I thought it really deserved. In reality, it was a straightforward analysis of a couple of dozen fatwas issued by Sistani in the post-2003 period. It struck me then that making an impression among Washington analysts was perhaps somewhat easier than it ought to be, considering not least the vast economic resources at the disposal of the world's only remaining superpower. Similarly when I was invited to my first Iraq conference in the United States in early 2006 I had expected to be interrogated as to the provenance of my sources and techniques for making the most of advanced, *exact-term Google searches in Arabic. Nothing of the kind ever materialized. Many of the analysts I met had experiences from entirely different parts of the world (such as Latin America) and knew no Arabic. There were all sorts of units with fancy names associated with the ongoing war effort in Iraq, including those engaged in "human terrain" analysis. Yet it was not until early 2009 that I finally met a U.S. Iraq analyst who used Google in Arabic in innovative ways to retrieve materials from obscure locations on the internet—but he did not have a security clearance to work on confidential materials for the U.S. government! To a considerable extent, then, there seemed to be a correlation between simplistic models for understanding Iraqi politics and a pronounced lack of resources—even in the midst of the Bush administration's wild spending spree in Iraq—for trying to understand Iraqi history and society.*

Towards Sectarian Separatism in Iraq?[1]
December 13, 2005

Threats to Iraq's territorial integrity are as old as the state itself. Kurdish demands for autonomy go back almost a century. Secular Basra leaders challenged the monarchy during the 1920s through a bid for a cosmopolitan city-state republic. There were even plans for a Christian enclave in northern Iraq in the interwar period.

Missing from this list is a scheme for a sectarian Shiite breakaway state. Even though outsiders frequently dreamt of this kind of scenario, the Iraqi Shiites themselves, throughout the twentieth century, appeared disinterested.

With one exception, that is. It occurred in 1927. After a savage clash between worshippers and Iraqi soldiers at Kazimayn, Shiite politicians whipped up a surge of sectarian discontent. At secret meetings, whispers of a Shiite state stretching from Baghdad to the Gulf were heard. But in the end, the attempt at separation proved abortive. The leading Shiite clergy rebuked the hot-headed radicals. One year later, the whole episode was forgotten.

The movers behind the Shiite separatist scheme were a diverse coalition. Some were disgruntled tribal leaders. Some were impoverished lower-rank clerics. The principal figure was Amin al-Charchafchi, a layman from a Baghdad merchant family, with strong links to the ulama. He may not have been the separatist architect, but his ability to gain access to the top clerics was all-important. At one point, he was close to securing their support.

Is the Charchafchi phenomenon present in Iraqi politics in 2005?

The most obvious parallel is the ongoing campaign for a single Shiite federal entity from Karbala to Basra. Launched last summer, this project uses sectarian identity to push for the unification of all provinces south of Baghdad. It has largely supplanted earlier Shiite calls for a federal Iraq with smaller, non-sectarian units.

Ironically, it seems as if the long-suffering Shiites are succumbing to sectarianism just as their prospects for securing a fair share of government in a democratic Iraq look brighter than ever.

The similarities to 1927 are numerous. Also today's movement is headed by professional politicians, not by the upper ranks of the clergy. Just like Charchafchi in 1927, these leaders have immense organizational skills. And like him they have no scruples about using sectarianism to boost their influence. With determination they approach the leading ayatollahs to elicit some sort of approval for their projects. Any signs of approval, however hesitant, are in turn employed to convince electors that they have a religious duty to give their support. The continuing terror attacks and anti-Shiite propaganda by Sunni Islamists can only fuel tensions; this echoes the harsh strictures on Shiite heritage by Sunni intellectuals seen in 1927.

The pro-federal Shiite politicians do not themselves promote separatism. Their own personal motives may be perfectly all-Iraqi. It is those on the fringes that challenge Iraq's territorial integrity. It is they who write on the internet about a single Shiite state from Samarra to Basra. It is they who see the pro-Shiite but technically multi-sectarian election ticket of the United Iraqi Alliance as essentially a "United *Shiite* Alliance". And it is they who are inclined to find inspiration in pamphlet literature where schemes for a "Shiite federalism" that would combine both Iran and Iraq are outlined.

The politicians' role is to build bridges between the higher clergy and grassroots radicals. In this they are astonishingly successful. Every single public statement by Grand Ayatollah Ali al-Sistani shows that the he is deeply concerned about the territorial integrity of Iraq and the dangers of sectarian warfare. And yet Shiite professional politicians somehow manage to maintain cordial relations with Sistani while at the same time pursuing policies that directly—if unintentionally—threaten the very unity so dear to Iraq's leading cleric. The most recent example is the last-minute green light from Najaf for a Yes vote to the new Iraqi constitution—a document devoid of real checks and balances against the forces of fragmentation. This sort of leeway is what Amin al-Charchafchi failed to achieve when he approached the ulama in 1927.

The upcoming elections may prove decisive. Sectarian factions among the Shiite Islamists persuaded the United States to accord them privileged status during the exile opposition meetings. They tenaciously held on to this position after the war, and translated it into electoral success last January by joining the "Sistani list"—so named after its assumed but taciturn sponsor. Today, they are again part of a wider Shiite coalition that frequently alleges it enjoys the top clergy's exclusive endorsement (but has yet to produce a fatwa or other unequivocal, signed and sealed statement to that effect). Will Iraqi electors once more allow these politicians a monopoly on expounding Sistani's reticent communications? Will those agitators themselves realize that their present course poses risks to the proud anti-sectarian tradition of Iraq's Shiites? Such issues could determine whether

Shiite separatism again gets relegated to parenthesis status in Iraqi history—or is transformed into a major theme.

A Disunited Iraqi Alliance Triumphs in the South[2]
December 22, 2005

On 20 December, the Iraqi election commission released partial elections results from the 15 December parliamentary elections based on more than 90% of the votes cast.

As many expected, the elections in the south were effectively reduced to a battle between two lists, the pro-Shiite, Islamist United Iraqi Alliance (UIA, list 555), and the secularist, anti-sectarian National Iraqi List (list 731). Many had predicted that the Islamists, who won massively in the last elections nearly a year ago, would meet with more effective competition this time. But the preliminary results indicate that the Islamist victory is now in fact even more resounding. The UIA has taken around 77% of the vote in Basra, 86% in Dhi Qar (the governorate to the north of Basra along the Euphrates) and a whopping 87% in Maysan (Basra's northern neighbor along the Tigris)—amounting to gains in the range of 5–15% on last January's poll. Ayad Allawi's secularists, on the other hand, have lost around 126,000 voters, or almost half of their support in Basra and Dhi Qar and three quarters of their voters in Maysan.

What has happened? Firstly, the UIA has seen its own ranks swell because more parties belonging to the radical Islamist Sadrist current chose to participate within the Alliance this time. But perhaps even more significantly, statistics suggest that the UIA may actually have won over large numbers of voters from Allawi since last January. In a pattern seen across Shiite-dominated governorates of Iraq, absolute numbers of Allawi supporters have consistently dropped although overall participation is now higher. (In governorates where Sunni majorities boycotted last January, Allawi has only managed to pick up 5 to 10% of the electorate that this time chose to participate). The very format of the electoral campaign may have stimulated this sectarian tendency: Regular debate was disrupted by the drama of Saddam Hussein's trial, before logistical issues of conveying voters safely to the polling centers took precedence and the country came to a standstill during the week before 15 December. In Basra there were allegations of police cars being employed for electioneering purposes on voting day; a testament to the influence of armed militias in the local administration. An atmosphere conducive to moderate debate of political issues it certainly was not.

In terms of parliamentary representation, the UIA looks set to walk away with 13 of 16 seats in Basra, 10 (possibly 11) of 12 in Dhi Qar, and 6 out of 7 in Maysan. Allawi's list will probably get 2 seats in Basra and 1 in each of the two neighboring governorates, whereas an independent Sadrist grouping (list 631) will compete fiercely with the UIA for the last seat in Dhi Qar. Finally, the Iraqi Accord Front, a mostly Sunni party with Islamist leanings, seems certain to get one seat in Basra, where the poor performance of Allawi's allies may indicate that Sunnis who boycotted in January now have voted largely along sectarian lines.

With the huge number of UIA deputies returned from the south, the focus will now inevitably shift to tensions within that heterogeneous bloc of politicians. It is often assumed that the Supreme Council for the Islamic Revolution in Iraq (SCIRI) is the leading force within the UIA. A closer look at the likely representatives for Basra, Maysan and Dhi Qar shows that while this interpretation may be true for the Baghdad leadership, it does not square with the party affiliations of UIA members in the south. Only 2 out of the 29 UIA candidates whose seats seem secure have a clear association with SCIRI, and an additional two from the institutionally independent Badr (formerly the Badr brigades) can be considered as being close to SCIRI. That means that more than 80% of UIA deputies from the south will have other, non-SCIRI, loyalties. Of these, 7 are Sadrists loyal to the radical Islamist Muqtada al-Sadr, 6 are members of the Fadila party (a competing Sadrist party whose spiritual guiding light is the cleric Muhammad al-Yaqubi) 5 belong to a breakaway faction of the Daawa party, 3 are from the mother branch of that organization (also the party of Ibrahim al-Jaafari, the current prime minister), and then there are 4 Islamist independents.

These patterns will have an impact on the struggle over southern regionalism which has simmered in the background of Islamist–secularist tensions in Basra and its environs over the past year and a half—and which will continue over the coming year as the constitution and other relevant legislation develop further. Within the UIA, SCIRI's Abd al-Aziz al-Hakim has taken the lead in calling for a single Shiite federal entity that would comprise all the land from Basra north to Baghdad. Southerners, on the other hand, are not so keen to merge their oil-rich territory with co-religionists further north and have established an alternative of their own: a smaller federal entity covering the triangle of Basra, Maysan and Dhi Qar. Crucially, at least three of the re-elected UIA deputies already have a record of creating internal dissension within the Alliance because of their particularistic demands for the deep south vis-à-vis the northern parts of the Shiite heartland. They are now being joined by Fadila representatives who have propagated the idea of isolating the "lesser southern region" during their past year in office in local government in Basra, thus effectively setting the stage for an internal UIA showdown over competing visions of federalism. (Among the non-UIA deputies, Ayad Jamal al-Din of Dhi Qar has indicated skepticism towards any federal project framed in sectarian terms, whereas Wail Abd al-Latif is a leading spokesperson for a smaller federal entity based on Basra.)

This southern battle over federalism has larger, national extensions that could influence power struggles in Baghdad. Importantly, the phenomenon of SCIRI hegemony within the UIA being challenged by non-SCIRI numerical superiority (in terms of new deputies) can be seen in most other governorates with the exception of Baghdad—and so Hakim and his plans for sectarian federalism may enjoy less support than is commonly thought. In addition to "southern regionalism" defectors, there are Sadrists from central parts of Iraq who are scornful of ideas of federalism altogether, and independents who are also more comfortable with the traditional idea of Iraqi nationalism defined in non-sectarian terms. Even nominal supporters of federalism like Ibrahim al-Jaafari and his Daawa party have at times hesitated in expressing active support for the concept, and have certainly signaled distaste for the sectarian specimens floated so enthusiastically by SCIRI.

All this means that despite the indications of an overwhelming UIA election victory in the south, the tripartite model of an ethnically divided Iraq federation may still get competition from older federal designs. These include the non-sectarian "administrative" federation of 5–7 medium-sized entities (with which the small-sized 3-governorate southern region plan would harmonize) as well as the long-established scheme for a bi-national Arab–Kurdish union. The election results also have implications for Abd al-Aziz al-Hakim and SCIRI: they may yet find themselves facing some quite unexpected obstacles in their struggle for supremacy over the Islamist political scene among Iraq's Shiites.

Beyond SCIRI and Abd al-Aziz al-Hakim: The Silent Forces of the United Iraqi Alliance[3]
January 20, 2006

With the release of final results from last December's elections, some reflections can be offered on the likely role of the largest winner, the United Iraqi Alliance (UIA) or list 555, in the next Iraqi parliament.

Crucial to any understanding of that role is an appreciation of the internal power games within the Alliance. One outstanding feature of the results for the "Deep South" of Iraq in the triangle Basra–Nasiriyya–Amara is the very weak representation of the party which has often been seen as the leading force within the UIA, the Supreme Council for the Islamic Revolution in Iraq (SCIRI). At first glance, this could seem like a localized phenomenon in the southernmost governorates, for the area has a strong tradition of creating internal north–south antagonisms among the Iraqi Shiites. But similar patterns, albeit slightly less pronounced, are now emerging in most areas all the way north to Salahaddin governorate, north of Baghdad. Only the Babel governorate and the Iraqi capital have returned delegations of more than two deputies from SCIRI and its close affiliate, Badr. The only remaining question is whether the scramble for the 19 compensatory or "national" seats won by the UIA can significantly change the balance. This is a murky process where the central coalition leaderships submit lists of candidates, and it has now emerged that the lists have yet to be handed in—thus possibly offering the SCIRI leaders a chance for reasserting themselves.

Unless SCIRI succeeds in completely dominating that final struggle, the new list of UIA deputies will warrant a rethinking of the Alliance's prospects in Iraqi politics. No longer is it possible to maintain the traditional image of the UIA as a tool completely at the disposal of SCIRI's Abd al-Aziz al-Hakim, with a sprinkling of wayward (but ultimately inconsequential) Sadrist renegades forming the only conceivable source of dissidence. Quite the contrary, the final results reveal vast zones of insecurity around Hakim, who himself commands the loyalty of only some 19% of the Alliance's confirmed parliamentarians. Supporters of the radical Muqtada al-Sadr, a Shiite cleric-to-be who has inherited a vast number of followers from his late father (Muhammad al-Sadr, assassinated by the former regime in 1999), emerge with 25 confirmed deputies to form one of the biggest one-party delegations in the new parliament—they will probably also get additional "national" seats. They are joined by another Sadrist group, the Fadila party, which is similarly inspired by the intellectual heritage of Muqtada's father but which has chosen to align with an independent cleric, Muhammad al-Yaqubi. Together, as of today, they account for around 36% of the UIA deputies, making it clear that the Sadrists in no way can be reduced to an ephemeral phenomenon in Iraqi politics. The second largest bloc within the Alliance identifiable by a modicum of shared political thought is also outside Hakim's direct control: the main faction of the Daawa will be accompanied by quite a substantial group of deputies representing a Daawa breakaway entity which has added the modifier Tanzim al-Iraq ("Iraq Organization") to the party name; combined they make up 23% of UIA's total of 109 confirmed deputies. A third grouping (22%) of independents and smaller parties is less homogeneous. But they too are unlikely to act as an uncritical mass of obedient placemen for Hakim. Although they include some pro-SCIRI politicians like Abbas al-Bayati, others have backgrounds that pull in different directions—Sami al-Askari (ex-Daawa) and Hussein al-Shahristani are examples of this.

What are the implications of this result? Naturally, there lies a danger in overestimating political cohesion within blocs like those made up by the various Daawa and Sadrist factions, whose experiences of internal splits have created considerable animosities between leading party personalities. It is also true that SCIRI are masterful coalition-builders whose maneuvers have left them in control of most if not all governorate councils in the Shiite areas. And quite substantial contingents of Sadrists have in fact been sitting in the outgoing parliament for almost one year without being able to unsettle SCIRI's hegemony. But the numerical strength of the clusters of non-SCIRI deputies will this time be more impressive. This seems bound to make some psychological impact and affect negotiating positions, and can in turn bring into play the ideological bonds that make the Sadrists and the Daawa current politically distinctive on many issues.

The most immediate decision likely to become affected by the UIA's internal structure is the ongoing negotiations for a new coalition government. Here, the strong Sadrist and Daawa representation emphatically points towards more whole-hearted overtures towards the Sunnis, as both groups have traditionally stressed anti-sectarianism and Iraqi nationalism as key features of their programs. (The Fadila more consistently so—grassroots elements within Muqtada al-Sadr's movement have been involved in some ugly anti-Sunni episodes, despite their leaders' often lofty rhetoric.) Last year, in local government in Basra, the Sadrist Fadila even entered into coalition with adherents of Ayad Allawi's secular Wifaq movement, completely sidelining none other than SCIRI in the governorate council.

Another potential impact concerns the federalism issue, expected to become important during the reassessment of the constitution scheduled for spring 2006, and a matter where simplistic media generalizations that "the Shiites all demand federalism and regional control of oil resources" are now becoming widespread. But just as the idea of a UIA perfectly submissive to Abd al-Aziz al-Hakim is overdue for revision, the notion of a homogenous "Southern Iraq" from Basra to Baghdad, united in a cry for the instant creation of a single Shiite federal entity, has now become obsolete. In the new parliament, there will be UIA representatives from the far south who, regardless of party affiliation, favor the creation of a smaller federal entity, the "Region of the South" (iqlim al-janub), limited to Basra and its two immediate neighboring governorates. And there will be representatives dismissive of federalism altogether: The Sadrist current in particular, but also the Daawa (both factions) have historically stressed the importance of a unified Iraq and voiced skepticism towards any project involving radical decentralization south of Baghdad, thus taking the traditional approach that sees federalism in Iraq as essentially an aspect of "the Kurdish question". The expected Kurdish–Shiite accord (more accurately, a PUK–KDP–SCIRI deal) that would create ethnic and sectarian enclaves in Kurdish and Shiite areas and leave a barren and oil-deficient rump Iraq in the Sunni west may therefore face competition from the original formula of a bi-national federation—in which the Arab parts of Iraq stay united, with a support base consisting of Kurds, Sunni Islamists, "northern" Sadrist and Daawa Shiite Islamists, as well as Arab secularists from all sectarian backgrounds.

With the elections results now finally released, it is tempting to speculate on how the misfit between public perceptions of the UIA and the actual patterns of party loyalties among its candidates came about in the first place. Why has the image of SCIRI as unrivalled kingmakers within the Alliance persisted, whilst some 80% of coalition members hitherto confirmed as deputies have remained obscure to outsiders? Why has there been so little interest in these huge swathes of uncharted political territory? Much is probably due to the slick and professional SCIRI leadership, who have been happy to reproduce the image of their own pre-eminence within the Alliance. The U.S. occupation authorities similarly have been content with a simplistic portrayal of the Shiite political scene: With a focus on a strong SCIRI as Washington's partners, there have been attempts at reducing Shiite dissent to "isolated" radicals in strictly delimited geographical areas—even though the attempts during 2004 at fencing in Muqtada al-Sadr in this manner proved just as futile as the venture to define a "Sunni triangle" without acknowledging populous Mosul as constituting a vital part of it. But the pro-SCIRI bias may also be the result of a more fundamental cleft in Iraqi politics: between the leading intelligentsia, who control the media and most contact with foreign journalists, and the larger masses of impoverished Iraqis and their young leaders, who are only now beginning to assert themselves in UIA elite politics. Last November and December, for instance, often-quoted Basra intellectuals turned the biggest local newspaper into a virtual election leaflet for their political party, the Popular Democratic Association. Reading the newspaper, one might easily get the impression that this party was the major political force in the Gulf city of more than one million citizens. In the event, the party received one hundred and ninety-eight votes in Basra. (The United Iraqi Alliance got 622,121.) Imams of neighborhood mosques may cut less impressive figures in the media world. But their impact on Iraqi politics in the early twenty-first century is formidable—and may well be a key to understanding both the provenance of the majority of votes cast on 15 December 2005, and the public enthusiasm for UIA figures who remain largely unknown outside Iraq.

SCIRI, Daawa, and the Sadrists in the Certified Iraq Elections Results[4]
February 11, 2006

After last month's distribution of 230 parliamentary seats won by candidates in Iraq's provinces, the United Iraqi Alliance (UIA) had 109 confirmed deputies, with supporters of Muqtada al-Sadr forming the largest bloc. The Alliance also received 19 "national" seats, but the allocation of these seats to individual deputies within the alliance was only announced yesterday, on 10 February.

Interesting statistics emerge from the distribution of these "national" seats. The Supreme Council for the Islamic Revolution in Iraq (SCIRI) and their close allies in Badr took no less than nine or almost half of the UIA's 19 seats. The Sadrists gained three seats; Fadila, two; Daawa (Tanzim al-Iraq), one; independents, four. The main faction of the Daawa received no "national" seats. In this manner, SCIRI managed to improve its overall share of UIA seats from 19% to 23%.

What enabled a single party to dominate this process so markedly? The explanation lies with a little-discussed peculiarity of the Iraqi election system. "National" and "compensatory" seats are common features in countries that practice proportional representation (PR) with multiple electoral districts (instead of a single district). The overarching aim of such devices is to achieve proportionality at the national level and to compensate for disproportionalities resulting from the introduction of districting into the process. In pursuing this goal, the Iraqi system shares features with several other PR systems; there is a particularly close parallel to the model adopted in Bosnia Herzegovina in 2000. But there is also one very important difference in the Iraqi system: here, the list order of the 45 seats awarded on a "national" basis is only decided by the political entities after the elections. (By way of contrast, in Bosnia these "national" lists, while not appearing on the ballots, are supposed to be publicly available in the period before the elections, all in the name of transparency.) The effect is of course that the Iraqi voter whose ballot ends up deciding a "national" seat never had the faintest idea about which candidate the vote would go to, except the name of the party and that it would be someone already on that party's lists—somewhere on a list, somewhere in the country.[5] Because the sole eligibility criterion for these seats is inclusion, in one way or another, on the list of the relevant political entity, party and coalition leaderships may horse-trade as much as they like with the seats that remain after "governorate" deputies have been named.

And the horse-trading among the UIA leadership appears to have been pretty intense. For instead of following any list-based logic, the UIA bosses have promoted relatively obscure SCIRI candidates from places far down on the lists, chiefly in Baghdad and northern Iraq, and thus from positions where they had been unlikely to succeed even if the UIA had performed better than they actually did. Technically, of course, these seats are meant to be "national" ones and thus detached from any geographical considerations. But the weak correlation between awarded seats and candidate electoral performance cannot escape notice. The new SCIRI deputy from Anbar province, for instance, has around 100 votes behind him, whereas the 300 or so UIA voters in Kurdish Sulaymaniyya were in a sense amply rewarded for their efforts: Two representatives to the new Iraqi parliament are from the UIA Sulaymaniyya list—the top Sadrist candidate and another SCIRI member who originally had ranked in fourth place on the ballot. Particularly instructive is what happened in Baghdad, where the UIA had 35 confirmed deputies before the distribution of "national" seats. First, number 36 and number 37 (non-SCIRI) on the list were bypassed by the coalition leadership. Numbers 38 through 41 did receive seats (one independent, one Sadrist, two Badr members), numbers 42 through 44 (non-SCIRI) were passed over, and then three seats were given to two SCIRI/Badr members and one member of Daawa (Tanzim al-Iraq) further down on the list. A candidate for Fadila and an independent placed at the very bottom of the list also received a seat each. In this way, the allocation of "national" seats has been completely detached from the ballot list order (instead of for instance employing a largest-remainders logic, which is often used in PR systems to address the problem of "wasted votes"). More appropriately, these seats could be termed "party seats", for the electorate has no influence whatsoever on how they are distributed to individual candidates within each political entity.

It is widely believed that some kind of pre-election formula on party quotas had been agreed inside the UIA and that this may have formed the leadership's rationale for an internal "redistribution" through "national" seats, but it is worth noting that had the UIA won a few more seats on a governorate basis, the coalition elite would have been unable to override the voters so effectively. If the aim is an electoral system where voters can better gauge the likely impact of their vote, other proportional representation (or PR hybrid) systems worldwide may offer features that could possibly be of relevance to the Iraqi system in the future, because they at least enable the electorate to make educated guesses about how the battles over "compensatory" and "national" seats are shaping up. In Scandinavian systems, this is done by pegging the distribution of compensatory seats to the ranking on provincial lists; in Bosnia voters may scrutinize the separate "national seats" lists before they cast their ballots; and there are of course countries that go all the way and explicitly acknowledge the dualism of district and "national" voting by giving the electorate two votes, as in Germany and Palestine. The tendency seen in Iraq today of back-room dealing in the distribution of the "national" seats seems distinctly at variance with the strong commitment to democracy otherwise prevailing among the general public in the country. (In fact, the precise modalities for creating lists for the "national" seats were not covered by the 2005 Iraqi electoral law at all; instead they appeared in a regulation issued by the Iraqi electoral commission, formally adopted as late as in November 2005 and apparently only made public on 6 December, 9 days ahead of the vote.)

Even after this impressive catch of seats by SCIRI, the internal UIA structure remains multiplex and without any obvious point of gravity (see Table 2.1). Recent political developments only serve to emphasize this. Complaints about the internal distribution of "national" seats have been loud, with some threatening to leave the coalition. The ongoing contest over the Alliance's candidate for prime minister has also taken a lot longer than UIA leaders had envisaged; some of the smaller parties such as Hizb al-Fadila have even fielded candidates of their own. And Sadrists have continued protesting against federalism, claiming that the issue should at least be postponed until all foreign forces have left Iraq. The Sadrist subtext seems to be that the whole course of Iraqi politics today is influenced by the presence of foreign troops (and their powerful diplomats, who are in the habit of paying frequent visits to a highly select pick of Iraqi politicians), and that normal conditions will only come once the external factor diminishes in importance. That point may conceivably even be aimed at the internal politics of the United Iraqi Alliance, where SCIRI is far ahead of everyone else in cultivating bilateral ties with Western embassies.

			Daawa			
Governorate	SCIRI	Independent	(Tanzim al-Iraq)	Daawa	Fadila	Sadrist
Basra	2	3	2	1	3	2
Maysan		1	1	1	1	2
Dhi Qar	2		3	1	2	3
Muthanna	1	1	2		1	
Qadisiyya	1	1	1	2	1	1
Babel	3	2		1		3
Najaf	1	2			1	3
Karbala	1	2			1	1
Wasit	2	2	1		1	1
Baghdad	7	8	2	6	3	8
Salahaddin		1				
Diyala		1		1		
Nineveh	1					1
National	9	4	1		2	3
Total	30	28	13	13	16	28*

Table 2.1: The intra-list structure of the United Iraqi Alliance

*Additionally, two Risaliyun deputies ran outside UIA but are expected to vote with the Sadrists.

The Maliki Government: What It Could Mean to Southern Iraq[6]
May 23, 2006

Despite shared bonds of Shiite Islam, the far south of Iraq—Basra, Maysan and Dhi Qar—was involved in some of the strongest criticism of the government led by Ibrahim al-Jaafari of the United Iraqi Alliance (UIA) in 2005. Is this internal friction within the Shiite camp likely to come to an end with the formation on 20 May 2006 of a new central government under the leadership of another UIA figure, Nuri al-Maliki?

A recurrent motive for southern resentment against a central government dominated by co-religionists from other parts of Iraq has been a sense of "marginalization" (tahmish). Government jobs, it was claimed, went to those Shiites who hailed from Baghdad and the holy cities of central Iraq—Najaf and Karbala. Development funds tended to end up in all other parts of the country. And even the ordinary democratic channel was blocked to the south, it was said. The January 2005 elections were carried out in a single national electoral constituency, and many southerners claimed that they were discriminated against in internal power struggles within the leading Shiite parties.

Statistics of ministers to the first post-2003 Iraqi governments confirm that there was some truth in these allegations, but also a degree of exaggeration. One example: two very senior UIA politicians who served as ministers, both from the Supreme Council of the Islamic Revolution in Iraq (SCIRI), are in fact of southern origin. But both Adil Abd al-Mahdi (born in Baghdad, but from a family of *sayyid*s from Shatra in Dhi Qar province) and Bayan Jabr Solagh (a Turkmen born in Maysan) may have spent too much of their careers in exile to be seen as "local" politicians first and foremost. Similarly, other representatives of the south in the interim and subsequent Allawi and Jaafari governments are individuals who returned to Iraq from abroad after 2003. They include Basrawis like Nuri al-Badran (interior minister in the interim government, resigned in early 2004) and Abd al-Falah al-Sudani (education minister under Jaafari), as well as Nasiriyya-born Qasim Dawud (national security advisor for Iyad Allawi from the autumn of 2004). Whilst the real significance of the cleavage between returnees and "domestic" Iraqis remains controversial, it is undeniable that a dichotomy of Iraqis classified as "the people of the outside" (*ahl al-kharij*) and the "sons of the interior" (*abna' al-dakhil*) is increasingly becoming a commonplace feature of Iraqi political discourse.

Some southerners with more long-established local connections did accede to government office after 2003; prominent among them was Wail Abd al-Latif (from Sharish north of Basra), a judge who served as minister for the provinces in Allawi's government. Others included Sami al-Muzaffar of Basra (of a Basra family of Shiite ulama) and Tahir al-Bakka (of Dhi Qar), but in both cases they held education ministries—posts that traditionally have been accorded limited prestige in Iraqi politics. (In the early days of the monarchy, this was the only portfolio the Shiites would get at all.) Nevertheless, at least one key government was allotted to someone from the south under Ibrahim al-Jaafari: the transportation ministry (involved in such grand projects as the projected Najaf airport and the upgrading of the port of Basra) was held by Salam al-Maliki of Basra, a Sadrist in his early 30s.

Two aspects of Maliki's government line-up stand out as far as relations with the far south are concerned. Firstly there are some remarkable exclusions. Most important is the marginalization of the Fadila party, which was squeezed out of the contest for the oil ministry on which its members had so high hopes—and who subsequently withdrew from the government negotiations. In isolation, this factor could strengthen southern discontent, because Fadila has played such a prominent role in regionalist propaganda over the past year, and because the demand for an oil minister to be recruited from the "oil region" has recurred—to no avail—ever since 2004. With access to the oil ministry as a source for spoils now blocked, Fadila will likely aim to consolidate its control over the structure currently remaining in its hands—the Basra governorate—and intensify its work to achieve a special federal status, either alone or with the two neighboring governorates. Similarly, the non-appearance of secularist Basra leader Wail Abd al-Latif in the final list of ministers is remarkable; for weeks he had been touted as a prominent ministerial candidate. Whereas infighting within the Iraqi National List of Ayad Allawi may have had something to do with this, media also reported a decisive "no" from the United Iraqi Alliance with regard to Abd al-Latif's candidature—in which case this would constitute a second major snub to a leader of southern regionalist senti-ment. Abd al-Latif had been involved in the first initiatives for a federal status for Basra, but had inclined towards a language of compromise in questions related to the management of oil revenue.

But there are also moves in the opposite direction, towards greater inclu-sion. Abd al-Falah al-Sudani, of the Daawa (Tanzim al-Iraq) in Basra, continues his ministerial career, this time in the trade ministry. During the early days of the monarchy this portfolio was known as a "Basra ministry"; today this kind of appointment resonates with Basra's mercantile traditions. Independent UIA member Safa al-Din al-Safi also continues in government, but remains in his old job as minister of state for the national assembly—undeniably one of the more contrived portfolios in a generally oversized cabinet (there are also posts for "national dialogue" and "civil society"). Much the same can be said of two other "southern" appointments, tribal leader Muhammad al-Uraybi, of the secular Iraqi National List and from Maysan, and Hasan al-Sari of Hizballah—a SCIRI-affiliated party with roots in the marshlands north of Basra. Both have been made ministers without portfolio.

One possible interpretation of all of this is that the Maliki government is reach-ing out for partners in the south who are not associated very strongly with the local regionalist trend. The choice of two tribal non-Sadrist ministers with connections to the Maysan area (Sari and Uraybi) stands out in this respect. Appointments of ministers of state without portfolio are by their very nature often suspect and could suggest ulterior motives that more than anything have to do with building power bases—in this case in a contested periphery, perhaps as a counterweight to Sadrist politicians who have often acted independently of those Sadrist leaders in central Iraq who are now Maliki's coalition partners. The exclusion of Fadila and other UIA individuals associated with the pro-southern current points in the same direction.

Will the alternative be a genuinely national direction of policy, and if so, will it succeed? So far, there is no evidence of Maliki backtracking from his party's long-standing commitment to Iraq's national unity and territorial integrity, or from the traditional Daawa skepticism towards potentially centrifugal forces. And in the south, despite all the talk of regionalism on the rise, such a policy could still have the power to succeed. Many southerners may be perfectly prepared to work within an Iraqi nationalist framework (and to abandon the regionalist frame of mind in assessments of the composition of the new team of ministers) as long as they feel that they are taken seriously by the center. If the central government acts in a truly national fashion (i.e., distributing services and investments equitably, bringing an end to the dreaded militia rule in Basra etc.) many in the south may respond by forgoing or at least postponing their plans for a federal mini-state in return. Indeed, several of the southern demands appear to be eminently negotiable: Southern under-representation in government bureaucracy and in Iraqi diplomatic missions abroad could be remedied, and southern demands for regional oil quotas could be addressed in a "softer" manner through long-term development funds set aside to address regional under-development—perhaps with some sort of international involvement in the assessment procedures, to address southern concerns about what is seen as the omnipresent and perennial problem of "northern" (whether Baghdad or Najaf) dominance. A steady flow of money will not extinguish southern grievances but may go a great way towards alleviating them.

Iraq Federalism Bill Adopted Amid Protests and Joint Shiite–Sunni Boycott[7]
October 12, 2006

Early reports about the adoption by the Iraqi parliament 11 October 2006 of a new Iraqi law for the formation of federal regions suggest that it was passed under rather chaotic circumstances. No more than some 140 parliamentarians—accounts vary from 138 to 141—or around half of the 275 members of the assembly turned up for the vote (all voted in favor of the bill), whereas most of the remaining deputies staged an organized boycott. At one point the session was reportedly closed to observers and journalists were not given access to the proceedings.

The boycott was largely inter-sectarian and Iraqi nationalist: It united all the Sunni parties of both secularist and Islamist colors and Shiite nationalist–Islamists, primarily supporters of Muqtada al-Sadr, as well as Fadila. At least one Turkmen representative also joined the main group of active boycotters, whose combined parliamentary strength is around 105 seats. Their objections range from virulent opposition to the principle of federalism (as seen among the Sunni groups), via preference for a system that would avoid sectarian federalism (Fadila; they also considered the adoption of the law at this time unhelpful to the process of national reconciliation) to rejection of federalism in a context of occupation (supporters of Muqtada al-Sadr). A conspicuous common denominator for many of these factions is their background as the "domestic" resistance to the former regime—as opposed to those deputies who are returnees from exile.

The principal backers of the bill were the Kurdish parties and the Supreme Council for the Islamic Revolution in Iraq (SCIRI), who together account for 88 seats. The balance of some 50 seats is believed to have come at least partly from Ayad Allawi's secularist alliance of 25 representatives—whose principal figures reportedly took part in the vote (Hamid Musa, Mahdi al-Hafiz, Wail Abd al-Latif, Safiyya al-Suhayl and Mufid al-Jazairi have all been specifically mentioned). The remaining votes that were required—perhaps between 30 and 40—must have come primarily from the "grey" middle segment of the Shiite United Iraqi Alliance (UIA), i.e. the 54 or so deputies who are neither SCIRI nor Sadrist and label themselves "independents" or come from one of the two main Daawa factions (an unspecified number of Allawi supporters protested against their leaders and stayed away from the vote). Lately the Daawa faction called Tanzim al-Iraq has changed its tradition-ally anti-federal rhetoric, and with its party mouthpiece now attacking those who "reject federalism on the pretext of national unity" it is very likely that it is drifting towards a pro-SCIRI position. On this particular vote they may have been joined by some members of the main Daawa branch as well as by independents, but the numbers make it clear that there must have been additional Shiite resistance to the bill on top of the protests by Fadila and the main Sadrist faction—despite the fact that there was reportedly enormous pressure on deputies to turn up for the vote.

SCIRI More Flexible on Federalism, but Fails to Resolve Khamenei Ambiguity[8]
May 12, 2007

The Supreme Council for the Islamic Revolution in Iraq (SCIRI) held its general meeting in Baghdad on 10 and 11 May 2007. The 49-point press release from the conference is noteworthy for at least two reasons.

Firstly, the document represents a notable softening of tone on the question of federalism in Iraq. In 2005 and 2006, SCIRI held a high profile in advocating the establishment of a single Shiite region of nine governorates from Basra to Baghdad. This region is not mentioned in the recent press release; instead there is general praise for the idea of federalism and emphasis on the need to follow the Iraqi con-stitution in this question, where after all a single Shiite region is but one of several possible outcomes (and, in fact, a rather unlikely one at that, given the complicated procedures for forming a federal region). Indeed, the explicit mention in the press release of "governorates" among the building blocks of the future federal Iraq sug-gests that SCIRI is now moving away from the view that the entire country should necessarily become subdivided into federal regions.

This coincides with an appreciable decline in propaganda in favor of the single Shiite federal region in early 2007, and with rumors of SCIRI members having sec-ond thoughts on the wisdom of any such large-scale federal entity—not least due to popular resistance from inside the Shiite community. Instead, forces close to SCIRI have begun re-exploring the old idea of several small-scale regions south of Baghdad, as seen for instance in the vision of Iqlim al-Janub (Region of the South) limited to Basra, Maysan and Dhi Qar—an idea that for the past years has been the preserve of SCIRI's archenemies in the south, such as the Fadila party. The sole mention in the press release of "the center and the south" (the key elements of the name of the projected Shiite mega-region, the Region of the Center and the South) is in a strictly geographical sense: in relation to a role for the tribes in ensuring local security, and as areas that have suffered particular deprivation in the past. Only when prompted by journalists at a news conference did SCIRI officials confirm that they were still in favor of the idea of a single Shiite region, but once again they stressed constitutionality and the role of the popular will above all. All in all, this could be signs of a constructive change of approach by SCIRI—and one that would be more in touch with Iraqi realities and the widespread skepticism among ordinary Iraqis to newfangled federalism ideas.

The second important point related to the press release is illustrated by the stark discrepancy between leaked information to the press by SCIRI officials prior to the publication of the document, and its actual contents on one key issue: SCIRI's relationship with Iran generally, and with that country's supreme leader, Ali Khamenei, in particular. Some early media reports suggested that SCIRI were about to formally renounce their ties to Khamenei, in favor of greater emphasis on the Grand Ayatollah Ali al-Sistani. That sort of loud and clear renunciation would have been immensely helpful to the Iraqi political process, and, along with a more flexible position on federalism, could have helped the party emerge as a true moderating force in Iraqi politics. Accusations against SCIRI of "pro-Iranian" and "Safavid" loyalties could then have been more easily consigned to the realm of conspiracy theories.

Ultimately, however, no such clarification of the party's position was included in SCIRI's press release, even though in the Western mainstream media there is already talk of a decisive "pledge". In fact, the only mention of Sistani in the press release was in a non-committal statement that SCIRI "valued" the efforts of the higher clergy in Iraq, including Sistani. (This of course reflects the fact that SCIRI does not have a reciprocal relationship with the leading Iraqi ayatollah; they need him more than he needs them.) True, the language of the press release is admirable and politically correct as such, with a condemnation of all external meddling in Iraqi affairs. But the failure to clarify SCIRI's relationship to Khamenei means that considerable ambiguity on this issue remains. After all, Muhammad Baqir al-Hakim (whose portrait dominated the conference room, alongside that of Sistani) is one of the few Shiite clerics in history to have made specific proposals for a greater Islamic union of countries with strong Shiite communities like Iraq, Iran and Lebanon under the leadership of a single supreme leader (*wali amr al-muslimin*, as described for example in the '*Aqidatuna* booklet from the 1990s). Since 2003, SCIRI have simply toned down their pan-Islamic and pan-Shiite rhetoric, instead of elaborating an alternative framework where they explicitly could have redefined their views on the concept of a single supreme leader. It is especially important in this context to distinguish between *wilayat al-faqih* as the particular model of government in Iran and the more general principle of submission to the *wali amr al-muslimin*: The late

Hakim is on record as saying that *wilayat al-faqih* may not be suitable for Iraq as an internal system of government due to the country's sectarian complexity, but that is not the same as a renunciation of the idea of loyalty to a single supreme leader, or even of pan-Shiite federalism of the kind propagated in *'Aqidatuna*—where the subunits presumably may retain separate systems of domestic government while at the same time somehow remaining under a pan-Shiite umbrella.

It is however interesting that the leaks prior to the publication of the SCIRI press release apparently came from SCIRI members who themselves were interested in marking some kind of break with Iran and Khamenei. This kind of desire among party members to stress their Iraqiness must have been the driving force behind some of the other points in the press release, such as the change of the name of the organization to the Supreme Islamic Iraqi Council (presumably SIIC; but later officially designated as ISCI by the group itself). It is an anomaly of Iraqi politics that there should be no well-organized party to represent the current associated with Sistani and his moderate Iraqi nationalist Islamism. The latest statement by SCIRI does not in itself quite suffice to fill that gap, but it does serve as an interesting indication that an internal debate on issues such as Iraqi nationalism and federalism may be underway within SCIRI. And if there has in fact been a real change in SCIRI's program on these important issues, SCIRI would win many friends in Iraqi politics by making this public in a coherent and comprehensive fashion, for all the world to see, instead of publishing bland documents like their latest press release.

The "Moderate Center" of Iraqi Politics[9]
October 7, 2007

Sunday 30 September 2007 saw a rare display of Iraqi–American unity in Baghdad: The U.S. embassy as well as scores of Iraqi politicians joined forces in condemning a U.S. Senate resolution to impose a federal state structure on all parts of Iraq. In general, there was agreement that the proposal which had been introduced by Senator Joseph Biden constituted gross interference in Iraqi internal affairs. Iraq already has a specific and very elaborate procedure for deciding the federalism issue, but both the timeline (nothing will start until 1 April 2008) as well as the size and number of the future federal entities (to be decided by popular referendums on the basis of grassroots initiatives) are clearly at variance with the Senate's proposal of an "international conference" intended to accelerate and simplify matters. For once, it seemed as if the Bush administration and the Iraqis were united in stressing the virtues of a unified Iraq capable of recovering from sectarian distrust.

There was one anomaly in this picture of Iraqi–American unity of purpose: The main forces that pulled together to condemn the Senate's decision were mostly from parties that are being largely ignored by the Bush administration.

They included Sadrists, the Fadila party, independents and Daawa members of the United Iraqi Alliance, the Tawafuq bloc, and secular groups like Iraqiyya and National Dialogue Front (Hiwar). All in all, they made up a strong Shiite–Sunni alliance accounting for more than a simple majority in Iraq's parliament. By way of contrast, all of Washington's principal allies in Iraq were absent: The Kurds enthusiastically welcomed the Senate decision, and the Islamic Supreme Council of Iraq (ISCI) wavered in its response, probably understanding some obvious parallels between the Senate proposal and their own scheme for a Shiite region, but also sensing a public opinion blowing in a different direction.

Could the message from Baghdad have been any clearer? Is there now any doubt as to where the real center in Iraqi politics is located? The reactions in Baghdad to the Senate decision convincingly demonstrate that there is in fact a majority of Iraqi politicians that are prepared to work for the Bush administration's goal of a unified and non-sectarian Iraq, independent from its neighbors while at the same time at peace with them. But this majority is different from the elusive "moderate coalition" that Washington has tried to cultivate over the past year—so far without any success in terms of "benchmark legislation" or national reconciliation. It is a majority that differs from the Bush administration's preferred allies in some key respects. It might for example be more restrictive towards foreign investment in the oil sector and would no doubt like to see a timetable for the withdrawal of U.S. troops. But they are the politicians who could deliver what should be the United States' primary objective in an Iraq of lowered and more realistic expectations: Maintenance of the country's territorial integrity, instead of its absorption into the realms of neighboring states as separate fiefdoms.

Engaging with this nationalist majority would require a rethink in Washington, above all with regard to federalism. It is now high time that U.S. politicians understand that ethnic and sectarian variants of federalism are simply considered unbeautiful by most Iraqis, and to insist on their implementation would only make matters worse. The alternative is to try to build on the majority potential that is so evident in these latest reactions in Baghdad to the U.S. Senate's proposal: Offer a timetable for withdrawal of U.S. troops in return for a revision of the constitution that would include some kind of limits on federalism. Yes, limits. It is such limits that have the potential to build bridges between Sunnis and Shiites in Iraq, to reinvigorate Iraqi nationalism, and to help heal sectarian conflict. They have repeatedly been proposed by nationalist forces in Iraq, but are routinely being blocked by Washington's "allies" among the Kurds and in ISCI who have jostled their way to key positions in the constitutional revision committee. True, this is the logical opposite of what Senator Biden has just proposed, but then again a viable way forward in Iraq will be one that enjoys a clear majority in the Iraqi parliament, rather than in the U.S. Senate.

CHAPTER NOTES

1 The original version of this text can be found at http://historiae.org/separatism.
asp.
2 See http://historiae.org/555.asp.
3 See http://historiae.org/UIA.asp.
4 See http://historiae.org/SCIRI.asp.
5 This should not be confused with the idea that voters did not know the names
of the candidates on the lists proper in the 2005 elections "for security reasons",
which is incorrect: All names were given on tables of correspondence in the election
centers. Also, even though voters were later given greater choice in terms of voting
for individual candidates in the 2010 elections (though they still did not appear on
the ballots but in publicly available registers), the old secretive system from 2005
remained in force for the distribution of these "national"/ "compensation" seats.
6 See http://historiae.org/Maliki-Government.asp.
7 See http://historiae.org/devolution.asp.
8 See http://historiae.org/khamenei.asp.
9 Op-ed published in *The News Journal,* Wilmington, Delaware (no longer available
online).

Chapter 3

The Turn to Nationalism in 2008

In early 2008, developments in Iraq appeared to be slowly turning in a direction more consonant with the long lines of the country's history: rapprochement between Sunnis and Shiites based on mutual, albeit often uneasy, commitment to Iraq as a shared territorial framework.

To some extent, this resonated with trends already discernible in the 2005 to 2007 period, with a particularly strong correlation between those parties that voted against the federalism legislation in October 2006 and those that eventually coalesced in the nationalist, cross-sectarian July 22 front in 2008. The new element in 2008 was the appearance of a rift between the key Shiite parties at the heart of the Maliki government—Maliki's own Daawa and ISCI (formerly known as SCIRI). This would gradually feed into the general tendency of growing nationalism and centralism as Maliki picked up many of the ideas of the nationalist opposition.

I began writing about Daawa–ISCI tension in February 2008, but it would take another half year before this conflict became fully visible. In the meantime, the key developments consisted of the discussion of the bill on provincial powers in February 2008; Maliki's increasingly visible role in security operations across Iraq subsequent to the U.S. "surge"—or at least his personal association with them; and finally the initial iteration of the provincial election law passed on July 22, 2008 (which eventually gave the new nationalist alliance its name). Both legislative projects included certain features associated with the embryonic cross-sectarian opposition, including a call for a timeline for local elections in the provincial powers law and a demand for special electoral arrangements in Kirkuk to compensate for perceived Kurdish highhandedness in the provincial elections law. At the same time, provisions reflecting the struggle between Maliki and ISCI made their way into both laws, with a stronger role for Baghdad than ISCI and the Kurds had wished for in the provincial powers law, and an open-list system and a ban on the use of religious symbols and places of worship during the election campaign in the provincial elections law—again against the wishes of ISCI. In this way, both the July 22 parties and Daawa and other centralists around Maliki won something and became wedded to the idea of persevering with the local elections against the preferences of the "establishment" that had done well in the previous local elections in 2005, notably the Kurds and ISCI. As autumn 2008 approached, the key question was to what extent the two forces would move closer together, either before the elections or in their aftermath.

I found this to be a fascinating period since certain positive tendencies that I had tried to highlight in the dark days of 2007 were beginning to assert themselves, if only very tentatively. In one moment of poetic justice in March 2008, some of the standard ethno-religious maps of Iraq that were decorating a conference room where I was presenting in Washington actually came off the wall as I switched to a Powerpoint slide showing an original map of the Ottoman province of Baghdad circa 1850, extending all the way from Basra to Mosul! But mostly my recommendations about diversifying U.S. policy beyond the dominant government parties (ISCI and the Kurds) fell on deaf ears. In February 2008, I told a gathering of U.S. analysts about the significance of the opposition parties in parliament coming together to demand provincial elections (this included Iraqiyya, Hiwar, Fadila, and the Sadrists). I stressed the need to reach out to Shiite Islamists outside ISCI before Iran did it. Fair enough, Washington actually did play a positive role when it came to the local elections, albeit in a rather forceful way: When ISCI and the Kurds in March 2008 tried to veto the law on provincial powers because of the timeline for local elections that had been inserted into it against their will, Vice-President Dick Cheney travelled to Baghdad to "talk" with the authors of the veto and miraculously it disappeared—probably the last occasion on which the U.S. government actually achieved something politically in Iraq through brute diplomacy. Months later, though, the U.S. would rather uncritically support the Maliki government as its bombs rained down on Basra, thereby starting the push of Sadrists and Fadila into the Iranian fold and preventing or at least discouraging the logical alliance between Maliki and the nascent July 22 forces.

At that time I briefly discussed with a National Security Council official the value of opening up a dialogue with the Sadrists—but to no avail. His take, which I found somewhat unrealistic, was that the Sadrists were extremely dangerous and that the Bush administration could instead rely on some kind of deal with the Shiite Grand Ayatollah Ali al-Sistani that would enable it to pass a Status of Forces Agreement (SOFA) to its own liking later in the year. . . . Another example of the contradictive "Shiite policy" of the Bush administration at the time was the stance of Ambassador Ryan Crocker, who publicly repeated the point that Iraqi Shiites would always be nationalists first and foremost and hence constituted some kind of "bulwark" against Iran, as had been seen during the Iran–Iraq War in the 1980s. But despite Crocker's fine words, the Bush administration was consistently choosing to cooperate only with those few Iraqis who had been fighting on the Iranian side during that war!

In Basra, Iraqi Nationalism Remains Proud and Articulate[1]

November 20, 2006

Today, analysts who emphasize the point about persisting Iraqi nationalism are routinely dismissed as utopians. References to long trends in history and warnings about the dangers of myopia are criticized for being out of touch with reality. Perhaps the best thing to do is therefore to stand back, and let some Iraqis speak for themselves.

In the 21 October issue of the Iraqi newspaper *Al-Manara*, several residents of Basra—a city characterized by deep divisions of opinion as regards federalism—expressed their views on the decentralization issue. The interviewees, who were identified by name and photograph, commented on the new law for implementing federalism in Iraq, as well as the more fundamental question of federal versus unitary models of government. Their articulate views and their heroic day-to-day efforts to combat sectarianism offer an effective counterweight to mainstream media reports about an Iraq divided into three mutually antagonistic monoliths.

According to Haytham Hashim, in principle there are no problems with federalism. In his view, "federalism and the law on the regions are part of family of successful and workable systems that have seen widespread application in the civilized world, including in Arab countries like the UAE, and I belong to those who say that federalism is unification not partition". But he is concerned about the way in which it will be implemented in Iraq: "The federal system should be demarcated in a spirit free from racism and sectarianism, by allowing governorates to become [uni-governorate] regions in their own right, or by combining with other governorates. But the adoption of this law at the present juncture I find somewhat hastened, because what the country is going through as regards security and economy does not permit the application of such a law. . . . I believe the fate of this law will depend on the will of the Iraqi people, and on their preparedness to live with this new system with which they are not familiar".

Nuha Zaki is more skeptical to the basic concept of federalism. She says, "I think the concept of regions is a bad idea, especially in the current situation with the sectarian winds and influences that are raiding our country, leading to the enshrinement of divisions at a time when we should do our utmost to combat sectarianism and make Iraq return to its past as a unified country and a unified people from north to south. The establishment of regions will lead to barriers that will have consequences for such areas as the economy and trade, which will be impeded by the creation of borders. . . . And at the social level, many Iraqi families are spread throughout the country from north to south and more borders will mean less contact within families. And politically speaking, I don't think we are in a sufficiently stable situation for our government to embark on this project".

Yet another Basrawi, Abu Usama, thinks that in certain settings, federalism may be a commendable political model. He describes it as a "developed democratic system of government". But he too is skeptical about its application in Iraq: "Iraq, the Land of the Two Rivers, was from the days of the monarchy a centralized state from north to south, and when the republic was declared, the late leader Abd al-Karim Qasim held on to every square inch of our dear fatherland of Iraq. But today we live under fire of the loathsome occupation which is aimed at splitting Iraq into races and sects. . . . Not everything that is workable in the West may be in harmony with Arab and Muslim Iraq. It is impossible to divide a unitary state and then reconstitute it as a federal state. . . . Today, Iraqi citizens don't need regions, they need security and services".

According to many Western analysts, these three citizens of Basra do not really exist. They are ghosts, raving about outdated ideas which "in reality" have been obliterated. Iraqi nationalism is supposedly dead; sectarian values rule supreme throughout the country. Why then, do Basrawis bother to appear in full public with their critical views on federalism? Why do they dare to suggest possible pitfalls concerning its implementation? And why do Iraqis sometimes mock the very sectarian categories they are supposed to belong to? ("I am a Sunni—at least that's how I am identified these days. . . . ") Oh, but those people are just Sunnis living as minorities in Shiite areas. . . . OK, perhaps some of them are in fact Shiites, but, you see, they are secularists, a dying sect. . . . Well, then, why is it that the leading Shiite cleric, the Grand Ayatollah Ali al-Sistani, in his latest pronouncement (15 October 2006) is at pains to point out that sectarian violence is more than just a problem of "Sunni extremists"? By hinting about sectarian malpractices on both sides Sistani risks quarrels with certain Shiite politicians who prefer to reduce the situation to a "Sunni *takfiri* problem", but he nevertheless sees a point in trying to transcend the sectarian divide.

Parliament Turns Nationalist[2]
February 11, 2008

Why is it taking so long to pass this the law on the powers of the governorates? During the repeated delays of the vote on the final package, two areas of disagreement have been at the forefront. The first concerns the right of the parliament in Baghdad to sack a local governor by an absolute majority, a somewhat surprising relic of centralism in a document which otherwise seems aimed at giving real powers to the governorates. On this issue, the anti-centralization parties (the Kurdish parties as well as the Islamic Supreme Council of Iraq or ISCI) have objected to the potential for interference by Baghdad that is implicit in the current draft.

The second point of dispute regarding the law concerns the timing of provincial elections, and has received even less public attention. But in a context where the Iraqi parliament has suddenly stopped issuing its daily minutes and opposi-tion parties such as the Iraqi Islamic Party criticize "parties inside the Maliki government" for "deliberate obstruction aimed at avoiding elections" but dare not mention their name, one cannot help wonder whether this is in fact the key issue. Again, it is the alliance of Kurds and ISCI that is making itself felt, but this time in a manner that seems less ideological: They flatly reject the idea of any timeline for provincial elections being inserted in the law, arguing that it would simply be out of place and should form the focus of separate legislation to be adopted at a later stage. Plausible at that may be from a purely judicial point of view, it cannot escape mention that early provincial elections is something which Iraq observers almost universally tend to highlight as a step in the right direction for the country. Significantly, the challenge to the ISCI–Kurdish axis on this issue comes from the cross-sectarian alliance in parliament that the United States routinely overlooks in favor of its own "moderate" government partners, and that includes parties like the (Shiite Islamist) Sadrists and Fadila, the (Sunni Islamist) Tawafuq and the (secular) Wifaq and Hiwar. Today, their "dangerous radicalism" is being expressed in a unified demand for a guarantee for local elections to be inserted in the gov-ernorates law (they complain that otherwise, the whole elections issue will tend to get further delayed), whereas Washington's "moderate" partners (who greatly benefited from Sunni and Sadrist non-participation back in the 2005 elections) seem to be deliberately slow-moving over the elections issue.

The Law on the Powers of the Governorates Is Passed[3]
February 14, 2008

The law on the powers of governorates not organized in a region was adopted by the Iraqi parliament on 13 February, but much of the reporting surrounding it in the Western mainstream media has been highly misleading.

In the first place, it should be emphasized that this is not an elections law and never was. It is a law that describes some of the powers of the existing administra-tive subunits in Iraq: the governorates or *muhafazat*. The idea of including a time-line for elections (1 October 2008 has been reported by several reliable sources) was creatively introduced by the opponents of the Maliki government; it was ferociously resisted by Maliki's most important backers, the Kurds and the Islamic Supreme Council of Iraq (ISCI). These parties argued that an election timeline would simply be out of place and should be postponed to separate legislation—an attitude many observers ascribe to the strong position these parties enjoy in the current governorate councils and the risk they run by holding elections. Their grudging accept of a timeline for elections thus represented a considerable triumph for the opposition, and at the same time exposed both the weak parliamentary fundament of the Maliki government and the anti-democratic strategies attempted by several of its coalition partners.

Secondly, the context of the bill's adoption has been grossly misrepresented in the Western media. The law was passed in a bundle with two other bills: the 2008 budget, and a law on amnesty for prisoners, including individuals suspected of insurgency activities but held without charge. Unsurprisingly, perhaps, leading newswires and U.S. papers have reported this as a "compromise between Shiites, Sunnis and Kurds", where each community supposedly favored one particular law! Nothing could have been further from the truth. The amnesty law was called for in particular by some Sunni parties as well as by the (Shiite) Sadrists, some of whom later complained that the law was not comprehensive enough. The law for the governorates, in turn, was not a "Shiite" demand, but a project that was sought by a broad alliance of groups which all had various motives for supporting it. Opponents of federalism—Shiites and Sunnis alike—have seen it as a framework in which the existing governorates can be given real powers and the holding of provincial elections can be accelerated. This explains why parties like the (Sunni Islamist) Tawafuq, the (Shiite Islamist) Sadrists and Fadila and the (secular) Wifaq and Hiwar have cooperated on the bill. They have faced resistance from ISCI and the two biggest Kurdish parties with regard to the demand for an elections time-line, but these anti-centralization parties, for their part, also see a potential in the law, by pushing for a maximum reduction of the powers of the central government in those areas of Iraq where their hopes for outright federalism are unlikely to be shared by the local population. Finally, parties representing all communities have realized the importance of passing a budget, although in this case an open "ethnic" dimension did materialize: the Kurdish demand for a 17% share of the federal budget has been criticized as being too high and out of touch with demographic realities and the compromise solution of a promised new percentage calculation for next year's budget survived in parliament but was nevertheless criticized by some non-Kurdish parties later on.

All in all, Iraqi criticism of the adoption of the bills has focused not so much on substance but rather on the procedure adopted by linking the three pieces of legislation in a single package. Critics see this as unconstitutional and a way of circumventing a more thorough debate about the Kurdish demands in particular—which probably passed because the two other bills to some extent mollified misgivings among parties with Iraqi nationalist agendas. Still, the passage of the governorates law means that the all-important issue of provincial elections is now firmly back on the agenda, and this cannot but have a positive effect on Iraqi politics. Hopefully, it will also involve more cross-sectarian politics of the kind witnessed in the Iraqi parliament over the past few weeks but so systematically overlooked by the Western press.

Maliki Begins Building a Power Base⁴

February 27, 2008

With the exceptions of oil-rich Basra and Maysan, the Shiite-majority governorates south of Baghdad are frequently referred to by observers as the loyal fiefdoms of the Islamic Supreme Council of Iraq (ISCI), America's and Iran's principal partner among the Shiites of Iraq. However, on the eve of Arbain—a holiday marked by the Shiites as ending the 40-day mourning period for Imam Hussein that starts on Ashura every year—Shiite Islamist politicians in the southern city of Nasiriyya have engaged in an intense internal struggle about the local security forces, casting doubt on the image of ISCI hegemony. On 25 February, a two-thirds majority of the governorate council decided to dissolve the local security council and transfer its powers to the local police chief instead.

This development is noteworthy for two reasons. Firstly, it is taking place in a setting—the provincial council—where no Sadrists are represented because they boycotted the January 2005 local elections. In other words, it is "other" Shiite Islamist forces, primarily Fadila but probably also at least some members of Daawa (Tanzim al-Iraq) that are behind the move. Whereas ISCI originally had managed to install their own man as governor of Nasiriyya, they are now being threatened from within in one of their supposedly "safe" constituencies. In this respect, Nasiriyya could be a bellwether for this autumn's provincial elections: Despite ISCI's dominance in terms of numbers of governors, many of "their" governorates south of Baghdad (including Karbala, Qadisiyya and Muthanna) have a rather complex party structure. The Sadrist challenge would come on top of this, as they are now signaling an eager desire to engage in electoral politics.

Secondly, it is significant that ISCI's opponents are deciding to strengthen the powers of the local police. This means that the image of full ISCI dominance in the security apparatuses of the south probably requires more nuance. In the case of Nasiriyya, it is actually ISCI who are now complaining about "party loyalties" exercising influence in the police force. That could be a result of increased local competition by other local parties asserting themselves in the security apparatus, but it could also be an expression of a conflict between ISCI and parts of the security forces that are more loyal to Nuri al-Maliki (and the central government) than to Abd al-Aziz al-Hakim—two leaders that increasingly have been at odds with each other over the past months.

The national aspect of this struggle was also emphasized today as the Iraqi presidency council issued a statement to the effect that it had vetoed the recent law passed by parliament on the powers of the governorates not organized in a federal region. The law and especially its provisions for early provincial elections had been resisted by ISCI and the Kurds, who control the presidency and two of the three vice-presidential positions. The presidency council today maintained that elections would go ahead on time, but the legislation is nevertheless sent back to parliament—ostensibly to sort out unspecified "constitutional" issues relating to the powers of the governors, but more likely because the elections themselves are seen as threatening by ISCI and the Kurds.

Maliki's Leap: The Second Battle of Basra[5]
March 26, 2008

On the surface, the story may look plausible enough. A provincial city rich in oil degenerates into mafia-style conditions affecting the security of citizens as well as the national oil revenue; the central government intervenes to clean up. This is how many in the media have been reporting the latest clashes between government forces and militiamen in Basra: the Maliki government has launched a security operation with the single aim of getting rid of unruly militias. Pundits with ties to the Bush administration have added that these are essential "preparations" for this autumn's provincial elections, or moves to forestall Iranian influence in Basra, or both.

But on closer inspection, there are problems in these narratives. Perhaps most importantly, there is a discrepancy between the description of Basra as a city ruled by several militias—which is doubtless correct—and the battlefield facts of the ongoing operations which seem to target only one of these militia groups, the Mahdi Army loyal to Muqtada al-Sadr. Surely, if the aim was to make Basra a safer place, it would have been logical to do something to also stem the influence of the other militias loyal to the local competitors of the Sadrists, the Islamic Supreme Council of Iraq (ISCI), as well as the armed groups allied to the Fadila party (which have dominated the oil protection services for a long time). But so far, only Sadrists have complained about attacks by government forces.

Others may suggest that rather than having to do with the rule of law, this is part of a wider operation in which Maliki in alliance with ISCI are doing their best to marginalize their political enemies locally—in preparation for local elections in October 2008, or with a view to dominate the process of forming federal entities (which could start next month, in April, when the moratorium on new federal regions agreed in October 2006 expires). Maybe it has been supported by Washington, as compensation for the bitter pill which Dick Cheney brought with him in the shape of a demand for early provincial elections despite the attempt at a presidential veto by ISCI and the Kurds? But whereas that sort of interpretation certainly seemed valid during the first battle of Basra (when Maliki arrived in Basra in late May 2006 and enforced a new security regime that was applauded by ISCI and denounced by Fadila), it does not quite make sense today.

Firstly, if the motive was the provincial elections or the federalism question, the target should have been Fadila and not the Sadrists. Basra is an exceedingly complex city (Shiite factions, Shaykhis, Christians, secularists, Sunnis, tribal groups etc.), and the overall electoral potential of the Sadrists there is probably considerably less than what many analysts have predicted. In the federalism question, the Sadrists are entirely on the sidelines, with the director of the Sadrist office in the city recently complaining that he was being kept in the dark about the project to make Basra a standalone federal unit (as propagated by Fadila and some of the secular leaders in the city in a scheme that challenges ISCI's vision of a single Shiite federal entity).

Secondly, there have been too many recent instances of conflict between Maliki and ISCI on these issues for that interpretation to make perfect sense. Increasingly, Maliki has associated himself with a more centralist current in Iraqi parliamentary politics, sometimes challenging ISCI directly, as seems to have happened during the process of adopting a law for the non-federated governorates. Whereas ISCI since early 2008 has been more outspoken in its attack on any interference by the central government in local affairs (much on the Kurdish pattern), Maliki has often defended the vision of a reasonably coherent and potent central government. In early March, ISCI demonstrators criticized Maliki's two handpicked security chiefs in Basra, General Mohan al-Firayji and Abd al-Jalil Khalaf, the police commander.

A less obvious explanation that may nevertheless be worth pursuing is Nuri al-Maliki's attempts to build an independent power base in the security services, to bolster his stature as prime minister (which ISCI repeatedly has attacked), and to compensate for his Daawa party's lack of strong militias. While the media over the last days have reported disagreements between Maliki and his two top security officials in Basra and even suggested their imminent dismissal, it may be more significant that for several weeks, both General Mohan and Khalaf (the police chief) had been talking about a forthcoming crackdown on militias (and on some occasions had singled out the Sadrists for criticism.) Prior to the current maneuvers, codenamed "the charge of the knights" or *sawlat al-fursan*, there were more limited operations against Mahdist followers of Ahmad al-Hasan in Basra back in January. Success in this kind of moves against internal Shiite enemies could conceivably make Maliki more immune against challenges to his premiership from ISCI although it still does not resolve the contradiction between his own centralism (where the Sadrists would be a logical partner) and the decentralism of ISCI. Also, the conciliatory statements by several Sadrist parliamentarians and directors of the provincial Sadrist offices in the first part of 2008 suggested that many of them would prefer politics to battlefield; it seems like a miscalculation by Maliki to spurn these overtures.

Still, there are probably few spots on this planet where the search for mono-causality is more futile than Basra. One key player that has so far refrained from showing its hand is Fadila, which controls the governor position. Back in 2007 the party frequently criticized Maliki's security operatives in Basra, at one point even signaling reluctance to the prospect of a handover from the British to the Iraqi forces. (The party may have feared that Maliki's attempt to oust them from positions of power locally—an attempt that was also supported by ISCI—would come to fruition as soon as the British forces were gone.) But then, after the December 2007 handover to Iraqi control and a subsequent "pact" between Basra's main political parties, the surface of local politics turned remarkably calm for a while. In January 2008, Fadila publicly supported the crackdown on the Mahdists, but the party has made no statement yet on the recent operations and very recently reiterated its preference for a non-sectarian form of small-scale federalism.

Perhaps the most useful approach is to compare the narratives of the parties involved. Maliki says this is a clampdown on illegal militias involved in "oil smuggling". ISCI also highlights oil smuggling and expresses support for "the state". The Sadrists complain about highhandedness by a government allied to "the occupation". This could all suggest that Maliki and ISCI, fundamental ideological tensions notwithstanding, have temporarily agreed to disagree about the question of federalism and instead resolved that the Sadrists are their common enemy.

Maliki, Hakim, and Iran's Role in the Basra Fighting[6]
April 9, 2008

The recent demonstrations against General Mohan al-Firayji in Basra can offer insights about Iran's role in southern Iraq. Alongside ISCI, another key participant in the demonstration was Daghir al-Musawi, leader of the small Sayyid al-Shuhada movement. Musawi's critics have long accused him of close ties to the leadership of the Iranian revolutionary guards. It is noteworthy that precisely in this context, Nuri al-Maliki's man, General Mohan, complained about "Iranian influence" in Basra. Similarly, as part of the Basra operations, Iraqi forces targeted the pro-Iranian Tharallah militia and arrested its leader. This less known casualty of the Basra fighting has been a loyal ally of ISCI in its campaign to unseat the Basra governor, Muhammad al-Waili of the anti-Iranian Fadila party. In 2006, black-clad members of Tharallah paraded through Basra identifying themselves as the "Martyr Muhammad Baqir al-Hakim Squadron", a reference to the previous leader of ISCI. Among the groups singled out by Ambassador Ryan Crocker for criticism in the 8 April U.S. Senate hearings on Iraq was "Hizbollah in Iraq", another stalwart local ally of ISCI (this Hizbollah should not be confused with "Hizbollah of Iraq" headed by Abd al-Karim al-Muhammadawi, or, for that matter, with the Lebanese Hizbollah).

In sum, it appears that Iran may have made an input on both sides during the Basra showdown. The smaller pro-Iranian parties within ISCI's umbrella organization put pressure on Maliki and may have nudged him towards taking stronger action against the Sadrists than originally contemplated. But the conclusion of a ceasefire on Iranian soil shows that Tehran's ability to influence the other end of the spectrum—the traditionally Iraqi nationalist Sadrist movement—may now be stronger than ever before, quite possibly the result of Muqtada's relocation to Iran at the beginning of "the surge", when he may have felt cornered by U.S. policy.

To the U.S. the good news is that Maliki still seems to insist on a certain independence vis-à-vis ISCI and Iran. A look at the composition of Maliki's entourage during his previous mission to Basra when he imposed emergency rule in May 2006 suggests that his power base is evolving. Then he arrived with the chief of the ISCI-linked Badr organization, Hadi al-Amiri, as well as a former Sadrist minister from Basra, Salam al-Maliki. This time his aides consisted of independents, interior ministry staff, and Shirwan al-Waili of the Tanzim al-Iraq branch of the Daawa. The constant in all of this seems to be Maliki's desire to come across as a strong leader: In 2006, he promised an "iron fist"; this time he announced "the charge of the knights". Through the process, he may well have rediscovered the usefulness of siding with ISCI, but there is nothing to suggest that Maliki acted as he did for the sake of the nine-governorate Shiite federal entity.

The bad news is that Maliki's current survival strategy does not appear to be compatible with the declared U.S. objective of achieving national reconciliation in Iraq. Maliki's vision of national reconciliation seems largely theatrical and not focused on profound constitutional revision. So far, it has failed to appeal beyond the small ruling minority of the Sunni Tawafuq bloc, the Kurds, and the Shiite ISCI—of whom the two latter also disagree deeply with Maliki on federalism. Conversely, Maliki's view of the Sadrists is altogether unrealistic. The Sadrists are far too deep-rooted in Iraqi society to be ignored; ideologically both they and the Fadila (which similarly criticized the Basra operations) can potentially be an important part of the center in Iraqi politics that Maliki is seeking. All too often it is forgotten that the benchmark of a fixed date for local elections was met mainly due to pressure from the Sadrists and Fadila in alliance with Sunnis and secularists, the very forces that are consistently being sidelined by Maliki and the United States.

Finally, there is Maliki's continued reliance on the support of the breakaway Hizb al-Daawa (Tanzim al-Iraq). Having been set afloat by Iran in 2002 (rather than being a product of the Iraqi underground, as is sometimes claimed) this chameleon-like outfit may well have as its principal objective to create as much confusion in Shiite Iraqi politics as possible. The party was probably designed as a counterweight to the mainline Daawa movement which always maintained a certain distance to Iran; whereas it supported ISCI's ideas about a single Shiite federal region back in 2006 it has gradually reverted to an Iraqi nationalist rhetoric, raising yet more questions about its own loyalties and aims.

To the U.S., the best way of rectifying these problems would be to abandon the current policy of unquestioningly going after whomever Maliki defines as a terrorist. Instead Washington could emulate the Iranians: Talk to as many Shiite factions as possible, which could be done simply by supporting free and fair local elections in October without giving in to very predictable schemes by Maliki and ISCI to exclude or obstruct the Sadrists and other undesirable competitors. Unfortunately, however, Washington appears headed in a different direction. The Bush administration fails to acknowledge that Iranian influences in Iraq operate through several channels, including some of Washington's best friends. In reality, the Iraqi nationalist component of Maliki's government is wafer-thin, and unless this problem at the Green-Zone level is addressed and anti-Iranian currents among the Shiites are better represented, no amount of bottom-up progress, "breathing room" or American material support in the provinces will be sufficient to achieve national reconciliation.

In sum, the Iraqi system is locked at the top level. The artificial constellation of the so-called "moderate coalition" under Maliki is to a large extent the result of a weaponry-focused American misreading of the many channels of Iranian influence. This was best summed up by Ryan Crocker's comments in the U.S. Senate on 8 April: In an attempt at playing down the significance of Mahmud Amadinejad's popularity in Iraqi government circles, Crocker referred to the staunch anti-Iranian attitude of the Iraqi Shiites during the Iran–Iraq War. What Crocker failed to mention was that his own administration's main Shiite partner in Iraq, ISCI, is the only sizeable Shiite party that fought on the Iranian side. Moreover, the confusion about the relationship between Iraqi Shiites and Iran is equally widespread among Democrats. Top Democrats are among the foremost proponents of the view that strong Iranian influence is a perfectly natural aspect of Iraqi politics and entirely unrelated to U.S. policy decisions, and that it cannot possibly be reversed. This particular kind of defeatism is an affront to those nationalist Iraqi Shiites who fought against Iran in the 1980s and whose marginalization is the result of U.S. policy decisions rather than of internal Iraqi dynamics. Nonetheless, it is a view shared by everyone who limits the discussion of Iranian influence to arms traffic and "special groups" and refuses to consider the Iranian influence in Green-Zone politics. In other words, it has the backing of George W. Bush, General Petraeus and Barack Obama alike.

Towards a More Unified Opposition?[7]

June 16, 2008

The new deadline set by Iraq's electoral commission for forming coalitions for this autumn's provincial elections is 30 June 2008. The deadline for registering political parties expired on 31 May; with some 500 entities having registered the main question today is whether any of these parties are capable of amalgamating into larger alliances that could mount a challenge to the established elites represented by the core components of the Maliki government. In the previous local elections in January 2005, it was mainly those elites—the Islamic Supreme Council of Iraq (ISCI) and the two biggest Kurdish parties—that excelled in the art of coalition building prior to the elections.

A look at the list of registered parties soon reveals the importance of coalitions. It is true that there has been an outpouring of nationalist sentiment in Iraq over the past year, often framed as opposition to the Maliki government and certainly as criticism against the ISCI–Kurdish axis which forms its parliamentary basis. In one way, the anti-sectarianism and anti-separatism expressed by this opposition is inspiring and could give ground for optimism. Its spirit is certainly reflected in the list of registered parties for the next provincial elections, with an abundance of names emphasizing Iraqi unity: "The One Iraqi People"; "The Bloc of Iraq's Territorial and Popular Unity"; "The Iraq First Association"; "I Am an Iraqi Independent". There is even a list dedicated to the memory of the slain police commander of Babel, Qays al-Mamuri, a staunch Iraqi nationalist who sacrificed his life by simultaneously challenging the militias of ISCI and the Sadrist movement. As on earlier occasions, south of Baghdad the only significant departure by smaller parties from the nationalist trend is regionalist rather than sectarian: "The Association of the Sons of the South", "The Southern Region List", "The Association of Southern Elites", "The Bloc of the Sons of the South", as well as the new party of Basra secularist Wail Abd al-Latif (Hizb al-Dawla). Most of these advocates of a special federal status for the "far south" (Basra, Maysan, Dhi Qar, in combination or as separate governorates) are explicit in their opposition to ISCI leader Abd al-Aziz al-Hakim's ideas of a much larger Shiite federal entity extending from Basra all the way to Baghdad.

And yet at the same time, the anti-sectarian current is also pathetic in its utter disorganization. For much of 2008, there has been talk about secularists and Islamists coming together across sectarian lines, with visions of a grand alliance of Sadrists, Fadila, Shiite independents, Sunni Islamists, Wifaq, Hiwar, and breakaway elements from the Daawa party. So far, however, while impressive in its legislative achievements (they single-handedly pushed through the demand for local elections against the opposition of the Maliki government), the moves to institutionalize this new trend have been something of an anticlimax. The formation of Ibrahim al-Jaafari's "National Reform Current" in late May is perhaps the most notable concrete result so far, but even this has not seemed to progress beyond the level of yet another Daawa breakaway faction whose political orientation seems to remain in flux. And as far as the list of parties registered for this autumn's elections is concerned, there are few signs of coalescence towards greater unity. All these opposition parties are registered separately, whereas the Sadrists are conspicuous by their absence altogether. (The Sadrists may still opt to support individual candidates, or throw their weight behind one particular party—the pro-Sadrist Risaliyun have registered, for example.)

But are parties really important, when there is a possibility for an "open-list system" in the forthcoming elections? The answer is Yes, and the reason is the maneuvering currently being undertaken by the Maliki government and its friends to minimize the possibility of challenges to its stranglehold on power. For some time, opposition parties have been pressing for a system in which the individual candidate, rather than the political parties, would become the focus of attention in the election campaign. However, the bigger parties have strenuously resisted this, marshalling an unholy list of arguments to avoid enhanced voter influence on the elections. Kurdish MPs have been particularly vocal during parliamentary debates, emphasizing the alleged "immaturity" of the Iraqi electorate and hence the "impracticability" of letting Iraqi voters do anything other than following the ranking set by the party elites. As arguments against an open system they have also mentioned "illiteracy" among voters, as well as the difficulties of guaranteeing female quotas. ISCI similarly prefers the closed-list system, and also stands out for its demand that the use of religious symbols and campaigning in places of religious worship be allowed during the run-up to the elections—again with reference to "illiteracy".

In the current draft of the elections law, these big parties have already achieved considerable results in strengthening their position. A hybrid system has been adopted (voters can choose between a list and an individual candidate), but the counting rules are clearly biased towards bigger entities. Whereas the votes for a party list will count towards a cumulative total score which will enable the party to maximize its share of all remaining seats available in a given province, votes cast for an individual representative will apparently become "redundant" once a candidate has received enough votes to win a seat for him/herself. This would be a major disincentive against voting for an individual instead of a standard list, because there is a very real chance that the individual vote can be wasted—incidentally, a kind of voter behavior against which an injunction by top Shiite cleric Ali al-Sistani was issued back in 2005. (A far more balanced arrangement would probably have been the "single transferable vote" system used for example in Ireland, where voters can rank a number of individual candidates in their preferred order.)

Also the "feminist" argument of the Kurds and ISCI seems somewhat disingenuous. After the female quota was introduced in Iraqi politics due to heavy American pressure in 2005, Iraq was propelled to a position where it currently ranks among the 30 countries in the world with the highest female parliamentary representation, way ahead of countries such as Canada, the United Kingdom, and indeed the United States itself. Earlier, in Iraq in the mid-1990s, female representation in parliament had been around 7%, slightly better than Greece: Surely it was the methods by which these women were "elected", rather than the gender issue as such, that constituted the fundamental problem of the old Iraq. All in all, if insistence on such a high female quota becomes an obstacle for the election of candidates with real popular support, the net result may well be that the praiseworthy ideal of higher female representation may stand to suffer as such, and that yet another imported and "artificial" feature is added to the new Iraqi model of government, thereby making it less durable.

Concurrently with these machinations inside the Iraqi parliament, the Maliki government also has cruder ways of wielding its power. Amara—the only Iraqi provincial capital run by a Sadrist administration—appears to be slated for an imminent large-scale security crackdown as Nuri al-Maliki increasingly seeks to portray himself as a strongman capable of ruling Iraq from the center. It has been suggested that his failure to support ISCI in their demand for permission to use religious symbols in the election campaign is a deliberate attempt to carve out a niche for himself, distinct from ISCI. Similarly, the recent refusal by a majority of the provincial council in Dhi Qar to accept the new police chief appointed by the interior ministry seems to indicate continued friction between ISCI and Daawa even as they cooperate in sidelining common enemies like the Sadrists (the Daawa members in Dhi Qar boycotted the vote in protest). This all suggests that even as Maliki's personal standing as a premier may be improving, his parliamentary base remains weak. For his project to work in the long run, either ISCI must abandon its sectarian federalism plans completely (there are some indications that this could be underway), or Maliki would eventually have to make friends with many of the forces that he is currently seeking to marginalize.

The Iraqi Parliament Passes the Provincial Elections Law[8]
July 22, 2008

The law on the Iraqi provincial elections was passed by the Iraqi parliament on 22 July. The adopted text largely reflects earlier drafts that have been circulating for weeks and months, with certain important amendments and clarifications:

- The hybrid system of lists and individual candidacies (single-person lists) is maintained. The adoption of this system means that the focus to some extent shifts from parties to politicians: voters can vote for a party list, or a specific person on a party list, or an individual candidate on a single-person list. However, the counting rules with no transferability mechanisms for "redundant votes" (i.e., surplus votes that accrue when a single-person list has reached the necessary number of votes required to secure election) still create a certain bias towards the established parties, because only multi-person lists will accumulate "party scores" that can give them additional shares of the last remaining seats.
- The female quota remains purely aspirational and has been subjugated to the increased focus on individual candidacies: there is a requirement for

the parties about nominating a certain proportion of women high on the lists, but this "enhanced visibility" notwithstanding many voters will vote for individuals on lists rather than the lists themselves. A murky paragraph authorizing the electoral commission to take undefined steps to secure a 25% female representation after the elections appears to have been removed.

- The ban on the use of religious symbols survives in a slightly more general version: the use of pictures or propaganda for persons who themselves are not candidates is disallowed. Hence any party that wishes an ayatollah to grace its elections poster needs to convince the cleric in question about the virtues of serving as a councilor in one of the Iraqi governorates. Also the ban on the use of places of worship for election campaigning purposes is upheld, alongside an unchanged and still highly hypocritical "ban" on the participation of parties who maintain militias.

- The explicit mention of the 1 October 2008 deadline has been removed (though it is of course still in place in the provincial powers law passed last February), and options for dealing with delays have been expressly mentioned: the existing councils will in that case continue to serve. The requirement of conducting the elections in a single day remains.

- Elections for Kirkuk have been postponed, but a power-sharing formula for the interim period has been envisaged in which key positions will be distributed between Kurds, Turkmens, Arabs and Christians in accordance with a percentage formula of 32-32-32-4. Security forces from "the center and the south" of Iraq will take charge of Kirkuk militarily in this period, while a committee of politicians will have until the end of the year to explore solutions to the conflict over the city. In a conundrum to Iraqi and Arab nationalists, it seems as if the insistence on the hated logic of quotas *(muhasasa)* in this case has been the most effective means of countering Kurdish nationalist ambitions.

- The "final provisions" of the law allocate a certain number of "minority" seats in certain parts of Iraq, without specifying the procedures for their election. In Baghdad there will be three seats, presumably mostly for Christians; in Mosul 2 seats, specified for Yazidis and the Shabak respectively; in the Kurdish areas two seats in each governorate (likely to go to Christians), and in Basra one seat which will probably go to a Chaldean or a Sabaean.

As for the exact voting patterns and the debate surrounding the elections law, information is beginning to filter through. It has emerged that the arrangements for Kirkuk to a large extent were supported by the bloc of opposition parties which had demanded the 1 October deadline for the elections in the first place when the provincial powers law was passed in February—a cross-sectarian alliance of Shiite Islamists (Sadrists, Fadila, some Daawa branches, independents), Sunni Islamists, secularists and minority representatives. Those who supported the Kurds over

Kirkuk were reportedly ISCI but also some United Iraqi Alliance independents. Thus, even if many aspects of the adopted law clearly carry the hallmarks of the more self-confident Nuri al-Maliki (especially in terms of challenging ISCI with the ban on the use of religious places of worship in the elections campaign), it seems that on the Kirkuk issue the government was actually overwhelmed by a cross-sectarian opposition less inclined to make compromises with the Kurds (for example, UIA independent Khalid al-Atiyya criticized the way the law had been adopted, reportedly with 127 votes out of 140 members present and with the Kurds and others having left the chamber). With the numerous reports from Iraq about Nuri al-Maliki being in the ascendancy as some kind of strongman with good ties to the security forces, this clear indication of parliamentary weakness as well as the obvious contradiction between his declared objectives as an Iraqi centralist and his choice of alliance partners (the Kurds and ISCI) certainly need to be taken into account as well. In fact, this is the second time in 2008 that the Kurdish–ISCI axis appears to have lost a parliamentary battle, once more forcing them to consider the presidential veto as a last resort.

CHAPTER NOTES

1 The original version of this text can be found at http://historiae.org/nationalism.asp.

2 See http://historiae.org/governorates.asp.

3 See http://historiae.org/provinces.asp.

4 See http://gulfanalysis.wordpress.com/2008/02/27/isci-faces-challenges-in-nasiriyya-provincial-powers-law-vetoed/.

5 See http://historiae.org/sawlah.asp.

6 See http://historiae.org/iran.asp.

7 See http://historiae.org/provincial.asp.

8 See http://historiae.org/muhafazat.asp.

Chapter 4

The 2009 Provincial Elections and Signs of Political Maturity

In autumn 2008, the cross-sectarian, nationalist front of the July 22 parties confirmed its influence with the passage of the final version of the provincial election law in September and the adoption of rules for the representation of minorities in November; during the same period the schism between the main Shiite parties was also confirmed as Nuri al-Maliki, along with a group of independents, launched the State of Law list separate from ISCI in late October. However, despite the significant points of convergence between Maliki and the July 22 parties, no further rapprochement took place ahead of the January 31, 2009, elections. Indeed, the July 22 parties themselves remained organized as separate entities, thereby dampening the earlier optimism that they might coalesce into a strong, antisectarian front.

Maliki scored some good nationalist points with the Status of Forces Agreement that he concluded with the United States in November 2008: It removed much of the U.S. leverage and provided Maliki with a reasonable timeline for U.S. withdrawal—the end of 2011—that balanced nationalist pressures for a full and speedy American pullout with his own need to benefit from U.S. military assistance in the short term. He went on to score an impressive victory in the local elections of January 2009. Since his campaign had to a great degree focused on bread-and-butter issues at a time when ISCI continued to appeal to voters on a sectarian basis (asking them to vote for good "Husayni", i.e., Shiite, candidates, and so on), his victory seemed to indicate a general turn on the part of the Iraqi electorate towards embracing the concept of a nonsectarian, strongly centralized state. Still, perhaps Maliki's most convincing moves came subsequent to the elections, in February and March 2009, when he initiated parliamentary cooperation with some of the July 22 parties on the issue of who should fill the vacancy of the parliamentary speakership and tried to establish coalitions with these parties in local assemblies across Iraq. These attempts included a tentative deal with Salih al-Mutlak of the secular Hiwar front in several areas, as well as proposed cooperation with Sunni leaders in Anbar and Mosul in anticipation of the next parliamentary elections.

Equally significant in this period, however, was the pushback against Maliki's promising nationalism, which came mainly from Iran and also—paradoxically— from the United States. Always concerned with maintaining a unified Shiite front, Iran put pressure on Maliki to give more posts in the provincial councils to its protégé, ISCI, which for its part used the de-Baathification card to criticize Maliki's rapprochement with secularists in the July 22 group of parties. For their part, the United States and Western ambassadors in Baghdad more generally were wildly enthusiastic about the emerging anti-Maliki candidate for the vacant speakership in parliament, Ayad al-Samarraie—the continuation of a policy that stretched back at least to 2007 when potential parliamentary supporters of Adil Abd al-Mahdi of ISCI as an alternative premier were being closely monitored and encouraged by those same ambassadors. On January 16, 2009, just days ahead of the local elections, The Washington Post *quoted an unnamed U.S. senior official who thought it important to make the point that Maliki could, according to this official's latest calculation of the loyalties of the parliamentary deputies, be dismissed as premier.*

What was going on in this period were two different alliance-formation projects. In the old, dysfunctional parliament from 2005, Western diplomats were busy abetting the comeback of the even older exiled elite of the Paul Bremer/CPA era from 2003 to 2004, probably contributing significantly to the increasing (but highly illogical) polarization between Maliki and the secular and nationalist Iraqiyya led by Ayad Allawi, himself a longtime exile. But meanwhile, in local councils across Iraq, Maliki was doing the exact opposite by reaching out to domestic leaders like Salih al-Mutlak, Ahmad Abu Risha and the Hadba front in Mosul.

The net outcome by May 2009 was the non-emergence of the projected alliance between Maliki and Salih al-Mutlak, and the gradual disintegration of the July 22 parties—whose Shiite components then became ripe for Iran's picking. One striking example was the case of Wail Abd al-Latif from Basra, who on May 7, 2008, in Al-Zaman *had criticized Tharallah (an ISCI affiliate) and two other unnamed parties close to the Maliki government for having their headquarters in Iran: One year later he would gravitate toward the very electoral alliance that had been created in Tehran a few months after ISCI was defeated in the January 2009 local elections, the all-Shiite Iraqi National Alliance (INA).*

One truly surprising development in this period was the way in which Maliki was able to reach out and occupy the nationalist political space that had been created by the July 22 front. This development was hard to detect in the results from the January 31, 2009, local elections themselves, where after all Maliki did not perform particularly well in any Sunni-majority areas apart from some parts of Baghdad. However, sources in the Iraqi opposition suggested that some kind of dramatic movement was afoot. At the time, I was engaged in a project with some Iraqi academics and politicians—mostly secular Iraqiyya supporters—and was quite impressed in January 2009 when all of a sudden we had to hastily delete several critical references to Maliki in our report because of overtures that had been going on between him and leading exiles in places like Amman. I still remained somewhat unconvinced about the depth of his conversion and continued to make this point at various conferences on Iraq even after the elections. I used to preface my presentations on the subject of "Maliki's newfound nationalism" with two almost identical photographs of Maliki meeting with the Iran's leader, Ali Khamenei, taken in July 2008 and January 2009. The sole difference between them was that in the first photo Maliki appeared tieless, Iranian-style, but by January 2009 he had donned a tie, thus presenting himself more in accordance with Iraqi custom and hence in a supposedly more nationalist way! However, when Maliki in March reached out to Salih al-Mutlak—a Sunni secularist who shared many points of view with Maliki on issues like state structure and relations with the Kurds—there seemed to be indications that he was about to become an Iraqi nationalist in more than a symbolic sense.

Communicating these developments to a U.S. audience remained as difficult as ever. In September 2008 I had been invited to preview the upcoming local elections at the National Defense University at Fort McNair in Washington and had been given the predictable charge of discussing "Basra and the south", with other speakers assigned, equally predictably, to cover the "Sunni center" and "the Kurds". I tried to point out that certain cross-sectarian national trends were in the making; yet I ended up, once more, discussing the "Sunni position" with an official of the Bush administration after the event. In meetings with European diplomats after the January elections there appeared to be general satisfaction that Ayad al-Samarraie was emerging as a "counterweight" to what was seen as an increasingly "authoritarian" Maliki. In Washington, among officials of the Bush administration who remained in charge pending the emergence of Obama's people, the fact that "Sunnis" (most of whom had boycotted the 2005 election completely) had done well in Diyala (where they constitute a majority) was given far more attention than the altogether more interesting development of cross-sectarian coalition building in multiple governorates.

Two Very Different Takes on Centralism[1]
September 20, 2008

Diverging opinions on the virtues of centralism as a principle of government have created tensions between the Daawa party and ISCI for some time, yet without escalating to the point where their alliance appears to have been under serious threat as such.

It is nevertheless interesting that over the past two days, the two opposing poles have expressed their conflicting views on the issue with almost perfect synchronization. In an interview in *Al-Hayat*, Nuri al-Maliki largely reiterated his position on federalism along the lines he described it an earlier interview back in November 2007: federalism is a constitutional option, but not something that should threaten the potency of the centralized state. Conversely, ISCI's Jalal al-Din al-Saghir expressed the exact opposite attitude in Friday prayers yesterday, describing "centralism" as a distinguishing feature of the old Baathist regime.

There can be little doubt that to Daawa, centralism remains a positive concept while to ISCI, it has negative connotations. This is interesting, because at least since the release of the main draft of the oil law in early 2007 it has been plausible to ask whether ISCI pursues a centralist plan B as an alternative to its severely-criticized scheme for a large federal Shiite region south of Baghdad. As of today, it seems as if ISCI still has some internal debating to do before the party can be at ease with the idea of centralism in the same way as the Iraqi premier and some of the circles around him. Oil minister Hussein al-Shahristani, for example, seems to belong to the latter camp in this question: In an interview in today's *Al-Sharq al-Awsat* he criticises the Kurds for obstinacy with regard to the oil law and contends that the only option left to "the Baghdad government" would be to revert to Saddam-time legislation. The symbolic significance of this kind of adoption of Baathist centralism by the new Shiite-dominated regime would be quite considerable.

Importantly, though, others see it in a different ways: In the context of the stalled debate over the provincial elections law and military operations by the central government in Diyala, Kurdish politician Qadir Aziz today speaks about a conspiracy against the Kurdish cause and he mentions both ISCI and Daawa as part of that conspiracy.

After Compromise on Kirkuk, Finally an Elections Law for Iraq's Governorates[2]
September 24, 2008

Iraq's parliament today approved the remaining article 24 of the provincial elections law that had been vetoed by President Jalal Talabani after its initial adoption on 22 July 2008.

The new article, which has been crafted in cooperation with the United Nations special representative in Iraq, Staffan de Mistura, delays the elections in the disputed Kirkuk province, but also establishes a committee which will deal with power-sharing issues in local government there. The committee will consist of 7 parliamentary representatives from Kirkuk—2 Kurds, 2 Turkmens, 2 Arabs and 1 Christian—and will have until 31 March 2009 to prepare its report. The Iraqi parliament will then proceed to create a special elections law for Kirkuk. (Or, if it fails to do so, the prime minister, the president and the speaker of the parliament will decree a suitable system for elections in cooperation with the United Nations!)

The new law is a compromise between federalists (in particular the Kurds) and nationalist centralists (now increasingly referred to as the "forces of 22 July"). Back in May this year, Kurdish politicians spoke in favor of postponing local elections in all disputed areas such as Kirkuk, arguing that their strong position in these areas—based on the heavily-boycotted January 2005 elections—would play to their advantage and could perhaps be a negotiating card towards a rapid settlement of territorial issues. The forces of 22 July, on the other hand, demanded more equitable power-sharing during a transitional period before elections, thereby seeking to shake up Kurdish dominance in the local council and to challenge what they consider to be a number of pro-Kurdish placemen and figureheads that have been anointed by the Kurds to serve as "Arab" and "Turkmen" representatives in Kirkuk despite having little support in the communities they purport to represent.

The compromise is more than a mere postponement: it keeps Kirkuk and the issue of power-sharing on the agenda, even if these issues are now lifted to the abstract realm of a parliamentary committee and with a timeline that stretches well into 2009. Also, it is noteworthy that the forces of 22 July scored at least a symbolic victory by gaining an explicit assurance that the central government would play an equally important role alongside the local authorities in facilitating the work of the parliamentary committee. The language on this disputed "fourth point" of article 24 is what held up the passage of the law for the last week or so; in a testament to the lingering conflict between centralizers and decentralizers in the Iraqi parliament, both Kurds and ISCI (Jalal al-Din al-Saghir) had criticized the nationalists for insisting on a reference to the central government.

In the end, the role of the central government was confirmed, thus in some ways also confirming the diminishing parliamentary clout of the federalists in Iraq. This has apparently enabled many of the component elements of the 22 July forces—including MPs from Iraqiyya, Fadila and the Sadrists—to feel satisfaction about the passage of the law, as seen in a number of positive statements in the aftermath. Perhaps the more important result of the process—in addition to the fact that provincial elections may now actually be held in late 2008 or early 2009—is the increased awareness, both inside and outside the Iraqi parliament, of this cross-sectarian bloc and the potential it represents. The big question now is whether the Maliki government is prepared to go ahead with free and fair elections given the increasing signs of a cohesive challenge from the opposition.

Finally: After having blown hot and cold—mostly cold—with regard to Kurdish participation in the elections, Kurdish leaders according to press reports now say that provincial elections will not be held anywhere in the Kurdistan region, as the right to legislate on those elections is seen as falling within the domain of the regional government. While the Kurds are the most pro-federal force in Iraq, Kurdistan itself is quite centralized (with two competing centers in Arbil and

Sulaymaniyya), with the local governorates having considerably less power vis-à-vis the Kurdistan Regional Government than their counterparts elsewhere in Iraq have towards Baghdad. This stance does throw into question the heavy Kurdish involvement in drafting the law, where they dominated parliamentary debates in long periods with their insistent demands that closed lists be used due to the supposed illiteracy of the Iraqi electorate—though they had no such qualms when it came to the constitution back in 2005, apparently!

ISCI and Maliki Go Their Separate Ways[3]
October 31, 2008

After a long series of extensions, it now seems as if the final deadline for forming coalitions for the next provincial elections in Iraq will be on 2 November 2008. The first announcement of coalitions among the Shiite Islamist parties is one of the indicators that suggest the coalition-forming process could be coming to an end.

The most newsworthy feature of the updated coalition list is that the main Shiite Islamist parties in the Maliki government are subdivided into two camps, "The List of the Martyr of the Mihrab and the Independent Forces", and "The Alliance of the Rechtsstaat" (*Itilaf dawlat al-qanun*—perhaps it could be called the State of Law Alliance in English). This could be a step towards a formalization of the growing tension between the alliance partners of Islamic Supreme Council of Iraq (ISCI) and Nuri al-Maliki's Daawa party, which form the nuclei of the two new lists. ISCI's list is named after the late Muhammad Baqir al-Hakim (Shahid al-Mihrab), and also contains a reference to independents. However, on closer inspection, this seems like old wine in a new bottle: apart from ISCI, the list consists of familiar names—Badr, "Hizbollah in Iraq" and the Sayyid al-Shuhada movement, all frequently accused of having particularly close links to Iran. The only "independent" element—"The Independent Society for the Sake of Iraq"—is in fact the personal creation of ISCI member Adil Abd al-Mahdi.

The Daawa coalition, on the other hand, has scored one important victory: It now includes the independent list of Hussein al-Shahristani alongside the two main factions of the Daawa. ISCI has long attempted to portray itself as a party with particularly close ties to the Grand Ayatollah Ali al-Sistani (who, for his part, has failed to reciprocate); to ISCI, the decision by someone like Shahristani to join the Daawa coalition must be something of a defeat, especially since the Iraqi oil minister is thought to have good relations with Sistani. Still, this merely emphasizes a division that dates back at least to February, when Maliki and independents of the United Iraqi Alliance (UIA) were at odds with ISCI over the provincial powers law. Other new elements in the Daawa coalition are smaller local parties from Dhi Qar and Qadisiyya as well as some Turkmen and Fayli Kurd parties.

So far, the only possible sign of a tribal awakening in the south being reflected in coalition politics is the emergence of a list that groups together Abd al-Karim Mahud al-Muhammadawi's "Hizbollah of Iraq" with smaller parties with head-quarters in Basra and Samawa.

Iraqi Minorities Get Special Representation in the Provincial Elections Law[4]
November 3, 2008

Today the Iraqi parliament finally passed a long-awaited modification of the pro-vincial elections law of 24 September which adds special representation for certain specified ethno-religious minorities in certain areas. The process towards agree-ment on these changes has been a tortuous one, involving basic disagreements on issues such as state structure and federalism, identity questions, and gerrymander-ing of key electoral constituencies.

To get a sense of what has been at stake in this, it may be worthwhile to revisit the first version of the provincial elections law that was adopted on 22 July 2008. In its article 50, 13 minority seats were specified, roughly half of which were in the Kurdistan region and Kirkuk and another three in Mosul, with two seats specifi-cally reserved for Yazidis and Shabak. While Kurdish objections against the law at the time above all focused on the contentious article 24 (which envisaged radical power-sharing in Kirkuk) it is easy to see that article 50, too, was a formidable chal-lenge against the Kurdish position. In the first place, it legislated detailed arrange-ments for the distribution of seats in the Kurdistan Regional Government (KRG) area. The KRG position is that the Iraqi parliament does not possess authority to make any decisions on those "internal affairs of Kurdistan" that are not enumer-ated in the constitution as shared powers or the exclusive powers of the federal government (hence, the "decision" to exclude Kurdistan from the next elections is not something that has been explicitly incorporated in the latest version of the elections law—as misreported by many news agencies—but rather a decision by the Kurdish leadership to ignore it in practice). Secondly, the specific mention of Yazidis and Shabak was seen as provocative by many Kurds, who often consider these peoples as Kurds with different religious and linguistic traditions. Some Kurds want to assimilate these groups under a wider pan-Kurdish umbrella, and areas inhabited by Yazidis and Shabak are annexation targets of the KRG.

The next version of the elections law, adopted on 24 September, focused on achieving some kind of *modus vivendi* on Kirkuk and thereby scrapped the whole issue about minority representation. This was followed by an outcry by Iraqi minorities and especially Christians, with swift declarations of solidarity from the entire Iraqi political spectrum from the Kurds to the Sadrists. It should be stressed in this context that there is a big difference between minorities and micro-minorities in Iraqi politics. Special representation for larger ethno-religious groups is frowned upon by most Iraqis except the Kurds. It is for this reason that ethno-religious quotas for Arab Shiites and Sunnis are dismissed as *muhasasa* (quota-sharing) and objectionable emulation of the Lebanese system. (The Turkmens constitute a grey-zone case, who mostly but not always prefer to compete within the national framework.) Conversely, special representation for the very small groups is a time-honored tradition which in the case of the Christians go back to Ottoman system when the only formal distinctions were between Muslims, Christians and Jews. The same logic has gradually become accepted with regard to the Yazidis and the Sabaeans (both of whom refer to religion as a carrier of their ethnic identity), and, in this last case, also the Shabak—a Shiite-majority group in northern Iraq whose language is similar to Kurdish but which claims to have a tradition and history as a distinctive ethnic group.

During most of October, it was believed that the final clauses on minority representation would follow closely the proposal by the UN special representative in Iraq, Staffan de Mistura. In its latest incarnation, this plan envisaged the creation of 1 special seat in Basra (for Christians), 4 in Baghdad (3 for Christians and 1 for Sabaeans) and 7 in Mosul (3 for Christians, 3 for Yazidis and 1 for the Shabak). On 30 October, the Kurds—who had hitherto strongly opposed the designation of the Shabak as an independent group and on more than one occasion described this as a plot to divide the Kurdish nation—expressed satisfaction with this kind of arrangement. Another report suggested that it was supported by both the Kurds and the Islamic Supreme Council of Iraq (ISCI). Also other members of the parliament expressed support, like Khayrallah al-Basri, a Wifaq representative from Basra who said it took some persuasion for the Sabaeans to accept the idea that they would be represented in Baghdad but not in their historical homeland in the south.

However, in today's version of the bill, different ideas prevailed. Yesterday, press reports suggested that the rest of the parliament had challenged the Kurds and ISCI and the de Mistura proposal, and instead wanted a decrease in the number of seats. And in the bill that was adopted today, minority representation has been cut by fifty percent. There is still one Christian seat in Basra, but no more than one Christian and one Sabaean seat in Baghdad, and one Christian, one Yazidi and one Shabak seat in Mosul.

A myriad of motives seems to have been involved in this process. For example, Iraqi nationalists have been divided as to whether the minorities should have special representation at all or should aim at becoming included through non-sectarian parties. Similarly, Christians have been divided as to the methods for calculating their number of seats and defining their identity: Some want to have a common "Assyrian" ethnic identity for all of Iraq's Christians, others—such as some of those who prefer to call themselves Chaldeans—tend to focus on their religious denomination which thus becomes more easily compatible with a wider Iraqi identity.

But above all, perhaps the contest over minority representation is best understood as an attempt to gerrymander the forthcoming elections in the hotly contested Nineveh governorate. In Basra and Baghdad, the minority quotas are so small compared to the total numbers of seats on the provincial councils that they are unlikely to have any major impact on the formation of the next provincial governments. Conversely, Mosul and the Nineveh area is home to many minorities, and if for example 12 seats had been agreed, it would have been almost a third of the members next provincial council. It is in this context the Kurdish change of position makes sense. The Kurds moved from intransigence on the question of recognition of Shabak identity to espousing the de Mistura proposal with 1 Shabak and 3 Yazidi seats, and with one Shabak member of parliament affiliated with the Kurdish parties even proposing 3 seats for the Shabak. Apart from the obvious advantages of staying on good terms with de Mistura, it seems that the Kurdish calculation has been that they might be able to stack these seats with pro-Kurdish representatives in a governorate where they have territorial ambitions, as they have also done in Kirkuk where nominally Arab and Turkmen representatives who owe their loyalties to the Kurdish parties serve as "Arab" and "Turkmen" representatives in the local government. The Kurds today expressed dissatisfaction with the rejection of the de Mistura plan, and it is likely that they were among the 50 or so representatives that voted for de Mistura and against the proposal that eventually prevailed.

Instead, those who wanted to reduce special minority representation overall won the day as 106 representatives voted for the new version of the law. At the time of writing it was still unclear whether ISCI had abandoned the Kurds in the last minute and joined with other representatives in adopting the more limited quotas. As late as yesterday, reduced quotas were seen as the alternative to the ISCI/Kurdish/de Mistura position (Daawa members, for example, had been advocating one seat only per community), although the battlefronts were far from clear-cut. Kurds did identify the nationalist "forces of 22 July" as an opponent in the battle, but there have also been examples of both members of Iraqiyya and Sadrists expressing themselves in favor of the proposal by de Mistura. The intricacies of the matter are perhaps best indicated through recording the position of Hunayn al-Qaddo. Qaddo is a Shabak who originally was elected on the United Iraqi Alliance (UIA) list but who at times has expressed sympathy for the more nationalist 22 July front. Fiercely critical of Kurdish attempts to assimilate the Shabak, he was also angry about the decision to exclude minority representation from the 24 September version of the minorities law. However, in a television interview with Al-Furat on 25 October he praised the position of UIA in confronting the Kurds, and especially highlighted Hadi al-Amiri of the Badr brigades for protecting the position of the Shabak. Today, some Christians have complained that they are the victims of an Arab–Kurdish struggle (and called for a presidential veto of the law), whereas Qaddo's supporters have celebrated the designation of a Shabak seat as a triumph for their small community, expressing satisfaction that they got one seat and that none of the other minorities got more than that. To them, at least, this was first and foremost about fending off the Kurdish challenge.

No Longer Supreme: After Local Elections, ISCI Becomes a 10% Party[5]
February 5, 2009

The provisional results of the Iraqi local elections held on 31 January 2009, released today, can be summarized in three main points as far as the areas from Baghdad and southwards are concerned: Maliki and his Daawa party are big winners everywhere and particularly so in the big cities of Basra and Baghdad; the Islamic Supreme Council of Iraq (ISCI) has been decimated across the country; fragmentation rather than the emergence of a clear secular "third way" is mostly the rule, with the exception of a respectable 9% for Iraqiyya in Baghdad and a couple of local secular successes (including Karbala).

Maliki's rise is spectacular. His coalition won Basra and Baghdad and came first in every Shiite-dominated governorate except Karbala (where the independent Yusuf al-Hububi won most votes), with results above 35% in Basra and Baghdad, around 23% in Dhi Qar and Qadisiyya, and between 10 and 20% in most other places. It should however be stressed that Maliki's increasing appeal to Sunnis, while often acknowledged by Iraqi Sunnis themselves, is not convincingly reflected in the results. There may have been Sunni votes for Maliki in places like Baghdad and Basra, but his coalition did not run in Anbar (though some suggest this may have been related to an agreement with Ahmad Abu Risha, a prominent Sunni leader in the area), and achieved only 3% in a heavily Sunni province like Salahaddin and less than that in Nineveh.

The decline of ISCI is equally remarkable. From a position where it dominated most governorates south of Baghdad it has fallen to a status of a 10% party or less in most places: It managed to hold on to 2005 levels only in Maysan, was strongly reduced in Baghdad and lost votes even in Najaf where its leadership in provincial government has been more valued by the inhabitants than elsewhere in Iraq.

Of the various pro-Sadrist lists, it is generally the "independent current" (list 284) that has done well, mostly scoring between 5 to 10%—hence, still a force to be reckoned with in Maysan, and with a better result than ISCI in Baghdad. Fadila lost seats across the country and was reduced to a humiliating 3% even in its stronghold of Basra (where its performance in the executive branch of the local government, won in 2005, has been criticized). Ibrahim al-Jaafari's breakaway faction of the Daawa, which has been courting Sadrists, did reasonably well with a consistent score between 5 and 10%.

There had been some talk of secularism emerging as an independent current this time; south of Baghdad this is generally reflected first and foremost in fragmentation of the vote in many councils, with lots of parties winning between 1 and 2%, and with further fragmentation and disproportionality expected to occur during the distribution of seats (when one-person lists are at disadvantage after they have secured a single seat because in contrast to the parties their surplus votes are not transferred anywhere and hence wasted). The exception, as far as voting and percentages go, is Karbala and to some extent Baghdad itself, where Iraqiyya got around 10%. (North of Baghdad, there is a good 13% result for Iraqiyya in Salahaddin and generally respectable figures for the list of Salih al-Mutlak and others challenging the more explicitly sectarian Sunni orientation of the Iraqi Islamic Party.) The emergence of the "Association of Justice and Unity" list in Basra with more than 5% seems a promising beginning for this party which originates with the Shaykhi community (a Shiite sub-sect) but appears to have been able to appeal to Basrawis at large.

Beyond the numbers, these elections have several implications for the overall atmosphere of Iraqi politics. One is that they to some extent mark a rejection of sectarian identity politics. The cleavage between ISCI and Daawa during the elections campaign ran precisely along these lines: Maliki tried to emphasize Iraqi nationalism; ISCI tried to emphasize sectarian Shiism. Maliki won. Secondly, the results clearly signify the triumph of centralism over pro-federal sentiments. Again, Maliki very explicitly emphasized this contrast between himself as favoring control by Baghdad and ISCI as the party of radical decentralization. Reflecting the poor result in the recent federalism initiative in Basra, no pro-federal Basra parties did well with the possible exception of the above-mentioned "Association of Justice and Unity" (5.5%).

Overall, this should serve as a wake-up call to the outside world, which tirelessly has sought to comply with the sectarian logic embraced by ISCI—in terms of ethno-sectarian quotas, sectarian variants of federalism, and the retrograde concept of "disputed areas". It is high time that Western politicians realize that the party they have been considering as the key to Iraq's Shiite community (and sometimes have singled out as the likely provider of the next Iraqi premier) actually commands less than 10% support in the constituency it purports to represent. In other words, for much of the period since 2003, America's policy in Iraq has probably not enjoyed the support of more than 25% of the country's population (represented by the two Kurdish parties and ISCI). Yet, still today, Iraqis continue to be the prisoners of the ethno-sectarian system of government that emerged in this period and was designed by the two Kurdish parties and ISCI. Even the UN special representative in Iraq, Staffan de Mistura, seems to miss the point when he in a recent *Washington Post* op-ed claimed there is a need for "greater willingness to seek national reconciliation at all levels and among all major groups: Sunni-Shiite, Shiite-Shiite, Sunni-Sunni, Arab-Kurd and Kurd-Kurd". What these elections go some way to show is that Iraqis are tired of these labels as such.

There are big tests ahead for Maliki's "centralism" or even "Iraqi nationalism" (it was these two features, rather than a sometimes-trumpeted "secularism", that dominated the campaign of his party). At the local level, will the Daawa engage in bold coalition-building outside the Shiite Islamist camp, or will it give in to advances from ISCI? And what about the parliamentary situation and the next speaker—will the Daawa think in terms of a "Sunni quota" or will it switch allegiance to the 22 July parties and the idea of a "nationalist" speaker of whatever sect? Finally, the next parliamentary elections scheduled for December: Will Maliki now seek to convert all his nice words about centralism into specific proposals for constitutional reform? Only then will the positive tendencies seen in this election create an enduring result for the long term. The "No Injuries Reported in Iraqi Elections", as per a recent *New York Times* headline, is in itself without much significance in the absence of true political reform.

Maliki and the 22 July Opposition Alliance[6]
February 8, 2009

The 22 July alliance, the much-overlooked nascent force of Iraqi politics that on 22 July 2008 voted in favor of an elections law that challenged Kurdish dominance in the disputed city of Kirkuk, could be rising again—this time in relation to the ongoing dispute over who should be the next speaker of the Iraqi parliament. Ever since the resignation of Mahmud al-Mashhadani in December 2008, the 22 July bloc has asserted itself as an Iraqi nationalist critic of the idea of restricting the vacant post to Sunni candidates only. Today, this sentiment was repeated, as a cross-sectarian group of parliamentarians from Fadila, the Sadrists and the two Hiwar factions (Ulyan and Mutlak) left the Iraqi parliament in protest as attempts were made to force through a decision on a new speaker. (Al-Iraqiyya is not mentioned in today's press reports; they normally follow the 22 July bloc.)

It is especially noteworthy that in its latest walkout from the Iraqi parliament, the 22 July bloc was accompanied by members of the two Daawa branches loyal to Nuri al-Maliki, the Iraqi premier. This is remarkable for two reasons. Firstly, it means that Maliki once more is emphasizing his ideological differences with his government coalition partners (ISCI, the Kurds and Tawafuq) over what Iraq's state structure should look like. The principal feature of the 22 July trend is rejection of key aspects of the post-2003 US-sponsored system of government in Iraq, including certain features of the 2005 constitution such as its latitude for a deeply decentralized state based on a system of ethno-sectarian quota-sharing. In relation to the debate over who should be the next speaker, the 22 July parties have once more emphasized this anti-sectarian approach, with outgoing speaker Mahmud al-Mashhadani firmly revolting against the system by proposing a (Shiite) Sadrist to succeed him instead of "whichever Sunni the Sunnis agree on"—the formula of the parties behind the 2005 constitution (KDP, PUK, ISCI). Secondly, Maliki's "defection" to the opposition should give pause to all those policy-makers in the West who have considered some kind of "balance of power between sectarian leaders" as the key to Iraq's future stability. Today, Maliki is of course spoken of by Western media as the big nationalist and even secularist. While some of this seems to be an exaggeration (especially the secularism bit), positive tendencies are certainly there, most convincingly in Maliki's turn to centralism and the vision of an Arab–Kurdish federation rather than wasting any more time in a labyrinth of possible and impossible federation schemes south of Kurdistan. But importantly, these positive tendencies are now accompanied by an attempt to reach out ideologically to the opposition, with which Maliki shares many preferences as regards state structure and anti-federalism. It cannot escape notice that these are all the parties that the United States have consistently chosen to ignore in its search for partners in Iraq.

Left behind in the Iraqi parliament sat representatives of the two Kurdish parties and the Islamic Supreme Council of Iraq (ISCI), Washington's (and sometimes Iran's) best friends in Iraq, still trying to convince the Americans that they have the necessary votes to get rid of Maliki. Except that they don't. It is high time that US policy-makers abandon any plans to make further concessions to this group of opportunists (such as a "big compromise on Kirkuk") in some kind of "final settlement" in Iraq. Instead, a more profound overhaul of the Iraqi political system is needed, with institutional checks against the quota-sharing system that a large group of Iraqi parliamentarians are now rebelling against. For whereas some Daawa figures now more openly than ever cultivate ties with the opposition, there are also more sectarian forces in motion in both Iraq and Iran seeking to revive the (all-Shiite) United Iraqi Alliance, something that could easily bring Iraq back to the backward political atmosphere of 2005–2006. Hence, only when Maliki moves in the direction of constitutional revision will his flirtation with the 22 July parties and his conversion to Iraqi nationalism become truly convincing.

The Provincial Elections: The Coalition-Forming Process Begins[7]
February 19, 2009

After today's official release by the Iraqi elections commission of the seat allocation in the new Iraqi provincial councils elected on 31 January, the process of forming new coalitions can begin in earnest. Since the provisional result was released two weeks ago, the various parties have had some time to calculate their likely share of the seats and initiate a process of negotiation with prospective partners, but small percentage differences can have dramatic implications for the mathematics of coalitions and hence the exact political landscape only became apparent today.

One general aspect of the results that will now become painfully clear to voters is that the modified Iraqi elections system—once hailed as an improvement on the previous one in that voters would have a greater impact on the ranking of individual candidates—remains heavily biased in favor of the bigger, established entities. As Sam Parker of the United States Institute of Peace has pointed out, the counting rules mean that lists fielding a large number of candidates will have comparative advantages in the battle for the last remaining seats, whereas on the opposite end of the spectrum, votes for one-person entities will have been wasted once a single seat has been secured. In general, this framework of disincentives for voting for smaller entities and one-party lists has been bluntly ignored by the Iraqi electorate, with the result that they today found out that a very high proportion of their votes might as well have been thrown directly in the dustbin. The most spectacular case is of course Karbala, where Yusuf al-Habubi's one seat is by far the priciest one of the election, coming on the strength of no less than 13% of the popular vote. In areas from Baghdad and southwards more generally, the gains in number of seats by Daawa and the State of Law alliance as a result of the system are quite dramatic, leaving them with an outright majority in Basra, and very close to majority in Wasit and Baghdad. Additionally, huge sectors of the electorate will realize that their votes were wasted in the sense that they yielded nothing to a seat-winning candidate. With the exception of the big constituency in Baghdad, this involves percentages for "unrepresented" voters ranging between 30 in Basra to as much as 60 in Hilla. ISCI, too, has benefitted somewhat during this process. Still, a comparison with 2005 underlines the extent to which the Daawa coalition has replaced ISCI as the dominant force across the Shiite-majority governorates.

In general, compared with the provisional result, the seat allocation (see Table 4.1) has served to produce a more stereotypic political landscape in the south, with Daawa in the lead, followed by ISCI and Sadrist as competitors for the second biggest chunk of votes, then followed by Jaafari and then Wifaq/Iraqiyya and/or some kind of local phenomenon—by which is meant both lists that have a genuine local character (such as The Justice and Unity Association in Basra or the Hope of Mesopotamia in Karbala) as well as lists that have been reduced to local phenomena against their own will (such as Fadila which won seats only in Basra, Dhi Qar and Qadisiyya).

The new councils will meet within 15 days to elect their new officials, and new coalitions will have to be formed in this period. Precisely because of the relatively homogenous political map now after the seat allocation, the ongoing negotiations among party elites in Baghdad could have enormous significance. By way of example, a deal between Maliki and the Sadrists would give the Daawa coalition

Governorate; total number of seats	Maliki	ISCI	Sadrist	Jaafari	Wifaq and other nationwide secularist parties	Local phenomena including minorities' seats
Basra (35)	20	5	2		2	2 + 2 + 1 + 1
Maysan (27)	8	8	7	4		
Dhi Qar (31)	13	5	7	4		2
Muthanna (26)	5	5	2	3		3 + 2 + 2 + 2 + 2
Wasit (28)	13	6	3		3	3
Qadisiyya (28)	11	5	2	3	3	2 + 2
Babel (30)	8	5	3	3	3	3 + 3 + 2
Najaf (28)	7	7	6	2		4 + 2
Karbala (27)	9	4	4			9 + 1
Baghdad (57)	28	3	5	3	5 + 4	7 + 1 + 1

Table 4.1: Results of the Iraqi provincial elections of January 2009 in Baghdad and governorates to the south

control of Maysan, Dhi Qar, Wasit and Baghdad. Adding Ibrahim al-Jaafari to his coalition alongside the Sadrists would give Maliki control of Qadisiyya and Najaf as well. This leaves a group of highly fragmented Middle Euphrates governorates where ISCI was once strong: Babel and Muthanna, plus the interesting case of Karbala, where the two "local phenomena", Yusuf al-Habubi and the Hope of Mesopotamia list, seem to be looking to Daawa and ISCI respectively as potential coalition partners. But whereas the Hope of Mesopotamia list is a significant bloc with 9 seats, Habubi has only one seat and Maliki would need the Sadrists in addition to gain a majority here.

One of the biggest questions now is whether there will be moves towards ideological or opportunistic alliances. Maliki has a golden opportunity to realign himself with opposition parties that share much of his ideology when it comes to centralism and state structure, such as the Sadrists, Fadila and Wifaq/Iraqiyya and other secularists. But there are also other tendencies at work. Recently, the secular Ayad Allawi has apparently been in dialogue with ISCI, and the heavily-decimated Fadila party has hinted at the possible reconstitution of the (Shiite-led) United Iraqi Alliance. These are both examples of moves that would negate the declared aim of these parties to move away from a political system of ethno-sectarian quota-sharing and would reverse the positive trends towards greater emphasis on issues and ideology in the latest local elections.

Iraq's New Provincial Councils[8]

April 13, 2009

With the election this weekend of the first batch of new governors in Iraq, the new political map of the country is also beginning to emerge. The Iraqis have already stretched the legal framework quite considerably—the "15 days deadline" from the publication of the final results on 26 March has apparently been interpreted as "working days", and the emphasis has been on holding meetings rather than necessarily electing all key officials—but around half or Iraq's provinces now have new governors.

It can be useful to discuss the emerging landscape on the basis of two different ways of looking at Iraqi politics. One is to emphasize ethno-sectarian divisions between Kurds, Shiites and Sunnis which in turn are seen as internally unified monolithic blocs. For a long time this sort of paradigm prevailed in U.S. policy-making circles, where it gave rise to such concepts as the "80% solution" (i.e., "work with friendly Kurds and Shiites who dominate the Iraqi parliament") and an "alliance of moderate sectarians" (the two Kurdish parties, the Islamic Supreme Council of Iraq or ISCI for the Shiites, and the Tawafuq bloc as a token Sunni representative).

The alternative view is to ignore the sectarian identity of Iraqi politicians and instead consider their position on key issues in Iraqi politics. From this perspective, the Iraqi political scene and the parliament have a highly different appearance, with the main cleavage between those ethno-federalists who favor almost all features of the 2005 constitution (KDP, PUK, ISCI, and, more reluctantly, the Islamic Iraqi Party or IIP) and those who criticize several aspects of it including federalism, ethno-sectarian quotas and how to deal with Kirkuk (the 22 July parties, including the Sadrists, Fadila, Iraqiyya, the Mutlak bloc and various defectors from the Tawafuq coalition). In the middle, leaning towards 22 July on most constitutional issues but still in government with the ethno-federal parties, are the Daawa factions and the group of independents that formed the State of Law coalition under Nuri al-Maliki's leadership in the January local elections.

At the national level, it has become increasingly clear that the ethno-sectarian approach is fast losing its relevance, especially with the emergence in 2008 of the nationalist 22 July front. How, then, is this playing out in local politics after the formation of at least some new provincial councils? North of Baghdad the picture is a mixed one. "New", issue-based coalition formation was certainly evident in Anbar, where Tawafuq was sidelined by Sunni contenders who are friendly to the Shiite prime minister (independents, secularists and tribal figures from the Awakening), leading to the election of the independent Qasim Muhammad as governor on 12 April. Arguably, much the same could be said for Mosul. Even if the election of Athil al-Nujayfi from the locally-based Hadba bloc as governor could be seen as a case of the old ethno-sectarian alliance (Shiite–Kurdish, made possible due to

Sunni non-participation in 2005) giving way to a new and possibly more hardened one (Sunnis mobilizing on anti-Kurdish sentiment), it is significant that Hadba members have been vocal in calling for a role for the Iraqi army in Mosul, thereby envisioning a truly national role for an army which critics sometimes portray as a mere instrument of Shiite sectarian dominance.

On the other hand, in Diyala, the new line-up of senior officials still reflects "old politics" and the mood of 2005. Here, an alliance of the Kurds, ISCI and Tawafuq succeeded in installing Nasir al-Muntasir bi-Allah as governor, whereas the other Sunni-dominated parties alongside the Shiite-dominated Maliki list chose to boycott the proceedings. (The dynamic is actually quite similar to the ongoing contest over who should be the next speaker of the Iraqi parliament.) In Salahaddin, too, Tawafuq, managed to get its own candidate, Mutashar al-Aliwi, elected with a 15 to 10 vote. Significantly, here, as well, an oppositional bid against Tawafuq was framed much in the spirit of the 22 July front, with other Sunnis, secularists, and Shiite supporters of Maliki attempting to create an anti-Tawafuq front, only to fail.

With the strong performance of the Maliki list in Baghdad, it is unsurprising that the two most sought-after posts in the Iraqi capital—those of governor and speaker of the provincial assembly—both went to people from his list, Salah Abd al-Razzaq and Kamil al-Zaydi respectively. Basra, too should be completely under the prime minister's control, with an outright majority for his list on the council, and a loyal candidate recently nominated (reportedly Shaltagh Abbud)—although so far the formal convening of the new council has been postponed until later this week.

The most interesting aspect of these proceedings, however, is the slow progress in a string of Shiite-majority governorates south of Baghdad. So far, only Karbala has had its new governor confirmed; this happened as early as last week when Amal al-Din al-Hurr from Maliki's list was elected governor, with a figure from the local list Amal al-Rafidayn or "Hope of Mesopotamia" (now Maliki's chief coalition partner in Karbala) as speaker of the local assembly. Karbala has particularly close ties to the Daawa movement and a figure close to the Daawa also served as governor after the previous elections even though ISCI enjoyed a majority in the local council.

In the remaining governorates south of Baghdad, no new governors have formally been elected. This is remarkable, because this part of the country was supposed to be a cakewalk for Maliki after he so roundly defeated his main internal Shiite challenger, ISCI, in the elections back in January. What happened? To understand this, it is probably necessary to revisit the atmosphere when the first provisional results were announced in February. Back then, two alternative paths seemed open to Maliki. Either, he could take a magnanimous line towards fellow Shiite Islamist parties—perhaps even ISCI—and opt for power-sharing and/ or independent governors in most places south of Baghdad, perhaps with the exception of Basra where his list won an outright majority. After all, being the incumbent in too many troublesome local councils could prove burdensome come election time at the national level (scheduled for December 2009), and he could stake his prestige on performing well in Baghdad and Basra. Alternatively, Maliki could try to make the most of his victory by building alliances that would secure Daawa dominance everywhere. Of these two options, Maliki appears to have chosen the latter.

Or at least, he tried to do so. February and March saw active coalition-building south of Baghdad that all seemed to be aimed at marginalizing ISCI as much as possible. The first step was to move closer to the breakaway Daawa faction of Ibrahim al-Jaafari, with whom a deal appeared to be ready in March. Then followed negotiations with the main pro-Sadrist list of Amir al-Kinani, who declared his preparedness to take part in coalitions as long as ISCI were excluded. By early April, tentative anti-ISCI fronts grouped around these three parties as a core and capable of winning majorities had been formed in Dhi Qar, Qadisiyya (also including Fadila and possibly even followers of Mahmud al-Hasani, the Sadrist breakaway leader), Babel, Wasit (almost a perfect copy of the 22 July and national trends, with an initial alliance between Jaafari, the Sadrists and Iraqiyya that was later joined by Maliki) and even Najaf in addition to Karbala. The only exceptions were Muthanna (where Maliki also formed an anti-ISCI front but where the council is split 50/50 between the two parties and their allies), and Maysan, where ISCI is particularly strong in some rural areas, and where an all-Shiite grand coalition almost resembling the United Iraqi Alliance at the national level in 2005 appeared to be in the making. To underline the anti-ISCI direction and Maliki's apparent revolt against "old politics", an alliance with the secularist Salih al-Mutlak also seemed to be evolving in Sunni-dominated areas north of Baghdad; this reportedly also included (Shiite-majority) Babel.

On the surface, problems became evident from mid-March onwards. First, it took forever for the elections commission to actually release the final results, which prompted rumors to the effect that Iraqi politicians applied pressure to the commission to prevent them from releasing the results before the parties had decided how they would distribute key posts among themselves. Then, from early April onwards came a series of setbacks for Maliki in various governorates. His slight majority on the 26-member Muthanna council shrunk to 13 representatives, prompting a query to the supreme federal court about how to proceed in the situation of a hung local assembly. On 8 April, a meeting of the new provincial assembly was scheduled in Qadisiyya, but members of Iraqiyya and Maliki's list preferred to stay at home. On 10 April, the Maliki–Jaafari coalition of 17 representatives in Dhi Qar met and elected their governor candidate, except that only 14 members were sufficiently supportive to show up, less than a majority of the 31-member Dhi Qar council. On 11 April, Tanzim al-Iraq members reportedly defected from Maliki's coalition in Wasit. On 12 April, the Maysan council met in closed session but postponed the election of leading officials; Sadrists complained that a promise from Maliki that they would get the governor position had not been honored.

Some of these problems may have to do with the practicalities of reconciling local interests with the preferences of leaders at the national level. The Maliki list—which campaigned with promises of a strong state—has been unabashedly centralist in its interference with the process of selecting governors, in some cases imposing its own candidates (as in Qadisiyya), sometimes even against the will of local politicians (as has been reported in Maysan). Reportedly, a complex deal between Maliki and (pro-Sadrist) Kinani involving several governorates south of Baghdad and stipulating party shares of mid-level officials in various localities has also been entered into.

But clearly there are also deeper forces at work. The rapprochement with Salih al-Mutlak can be described as some of the bravest (and arguably most quintessentially Iraqi) that Maliki has done as premier. But so far, the new political map does not show much trace of that alliance, which reportedly had been underway in Salahaddin, Diyala, Baghdad and Babel. At the same time, the failure of Maliki to impose his will on the Shiite-majority areas of the south could mean that there is more competition than a mere glance at the elections results would suggest. With its anti-Baath message, ISCI (which remains powerful in many branches of government including the security apparatus and the integrity commission) has been at the forefront of the pushback against Maliki's overtures to Mutlak, and there are forces inside both his own party and among the Sadrists that are tempted to go along with the kind of criticism offered by ISCI. Iran, for its part, makes no bones about its preference for politics in Iraq to be based on sectarian identity rather than a national Iraqi one, and is likely to have played a role in the recent revival of the idea of a reunited Shiite alliance of the kind that would pose a clear challenge to any deal between Maliki and Mutlak.

In sum, while the advances of a more national kind of politics in Iraq over the past year have been impressive, the forces that seek to enshrine ethno-sectarian divisions remain strong, and it is particularly remarkable that they have managed to continue to offer so much resistance after their massive defeat at the ballot box in January. This can already be observed in the new political map of Iraq north of Baghdad in places like Diyala, and it will be particularly interesting to see how the struggle unfolds as governor elections take place in all the remaining white spots south of Baghdad over the coming weeks, not least in battleground mid-Euphrates governorates like Dhi Qar, Muthanna, Qadisiyya and Babel.

Maliki Suffers Setbacks as Samarraie Is Confirmed as New Speaker[9]
April 19, 2009

Iraq's parliament finally has a new speaker, whereas the basic structures of local government in all governorates south of Baghdad except Muthanna emerged during the past week. Both the election of Ayad al-Samarraie by the Iraqi parliament today as well as developments in at least two governorates (Maysan and Wasit) appear to be at variance with the overall strategy pursued by Maliki over the past months.

The highly significant setback for Maliki in the contest over who should be speaker of the parliament is likely to drown in Western newswire reports which rather misleadingly portray the whole affair as a case of "Sunni Arabs bickering about who should represent their community" and even allege that somehow the Iraqi constitution imposes sectarian criteria for membership of the post, i.e., one has to be Sunni in order to hold this job. But the assertion that this was an "internal Sunni affair", whether legally or politically, is highly inaccurate. In fact, Maliki was deeply involved from the beginning. The speakership became vacant back in December 2008 in an atmosphere where the incumbent, Mahmud al-Mashhadani, was forced out in rather murky circumstances but clearly to the applause of forces that were critical of Maliki and his increasingly assertive centralism—including most prominently the "decentralist"/ethno-sectarian alliance of the Kurdish parties (PUK and KDP), one of the Shiite Islamist parties (the Islamic Supreme Council of Iraq or ISCI), and, more reluctantly, one of the Sunni Islamist parties (the Iraqi Islamic Party or IIP). Mashhadani's backers were a cross-sectarian coalition that shared his view on the virtues of a strong state, including the Sadrists, Fadila, the secular Iraqiyya and breakaway elements from the IIP-led Tawafuq front—all collectively known as the 22 July parties in reference to their common, Iraqi nationalist stance on Kirkuk.

As for the legal aspect, the idea that there is any constitutional requirement for the speaker to be a Sunni is pure nonsense. Whereas there are certainly several sectarian elements in the constitution that was adopted back in 2005 (including most prominently the tripartite presidency that was adopted for the first parliamentary cycle, as well as the constant references to the "components" or *mukawwinat* of the Iraqi people instead of the whole), the speakership of the parliament is not affected by this at all. Quite the contrary, the fact that the speaker can be elected with an absolute majority made this post into an obvious focus for those who wanted to challenge the system of ethno-sectarian quota sharing. Neither do the "house rules" of the Iraqi parliament impose any particular sectarian formula for the election of the speaker; the reference to a requirement that the speaker should reflect the "balance" of the parliament could plausibly be interpreted as referring to ideology as much as to sectarian identity. Quite in line with this, then, the first suggestion by the ousted Mashhadani himself on 24 December 2008 was actually that he should be replaced by someone from the (Shiite) Sadrist bloc. On 6 January 2009, a Shiite from Iraqiyya and the 22 July bloc, Mahdi al-Hafiz, presented himself as a candidate and on 13 January received the support of Jamal al-Batikh, a prominent Iraqiyya politician.

In this way, the Mashhadani resignation in December highlighted the contradiction between Maliki's alliance with the ethno-federalist parties in government (whose alleged plan to backstab him was referred to publicly by Maliki's confidant Sami al-Askari on 27 December 2008) and his ideological stance on key constitutional issues, where his closeness to the 22 July group of parties was becoming ever clearer as the 31 January 2009 local elections approached. But the way the Daawa handled the issue brought into the open the deep internal fissures in the question of whether to pursue a sectarian or a non-sectarian agenda. For, despite the tendencies by the Maliki list in the local elections campaign to de-emphasize sectarianism, several Daawa party spokespersons repeatedly expressed sectarian points of view as far as the speakership of the national assembly was concerned. For example, on 12 January, Kamal al-Saadi said that the (Shiite-dominated) United Iraqi Alliance would support any candidate that "the Sunnis" themselves could agree upon. Conversely, though, when the 22 July parties protested against the attempt to impose a Sunni candidate from the IIP shortly after the local elections, Daawa joined them in boycotting a parliamentary session on 8 February, and reportedly were among those voting blank or supporting the 22 July candidate (Khalil Jaddu al-Shayhawi) when on 20 February the ethno-federalists tried to force through Ayad al-Samarraie of the IIP but obtained only 136 votes, two votes short of the absolute-majority requirement of 138.

By mid-February, the process of forming local councils took precedence and parliament went into recess. In a sign of desperation, the IIP appealed to the Iraqi federal supreme court for their legal opinion on "what constituted an absolute majority" (with the intention of redefining it so that 136 out of 275 votes would qualify to settle the speakership), a somewhat futile bid because this is one of the few areas where the Iraqi constitution is really perfectly clear and not open to imaginative interpretation. Meanwhile, Maliki appeared to embark on a grand strategy that had the potential to bring his alliances at the provincial level into harmony with the signs of cooperation between himself and the 22 July parties on constitutional issues as well as in the speakership question. Basically, the plan seemed to be to make alliances with secularists, anti-Tawafuq and/or anti-Kurdish Sunni Islamists as well as Shiite Islamist opponents of ISCI wherever possible, and by late March tentative coalitions on this pattern had indeed been formed in most areas.

But the new political map of Iraq that has emerged as new governors have been chosen over the past weeks deviates quite considerably from what would appear to be Maliki's preferred scenario. In Anbar and Nineveh, where councils were formed more than a week ago, Maliki is probably satisfied with the fronts formed on an anti-Tawafuq and anti-Kurdish basis respectively, but in both Diyala and Salahaddin people from his list tried to challenge Tawafuq without any success. Then came a number of crucial decisions in governorates south of Baghdad over the past week. The case with the closest fit to the grand strategy may be Babel, where on 18 April a Maliki-friendly independent governor was elected with support also from Sadrists and Iraqiyya, with ISCI abstaining. Then follow those areas where Maliki either did not manage to work with the secularists or there weren't any to work with, but where he still managed to put together majorities of Shiite Islamists with an anti-ISCI orientation. This includes Qadisiyya (where by mid-April Iraqiyya appeared to have dropped out, but where an agreement on power-sharing that excludes ISCI was reported today) as well as Dhi Qar (where a pro-Maliki governor and a Sadrist council president were elected on 16 April).

But with the exception of Basra (where things could hardly go wrong given the clear majority for Maliki and where two loyalists, Shaltagh Abbud and Jabbar Amin, were elected as governor and council speaker respectively on 15 April), most other areas south of Baghdad have seen problems, even when the arithmetic of seats looked good initially. Muthanna, of course, was always going to be problematic, with ISCI and Maliki each leading coalitions of 13 representatives, with one of the local lists even internally divided between these two coalitions. But in Najaf, Maliki could in theory have allied with Ibrahim al-Jaafari and the Sadrists to marginalize ISCI but he opted instead for an even bigger coalition also including local lists—which in turn began to quarrel internally. Whilst a president of the local council from Maliki's list has now been elected, there is still no governor and there has even been talk about the incumbent ISCI governor making a comeback. Similarly, in Maysan, Maliki had the numbers for an alliance with Jaafari and the Sadrists on the standard pattern, but opted instead to drop his cooperation with the Sadrists and instead work with ISCI (whose ally, "Hizbollah in Iraq" had its candidate as speaker of the local council confirmed on 14 April, with a pro-Maliki governor, Muhammad al-Sudani). And in Wasit, too, everything seemed ready for a coalition inspired by the 22 July formula, with Maliki initially joining a subcoalition of Iraqiyya, the Constitutional Party and the Sadrists. But on 15 April, the new council elected a speaker from ISCI and decided to keep the incumbent governor—from the bloc of independent Shiites associated with Khalid al-Atiyya—in office. The Constitutional Party, Iraqiyya and some members of Maliki's local branch of Daawa (but not Tanzim al-Iraq or the independents) refrained from supporting the new arrangements!

What is going on here? The resultant political map looks rather schizophrenic, with Maliki taking part in coalitions with a clear and aggressive anti-ISCI edge in places like Karbala, Babel, Qadisiyya and Dhi Qar, but apparently making unnecessary concessions to the same ISCI in Maysan, Wasit and possibly even Najaf. In some cases, of course, at least some of the lack of policy coherence may have to do with local politics—as in Wasit, where the decision to ally with ISCI and keep the current governor in office reportedly had been approved by Maliki himself but was resisted by members of the local branch of the Daawa. Also, at least in two cases, the problems came from within Maliki's own list, with the Tanzim al-Iraq branch apparently the main culprit.

But perhaps it is necessary to see this also in relation to the parliamentary struggle about the speaker, which came to the fore again last week and was settled today—and where the contradiction in Daawa policy once more has become evident. On 15 April, a Daawa spokesman declared his opposition to any election of Ayad al-Samarraie of the Iraqi Islamic Party (who was backed also by the Kurds and ISCI), and instead discussed compromise candidates from Iraqiyya, Hiwar and independents, apparently in the spirit of the opposition to Samarraie shared by the 22 July opposition. As late as yesterday, Daawa leaders said Samarraie should not be allowed to run for a second time (but at the same time showed their differences with the 22 July parties by stressing their view that the post should go to a Sunni and a Sunni only). In the end, one of their suggested "compromise candidates", Mustafa al-Hiti, did indeed run against Samarraie today, but received only 34 votes against 154 for Samarraie, with 45 blank votes reported, probably including the Daawa. Altogether, then, only 79 parliamentarians backed the anti-Samarraie stance articulated by Daawa members just days ago.

When using these indicators to discuss Maliki's strength and his room for maneuver, certain caveats need to be kept in mind. The current parliament is an anachronism from 2005 and, in theory at least, in its dying days. Hence, a parliamentary defeat for Maliki on the speakership issue does not necessarily mean that he will give up fighting the next parliamentary elections in December on the same message of a strong (and even non-sectarian?) state that he seemed inspired by back in January. Also, with regard to the speaker, some parliamentarians may have been swayed simply by the acuteness of the issue and the need to get the system up and running again before the whole issue turned farcical; this too suggests that Maliki and his Daawa party will simply put on a brave face and get on with it. Still, the fact that around 20 parliamentarians changed their views on the same candidate within a month is somewhat remarkable, and could suggest that a certain degree of deal-making has taken place.

As for the coalition-forming processes in the provinces and the apparent failure of Maliki to make the most of the elections results, two interpretations are possible. One may ponder why ISCI is doing better than expected in two governorates that border on Iran, and also ask why they appeared to benefit from the antics of the Tanzim al-Iraq branch in at least two governorates (this Daawa faction is thought to be closer to Iran than Maliki's main branch). That kind of search for a hidden hand trying to balance the Shiite Islamist factions against each other is, admittedly, something of a conspiracy-oriented approach. But is it really more plausible to choose the alternative interpretation, i.e., this is all due to the complexities of local

Iraqi politics and Iran is sitting idly by, in splendid isolation, frustrated by its lack of influence, and having no other options left but to plot the next IED campaign through its sole remaining instrument, the "special groups"?

CHAPTER NOTES

1 The original version of this text can be found at http://gulfanalysis.wordpress. com/2008/09/20/two-very-different-takes-on-centralism/.
2 See http://historiae.org/22_July.asp.
3 See http://historiae.org/coalitions.asp.
4 See http://historiae.org/minorities.asp.
5 See http://historiae.org/ISCI.asp.
6 See http://gulfanalysis.wordpress.com/2009/02/08/the-22-july-opposition-alliance-is-still-alive-and-well-and-gets-some-support-from-maliki/.
7 See http://historiae.org/allocation.asp.
8 See http://historiae.org/Provincialcouncils.asp.
9 See http://historiae.org/samarrai.asp.

Chapter 5

Sectarian Repolarization during 2009

Nuri al-Maliki failed in his attempt to establish a parliamentary front against Ayad al-Samarraie, the new speaker, in April 2009. This meant not only the collapse of any potential alliance between Maliki and the nascent July 22 nationalist forces with which he held much in common. It also involved a collapse of the July 22 front itself as some of its members, notably Iraqiyya, reverted to patterns of political behavior seen during the "old days" of Bremerian politics during the governing council in 2003 to 2004 in which allies would be chosen not on the basis of common views on political issues, but with reference to old friendships and personal relations, often formed during long decades in exile. Subsequently, Maliki came under immense pressure from Iran to join its newly reconstituted Iraqi partner, the Iraqi National Alliance (INA) which came into existence in Tehran around May. One notable feature of summer 2009 was the massive pressure on Maliki to make him join in an all-Shiite alliance for the 2010 parliamentary elections.

Maliki resisted. In October he decided to contest the elections on a separate ticket, apart from the other Shiites. However, during the process, he had become increasingly embattled and lost much of the nationalist credibility that he had managed to establish in the previous local elections. One issue that had a particularly fateful impact was his reaction to a series of terror attacks in Baghdad in August, which he blamed squarely on Syria and "Baathists" without appearing to have the proof to support his claims. This certainly did not win him any new and much-needed friends in Sunni-majority areas to the north of Baghdad. Thus was reversed the positive trend in which, since 2008, Maliki had increasingly dared to challenge fellow Shiites on issues like militias (the Sadrists), state structure (ISCI's federalism), quota-based power-sharing (tawafuqiyya), and finally the constitution itself (supporting reform towards greater centralism—a goal shared by many Sunnis).

But above all it was the collapse of Maliki's credentials on issues related to the northern parts of Iraq that hampered the prospect of some kind of decisive pact with key Sunni and nationalist–secularist politicians that could have altered the political map of the country fundamentally. Back in 2008, Kirkuk had been the issue that allowed the nationalist July 22 forces to emerge, and Maliki now had the option of aligning himself with these tendencies as the election law came up for debate in autumn 2009. However, during that process, his State of Law alliance never opted to press for any kind of strong special arrangements for Kirkuk on the pattern of what had been achieved by the July 22 parties previously. Hence, a repeat of the cross-sectarian consolidation seen in 2008 simply failed to materialize, and all the (mainly Sunni) nationalist forces of the north now gravitated toward the secular Iraqiyya instead. Indeed, after the initial version of the election law had been vetoed in early November by Tariq al-Hashemi, the Sunni vice-president, Maliki joined with other Shiite and Kurdish politicians and struck back—at first, by attacking the veto itself in an unconstitutional way; later, by inserting a distribution key for seats more amenable to Kurdish interests. That brought the pattern of alliances inside the Iraqi parliament largely back to the sectarian situation in early 2006.

It should also be added that once more, at this critical juncture, the international community—and the United States and UNAMI, the UN agency in Iraq, in particular—played key roles in preventing nationalist mobilization on the Kirkuk issue. Fearful of breaking any eggs in their attempts at preparing an Iraqi omelet, the Obama administration fervently discouraged any discussion of Kirkuk in relation to the election law, focusing, as ever, on the very short term and the election timeline. This period also saw the beginnings of remarkable moves by one of the key July 22 parties, the secular Iraqiyya, toward dialogue with one of the least plausible conversation partners they could have found on the Iraqi scene, the Shiite-led INA alliance. Resulting first and foremost from personal antagonisms between Maliki and the leader of Iraqiyya, Ayad Allawi, these moves served to widen further the gap between State of Law and Iraqiyya (whose alliance would have been eminently logical from the political viewpoint). Though the split originated in differences that were solely personal, a whole discourse of antagonism was developed by Maliki's opponents in which the idea of Maliki as a dangerous strongman formed a central component. This discourse did not make much sense since the idea of a strongly centralized government remained important to many Iraqiyya supporters, but the personal differences were so intense that Iraqiyya's ideological differences with the newfound INA partners (pro-federal, pro-Iranian, pro-Kurdish) were conveniently laid aside.

In a report released via the New York–based Century Foundation in February 2009, I tried to warn about the Iranian-inspired project to reconstitute the all-Shiite alliance. This project was clearly Iran's attempt at regaining initiative after its protégé, ISCI, had performed so poorly in the January local elections. But to try to communicate this to the newly installed Obama administration in spring 2009 was like banging on a closed door. I participated in a group of Iraqi and Norwegian academics who wrote a report on strategies for achieving a post-sectarian climate for the upcoming 2010 parliamentary elections and presented it at the United States Institute of Peace in early March, with separate meetings at the State Department, the National Security Council, and the Pentagon. Our recommendations included proposals for a public U.S. apology for the way in which sectarian politics had been enshrined in the Iraqi governing council fashioned by Paul Bremer in 2003; an end to the passive or active reproduction of the sectarian narrative on Iraqi politics that Iran so clearly preferred; and a clear U.S. statement that Iraq would never become a negotiating card in U.S.–Iran relations. (It is a common fear among many Iraqi nationalists that Iran is being granted influence in Iraq by the U.S. in exchange for a détente between Tehran and Washington.) We were basically asking for measures that would not cost a dime of U.S. taxpayers' money. We were asking for a change of mind-set and for Washington to start a normal conversation with Iraqi politicians without preconceptions about sectarian representation.

Throughout this process, however, we were dismissed as alarmists for pointing to the danger of Iran using the sectarian card to regain influence in Iraq. "You are very afraid of Iran, are you?" one State Department official enquired, as if this constituted some kind of particular Scandinavian disease. (This particular official was even a holdover from the Bush administration.) He declared, "2008 was a bad year for Iran in Iraq," highlighting as the supposed U.S. triumph the Status of Forces Agreement (SOFA) of November 2008. We tried to point out that the SOFA was not particularly valuable if the Iraqi government was aiming at cooperation with Iran once the U.S. forces were gone in 2011, but American military experts assured us that the nascent Iraqi military was "organically tied" to the United States, unable to operate without U.S. assistance; hence, an informal U.S. sphere of influence for the next decade was guaranteed. "We're gonna have a pretty firm hand on power in Iraq for five to 10 years." But in that same period, as the Obama administration was just beginning to think hard about Iraq, press reports out of Baghdad featured more claims than ever that Iran and the Badr brigades were behind an upsurge of terror attacks in Shiite areas in an attempt to put pressure on Maliki to join the ongoing Shiite unification attempts.

I made another attempt at getting my skepticism across at a major U.S. government conference on Iraq in May 2009—but again to no avail. I made the point that because of the general turn to nationalism in the local elections, pro-Iranian Shiite groups would be likely to proceed more subtly with respect to their sectarian ambitions, for example by using fear-mongering about former Baathists as an election strategy instead of mobilizing on themes that explicitly stoked Sunni–Shiite conflict. However, as if to legitimize the de-Baathification camp even at that early stage, senior U.S. diplomats present at the meeting retorted that fear was "deep and very real" in Iraq, reiterating the now-familiar "bad-year for Iran" chorus and highlighting the prospect for future Fulbright scholar exchanges. . . . A couple of months later, I took part via video-link in a smaller Iraq conference in Washington, where the focus was on the possibility that the disturbances after the Iranian presidential elections in June might weaken Iran's influence in Iraq. I suggested it was the other way around but most speakers maintained that Iran was playing a straightforward, "soft power" game in Iraq. Few empirical points were offered; in fact it was difficult to avoid the feeling that some of this was based on a widespread worry among U.S. academics concerning their potential roles as crown *witnesses in an imaginary war against Iran—in itself a perfectly understandable worry after all the war-mongering of the Bush era.*

As for the stunning turn of Iraqiyya to the ideologically contradictive attempt at alliance with the newly constituted, all-Shiite INA, I had a number of conversations with leading politicians on the Iraqiyya side in an attempt to clarify what was going on. This, of course, was an area where the Americans are not the ones that are primarily to blame, although it has been reported that Iraqiyya leaders were denied audiences with central members of the Obama administration in summer 2009 and more generally were always encouraged by U.S. think-tankers to worry as much as they could about the prospect of Nuri al-Maliki getting "too strong." Rather, it was a matter that seemed to derive almost wholly from the personal animosities between Allawi and Maliki. Iraqiyya people gave me long lectures about Maliki's insatiable appetite for power, replete with stories about how, during the Saddam years, people from Maliki's Daawa party who were living in exile in London would express authoritarian tendencies in the way they interacted with the rest of the Iraqi diaspora. There were poorly camouflaged hints that the Daawa were untrustworthy because of their comparatively lower-class status. ("Only Haydar al-Abbadi is a really good man; he is rich.") They would add ceaselessly to this anti-Maliki narrative. However, those efforts could not disguise the fact that their proposed alternative, INA, disagreed with Iraqiyya on every issue of significance in Iraqi politics, including most signally federalism and the management of the all-important oil sector. That was certainly the case with the most "indigenous" elements of the heterogeneous Iraqiyya alliance that eventually came into existence, such as the Hadba group of Mosul and Salih al-Mutlak's party. The main exception that might perhaps explain the seemingly illogical turn to INA would be the more exile-oriented Wifaq, which comprised several individuals who seemed more interested in free trade and the oil business (including Crescent Petroleum) than in anti-federalism and combating Kurdish encroachments on the prerogatives of the central government in Baghdad.

Notes on Iranian Strategy after ISCI's Failure[1]
March 18, 2009

- While the common notion of Iraqi Shiites as Iraqi nationalists appears to be true with regard to the Shiite population of the country as a whole, it is not historically correct with respect to the pro-Iranian exiled Shiite Islamists that were installed as leaders of Iraq by the United States since 2003, such as ISCI and at least some of the Daawa factions.
- The irreducible minimum of Iranian desiderata in Iraq appears to be the

maintenance of a system in which politics remains defined on the basis of sectarian identity, regardless of state structure more generally. Thus, while Tehran may be only experimenting as far as territorial partition in the shape of federalism is concerned (as exemplified by the increasingly ambiguous position of ISCI), psychological partition in the shape of ethno-sectarian quotas and power-sharing seems to be a more permanent goal. For this reason alone, a post-sectarian agenda seems the most promising avenue for a counter-strategy against excessive Iranian influence in Iraq.

- Accordingly, the reconstitution of the United Iraqi Alliance—possibly dressed up as a "national" and more centralist alliance under the leadership of the Daawa and the Sadrists but still a clearly Shiite Islamist project— could be a natural priority for Tehran when faced with ISCI's declining popularity.

- While Nuri al-Maliki has taken a number of valuable steps towards emphasizing the virtues of a functioning centralized state, only institutional change and constitutional revision can consolidate these positive tendencies in a way that would make Iraq more corrosive against external influences. Today, the Washington narrative of Maliki as an Iraqi nationalist and even secularist with widespread popular appeal remains problematic in many ways—including the continued importance of some pro-Iranian elements within his electoral coalition, his poor performance in Sunni areas north of Baghdad in the recent local elections, as well as renewed flirtation even inside his own Daawa branch with policies that can only benefit Iran in the long run (like pursuing a sectarian logic in the appointment of the next parliamentary speaker, or working to reconstitute a broader Shiite sectarian alliance).

- The United States seems to underestimate the scenario that a future pro-Iranian Iraqi regime may elect to speak a perfectly Iraqi nationalist language on issues such as complete withdrawal of foreign troops while at the same time coordinating pragmatically with Tehran for the long term. By way of example, for decades, Syria's government has been impeccable in its ideological attachment to Arab nationalism but without jeopardizing its long-standing ties to Iran.

Hammudi Tapped for Leadership Role in Reviving the United Iraqi Alliance[2]

May 13, 2009

According to a brief press release of today's date described as "very important" by the Islamic Supreme Council of Iraq (ISCI), Abd al-Aziz al-Hakim has charged another prominent ISCI figure, Humam Hammudi, with the job of reviving the (all-Shiite) United Iraqi Alliance (UIA). The communiqué lists the achievements of the UIA until this date but warns that Iraq's future challenges, and especially the threat from insurgents (whether Islamists or Baathists), are such that no disunity between the UIA components can be allowed.

Of course, disunity inside the UIA has been the dominant theme since at least the summer of 2008 (when even its perceived center of Daawa and ISCI began to crumble), to the point where the alliance today is almost defunct. But when Maliki in March tried to go ahead with forming provincial councils on an anti-ISCI platform and reached out to secularists and Sunni parties that are unfriendly with ISCI, criticism from inside the Shiite community soon manifested itself. Going forward, the fate of Hammudi's UIA mission will be an important indicator of what kind of political climate we can expect from the next parliamentary elections in Iraq, and above all whether the politics of fear will continue to prevail.

After Sadr–Badr Compromise in Tehran, the Iraqi National Alliance (INA) Is Declared[3]
August 24, 2009

After a bit of juggling with adjectives and word order, the Iraqi National Alliance was launched in Baghdad today (INA, in Arabic referred to as Al-Ittilaf al-Watani al-Iraqi), thereby becoming the first publicly confirmed major electoral alliance for next year's parliamentary elections in Iraq. Essentially, the new coalition consists of the two largest blocs of the previous Shiite alliance (the United Iraqi Alliance or UIA)—the Islamic Supreme Council of Iraq (ISCI) and the Sadrists—plus certain breakaway elements from Daawa/Tanzim al-Iraq (the most pro-Iranian of the two Daawa factions), as well as Ibrahim al-Jaafari's breakaway faction. The only significant components from outside the old UIA are the Anbar Salvation Council headed by Hamid al-Hayis (a breakaway group of the Anbar Awakening which received only a modest share of the votes in the last local elections) and Khalid Abd al-Wahhab al-Mulla, the president of a Sunni group of Islamic scholars from Zubayr outside Basra. Additionally, the party of the Shiite Bahr al-Ulum family, which was sometimes separate from the old UIA, has been reintegrated.

It may be useful to briefly recapitulate how the new alliance evolved. The idea of a "revived" Shiite alliance with a more "national" orientation was first intro-duced publicly by Muqtada al-Sadr in Qum, Iran, in mid-February 2009, when he requested a full makeover of the UIA which in the future should be referred to as the "United National Iraqi Alliance". Sadr was responding to the results of the January local elections, in which the Daawa party of Prime Minister Nuri al-Maliki was rewarded by voters for a rhetoric in which the sectarian agenda was pushed into the background and the focus on national and centralist values was strengthened. After Sadr's initiative, other forces in the old UIA, including the pro-Maliki independent Abbas al-Bayati as well as Ahmad al-Chalabi, soon offered their support, but it was not until May that the project got going in earnest. By that time, ISCI—which had been punished particularly hard by voters in the January polls—had taken over the initiative, and within weeks several dozen key UIA members paid their visits to ISCI's ailing leader Abd al-Aziz al-Hakim at a convalescent home in Tehran where details of the new alliance were discussed. Reportedly, Muqtada al-Sadr also made the journey from Qum to reconcile with Hakim, a long-time opponent, apparently seeing the symbolic change of name as a "concession to a Sadrist demand" that could justify their return to the UIA.

At one point, it seemed as if the new alliance was on course to co-opt Maliki and thereby could hope to reclaim lost voters. However, once more old disputes between Maliki and ISCI came to the fore in June and July. Far from preaching ecumenism towards ISCI, Maliki held on to his centralist discourse on several occasions, focusing on the limits of the power of the governorates at a time when ISCI along with the Kurds kept talking about unrestrained decentralization. Similarly, at the recent general conference of the Daawa party, Maliki's distaste for militias was emphasized ("we don't have militias because we believe in the state"), another indication that he did not mind his differences with ISCI and the Sadrists remaining on display in the public domain. While Maliki talked about "no alliances for the sake of alliances", ISCI seemed prepared to ignore ideological differences if only Maliki would join their new alliance and thereby keep the Shiites unified at any cost—Maliki's disinclination to do this was ascribed to personal ambitions regarding the premiership and the Daawa share of seats in the new alliance. Last week, the entire process seemed to be in complete disarray: During the course of a single day, no less than four different dates for the forthcoming announcement of the alliance were cited by various UIA members; simultaneously, at the level of local government, Maliki supporters were allegedly expelled from the provincial council of Diyala by an ISCI-friendly coalition while ISCI partisans complained of their marginalization by the Maliki-dominated council in Diwaniyya. However, not even the latest string of bomb attacks in Baghdad—no doubt designed to hurt Maliki's vision of a normalized Iraq where concrete barriers could be safely removed, and even blamed on Iran by at least one senior intelligence official— seems to have changed his mind. As a consequence, the Maliki branch of the Daawa was the notable absentee at today's announcement.

A footnote on the perennial subject of Daawa subdivisions seems appropriate at this point. During the summer there have been several of them, mostly neglected by the international press. First, in late July Diyya Amin al-Sayyid Nur abruptly declared a complete change of leadership in Harakat al-Daawa, one of the smallest (and oldest) wings of the Daawa, with particularly close ties to Basra (the late Izz al-Din Salim was perhaps the most prominent representative of the party). A few days later, Muhammad Jasim Khudayr al-Maksusi, another party member, categorically rejected the move. Then, in early August, an apparent coup attempt took place within the Tanzim al-Iraq branch of the Daawa. The party is of far more recent origin, and while it is often misinterpreted as some kind of "domestic Daawa" it seems clear that it was created by Iran shortly before 2003 in order to regain lost control within the Daawa movement, operating out of offices in Qum and London before it came to Baghdad after the American invasion. Earlier this month, while many leading parliamentarians were on summer holiday, Abd al-Karim al-Anizi arranged a party conference in Baghdad and elected a new leadership, to loud protest from other party members including the party chairman Hashim al-Musawi, but with the support of Isa al-Firayji, the head of the television channel al-Masar (which has since physically occupied the Tanzim al-Iraq website). Significantly, after this incident, Anizi has remained particularly central to the formation of the new INA. He is considered among the most pro-Iranian elements in Daawa (Tanzim al-Iraq) and has also been emphasizing sectarian solidarities with the Sadrists. His role in reconstituting the UIA was highlighted by ISCI preacher Jalal al-Din al-Saghir a few weeks ago, and today during the formal launch of the INA he was once more prominent, whereas most other Tanzim al-Iraq leaders were absent, signaling their solidarity with Maliki instead.

The centrality of people like Anizi to the INA project is one among several factors that raise certain doubts about the sincerity of its new "national" agenda. Of course, some will ask how there could possibly be anything sectarian about a new alliance that actually leaves out some Shiites (Maliki) to the advantage of Sunnis (such as al-Hayis)? But while new constellations of this kind in themselves doubtless are of immense value to the maturation of the Iraqi political process, in this case, the basic facts of the genesis of the alliance simply speak a lot louder than rhetoric of national unity. Agreement on the new alliance seems to have been arrived at in Tehran, and it is basically a case of Shiite Islamists with long-standing Iranian sympathies like Abd al-Aziz al-Hakim and Abd al-Karim al-Anizi reaching an understanding with other Shiite Islamists whose turn to Iran is of far more recent date (and probably is still disputed by many of their adherents in Iraq), as in the case of Muqtada al-Sadr. Already in May, full lists of the new alliance circulated; they included the entire old UIA, with unspecified "independent" and "tribal" Sunnis forming a beautifying addendum. Last week, ISCI even let it be known publicly that there had been a visit to the Grand Ayatollah Ali al-Sistani in Najaf, the world's most prominent Shiite leader, to "confer" about the new alliance. And while most elements of the new program and "principles" of the alliance published today come across as rather bland, unobjectionable and therefore also unremarkable (fostering civil society, protecting the environment etc.), one item will be difficult to stomach for those with more secular inclinations or non-Shiite backgrounds: The new alliance will "adhere to directions from the *marjaiyya*", which could mean the higher Shiite clergy in its widest possible sense (even the usual restriction to "the *marjaiyya* of Najaf" or "the *marjaiyya* of Iraq" is omitted). In this context, Hayis and other elements from outside the old UIA run the risk of becoming figureheads and stooges for Shiite Islamist interests first and foremost. The invitation to other forces to "join" now looks somewhat tongue-in-cheek given that the party program has already been decided, and seems mainly aimed at the possibility of Maliki joining at a later stage.

The attention will now shift to those forces that have yet to declare their alliances for the parliamentary elections that are scheduled for 16 January 2010: Maliki as well as the various nationalist opposition parties. If Iraq is to make a meaningful transition to a less sectarian form of politics, it is important that the anticlimaxes of 2008 are not repeated. During the spring if 2008 there was a lot of cross-sectarian cooperation in the Iraqi parliament, but while this resulted in victories like the provincial elections law, nothing durable came out of all the promises of a monster national alliance. Maliki, for his part, will also need to go beyond what he accomplished in the local elections, which was more of a shift in rhetoric than a real integration of new political forces outside the Shiite Islamist core. So far there has been talk about an alliance between Maliki and the awakening forces of Anbar. As for the nationalists, there are signs of growing cooperation between forces like Iraqiyya, the Constitutional Party of Jawad al-Bulani, Tariq al-Hashimi, Salih al-Mutlak, Nadim al-Jabiri (a defector from Fadila, which early on rejected the UIA makeover as political theater but which now is reported as a last-minute convert to the project) and Mahmud al-Mashhadani (the former speaker of parliament, associated with the 22 July movement)—a trend that seems particularly significant in that it could potentially reverse a tendency of Iraqiyya to sometimes support ISCI in parliament even in cases where this runs counter to its own declared ideological principles. If two such grand cross-sectarian coalitions should emerge then the next elections could indeed become a step forward for Iraq. And in that context, the INA in its unfinished state (and therefore in practice somewhat less sectarian than originally intended) could also play a constructive role.

Why an Allawi–Hakim Alliance Would Mean Retrogression in Iraq[5]
September 21, 2009

The rumors are so persistent that they are getting quite difficult to ignore: Ayad Allawi, leader of the Wifaq movement and the Iraqiyya coalition—the most sizeable, enduring and electorally successful secularist entities in post-2003 Iraq—keeps spending time talking to Ammar al-Hakim and other leaders of the newly (re)formed, Islamist and Shiite-dominated Iraqi National Alliance with a view to possibly joining their ticket for the upcoming 2010 parliamentary elections. Or rather his lieutenants in Baghdad keep these discussions going; Allawi himself has actually spent parts of Ramadan in the United States.

Some Iraq watchers are likely to construe any such alliance as a wonderful sign of progress in Iraqi politics. Is it not great that Allawi, a secularist, can get together with Shiite Islamists in a businesslike manner? Is this not proof that sectarianism is on the decline, since Allawi, while himself a Shiite, is popular among many secular Sunnis as well?

Alas, no. Political maturation requires a little bit more than people of different backgrounds getting together on the same coalition list. In particular, it would be nice, especially for voters, if the components of that kind of list had a minimum of ideological coherence and common issues on which they agreed. But unfortunately, such coherence is in short supply when it comes to the Iraqi National Alliance. Already, there is pronounced tension between the two main components, the Sadrists and the Islamic Supreme Council of Iraq (ISCI). The former subscribes to the vision of a strong, centralized Iraqi state; the latter has been the main protagonist of the decentralization in Iraq and giving concessions to the Kurds. Where the two agree is with regard to the need to Islamize Iraqi society, as seen for example in Basra where Sadrists and ISCI figures have been trying to outbid each other in imposing Islamic dress codes and Islamic behavior. Also, they are unified in their desire to keep Iraq free of Baathists and what is described as remnants of the old regime more generally. In fact, this is probably the single issue where there seems to be perfect agreement inside the alliance: Among the few specific points offered in the INA program is a promise to voters to "cleanse the institutions of the state of Baathist and Saddamist elements".

This anti-Baathism was the unifying theme in the previous Shiite alliance (the United Iraqi Alliance or UIA), and ISCI preacher Sadr al-Din al-Qabbanji—the figure who communicates with the popular base of the party—has promised that it will be central to the new alliance as the 2010 elections approach. And so it seems clear that to add Allawi to this mix would turn things into a complete parody. In fact, such is the antipathy towards Allawi in the core electorate of the Shiite coalition that the first UIA elections poster featured pictures of him as well as Hazim al-Shaalan with the text "the Baath is coming back—will you allow it"? In other words, it was believed that dislike of Allawi would be the best way to mobilize UIA voters. Remove the anti-Baathism issue and it becomes incredibly difficult to define what the Iraqi National Alliance really stands for.

That exposes the only remaining glue in the Shiite-led alliance: thirst for power, without the slightest regard to ideology. Over the past weeks, the alliance has signaled readiness to include anyone who is willing to sign up, including other past foes like Wail Abd al-Latif from Basra who antagonized ISCI with his drive to make Basra a standalone federal entity and his constant criticisms regarding their ties to Iran. As for Allawi himself, it is easy to contemplate his fate if he should sign up for the new alliance. The Iraqiyya movement would break apart—you just cannot fool all of the people all of the time. (In fact, this kind of outcome may well be exactly what the alliance leaders are hoping to achieve.) And even in the unlikely event that this trick succeeds among the Iraqi public, Allawi will likely end up as a disillusioned casualty of unbridgeable ideological divides, at best rewarded with a honorary ministry in the next Iraqi government. In short, the ascendancy of this kind of alliance would signify a return to the nonsense of 2003, a Paul Bremer logic with oversized, non-technocratic and corrupt governments in which each powerful player is accorded a ministerial vantage point from which to scavenge on the decaying Iraqi state.

Maliki Re-Launches the State of Law List: Beautiful But Is It Powerful Enough?[6]
October 1, 2009

Today, Prime Minister Nuri al-Maliki has put together a new line-up for his State of Law list (*dawlat al-qanun*) that will contest Iraq's parliamentary elections in January 2010. In terms of Iraq's maturation from a sectarian to an issue-based kind of politics, Maliki's list represents considerable progress, although it was not quite as wide-ranging as some had hoped for.

Before discussing the potential of the new iteration of the State of Law coalition, it can be useful to recap what the previous version was and what it wasn't. True, Maliki's electoral performance last January was impressive, and his wins in the two big cities of Basra and Baghdad stood out in particular. But despite all the spin, the composition of his list back then was still heavily Shiite Islamist, with most leading candidates coming from the two main branches of the Daawa and the bloc of independent Shiite parliamentarians affiliated with the oil minister, Hussein al-Shahristani. Also, its electoral performance in Sunni-majority areas north of Baghdad was dismal, with just a couple of percent of the votes at best; on the whole, Sunni votes for Maliki materialized in few areas outside Basra and Baghdad. While sometimes described in Western media as a new, anti-Iranian and even secular strongman of Iraq, Maliki in reality had won an ambiguous victory that was subsequently reflected in problems of coalition-forming in several governorates and considerable kowtowing to hardliner Islamist demands by some of his local councilors in both Basra and Baghdad.

Since the local elections in January, Maliki's political strategy to boost his chances of winning the next parliamentary polls has apparently followed two tracks. The first is to expand the range of parties that take part in his coalition, especially to bring in more secularists and Sunnis. At its bravest, back in March, this included talks with the secularist Salih al-Mutlak and cooperation with the secular Iraqiyya list in several provincial councils, reflecting the fact that on many key issues relating to the design of the optimal basic state model for Iraq, Maliki's centralist ideals correlate fairly well with the preferences of those secularist parties. It also involved more recently a long overdue rapprochement with other national-ist forces associated with the 22 July trend that grew out of opposition to Kurdish policies in Kirkuk and today is embodied primarily in the Nationalist Independent Trend headed by Mahmud al-Mashhadani and Nadim al-Jabiri, but which also has a certain affinity to local movements like the Hadba list in Mosul headed by the Nujayfi brothers, the independent Yusuf al-Habubi in Karbala, and the Iraqi Constitutional Party of the minister of interior, Jawad al-Bulani. Another new idea in Daawa circles over the summer consisted of reaching out to reformist forces in Kurdistan like Goran, which recently have been empowered by growing Kurdish dislike of the stranglehold of their two biggest parties (as witnessed for example in the regional elections there in July).

On this dimension, the roster of parties that were reported today as actually having signed up for the new State of Law coalition seemed to include a good deal of second-best leftovers. There appears to be no Iraqiyya, no Hiwar, no Nujayfi, no Habubi (although some reports say his new-found partner of the Dulaym tribe, Ali Hatim Sulayman, was present), no Mashhadani, no Jabiri, no Bulani and appar-ently even no Ahmad Abu Risha (the Anbar leader with whom Maliki appeared to have a tacit alliance at the time of the last local elections). Instead, in addition to the expected Daawa/Shiite Islamist core (this includes the main faction of the Tanzim al-Iraq branch), there are a collection of breakaway elements. For example, from the Iraqiyya coalition there are defectors such as the Iraqi Communist Party, as well as independent representatives like Mahdi al-Hafiz and Safiya al-Suhayl (who are sometimes described as defectors and sometimes as casualties of expul-sions). Similarly, there are splinter elements with a past association with Hiwar or the 22 July trend generally, like Abbad Mutlak al-Jibburi, ex-Tawafuq members with links to Kirkuk like Hajim al-Hasani, and Sunni tribal figures who have tried to cooperate with Shiite Islamists earlier, such as Khalid al-Yawir. The presence of a Fayli party will probably be highlighted as a new "Kurdish" dimension although it has to be stressed that many Faylis have a fairly distinct sense of separate identity also rooted in their Shiite links. Jaafar al-Sadr, another figure now highlighted by the new coalition, is the only son of Muhammad Baqir al-Sadr, Iraq's iconic cleri-cal activist in the 1970s. In the late 1990s the young Jaafar al-Sadr was involved in creating an office for the Sadrist movement in Iran and may perhaps appeal to some in the Sadrist camp for that reason, although his personal relations with Muqtada have been poor at times.

We should however keep in mind the second track of Maliki's overall strategy in building support, which is less in the news and therefore less easy to keep track of. Basically, it consists of strengthening Daawa influences in local communities also outside the field of electoral politics. Back in the last local elections, this became controversial with respect to the so-called "support councils" (*majalis isnad*), associations of supposedly unarmed tribesmen with somewhat elusive mandates aimed at "strengthening the state" in the local community. More recently, there has been an increasing focus on the efforts of the Daawa party to install individuals loyal to themselves in the Iraqi public bureaucracy. This dimension may well be part of the new coalition effort too, as it is difficult to know exactly who the unnamed tribal participants from various governorates north of Baghdad are and how much influence they actually have. But anecdotal evidence suggests that this process is ongoing; as recently as yesterday a high-level defection from Hadba to the State of Law list was reported in the Sinjar area in Nineveh province.

On the balance, then, the new list is a courageous move by Maliki, but there is still a feeling that one or more additional elite allies from the secular or Sunni-oriented parties could be needed for a big success. For sure, just the mere fact of going it alone, separate from the Shiite-dominated Iraqi National Alliance, is in itself a brave choice. The new list is very different from the Iraqi National Alliance in that it looks less sectarian—the Sunnis and secularists in it seem like real representatives in the total picture, whereas in the Iraqi National Alliance they come across as ornaments that will never have real influence—and it has got more ideological coherence, focused on the vision of a functioning centralized government in Iraq. It seems clear that Maliki is determined to get out of his dysfunctional relationship with the anti-centralist groups that currently make up his cabinet (especially the Islamic Supreme Council of Iraq and the Kurds). Vague talk of "super-alliances" between the two coalitions in the future cannot detract from the fact that Maliki's decision to go it alone was something neither the Iraqi National Alliance nor Iran wanted.

On the other hand, it seems that a series of recent unfortunate events, most of which were probably not of Maliki's own making, may have helped sour his relationship with potential Sunni and secularist allies. In the first place, there were the "Black Wednesday" bombings in August and the subsequent drive by Maliki to accuse Syria and Baathists, which may have alienated some prospective allies. This whole development is slightly ironic in that criticizing Baathists and neighboring Arab states for a long time has been the preserve of ISCI, but on this occasion they stood back and let Maliki go all the way. Secondly, there was the conflict with Abd al-Karim Khalaf, a top-level ministry of interior official who in the past has been considered an astute nationalist by many secular Iraqis. And of course, there was the case of Muntazar al-Zaydi who became a nationalist hero in the shoe-throwing incident last year where Maliki was standing rather uncomfortably shoulder to shoulder with George W. Bush; his recent release from prison prompted accusations of highhanded action by Maliki's security detail in the past. While at least two of these conflicts may ultimately well be the results of intrigues by his enemies in the Shiite camp who had wanted him to join their coalition, Maliki needs to remember that he cannot afford to alienate too many secularists and people with a degree of pan-Arab sympathies either. After all, the magnitude of his victory in the last local elections was caused primarily by watershed victories in urban areas where Iraqis saw him as an inspirational figure; the other strategy of building tribal support in the countryside did not produce such convincing results in terms of votes for the State of Law list.

And so the next few weeks will probably see the most decisive developments. What will happen to the rumored negotiations between the Iraqi National Alliance and Iraqiyya? How will the question of Kirkuk in the elections law affect the coalition-forming process? Will more Iraqi nationalists see the potential strengths of the State of Law list and join, or will they use the opportunity to coalesce into a third big coalition? Unfortunately, some may well feel inclined to choose the unrealistic alternative of dreaming about a solo win, in which case it will be fairly easy for Iran to create conditions conducive to the re-formation of a Shiite sectarian majority come January 2010. But with his new list, Maliki has at least made a tentative step and a bold contribution towards extricating Iraq from the politics of sectarianism.

Allawi–Mutlak: Consolidation at the Center of Iraqi Politics[7]
October 27, 2009

After the announcement last week of the Unity of Iraq Alliance led by Interior Minister Jawad al-Bulani and Anbar *sahwa* (Awakening) leader Ahmad Abu Risha, it has been a dizzying period for the remaining nationalist parties that are still trying to form some kind of large-scale coalition and/or considering joining either the Unity of Iraq Alliance or Maliki's State of Law.

All the logically possible combinations have by now been exhausted more than once in press reports, so it was perhaps to be expected that the first step with some substance to it took place in the darkness of night yesterday, in decidedly low-key style. It consisted not of the announcement of another big alliance, but simply of a press release from the Wifaq movement of Ayad Allawi to the effect that it had joined with the Hiwar movement of Salih al-Mutlak to form a new entity, called the Iraqi Nationalist Movement.

The new movement (*haraka*) is referred to sometimes as a "party" (*hizb*) or "organization" (*tashkil*), but is apparently not reckoned as an "alliance" yet, meaning negotiations with others are still going on—and may well continue until the expiry of the deadline for forming coalitions. "Others" in this case means above all Usama al-Nujayfi who is affiliated with the powerful Hadba movement of Mosul, but to some extent also Tariq al-Hashemi (who has broken away from the Tawafuq bloc, a more Sunni-oriented entity) as well as Rafi al-Eisawi (the deputy premier, also a Sunni). Interestingly, the objections against the two latter individuals joining the alliance appear to have come above all from leaders in the Hiwar movement, who reject the way Hashemi and Eisawi have been "playing the game of sectarianism and quotas [*muhasasa*]" by accepting high offices in the Maliki government in what critics say amounts to roles as Sunni figureheads.

Some of that criticism seems easy to understand, even if Hashemi at times has been a robust critic of the system "from within". Hiwar, for its part, has been a prominent player in the 22 July front that has driven forward many of the important changes in Iraqi politics over the past year—such as demanding local elections on time and focusing on Kirkuk as an issue of national significance. Also Iraqiyya, especially since it left the Maliki government in August 2007, has increasingly contributed to this nationalist opposition which played a key role in changing the climate in Iraqi politics in 2008 (and to some extent created space for the more nationalism-oriented Maliki to emerge). Against that background, the by far most important omission from the line-up is Nujayfi, whose Hadba movement totally overshadowed all the other nationalist parties in Mosul during the last local elections. In American discourse on Iraq, Anbar is often seen as the key to the "Sunni scene", but Hiwar and Iraqiya probably realize that there is more to lose in Mosul, which historically is home to many of the important nationalist movements in Iraq.

Some will say that a simple merger of Wifaq/Iraqiyya and Hiwar was the very minimum a secular and nationalist Iraqi voter could ask for. That is true, but it is nevertheless important in itself that such an act of consolidation did take place, especially given the hopeless fragmentation of these forces during the previous elections in 2005. Back then, under adverse circumstances, the two managed to win altogether 34 parliamentarians; last January they won 45 councilors across Iraq from Basra to Ramadi. But with the emerging dynamic of perhaps five medium-sized blocs (The Kurds, the Iraqi National Alliance, the State of Law, the Unity of Iraq Alliance, and most recently the Iraqi Nationalist Movement with or without Nujayfi and friends) we could be headed towards a parliament with no clear winners. Right now no list looks like an obvious potential winner in the way that for example a Maliki/Nujayfi ticket or Allawi/Mutlak/Bulani/Abu Risha would. Competing prime-ministerial ambitions may prevent such alliances from taking place, but the net outcome of a failure to coalesce could be that many of these parties gain no power at all. Which is something to think about as the coalition deadline of 31 October comes closer.

The Election Law Is Passed[8]

November 8, 2009

With 141 votes out of the total of 195 deputies that were present, the Iraqi parliament finally passed a revision of the 2005 election law this evening around 8 p.m.

in Baghdad. The session was not without drama and at one point was about to derail because of a dispute about whether the five minority seats for Christians should be considered as a single constituency or five different ones! However, despite this, as well as attempt by pro-Kurdish representatives among the Shabak and Yazidis to increase their quotas in the last minute (in the former case against the wishes of other, anti-Kurdish Shabak), each of the amendments was voted on, followed by a separate vote for the whole package.

The broad outline of the revised law has already been known for a long time and contained few surprises as such: Open lists, governorate-level constituencies and minority seats for Christians (5), Sabaeans (1), Yazidis (1) and Shabak (1). In other respects, most features of the 2005 law (including the procedures for allocating compensatory seats, which this time make up 5%) are kept in place. However, two sections of last year's campaigning rules, including the ban on the use of images of (non-candidate) religious leaders, have been included in the revised law for the parliamentary elections through the insertion of a brief reference to the 2008 provincial election law. The law does not specify the exact number of representatives and only says it will follow the constitutional quota according to the latest official statistics (there is no updated census); however it is generally expected that there will be an increase of seats from 275 to around 310. Voting for internally displaced will be based on residence according to the ration-card registers (meaning some will vote where they have sought refuge which is potentially controversial) and for exiles it will be at Iraqi embassies abroad based on rules from 2005 that only give them a say in deciding the compensation seats (where these votes will be pooled with all the governorate votes).

The controversy for the three past weeks has focused on how to hold elections in Kirkuk, where the non-Kurdish population complains that the electoral registers have been tampered with by the Kurdish-dominated local government in the period from 2004 until now, with the aim of securing a Kurdish victory in any future referendum about the inclusion of the city in the Kurdistan federal region. For this reason, Arabs and Turkmens in Kirkuk as well as Iraqi nationalists from all parts of the Iraq have been eager to secure special arrangements that would ensure extra scrutiny in the electoral process in Kirkuk; the Kurds, for their part, have been equally adamant that any special status for Kirkuk would be anathema and that they would not support any law that mentioned the word "Kirkuk".

What was agreed in the end is a compromise that gives something to each side. Kirkuk is indeed mentioned in the bill several times, as an area whose electoral registers are recognized as being "dubious" and therefore should be subject to extra scrutiny in a one-year investigation after the elections, with a possibility of modifying the results. As a result of Kurdish insistence, that kind of arrangement is also enabled for any other governorate whose registers are deemed dubious (and the Kurds will probably try to nominate several other governorates for this status); however Kirkuk is the only such explicitly recognized governorate in the law—

which therefore in some ways preserves the "special status" that the Kurds fought against. If any other governorate is to be treated on par with Kirkuk it would need to be demonstrated that the statistics show a "suspicious" annual population growth of more than 5%, and each case must be approved by a simple majority in the Iraqi parliament after a request by more than 50 deputies.

At the same time, this is a highly symbolic and therefore weak kind of special status. Most crucially, the entire reasoning that the initial election result in Kirkuk can be decoupled from the broader debate about Kirkuk's future is faulty. The future disposal of Kirkuk is likely to be settled by the next parliament whose job it will be to fulfil the promise of a one-off revision of the 2005 constitution; the composition of the next constitutional committee, in turn, may well be influenced by the composition of the parliamentary delegation from Kirkuk. Those seeking to dismiss the significance of the Kirkuk issue in the context of the election law portray it as a "a matter of a couple of seats only", but the truth is that it does matter whether Kirkuk returns a contingent of deputies broadly supportive of the Kurdish position or whether it includes several representatives with an Iraqi nationalist orientation. Not least because of its expected centrality in the constitutional revision process, there will be a particular focus on how Kirkuk is represented in the next committee charged with handling this issue.

Additionally, in the final version of the bill the process of scrutiny seems first and foremost focused on establishing the correct number of representatives for Kirkuk, apparently just reclassifying any undue "surplus" representatives as "national" ones. This leaves the focus on the only other "hard" implication of the arrangements: "That the result should not form the basis of any future electoral process or serve as precedent for any political status before the conclusion of the investigation of the registers", which in turn means that the 2010 results cannot be used in an argument about Kirkuk's future. But in addition to misrepresenting what is actually going to happen (in terms of the political impact of the deputies that obtain representation next January and will sit for at least one year), this stipulation also ignores the fact that the fate of Kirkuk will be decided either by article 140 of the constitution (which demands a new census, thus making the election result entirely irrelevant), or, alternatively, whatever other solution the next constitutional review committee may manage to come up with.

The parliamentary developments that enabled the Kirkuk compromise to emerge apparently started with rapprochement between the Kurds and those non-Kurdish parties in the assembly that do not seem to worry too much about what happens to Kirkuk: Above all the (Shiite) Islamic Supreme Council of Iraq (ISCI) and the (Sunni) Iraqi Islamic Party (IIP), but more recently also the Sadrists and apparently even Maliki's State of Law coalition. The Sadrists used to be quite nationalist about Kirkuk, as did Maliki's party, but yesterday Zafir al-Ani complained that the Daawa had been among the strongest forces in calling for an immediate vote. In a move somewhat reminiscent of the old Kurdish–Shiite–IIP alliance, those groups prepared a revised draft of the law which included the Kurdish demand for other governorates as potential and theoretical candidates for additional scrutiny, and the compensatory seats earlier promised for Arabs and Turkmens were unceremoniously dropped. Bahaa al-Aaraji, the Sadrist head of the legal committee in parliament, tried to gather enough deputies for a quick vote before other parliamentarians had had the time to acquaint themselves with the new proposals. In another possible echo of the past, Aaraji also quoted support for Iraqiyya in hammering out the latest proposal; whether this is in fact correct remains unclear (some Iraqiyya deputies have criticized the proposals on Kirkuk from a nationalist point of view), but if true it reflects more or less the same and rather surprising constellation that in April enabled the current speaker of parliament Ayad al-Samarraie to replace Mahmud al-Mashhadani who was ousted a year ago (Samarraie mysteriously decamped to Qatar for an official visit only hours before the vote). Mashhadani was of course a central figure in the nationalist 22 July movement, whose crime it was to care too much about Kirkuk.

The Hashemi Veto Backfires, Parliament Ups the Ante[9]
November 23, 2009

In a dangerous development, with barely a quorum, the Iraqi parliament has voted 133 against 19 for a new amendment to the election law after the first batch of amendments passed on 8 November was rejected by Vice-President Tariq al-Hashemi. Originally, around 190 deputies had been present when the parliamentary session started this morning.

In their first press briefings subsequent to the vote, the prime movers behind the second amendment—the Iraqi National Alliance (Hakim/Sadr/Jaafari), the State of Law Alliance (Maliki), and the Kurdistani Alliance (PUK/KDP)—have tried to highlight the most palatable aspects of the amendments. The idea of linking the exiled vote to specific governorates (i.e., governorates of origin) is progressive in that the weight of the exiled vote will be more equal to that of domestic Iraqis, even if this solution probably means a logistical nightmare for those tasked with organizing the vote abroad, depending on what exact "special procedures" are adopted by the Iraqi election commission. Also, the ad hoc parliamentary alliance that favored the amendment tried to highlight minor modifications to the procedures for electing the Christian minority seats, primarily in the shape of a single electoral constituency (thought to be a concession to demands by Christian leaders).

The part of the amendment that is not talked about so much by these parties is the real bargain that lies behind it: A reversion to the distribution of parliamentary seats according to the 2005 allocations, with an overall 2.8% annual growth rate reckoned across the country. This replaces the arrangement adopted on 8 November, whereby statistics from the trade ministry would form the basis for a new distribution of seats. Those statistics reflect population movements in the period 2005–2009 and in contrast to the figures used in 2005 relate to total population rather than registered voters. They had been known to Iraqi politicians and the Iraqi public prior to the vote on 8 November, but were officially confirmed only on 11 November. The fact that the trade ministry, dominated as it is by loyalists of Prime Minister Nuri al-Maliki, published statistics that showed the strongest growth in Sunni areas (and especially Nineveh), was taken as an indication that there was a degree of neutrality to them. However, the statistics were criticized by the Kurds for the low growth figures they provided for Kurdistan, and Masud Barzani even threatened to boycott the elections unless they were changed.

That situation in turn created a context in which a veto by Hashemi was always going to be a hazardous proposition. The substance of veto itself is perfectly understandable, and relates to discrimination of exiled voters in the old law that was real and serious. But Hashemi then tried to pretend that it was possible to present a "partial veto" and went ahead with this kind of innovation in a context when he knew that the Kurds were interested in revisiting perceived losses in the seat allocation. As was inevitable, perhaps, the Kurds saw a chance to do some further bargaining over the seat distribution and on this issue rediscovered their old friends in the mainly Shiite Islamist parties, who now care less about the exiled voters than in 2005 and certainly do not see any reason to allow Nineveh disproportionate growth rates in the 2005–2009 period if this can be avoided. As a result—and as the rawest expression of the horse-trading that was involved in this amendment— the updated ministry of trade statistics from 2009 have been promptly shelved and replaced by the old distribution key from 2005 which almost everyone knows has a weaker correlation with current demographic realities. In other words, Hashemi's move ultimately backfired regardless of whether he considers himself an Iraqi nationalist or a Sunni first. Yesterday, even Mosul representatives pleaded with him to withdraw his veto, because they saw what was coming.

Unlike the Kirkuk issue which tends to unite groups of different ethnosectarian backgrounds against the Kurds, the Hashemi veto with its focus on the exiled vote has brought back, at least temporarily, old lines of division in the Iraqi parliament that are more clearly sectarian. It should be added that many nationalists of whatever sectarian description still support Hashemi (for example, Hiwar and Wifaq did come up with a second alternative that involved a separate electoral district for the exiles), but Shiite Islamists tend to agree with the Kurds over this issue to a greater degree than they do in the Kirkuk question. Ironically, then, with the "new" seat allocation according to the 2005 key, Hashemi is now likely to come under much greater pressure from below for producing a second veto than was the case before the first veto. This time, Mosul politicians will feel that the clock has been turned back to 2005 in more than one sense: Not only is the "new" distribution key a relic from that period, but for the first time in a long while the configuration of their opponents—an alliance of Kurds and Shiite Islamists—is looking more similar to the situation in 2005 as well.

CHAPTER NOTES

1 The original version of this text can be found at http://www.tcf.org/publications/internationalaffairs/Visser.pdf.

2 See http://gulfanalysis.wordpress.com/2009/05/13/hammudi-tapped-for-leadership-role-in-reviving-the-united-iraqi-alliance/.

3 See http://historiae.org/INA.asp.

4 Hakim died in Tehran two days later, on 26 August 2009.

5 See http://gulfanalysis.wordpress.com/2009/09/21/why-an-allawi-hakim-alliance-would-mean-retrogression-in-iraq/.

6 See http://historiae.org/state-of-law.asp.

7 See http://gulfanalysis.wordpress.com/2009/10/27/allawi-mutlak-consolidation-in-the-centre-of-iraqi-politics/.

8 See http://historiae.org/election-law.asp.

9 See http://gulfanalysis.wordpress.com/2009/11/23/the-hashemi-veto-backfires-parliament-ups-the-ante/.

Chapter 6

The 2010 Parliamentary Election

By December 2009, much of the progress seen in Iraqi just one year earlier had been reversed. After the Kirkuk issue with its potentially cross-sectarian appeal ended up less politicized than expected, voting patterns on the election law in parliament had at times seemed strikingly similar to the Kurdish–Shiite alliance of 2005. Prime Minister Nuri al-Maliki still remained separate from the other Shiites, but this was now more a case of him having lost all friends than any attempt to create new bold alliances outside his traditional Shiite Islamist camp.

The striking features of the period leading up to the March 7, 2010, election were, first, the de-Baathification blitzkrieg initiated by the Shiite Islamist Iraqi National Alliance (INA) with the obvious goal of weakening both of its two main political competitors, Maliki's State of Law Alliance (SLA) and the secular Iraqiyya and, second, the spectacular failure of both these victims to burn all bridges to INA in an adequate response. The intense de-Baathification campaign had clearly been inspired by the most Iran-friendly forces within INA, including Sadrist parliamentarians who less than two years earlier had been involved in dialogue with secular political forces. An unexpected and subtle move, it succeeded in sidelining every other issue in Iraqi politics from January 2010 until well into the counting process that followed the March 7 elections. It thereby established a very different atmosphere for these elections from the focus on bread-and-butter issues that had marked the local elections of January 2009 (in which many INA parties, and ISCI in particular, suffered serious losses.)

The legal basis for the de-Baathification proceedings (discussed in greater detail in chapter 9) was shaky, to put it diplomatically. Politically, the effect was a repolarization of Iraqi politics along sectarian lines since Maliki, in particular, failed to rise above the issue in the same nonsectarian way that had characterized his handling of the security file in 2008. Instead, his State of Law allies actually emulated the savage INA policies and rhetoric on de-Baathification throughout the governorates south of Baghdad, ironically doing so even as their own alliance was being subjected to de-Baathification by the INA-dominated de-Baathification committee on the eve of the elections. It should be added that the rest of the Iraqi political establishment, in addition to the INA and SLA, became complicit in the de-Baathification maneuvers, including such American favorites as the Kurdish president Jalal Talabani and the Sunni speaker of parliament Ayad al-Samarraie. In short, there was a complete lack of opposition in the system against the outrageous attacks on legal principles that took place at the time, signifying that the level of maturation in Iraqi politics still remained disconcertingly low.

In terms of alliances, this climate led to a second illogical development with consequences for post-election coalition forming, following the earlier, tentative rapprochement between INA and Iraqiyya in autumn 2009. Nuri al-Maliki, feeling cornered, tried to clinch an alliance with the Kurds. In principle, the Kurds rejected every move Maliki had made as prime minister since 2008 in terms of "bringing the state back in." But now, having no other friends, Maliki appeared to find comfort in meetings with Jalal Talabani, the Kurdish president of Iraq. In January 2010 he was rewarded with a Kurdish decision to avoid creating problems for him over the budget and a projected "law on electoral behavior," which had been planned by INA and Iraqiyya in order to restrain the spending power of Maliki in the lead-up to the March 7 vote.

The failure of the international community to stand up against the blunt attack on basic principles of rule of law during the de-Baathification witch hunt was striking. I got some disturbing personal experience of this during visits to Washington and through my correspondence with U.S. officials in Baghdad in February. At a meeting with the Iraq staff of the National Security Council in late February, I tried to make the point that the United States, as a guarantor of security in Iraq during the time of the elections, was a legitimate participant in the debate about the democratic quality of those elections and that it could well make some noise without being accused of interfering. The officials appeared to be listening attentively but at the end of the meeting one of them handed me his own personal copy of recent public remarks by the UN representative in Baghdad, Ad Melkert, which basically white-washed the whole de-Baathification affairs, belittling the de-Baathification cases as "150 candidates on the overall more than 6,000 that will stand." Judging from the enthusiastic use of text-marker throughout this highly apologetic document, I couldn't help getting the impression that the Obama administration was more eager to have the elections on time than to create further delays over procedure. It was pretty much the same story with the U.S. military. A high-ranking general in Baghdad initiated correspondence with me around the same time and clearly appeared concerned. However, a few days before the elections he wrote to me and said he finally had good news: The special vote of the military and prisoners had passed off peacefully!

Perhaps the most revealing comments came during a session with the Iraq section in the Near Eastern Bureau of the State Department. At first there seemed to be some interest in how the de-Baathification process violated both the Iraqi constitution and general principles of due process. But at the end of the discussion, after I had suggested a tougher U.S. response, a high-ranking official seemed to sum up the prevalent mood when he said, "But, what can we do"? I was not, however, entirely convinced that they truly wanted to do anything. I made the point that the whole de-Baathification campaign seemed aimed at recreating a sectarian front by attacking Allawi and making Maliki less nationalist. The response was a rhetorical question: Would it not involve more work for the United States to support a nationalist coalition in Baghdad instead of yielding to a Shiite–Kurdish coalition that was friendly to Iran?

In addition, everywhere you turned in Washington, the diehard tripartite paradigm of Iraq remained present. Even as Iraqi parties were still trying hard to present themselves as non-sectarian, key officials of the Obama administration like the deputy assistant secretary of state for Iraq, Michael Corbin, were primarily concerned with having a united Sunni front! On March 17, 2010, he told a gathering of experts that "the Sunnis had a claim on the presidency, but because they couldn't all get together and support one candidate, or . . . get into alliances that would be stronger, they have diminished their ability to get that. So what we'll see [in] this process now is that Talabani, the Kurd, may keep on as president." Similarly, exactly one year after we had visited the Pentagon to brief Colin Kahl, the deputy assistant secretary of defense, on our post-sectarian "More than Shiites and Sunnis" report, I heard Kahl give remarks on the forthcoming elections in which, within the space of 20 minutes, he made no less than three calls for a "representative government that includes Shiites, Sunnis, and Kurds." Little wonder, then, that secular visions for Iraq were at disadvantage when faced with that kind of public diplomacy from the U.S. government.

Some others, especially former officials of the Bush administration, seemed to believe genuinely in the importance of transcending these divisions instead of reifying them as per the policy of the Obama administration. Still, though, I thought many of their presentations of the situation erred on the side of optimism. I heard both Meghan O'Sullivan (formerly with the NSC) and former Ambassador to Iraq Zalmay Khalilzad give reasonably upbeat assessments at the Jamestown Foundation in early March, just days before the poll. My own take was less optimistic: I warned that the sectarian repolarization brought about by the de-Baathification debacle had made Maliki look a little too weak north of Baghdad and Allawi a little too weak south of it for them to emerge as true Iraqi nationalists.

No Second Veto: The Election Law Is Approved[1]

December 6, 2009

In a bazaar-style compromise, the Iraqi parliament has kept the best parts of the amended election law and thrown out the more dubious ones, thereby averting a second veto by Vice President Tariq al-Hashemi.

The first veto of the election law by Hashemi caught most observers by surprise. The veto itself was perfectly logical, and, contrary to what the international mass media has written, not particularly sectarian in origin or outlook. It included several elements, but the most important one focused on the procedures for exiled voting (in the media this was misleadingly portrayed as something that catered for Sunnis exclusively). This demand, in turn, was actually addressed by parliament in a very constructive way, since the new procedures—exiled voters will vote according to their "home" governorates—restore the rights of the exiles and put them on more or less the same level as domestic Iraqis instead of reducing their influence to the compensation seats only. But Hashemi's big gamble related to the possibility that parliament might use the opportunity to pick apart other aspects of the law that they had second thoughts about. And that was exactly what happened: Specifically, the Kurds, who had been focusing their energies on securing arrangements for Kirkuk that would not involve too much extra scrutiny of the disputed election registers there, moved down to the next item on their list of priorities: The distribution of seats between governorates. The Kurds were unhappy with the apportionment that had emerged on the basis of the up-to-date statistics from the ministry of trade, and instead sought a reversion to the 2005 statistics as starting point, allowing for an annual 2.8% increment across Iraq. Many Shiite Islamists—who are generally eager to get on with the elections immediately after the holy month of Muharram in January 2010—agreed to the Kurdish demand even though this did involve significant seat reductions for some Shiite-majority governorates.

The reversion to the 2005 statistics left Iraq with an election law full of contradictions. In the first place, an earlier federal supreme court ruling had specifically stated that the seat distribution should take into account the full Iraqi population (for this reason it specifically criticized the 2005 law in which the seat distribution was based on registered voters), meaning that the reversion to five year old data in theory could be construed as unconstitutional given the availability of more up-to-date numbers. Additionally, in a much overlooked detail, the new arrangements really made a mockery of the provisions for Kirkuk that had been arrived at in the first iteration of the law (and more theoretically applicable to any other governorate suspected of unnatural population growth), according to which the whole point was to investigate discrepancies between the registers for 2005 and 2009 with a view to adjusting the total quota on the basis of 2009 realities! That entire provision obviously lost most of its relevance as soon as 2005 was adopted as the point of reference, but the Kurds were happy to ignore the contradiction as long as they were allowed to use the 2009 registers for defining the electorate of Kirkuk. Thankfully, though, today's agreement in the Iraqi parliament involves a return to the seat distribution largely as defined by the first ministry of trade statistics from 2009 to which the Kurds objected. The difference is that this time the distribution key is written into the law through a "decision" in the Iraqi parliament, and the

Kurds have been awarded 3 additional seats as in Dahuk and Sulaymaniyya as compensation for accepting the new statistics.

The bargain itself was reminiscent of the atmosphere of a bazaar: Some weeks ago, Mahmud Uthman, often a bellwether of the Kurdish maximalist position, said he had expected some 10 to 15 extra Kurdistan seats in the 2009 apportionment. When Hashemi demanded that the original 2009 statistics be applied as precondition for averting a second veto, other blocs in the parliament first suggested that the Kurds could be given two extra seats to compensate for grievances they might have relating to the most recent statistics. This quota was increased to three seats today, with some suggestions that there had been pressure on the Kurds by the Americans to accept it. The Kurds thereby keep the number of seats they would have received by a reversion to 2005, but the other governorates also keep the quotas they had originally been awarded, hence in some cases still improving their relative weight vis-à-vis the KRG (Kurdistan Regional Government) governorates. For example, the contentious ratio of KRG seats to Nineveh seats (the biggest Sunni Arab majority governorate) was 1.84 in 2005 (based on registered voters); it was changed to 1.22 in the first apportionment based on 2009 statistics; then to 1.41 as a result of a reversion to 2005 figures of the total population; it now stands at 1.32 as a result of the latest compromise. Technically speaking, the whole package has been dressed up as an "interpretation" (*istifsar*) of the awkward language in the previous iteration of the law that involved the old 2005 statistics.

The most significant aspect of this compromise is that in the end the Kurds and the Shiite Islamists who had voted in favor of the second batch of amendments eventually backed down from their threat to ignore Hashemi altogether and push through a law according to their own preferences with a three-fifths majority in parliament—which was theoretically possible and would have been veto-proof. That they instead chose to take the veto seriously is in itself quite important, because the atmosphere in Iraqi politics over the past weeks has been heated, with frequent attempts by politicians to label anything they don't like as "unconstitutional". Remarkably, in addition to the Kurds, this time Daawa leaders have been at the forefront of the campaign to simply ignore Hashemi, with frequent hints that they had the votes to guarantee a super-majority, and with Haydar al-Abbadi even trying to overrule the federal supreme court by expressing his personal view that the veto deadline actually expired last night. To some extent they received help from other Shiite Islamists, including Sadrists like Bahaa al-Aaraji (who yesterday encouraged MPs to stay away from the emergency sessions in parliament), as well as ISCI leaders like Jalal al-Din al-Saghir (who last Friday returned to his usual sectarian theme of the importance of "the majority" in Iraq to be united through a pact between Maliki's State of Law and his own, all-Shiite Iraqi National Alliance). But it is noteworthy that some ISCI members and Sadrists—specifically Hadi al-Amiri and, according to some sources, Nassar al-Rubaie—did take part in emergency meetings with Sunni and nationalist leaders including Hashemi and Rafi al-Eisawi at the house of Ayad Allawi last week, with a follow-up meeting today that involved Amiri plus Khalid al-Atiyya (who is closer to Maliki). Additionally, some of the mid-Euphrates governorates saw their quotas reduced under the second version of the bill, which may have prevented a more clear-cut Kurdish–Shiite alliance.

The unusual constellation involving nationalists and Shiite Islamists, in turn, is of interest in relation to the latest talk in Iraqi politics of the need to have a "caretaker government" in case parliamentary elections are delayed. Such ideas of shaking up the system are popular with everyone who is not close to Maliki—ISCI, in particular, seems to be blowing hot and cold in that regard right now—not least because of accusations that Maliki may try to exploit his powerful position during and after the elections. The remarkable thing, however, is that like so much else in Iraqi politics right now, talk of this kind completely ignores the Iraqi constitution. There simply is no "caretaker government" option in the constitution. Unless parliament decides to sack the entire government—which of course it can do if it pleases, anytime—the only emergency scenario in the constitution other than a premature dissolution of parliament itself is the one-month, renewable declaration of an emergency, which requires a joint initiative by the premier and the presidency council and a two-thirds parliamentary majority. Hopefully, though, today's development will get everyone's minds focused on the inevitability of early elections, and lead to greater focus on the political issues at stake.

The Official Coalition List Is Out[2]

December 9, 2009

The deadline for registering coalitions for the 2010 parliamentary elections expired in mid-November. But even though all the parties had submitted their lists by then, the Iraqi elections commission, IHEC, kept postponing the publication of the lists pending the final passage of the election law. However, now the official list has been released.

The list contains relatively few surprises. There are only 12 coalitions, of which not more than around 6 seem truly competitive: Kurdistan Alliance, Tawafuq, the Iraqi National Alliance, State of Law, Unity of Iraq and Iraqiyya. For these, in turn, the line-up is more or less as expected, even though a few entities remained in doubt about their loyalties until the very end. Eventually, it was Maliki (and not Unity of Iraq) who got the amir of the powerful Rabia tribe of the Tigris on his side; the Iraqi National Alliance, for its part, has managed to enlist the support of the Shaykhi community of Basra. Also, as has been widely reported, the Independent Nationalist Trend of Mahmud al-Mashhadani and Nadim al-Jabiri opted to join Unity of Iraq alongside Wathab Shakir; the same list also suffered a defection by

Nehru Abd al-Karim who joined Khalaf al-Ulyan and the Shiite *mujtahid* cleric Fadil al-Maliki to form a smaller coalition named the National Unity Alliance. Finally, Iraqiyya has now been confirmed in the shape that everyone has been talking about for weeks: To the Allawi–Mutlak core have been added powerful politicians like Tariq al-Hashemi, Rafi al-Eisawi and Usama al-Nujayfi, plus Tawfiq al-Abbadi, a businessman from Basra, Iskandar Witwit from the mid-Euphrates region and Abd al-Karim al-Muhammadawi (the "Lord of the Marshes", no longer calling himself "Hizbollah of Iraq"). A more formal launch of this expanded list is still expected to take place.

Of these, in turn, only the Kurdistan list is perfectly forthright and clear about its program. All the others play the now predictable message that they represent all the elements of the Iraqi people from north to south and generally favor a vague program of "national unity" and "anti-sectarianism", often backed up by a symbolic parade of tribal chiefs from all parts of the country and religious leaders typically representing even the smallest of these components, such as Chaldean priests or Mandaeans. However, if one probes further, it makes sense to distinguish also between these remaining five coalitions in a number of ways. For example, in addition to the Kurds, both Tawafuq and the Iraqi National Alliance often mix their political message with a focus on ethno-religious sub-identities (Sunni and Shiite respectively); the three others seem to be more determined to avoid this. Similarly, both the Kurds and the Iraqi National Alliance highlight decentralization as a virtue, and the latter has recently recruited both the pro-federal Turkmeneli party as well as Fawaz al-Jarba, a Sunni tribal leader of the Shammar who has reportedly expressed an interest in decentralization more recently (he was also part of the old UIA in 2005 but had been negotiating with Maliki). De-baathification is particularly important for State of Law and the Iraqi National Alliance.

In terms of control of the state apparatus, State of Law is in a unique position, but the Unity of Iraq Alliance also has some influence through the interior ministry. The Iraqi National Alliance used to be well-entrenched within the system, but after its latest quarrels with Maliki it has sometimes found itself in an unusual alliance with Iraqiyya and the remnants of Tawafuq that increasingly have lost some of the influence which they enjoyed previously when they participated more fully in government. Often overlooked is the fact that the elections commission (IHEC) in practice is owned by the Kurds, the Shiite Islamists and Tawafuq, who effectively control 8 out of 9 commissioners. Iraqiyya is thought to have influence over one member of the commission whereas Unity of Iraq—a relative newcomer—has no representatives in the commission at all.

This all makes for a rather complex picture as Iraq moves forward towards the elections, now set for 7 March 2010 according to the latest reports from Baghdad. For voters, the fear must be that post-election coalition-forming becomes so important that few parties are willing to be clear about issues and prospective partners, simply out of fear of alienating anyone. For the United States, the new timeline could be a course of concern, since an election date in March means summer will come closer as a new government is being formed, and Ramadan next year falls in the late summer (around 10 August–10 September), thereby potentially prolonging the period of standstill in Iraqi politics.

Why Ad Hoc De-Baathification Will Derail the Process of Democratization in Iraq[3]

January 8, 2010

Considerable confusion has erupted after news began leaking yesterday about a move to bar Salih al-Mutlak, a prominent secularist leader of the Hiwar front which is now part of the Iraqiyya movement and coalition, from standing as a candidate in the March parliamentary elections.

Much of the lack of clarity relates to the essentially transitional character of the Iraqi de-Baathification bureaucracy. The old de-Baathification committee, created on the basis of ideas from Paul Bremer and headed since 2004 by Ali Faysal al-Lami—a Shiite political operator with particularly close ties to Iran—is supposed to be replaced by a new "accountability and justice board" pursuant to the "accountability and justice act" passed in early 2008. However, Iraqi parliamentarians have been wrangling about who should sit on the new board, with a government proposal for a Maliki ally (Walid al-Hilli) to take over its leadership so far having been rejected in parliament, partly due to internal Shiite opposition. In the meanwhile, Lami, together with the "accountability and justice committee" of the Iraqi parliament, continues to wield considerable influence in issues relating to de-Baathification.

It is Lami and the committee that appear to be the driving force behind the latest proposal to exclude Mutlak. It may be useful, therefore, to have a brief look at the political affiliations of these individuals. Lami has ties to Ahmad Chalabi, the Sadrist breakaway faction Asaib Ahl al-Haqq (involved in the Qays al-Khazaali case and the abductions and murder of British hostages), and Iran. As for the parliamentary committee, it is headed by a Sadrist, with a Badr member as number two. The other members are from the PUK, Daawa and yet another Sadrist who together form the majority (hence, Iraqi National Alliance is stronger on the committee than Daawa/State of Law as far as the Shiites are concerned). Additionally, there is a minority of two secularists on the committee, plus Rashid al-Azzawi who represents Tawafuq—a Sunni Islamist who on some issues may well find common ground with the Shiite Islamists rather than with the secularists.

The main problem with the proposal to exclude Mutlak is of course its abrupt, ad hoc nature, and the fact that it emerges in the middle of a period of transition for the de-Baathification bureaucracy. Firstly, why has not this been dealt with earlier? The fact is that Mutlak and his party have been an important part of Iraqi democracy for four years, and that they have played a key role on numerous occasions in furthering the democratic process—for example when they along with other opposition parties demanded a timeline for local elections when the provincial powers law was adopted in February 2008. Mutlak has also been crucial in keeping the issue of Kirkuk on the agenda as a question of national concern, and was talking about "putting Iraq first" when this kind of approach was very unfashionable back in 2006 (of course, in a very predictable way, the Western mainstream media is still today obsessed with him as a "Sunni"). Thus, the very sudden singling out of him as a potential neo-Baathist (ostensibly on the basis of "new documents" that, unsurprisingly, have not been made public) smacks of a highly politicized decision that can only weaken the public trust in the democratic process. It took more than two weeks before the the Shiite Islamists began reacting in an audible fashion to the Iranian occupation of the border oilfield al-Fakka, and one cannot help wonder whether this latest move may reflect a certain panic over the way this issue has played into the hands of nationalists like Mutlak. Conversely, Mutlak's bloc, Iraqiyya, has once more highlighted its non-sectarian, Iraqi nationalist orientation by promptly and strongly rejecting slander by Saudi clerics against the (Shiite) Grand Ayatollah Ali al-Sistani.

More fundamentally, the question of "selective de-Baathification" comes on the agenda here in a big way. It is a historical fact that Shiites and Sunnis alike cooperated with the old regime in their millions, and many Shiite tribes participated in cracking down on the "Shiite" rebellion in the south in 1991. Nonetheless, the exiles who returned to Iraq after 2003 have tried to impose an artificial narrative in which the legacy of pragmatic Shiite cooperation with the Baathist regime is simply forgotten; instead one singles out political opponents (often Sunnis) as "Baathists" and silently co-opt political friends (especially if they happen to be Shiites) without mentioning their Baathist ties at all. The result is a hypocritical and sectarian approach to the whole question of de-Baathification that will create a new Iraq on shaky foundations. For example, the Sadrists have been in the lead in the aggressive de-Baathification campaign, yet it is well known that many Sadrists in fact had Baathist ties in the past.

The proposal concerning Mutlak now apparently goes to the Iraqi elections commission (IHEC), which is supposed to be more independent, but whose members were in reality also elected on the basis of loyalties to political parties—and with an even poorer representation for secular Iraqis (only one of the nine commissioners is believed to have ties to Iraqiyya). This is going to be a test case not only for IHEC but for the whole Iraqi political process.

The Bloc That Has No De-Baathification Worries[4]

January 17, 2010

For weeks, we have been waiting for the formal release of the parliamentary candidate lists by the Iraqi elections commission (IHEC), at which point campaigning for the 7 March elections is expected to start in an official way. Pending the formal certification by IHEC, Iraqi political parties have mostly refrained from discussing the details of their candidate lists in the various provinces. There is however one exception: The Shiite-led Iraqi National Alliance (INA), which last week began circulating its candidate lists in full.

How can INA be so confident and go ahead with the publication of its candidate lists even before IHEC has formally approved them? The explanation is very simple, and is contained in the INA lists themselves: Its candidate number twenty-four in Baghdad is named Ali Faysal al-Lami and belongs to the Iraqi National Congress headed by Ahmed Chalabi. Sounds familiar? Yes, that's right, Lami is the director of the accountability and justice board that recently moved to bar several hundred candidates from taking part in the elections. No resistance was offered, and today no one in Iraq seems to be making a big point of the fact that he himself is a candidate in the elections! Little wonder, then, that the INA leaders seem confident about proceeding with the release of their list: It is they who effectively control the vetting process for the entire elections process. They enjoy full support in this from Iran; meanwhile their leaders are being feted in Washington, where Adil Abd al-Mahdi has just been visiting.

As for the candidate lists for the rest of the parties that are not as lucky as the INA when it comes to controlling the system, it seems we will have to wait a few more days. IHEC declared on Saturday that Iraqi newspapers would publish the lists of banned candidates on Sunday, which in turn would probably have paved the way for a release of the candidate lists. But who is the head of the "independent" IHEC to make such decisions? It emerged that Ali al-Lami wanted to de-Baathify just a little bit more, so Haydari was apparently ordered to hit the "stop press" button while another batch of last-minute exclusions are under consideration by IHEC. The lists of those excluded are now expected for Monday instead.

The 511 De-Baathification Cases: Sectarianism or Despotism?[5]

January 20, 2010

Late Tuesday night, the Iraqi television station Sumaria published the full list of 511 Iraqis that have been barred from standing as candidates in the 7 March parliamentary elections with reference to the de-Baathification procedures. The list says a good deal about the nature of the recent decision by the de-Baathification board and what it means in terms of unexpected complications for the Iraqi elections process at a time when many observers thought the institutional framework had been safely locked in place.

As soon as one proceeds beyond the few cases that are already famous from having been repeated in the media all the time—the exclusion of people like Salih al-Mutlak of Iraqiyya and Nehru Abd al-Karim, an Iraqi nationalist of Kurdish origin—many of the other names are not particularly prominent (and, no, the Nujayfi brothers are not on the list). For example, a few weeks ago, many Shiite websites circulated lists of 40 alleged Baathists that were expected to be banned. However, out of these 40, only around 10 actually appear on the final list of banned candidates. They include people like Saadi al-Jibburi, an independent candidate, Ahmad Hamid Ahmad Jirjis, an independent nationalist from Kirkuk, Muzahim al-Tamimi, a Shiite tribal leader from Basra affiliated with the secular-nationalist Unity of Iraq bloc of Jawad al-Bulani, as well as Abdallah al-Muhammadawi and Jawhar Mahi al-Din, also both from Unity of Iraq. With the exception of Nehru Abd al-Karim (who heads the Coalition of National Unity) and Salih al-Mutlak (who used to head the Hiwar but is technically no longer a party head after its merger with Wifaq), most heads of political entities that have been excluded appear to belong to the Unity of Iraq coalition.

A second dimension that needs to be taken note of relates to sectarian issues. American analysts branded the list as an overt "anti-Sunni" measure before it had even been printed. What the list actually shows is a typically Iraqi, far more complex picture. There are certainly Shiites and Kurds on the list, too, as shown by the prominent examples of Nehru Abd al-Karim and Muzahim al-Tamimi. And even from the grey mass of this material it is possible to conclude without being too essentialist that the presence of more Shiites is attested to by five instances of the name Abd al-Hussein, two of Abd al-Hassan and one Abd Ali, to give just a few examples of highly obvious Shiite personal names. There are likely hundreds more Shiites here; the key point is that this is not quite as black and white as the media would like us to believe.

As regards the level of party affiliations, as expected there seems to be a tendency of hitting at the secular and nationalist parties. Still, Maliki's list has taken a few casualties: Some had expected Abbad Mutlak Hamud to be banned but he wasn't; conversely Salih Jaafar has been excluded. Even the Iraqi National Alliance, which controls the whole process through Ali al-Lami, has de-Baathified at least one of its own, although this has apparently been done for good measure and affects a candidate far down on its Basra list: Rashash al-Imara, an independent candidate with a past in the Iraqi security forces.

The main problem with the de-Baathification measures, then, refers not so much to systematic and overt sectarianism or partisanship as such as to despotism more generally, albeit clearly with the ulterior goal of perpetuating a sectarian political atmosphere. The basic problem here is the attempt by the accountability and justice board to portray its decisions as "legal" and "constitutional" when they clearly are not—and the failure of the rest of the "democratic" system in the new Iraq to offer any meaningful resistance. Previous developments have shown that the accountability and justice board is an anachronism that lacks a clear legal basis after the passage of the accountability and justice law in 2008; that the formation of a seven-judge appeals court (to which these decisions may be appealed within three days) remedies this situation only in a partial way since the deadline for appeals is not in conformity with the relevant law; that the Iraqi elections commission seems to be in league with the accountability and justice board in this matter; and that even if one accepts the dubious legal rationale of the current de-Baathification board, its application of the relevant laws appears to be both partisan and selective in the extreme.

In sum, rather than being an attempt at the complete exclusion or elimination of political enemies, these de-Baathification measures seem aimed at intimidating and terrorizing, with the overarching motive of keeping sectarian issues on the agenda. Any attempt at remedying the situation must keep this aspect in mind: What is at stake here is not a question of "Sunni participation" versus a "Sunni boycott"; rather this is about the very fundamentals of the post-2003 system of government in Iraq and the importance of offering hope to those Iraqis who wish to get rid of the narrow sectarian categories altogether. Hence, even if the United States should miraculously succeed in reversing or postponing the de-Baathification moves, the ball will simply be kicked further down the road: The so-called independent elections commission (IHEC) which will oversee the elections is in practice owned by the same Shiite Islamist parties that control the accountability and justice board and that authored the decision to exclude 511 candidates with reference to de-Baathification and with support from Iran. To really make a difference, what is needed today is some kind of appeals institution that does not mechanically replicate the structures of power in Iraq that have emerged since 2003 on an ethno-sectarian basis and their underlying sectarian logic, which after all is what the accountability and justice board is fighting so hard to preserve. An internationalized complaints procedure for the elections inspired by the one used in Afghanistan could be one possible option. On the whole, it is of course a good sign that US policy-makers today seem concerned about the gravity of the situation, but if they are really serious about solving it then they should realize that none of their current friends in Baghdad are capable of doing so in a truly sustainable fashion.

The Backlash from the Hardliners[6]

February 4, 2010

Perhaps the most surprising aspect about yesterday's key developments in Iraq—the apparent green light from the de-Baathification appeals court for more than 500 banned candidates to take part in the elections after all—was that the whole thing was allowed to proceed quite far before a reaction materialized. However, when it came, it was just as ferocious as one would expect.

Part of this confusion may have to do with the fragmented character of the communications from the Iraqi elections commission (IHEC) on the issue. For once, we heard a lot from Amal al-Birqadar, who is thought to be the only commissioner with ties to Iraqiyya. She said the appeals court had "cancelled" the decision by the accountability and justice board to exclude more than 500 candidates. Hamdiya al-Husayni, who is considered to be close to Nuri al-Maliki, also conveyed the decision of the appeals board mostly as a fait accompli, although she did present it as a postponement rather than as an outright annulment. The head of the commission, Faraj al-Haydari who has a past in the Kurdish KDP, went further then Birqadar and Husayni in expressing doubt about the decision; none of the commissioners with ties to the Shiite-led alliance known as the Iraqi National Alliance—including Qasim al-Abbudi, who is the most prominent of them—made any public comment at all.

Since IHEC on many occasions has followed the diktats of the accountability and justice board rather robotically, its apparent recognition of the reinstatements for some hours yesterday could conceivably have been interpreted as a signal from powerful figures in the Iraqi government (Kurds? Pro-American Daawa figures?) that enough was enough and that there had to be limits to a de-Baathification process that has been spinning out of control. And for a while, the Daawa was silent whereas the Iraqi National Alliance including Chalabi, Lami and their partners in ISCI and the Sadrists took the lead in condemning the decision and branding it "unconstitutional". However, towards the end of the evening, Maliki, too, joined this chorus, and even some of his more pro-American advisors like Sadiq al-Rikabi went on record with criticism of the decision to reinstate candidates. It was, in other words, becoming clear that the Shiite Islamists were singing from the same sheet, probably to the satisfaction of the forces behind the de-Baathification drive.

IHEC says it will seek the opinion of the federal supreme court on the legal implications of the decision by the appeals court. Crucially, according to a statement by the head of IHEC, Faraj al-Haydari, it will only ask whether the decision is "binding" or not (figures in the accountability and justice board like Ali al-Lami and Khalid al-Shami have already expressed the view that it is not). Since the wording of the decision by the appeals board is not in the public domain, it is a little difficult to predict how the supreme court will react to this kind of query. However, if it is indeed correct that the board has tried to rule on the right of the banned candidates to take part in the elections (i.e., by stipulating a procedure for postponement until after the elections instead of simply ruling on their de-Baathification status) there is a danger that this may be seen as overreach with respect to the prerogatives defined in articles 15 to 17 of the accountability and justice act of January 2008. On the one hand, there is no doubt that the appeals court has the right to reverse decisions by the accountability and justice board, and that its decisions are "final". It can clearly trump the accountability and justice board and IHEC on the question of whether someone is subject to de-Baathification (in Arabic *mashmul* versus *ghayr al-mashmul*), and it would be scandalous if either of them tried to overturn the decision of the appeals court in this respect. But if the court has gone further than that in its decision by prescribing modalities for participation in the elections and for a post-election reassessment of the cases (as reported by Husayni), then things become more complicated and the decision may be more vulnerable to an attack on purely procedural grounds. It has to be remembered that whereas the federal supreme court is often referred to with optimism by secular Iraqis, it did produce a rather weak ruling last December when it had the opportunity to strike harder against the accountability and justice board and IHEC. That said, it would be thoroughly shameful if the court simply opted to describe the latest ruling as "non-binding" on procedural grounds while turning the blind eye to the many procedural infractions by the accountability and justice board itself, including most flagrantly the abrupt and unexplained reduction of the appeals period stipulated in the accountability and justice law from 30 to 3 days.

Meanwhile, IHEC has announced that the start of campaigning, previously scheduled for 7 February, has been postponed until 12 February.

"The Four Presidencies" Overturn the Ruling of the Judiciary[7]
February 6, 2010

Those who had wanted a purely legal solution to Iraq's de-Baathification crisis experienced a setback today. In a rather blunt attack on the principle of separation of powers, "the four presidencies", i.e., the president proper (Talabani) plus the "presidents" of the cabinet (Maliki), the parliament (Samarraie) and the higher judicial council (Midhat al-Mahmud) had been summoned to a meeting that probably was aimed at pre-empting any independent decision by the federal supreme court on the query from the elections commission (IHEC) regarding the latest decision by the special appeals court for de-Baathification cases to let all the banned candidates take part in the election. In the event, Talabani absented himself but Maliki and Samarraie were joined by one of the deputy speakers of parliament (Khalid al-Atiyya) and one of the deputy prime ministers (Rawsch Shaways, a Kurd), ensuring a setting that was entirely dominated by politicians from the big parties.

Unsurprisingly, perhaps, this quartet apparently strong-armed Judge Midhat into accepting the procedure they had been advocating all along: That the appeals process must run its course in a normal way, with the added caveat that the work of the appeals court must now be completed before the start of the electoral campaign on 12 February. That probably means good bye to any idea of due process given the short period that remains, which had been a main argument in the decision to postpone the appeals (incidentally, it is also a violation of the 60-day period for consideration of appeals stipulated in the relevant legislation). Still, article 17 of the accountability and justice law does provide the appeals court with rather unambiguous powers to decisively reverse any decision by the accountability and justice board as far as the de-Baathification status of an individual is concerned. The court is also protected by the absence of any mechanism for its dismissal in the accountability and justice law. This latter point was apparently lost on members of the legal committee of parliament who earlier today called for a "withdrawal of confidence" in the court, thereby just confirming a growing tendency of Walt Disney–style behavior that has also included calls for de-Baathification of figures like Vice President Tariq al-Hashemi and even General David Petraeus! Unfortunately, parliament is still scheduled to meet tomorrow to make "adequate decisions" in the matter, suggesting that there may be yet more theater to come.

It seems likely that the relatively strong character of the initial ruling by the appeals court (with a direct attempt at reinstating candidates) was an attempt at pre-empting moves by Ali al-Lami of the de-Baathification board to pressure IHEC to ignore the court's decisions on individual appeals (this had already been publicly hinted at by Lami prior to the release of the decision by the appeals court). The minimum the international community can now do is to send a clear signal that any attempt by IHEC to override the decisions of the appeals court in individual cases next week will make it exceedingly difficult for the outside world to continue to classify Iraq as a "democracy" in any meaningful sense of the word.

IHEC Publishes the Names of 6,172 Approved Candidates[8]
February 10, 2010

It is a little unclear why this is not all over the newswires, but at any rate: The Iraqi elections commission (IHEC) today released the list of 6,172 approved candidates for the 7 March elections. This supposedly includes all candidates whose documents were found to be in good order and who are not subject to de-Baathification.

Until now, the Iraqi National Alliance (which enjoys a "special relationship" with IHEC through Ahmad Chalabi and Ali al-Lami) has been the sole entity to publish all its candidate lists. The newly released material obviously includes thousands of names that are relatively unknown, but at least some characteristics of the competing top candidates in various provinces can be sketched out at this point. Starting in the south, in Basra the big battle will likely be between the Iraqi National Alliance (INA) and State of Law (SLA). As has emerged earlier, INA has put a Sadrist plus the ex-Iraqiyya representative Wail Abd al-Latif at the top of their list alongside some important local figures like Amir al-Fayiz of the Shaykhi community. Maliki's top candidate in Basra is Safa al-Din al-Safi, a long-time minister (most recently acting planning minister); Abd al-Hadi al-Hassani, an influential figure in the oil and gas committee is relatively far down the list at number eleven; Khayrallah al-Basri, previously with Iraqiyya, is number eight. Elsewhere in the "deep south", INA already has revealed a list of well-known figures in the second-biggest prize to be won—Dhi Qar—including Adil Abd al-Mahdi of ISCI, the Sadrist Bahaa al-Aaraji and ex-governor Alwan, another ISCI/Badr figure. SLA has now placed an independent candidate from a local religious family, Muhammad Mahdi al-Nasiri, at top of their list, with minister of state Shirwan al-Waili third. In symbolically important Najaf, INA has Nassar al-Rubayi, a Sadrist, on top whereas Maliki has put the independent Khalid al-Atiyya as his number one candidate in Qadisiyya.

Across the Shiite-majority areas south of Baghdad, the big question will be to what extent more secular and nationalist parties such as Iraqiyya and Unity of Iraq will be able to eat into the Shiite Islamist vote and go beyond the 10% threshold that has seemed pretty constant in many areas in recent years. A cursory glance at the list indicates that the secular parties could have needed a few more top candidates to radically change that picture, although incumbency and fame are of course not necessarily the best determinants of electoral success in today's Iraq. It is noteworthy that some of the few famous "southern" names in the secular coalitions do not seem to have put themselves forward as candidates proper. For example, the Lord of the Marshes (Muhammadawi) does not appear to be on the Iraqiyya lists anywhere in the three southernmost governorates. Abbas al-Mamuri is running as top candidate for Unity of Iraq in Babel, and Jamal al-Batikh for Iraqiyya in Wasit, but where is Ayad Jamal al-Din, the leader of the Ahrar party and a natural Dhi Qar candidate? Another notable omission in this category is of course the secular independent Yusuf al-Habubi, the big sensation of the last local elections in Karbala. An ex-Baathist who did well on the basis of a good reputation and an ability to get things done, his performance in religious Karbala was seen as a sign of pragmatism among the heavily Shiite electorate there and it had been expected that he would run again for national office in the 7 March elections. But even though his "Flags of Iraq" alliance technically became part of Maliki's SLA, his name is apparently nowhere on these lists—possibly another bad sign in terms of a potential shift back to a more sectarian political climate compared with 2009. Similarly, the Iraqiyya contingent from Basra in the outgoing parliament has bifurcated, with Khayrallah al-Basri now as an SLA candidate and Wail Abd al-Latif having joined forces with lots of old enemies in INA.

The truly big battle is going to be Baghdad, with 68 seats and some 1,800 candidates, almost a third of the whole list. This is where all the major celebrities congregate. INA has already presented a Bagdhad list comprising two potential prime ministerial candidates (Jaafari and Bayan Jabr Solagh); they will now get serious competition from both SLA (Maliki on top, followed by Haydar al-Abbadi, Hussein al-Shahristani and Jaafar al-Sadr, the son of the Shiite Islamist icon Muhammad Baqir al-Sadr, as number five) as well as Iraqiyya (Ayad Allawi is number one, other top candidates include Hasan al-Allawi, Ahmad Radi, Tariq al-Hashemi and Aliya Nusayf). Unity of Iraq has also put most of its top candidates in Baghdad, including Jawad al-Bulani on top, followed by Mahmud al-Mashhadani, Hashim al-Habubi, Wathab Shakir and Nadim al-Jabiri.

North of Baghdad, in Anbar, Iraqiyya has Rafi al-Eisawi as their number one candidate. But it may seem as if Ahmad Abu Risha, of Unity of Iraq, has opted not to run for office here and instead has chosen to stay on the sidelines? SLA has the lesser known Abu Risha (Saad) as their number one here, and INA is fronted by Hamid al-Hayis; neither is expected to attract enormous numbers of voters. Further east, in Salahaddin, Maliki is running with his sports minister as top candidate. With several other Shiites following on the next places it does seem that much like INA he is trying to maximize the Shiite minority vote in Salahaddin instead of making a deliberate effort to come across as more "national" in this governorate. For its part, the Sunni-oriented Tawafuq has placed its party chairman on top of the list here and interestingly has also included its controversial (ex-) governor here, as number three. Iraqiyya has Falah al-Naqib, a former minister of interior under Ayad Allawi, as its number three candidate in Salahaddin. Up in Kirkuk, Iraqiyya is looking strong with Muhammad Ali Tamim as first candidate (he is from the Hiwar front of Salih al-Mutlak and an outspoken leader of the nationalist current that is seeking to retain the disputed governorate under central government control). SLA has Abdallah Iskandar as their number one in Kirkuk, to some extent perhaps an attempt at reaching out to the Iraqi nationalist segment—but weren't Abbad Mutlak al-Jibburi and Hajim al-Hasani supposed to be here too instead of in Baghdad? Finally, in Mosul, unsurprisingly, it is Usama al-Nujayfi on top of the Iraqiyya list. SLA is running with the independent, Sunni Kurdish minister of planning Ali Ghalib Baban as number one; like in Kirkuk Maliki in other words comes across as slightly more "national" in orientation than INA.

The lingering question is of course what, if anything, this release says about the ongoing de-Baathification process. Many had expected that no lists would be published until the appeals process had been exhausted. But the strange thing is that from a sample of 22 banned Iraqiyya candidates from Baghdad, at least 4 have been reinstated on this new list of 6,172 candidates. Nonetheless, since most of the top candidates whose cases are currently being reviewed by the appeals court (such as Salih al-Mutlak) have not been reinstated on this list—and since there has so far not been any major outcry by Iraqi political parties this evening—we must assume that the appeals process is still ongoing and that the limited number of reinstatements may relate to technicalities. Hopefully, the picture will soon clarify, because at the end of the day the general atmosphere of the election debate is probably going to mean much more for the overall outcome than the individual characteristics of these 6,000 plus candidates.

Governorate and Party-Level Indicators of De-Baathification[9]
February 16, 2010

Since the Iraqi elections commission flatly refuses to release aggregated statistics at the party/governorate levels of its recent exclusions with reference to the de-Baathification procedure, the temptation to try to interpret the more indirect indicators of de-Baathification that exist in the public domain is irresistible.

The most promising source in this regard may be the list of 6,172 candidates for the 7 March elections that was issued last week. Or, more specifically, the lacunae in that list. As a rule, candidates are listed for each electoral list from number one right down to the last candidate (in Baghdad, some lists have more than one hundred candidates); where the numbered sequence of candidates is broken and someone is missing, IHEC has indicated that there is a problem with that person's candidacy. In the majority of those cases, probably around 170–200 of the some 350 that can be identified in a rough count, the omission will relate to a de-Baathification appeal that was pending at the time the list of approved candidates was published. The remainder likely relates to other sorts of procedural problems that may have delayed or prevented the approval of a candidate (including document forgeries), although there is so much contradictory information about a second batch of de-Baathification exclusions that it is not inconceivable that at least some such cases are also included. What we have, at any rate, is not a perfect measurement of de-Baathification as such, but a somewhat more messy indicator of "conflict level with IHEC". Predictably, in the few cases where actual de-Baathification statistics can be found for a party or a particular governorate, the numbers that emerge using these methods show similar trends but are not identical.

Some additional methodological points are in order. Obviously, if an individual was originally placed at the bottom of the list but then got excluded then the exclusion will not be discovered using this method since the numbering will not be broken. Similarly, one-person entities that fail to appear in the list for reasons of exclusion will go unnoticed. More related to the interpretation of the data: Out of 511 exclusion cases originally reported, several hundreds prompted the affected entities to voluntarily replace their candidates, whereas a more limited number simply led to withdrawals. In other words, the numbers reported here

Table 6.1: Number of candidates who have yet to receive IHEC approval, by electoral list and governorate

Governorate	Tawafuq	Alusi	Kurd	INA	Ahrar	SLA	Unity of Iraq	Iraqiyya	Other Secular & Nationalist	Total
Basra		2		3	1	1		3	3	13
Maysan		1				1		2	1	5
Dhi Qar		2		1	2			3		8
Muthanna		1			2			2	3	8
Qadisiyya										
Babel	2	1	2					2	5	12
Najaf								1	4	5
Karbala							1	3		4
Wasit		1				1			3	5
Baghdad	3	4	7	3	6	9	18	20	31	101
Anbar				1	1	2	4	2	25	35
Salahaddin		1	2		1	1	2		14	21
Mosul	5		2	2		3	12	2	9	35
Diyala			1	2	4	2			3	12
Kirkuk	1			1		1	2	4	10	19
Sulaymaniyya				4	1		1	3	1	10
Arbil			1	1						2
Dahuk			1	5						6
Total	11	13	16	23	18	21	42	50	107	301*

Note: These figures exclude around 55 cases related to local, smaller, or single-member lists.

(see Table 6.1), which are mostly related to appeals, do not tell the full story about intimidation of electoral candidates by the accountability and justice board.

Nonetheless, even if aspects related to these caveats conflate the figures somewhat, the picture that emerges is a rather remarkable one. Out of the big coalitions, the Kurdish list as well as Tawafuq—the Sunni Islamist entity that is seen as most oriented towards compromise with the Maliki government—rank top of the class in terms of a frictionless relationship with IHEC. They are followed closely by the Shiite-oriented alliances, the Iraqi National Alliance and State of Law. Both of these have certain lacunae in their lists, but it is noteworthy that this occurs mostly in governorates that are rather unimportant to these parties (such as the Kurdish ones for INA), and tends to involve candidates far down on the list (suggesting the omissions may well involve problems with documents rather than de-Baathification). Due to its intimate relationship with IHEC and the accountability and justice board, INA was in fact able to exclude many of these names when they published their own electoral lists before they were approved by IHEC—conceivably because INA may have had inside information about potential problems related to some of their candidates in the more marginal constituencies!

The picture is sharply different for the secular and nationalist lists. Even after the process of replacement of candidates, Iraqiyya and Unity of Iraq still account for a third of all exclusions. Additionally, in their cases, it is often top candidates in key constituencies that have been struck from the lists. In terms of having problems with IHEC, these parties are followed by other, smaller secular lists that also experience problems that are disproportionate to their party size. Ahrar of Ayad Jamal al-Din and the list of Mithal al-Alusi stand out, but there are also others. In fact 8 lists (310, 324, 327, 348, 349, 357, 358, 373) about which less is known—except that they have a secular and/or nationalist orientation and some of them with a particular strength in Sunni tribal areas—account for another third of the lacunae in the list of candidates. Geographically speaking, the patterns of discrimination also seem clearer than was the case with the original 511. In this material, Anbar, Salahaddin and Kirkuk have been targeted in a way that is disproportionate to their population size and more detailed information from Kirkuk confirms that it is the anti-Kurdish blocs that are suffering. The areas south of Baghdad have been left comparatively untouched.

Pathophysiological Aspects of a Dysfunctional Democracy[10]
March 2, 2010

The last couple of days have seen an outpouring of cheerful comments by optimistic observers of the Iraqi election campaign. The high number of candidate posters, it is argued, is testament to a vibrant democracy!

Perhaps the assessment of the Iraqi political process would become more realistic if observers went beyond counting the posters and started actually analyzing what is written on them. And a good place to start is of course the wonderful placard for candidate number 24 on list 316 (Iraqi National Alliance) in Baghdad, Ali Faysal al-Lami. Immediately following Lami's name, the principal item of his resume is indicated: "Executive director of the accountability and justice commission", also known as Iraq's de-Baathification board. At the bottom of the poster is a slogan, "For the sake of preventing the return of the oppressive Baath".

Lami's poster highlights the way in which the legacy of the de-Baathification process is deliberately being inserted in the Iraqi election campaign, effectively overshadowing many more important issues in Iraqi politics. And even at this late stage, Lami and his allies have the audacity to shamelessly employ the accountability and justice board—which in theory was supposed to be a politically neutral institution—to keep up the pressure as far as de-Baathification is concerned, all the way to election day it seems. On the last day of February, Candidate al-Lami, this time wearing his hat as de-Baathification director, dramatically announced that his commission would publish the evidence against the excluded candidates "at some point before the 7 March elections", suggesting a crescendo towards a grand anti-Baathist finale on the eve of the poll.

Also the supposedly more neutral state bureaucracy is succumbing to pressure by Lami and his allies. Judge Abd al-Sattar al-Birqadar, the spokesman of the higher judicial council, recently dismissed as "unrealistic" the attempt by Salih al-Mutlak to mount a legal challenge against the de-Baathification board, claiming that the appeals board constituted by parliament was the highest authority in the matter. What he failed to mention—and what the higher judicial council has so far not responded to in a judicial way—is the problem that neither the de-Baathification board nor the appeals court constituted to deal with its proceedings has any authority to rule on exclusions related to article 7 of the Iraqi constitution, which in legal terms simply has yet to be implemented since the special legislation called for in the constitution has yet to be passed. IHEC and UNAMI seem more focused on how to replace the banned candidates instead of considering the far more fundamental problem concerning the implementation of article 7; the Americans, for their part, now appear to be primarily focused on asking the losers of the elections to behave in a polite manner, i.e., that they should go quietly. The outcome of all this is elections whose legitimacy is in doubt even before the first votes have been cast. The secular and nationalist forces keep asking critical questions about the process and have signaled that they may boycott the political process in the next parliament if the election is fraudulent.

Isn't it reductionist to focus so exclusively on the de-Baathification process? Yes and no. Often overlooked in the west is the often Delphic character of the political discourse of Iraqi electoral candidates, even in this new age of democracy. It is for example slightly disconcerting that the number one candidate of State of Law in Nasiriyya in a recent, much profiled interview with an American journalist was unable to proffer any substantial description of his party's political program whatsoever. Other agendas that transpire in the election debate are disconnected from national politics altogether. Why don't we take a look at the activities of the counterpart of Lami in Basra, INA's number 24 there, Wathib al-Amud. He recently began campaigning for the creation of two new governorates to be parcelled out from Basra itself: Qurna and Mudayna/Madina. Candidate al-Amud says the two northernmost portions of the governorate do not receive a fair share of the Basra budget. More than 750,000 people live here, he says, which is more than both Dahuk and Muthanna (which in turn enjoy governorate status). If 100,000 signatures are collected, the Iraqi parliament will have to grant them governorate status! It doesn't matter one iota, it seems, that no such procedure for sub-governorate secession actually exists anywhere in the constitution. No, Amud, who is propagating a scheme that first appeared around December 2008 in the sub-governorate council of the oil-rich Qurna area, is making it all up and no one seems to care. Much like the situation at the national level, the Iraqi "democratic" process in Basra is full of fantasy and unencumbered by the tiresome inhibitions of law and due process.

Some observers will no doubt see the Amud phenomenon as yet another indicator of the prospering and deliciously messy character of Iraq's new democracy.

Down to the Wire: Maliki Advisor Reportedly De-Baathified[11]

March 4, 2010

The big news out of Iraq today is a report that sources in the accountability and justice board say they have written to the Iraqi elections commission (IHEC) to have the name of candidate number 10 for the State of Law list in Najaf, Abbud Wahid al-Eisawi, struck from the ballot paper. Eisawi is a tribal advisor to Nuri al-Maliki.

Regardless of whether this will actually come to pass or not, the case has two dimensions. Firstly it proves that the forces behind the de-Baathification process wanted this issue to define the Iraqi political climate throughout the period leading up to the elections. With exclusions—or possibilities of exclusions—still being discussed at this late stage, one senses a kind of quasi-competitive politics that is characteristic of neighboring Iran, rather than one that is reminiscent of democracy in the liberal tradition.

Secondly, this development underlines the extent to which the Iraqi National Alliance was always in the lead in the de-Baathification process, and that Maliki was following after. Of course, eventually some Maliki adherents in the governorates went even further than INA in inventing new procedures for excluding political enemies.

The question now is whether Maliki will use this affair to make a last-minute, much-overdue public verdict on the whole flawed de-Baathification process. Reinstating some former officers in the army isn't enough; it is the collapse of the rule of law that needs to be addressed. Conversely, the stance of Iraqiyya, which has been critical of de-Baathification all the way (and one of its major victims) will also be interesting. Rumors continue to swirl as to its possible post-election alliance with INA, which would be a veritable sell-out and a sorry end to the whole de-Baathification affair—an INA creation where Iraqiyya has always been at the receiving end.

The Iraqi elections still feature intra-Shiite competition. But they are a competition in de-Baathification rather than a contest in national leadership.

CHAPTER NOTES

1 See http://gulfanalysis.wordpress.com/2009/12/06/no-second-veto-the-election-law-is-approved-by-tariq-al-hashemi-and-the-iraqi-presidency/.
2 See http://gulfanalysis.wordpress.com/2009/12/09/the-official-coalition-list-is-out/.
3 See http://gulfanalysis.wordpress.com/2010/01/08/why-ad-hoc-de-baathification-will-derail-the-process-of-democratisation-in-iraq/.
4 See http://gulfanalysis.wordpress.com/2010/01/17/the-bloc-that-has-no-de-baathification-worries/.
5 See http://historiae.org/de-Baathification.asp.
6 See http://gulfanalysis.wordpress.com/2010/02/04/the-backlash-from-the-hardliners/.
7 See http://gulfanalysis.wordpress.com/2010/02/06/back-to-work-for-the-appeals-court/.
8 See http://gulfanalysis.wordpress.com/2010/02/10/the-ihec-publishes-the-names-of-6172-approved-candidates/.
9 See http://gulfanalysis.wordpress.com/2010/02/16/governorate-and-party-level-indicators-of-de-baathification-plus-some-breaking-news/.
10 See http://gulfanalysis.wordpress.com/2010/03/02/pathophysiological-aspects-of-a-dysfunctional-democracy/.
11 See http://gulfanalysis.wordpress.com/2010/03/04/down-to-the-wire-maliki-adviser-reportedly-de-baathified/.

Chapter 7

The Government Formation Process, 2010

The election of March 7, 2010, produced no clear winners. Rather, four slates made a strong showing. The secular Iraqiyya had a narrow lead, with 91 seats compared with 89 for Nuri al-Maliki's State of Law (SLA). INA, the most outspokenly Shiite alliance, came third with 70 seats and the Kurdistan Alliance got 43. Additionally, the Kurdistan Alliance seemed confident about parliamentary support from another 14 Kurdish deputies from smaller Kurdish parties, as well as at least some of the 8 minority deputies, most of whom hailed from northern parts of Iraq. The only remaining blocs in parliament, Tawafuq, a Sunni Islamist coalition with 6 seats and Unity of Iraq, a more secular, nationalist alliance with 4 seats, remained uncommitted vis-à-vis the bigger blocs.

All in all it was clear that the de-Baathification trick introduced by INA had paid off: Maliki did miserably in Sunni areas north of Baghdad and Allawi may have done worse south of Baghdad than he would under normal circumstances because his voters experienced gross intimidation there—although Iraqiyya none-theless did achieve a respectable and unmatched level of representation from Basra in the south to Mosul in the north. Despite the fact that SLA and Iraqiyya had tried to run as nonsectarian lists, they ended up with support bases that looked increasingly sectarian. For SLA, this represented a reaffirmation of the situation that had evolved since the creation of the alliance in 2008—it should be remembered that Maliki did not even start to reach out to non-Shiites in any serious way until after the local elections of January 2009. Regarding Iraqiyya, however, it is possible to speak of a degree of Sunnification having occurred with the co-option since autumn 2009 of numerous prominent politicians from the northwestern parts of Iraq. In terms of intra-list fragmentation, it was INA that stood out since dexterous strategizing by the Sadrists enabled them to capture no fewer than 40 of the 70 seats won by the alliance, leaving ISCI as clearly a junior partner with fewer than 20 seats.

The subsequent process of government formation can be described as a series of distinctive, if partially overlapping, phases. The first of these stages was the battle about the results themselves, consisting primarily of an attempt by Nuri al-Maliki to mount challenges to the allocation of deputies so that he, rather than Ayad Allawi, would come first and thereby gain the right to form the next government. State of Law started legal battles to have candidates from the other lists disqualified and their votes canceled (including using post-election de-Baathification as a tactic); they also demanded a full recount in Baghdad, which was granted but did not produce any change in the result. The battle lasted from the publication of the preliminary result on March 26 until the certification of the results on June 1, with no changes to the allocation of deputies taking place. It is noteworthy that in this period, two other developments indicated an alternative path to a second premiership for Maliki. First, a ruling by the federal supreme court in late March put pre-election and post-election coalition forming on the same legal footing in terms of defining the right of the biggest bloc to form the next government. In other words, theoretically, at least, the pan-Shiite alliance combining State of Law and the Iraqi National Alliance was now a possibility. In a second key development, such an alliance was indeed announced in early May. However, at this stage, Maliki was clearly still fighting for the possibility of a change in the results, and appeared lukewarm to the pan-Shiite project at first.

After the certification of the result in June, Maliki's sole remaining path to power consisted of some kind of post-election alliance—either with INA or with Iraqiyya. For Iraqiyya, the situation was slightly different: It could still hope to obtain support from other blocs in case the projected all-Shiite alliance should fail to agree on a single premier candidate. This second phase—in practice the battle between different legal definitions of the right to form the government represented by a pre-election bloc (Iraqiyya) and a still-putative post-election bloc (the National Alliance, or NA)—lasted from June until Ramadan in early September. SLA and INA claimed to have an alliance but could not agree on a premier candidate and were thus unable to move ahead with forming a government. While those two blocs continued their tug-of-war, each was also meanwhile conducting negotiations with Iraqiyya in an attempt to put pressure on the other and win the intra-Shiite struggle between them. Iraqiyya, for its part, pretended the Shiite alliance did not exist, and, having apparently already forgotten the whole recent record of the de-Baathification campaign, spent much of its time negotiating with INA in the hope that INA would ultimately accept Allawi as its premier candidate. Apparently because of the considerable personal animosities between Allawi and Maliki, the eminently logical alternative of Iraqiyya and State of Law combining in an alliance to exclude the others did not gain any significant traction; Iraqiyya instead clung to the rather unrealistic dream that the Sadrists, with Syrian mediation, would somehow help swing INA—half of the projected Shiite alliance—behind Allawi as premier candidate.

By September, it became clear that both INA and SLA were after all going to focus their energies on their own Shiite alliance. This third stage—the intra-Shiite struggle—was comparatively swift. INA in early September nominated Adil Abd *al-Mahdi of ISCI to face off against Nuri al-Maliki as the premier candidate of the SLA. On October 1, Maliki was declared the winner in the internal contest by acclamation (but with some significant abstentions) and hence formally became the prime ministerial candidate of the combined, all-Shiite National Alliance. It appeared that a sudden change of heart in late September by the Sadrists—who had been consistently anti-Maliki for months—clinched the deal. This mysterious maneuver, in turn, seemed to indicate a degree of Iranian involvement as well as a slight change in the Iranian position. Up until September 2010, Iran had generally considered Maliki a little too independent-minded and uncontrollable, and there were indications that both Tehran and the Sadrists instead favored some kind of "compromise candidate" to be the premier candidate of the NA, such as Ibrahim al-Jaafari. What prompted the Iranians to rather suddenly shift to Maliki remains unclear, although it is possible that their fear of the scenario of some kind of bilateral pact between Maliki and Allawi—which temporarily had been the subject of some renewed discussion in August—may have played a role.*

The fourth stage of the process commenced in October. Because of the way the intra-Shiite struggle had played out, the Kurds were for the first time made king-makers in the battle for the premiership. The reason was simply that the defection by Maliki's opponents inside the Shiite alliance was greater than expected and seemed to include most of ISCI, Badr, possibly Fadila and some independents—10 to 20 deputies altogether. This was sufficient to kill any hopes on the part of Maliki to form a government with the smaller Sunni-oriented parties (Tawafuq and Unity of Iraq) and minority representatives alone; he would definitely have to rely on Kurdish support. Accordingly, the "Kurdish drama" was played out in October, and the Kurdish list of demands for joining the government—19 points—became the focus of a strange process in which Maliki and Allawi (who due to the size of the NA defection was still in play as a candidate, at least theoretically) appeared to be outbidding each other in terms of satisfying the Kurdish demands. Iraqiyya even went as far as indicating its willingness to nominate Adil Abd al-Mahdi of INA as its own premier candidate (instead of Allawi) because it was thought Abd al-Mahdi's personality and decentralization agenda might serve as an added incentive for the Kurds. It was a remarkable scene indeed, since both Allawi and Maliki headed political movements committed to centralist and nationalist values—the very antithesis of the Kurdish agenda. All of a sudden they seemed prepared to make promises that would contradict their own programs: The 19 Kurdish demands included measures of radical decentralization that would weaken the Iraqi state even beyond the concessions to the periphery in the constitution adopted in 2005, including an oil and gas law with strong regional rights, a perpetuation of the veto-wielding, ethno-sectarian presidency council until the formation of a senate, and a dilution of the powers of the prime minister.

By late October, there was nothing left to prevent the Kurds from picking one of the competing premier candidates as a winner, and a ruling by the federal supreme court in the last week of the month to end the "open session" of parliament added more pressure on them to make up their minds. Maliki (who now enjoyed firm Iranian support) had gone further than Iraqiyya in making promises to the Kurds, and though they still had some doubts about his sincerity they swiftly joined him in rejecting a last-minute Saudi attempt to forestall his formation of a government. The first week of November was then dominated by the so-called Barzani initiative, a political roundtable of all blocs, as the Kurds worked to maximize their own benefit from the second Maliki government that increasingly seemed to be a fait accompli. During this process, Maliki got the second term he wanted, the Kurds got promises, and Iraqiyya—now with more U.S. backing than before, since the fear of "Sunni exclusion" had become its main concern—was awarded a promised "national council for strategic policies" that had no basis in the Iraqi constitution and no prerogatives defined by any existing laws. The whole package was finalized in Baghdad on November 10, with a parliamentary session convened for the following day to formalize the agreement. Thus, on November 11, 2010, Usama al-Nujayfi of Iraqiyya was elected speaker of parliament, Jalal Talabani of the Kurdish alliance became president with ceremonial powers, and Nuri al-Maliki was nominated for a second term as prime minister. Even as the meeting was under way, problems erupted in the shape of a partial Iraqiyya walkout, signaling the fragility of the new arrangements and potential pitfalls ahead. Instead of real integration, Iraqiyya seemed to be dragged into the process only to be awarded what was still only an informal (indeed, unbuilt) garden shed in the sprawling Iraqi political architecture.

At least some of the blame for the long delay must be placed with the United States, which consistently seemed to favor the most time-consuming and complex scenarios. There was a period in summer 2010 when they could have pushed for an alliance between Allawi and Maliki. However, instead of pressing for a straightforward deal in which only Iraqiyya and State of Law would have formed the government (an arrangement that would have kept Iran at more of a distance from Iraqi decision making), Washington kept pressing for the inclusion of all four of the larger blocs and kept suggesting convoluted power-sharing formulas that would all have required legislative action or even constitutional change and confirmation by popular referendum. These suggestions included, first, the Byzantine scheme for a revived "political council for national security," and later, the idea of an empowered presidency. As late as September 2010, leading officials of the Obama administration were informally describing this latter formula as offering a valuable "Sunni cushion." These officials also spent considerable energy trying to convince the Kurdish nominee for president, Jalal Talabani, to yield to Ayad Allawi. In the end, a slightly modified version of the proposal for a national security council did win acceptance; it was that proposal that secured Iraqiyya's participation in the inaugural session of parliament on November 11. This was promptly celebrated as a triumph by the U.S. government even though the powers of the council—and *hence the reality of the "integration" of Iraqiyya that was achieved in the dying days of Pax Americana in Iraq—remained undefined even as Maliki was nominated to a second term.*

In this way, the Iraqi government-formation process of 2010 came to be focused almost exclusively on power-sharing formulas catering to ethno-sectarian special interests. Proposals for institutionalizing new positions to counteract an independent-minded premier received much attention, not least from the United States and supposedly "progressive" international players like the UN agency in Iraq, UNAMI, which effectively encouraged the Iraqis to violate the 2005 constitution as much as possible to get a government in place. In the end, almost regardless of how it would work in practice, the power-sharing deal that was eventually agreed to in November 2010 stood in contradiction to the constitutional vision proclaimed in 2005: that of the next five years seeing a transition to a more progressive form of politics in Iraq. If it should succeed, the November 2010 power-sharing deal would put in place new checks and balances that were still, however, framed in vaguely couched ethno-sectarian terms (with the allocation of the national council for strategic policies to Iraqiyya signaling an intended "Sunni inclusion.") If the November deal failed, that would probably result in a situation of ethno-sectarian dominance (whether all-Shiite, or Kurdish–Shiite), based on Iranian support. There remained, of course, a small possibility that Maliki might one day try a repeat of what he did in 2008 in terms of liberating himself from his coalition partners (this time, the Kurds and the Sadrists) and play the Iraqi nationalist card again. But with a political system still based far more on regional interests, ethno-sectarian factions and personal friendships than on political issues, by the end of the "transitional" period in November 2010 Iraq's democratization could hardly be described as anything other than a failure.

The Uncertified Election Results: Allawi Comes Out on Top[1]
March 26, 2010

The Iraqi elections commission, IHEC, has today released the full, uncertified results of the 7 March parliamentary elections. The distribution of the seats has been specified at the entity level for all the 325 deputies in the next assembly.

The secular-nationalist Iraqiyya (INM) comes out on top with 91 seats (89 ordinary and 2 compensation), followed by State of Law (SLA) headed by Nuri al-Maliki second at 89 seats (87+2), the Iraqi National Alliance at 70 seats (68+2) and the Kurdistan Alliance at 43 seats (42+1). The full distribution of seats is as shown in Table 7.1.

The names of the winning candidates (based on how the electorate used the open-list option to promote individuals within a list) have yet to be published; this

Table 7.1: Results of the Iraqi parliamentary election of March 2010								
Governorate	INA	SLA	INM	Unity of Iraq	Tawafuq	Kurdistan Alliance	Other Kurdish	Minority
Basra	7	14	3					
Maysan	6	4						
Dhi Qar	9	8	1					
Muthanna	3	4						
Qadisiyya	5	4	2					
Babel	5	8	3					
Najaf	5	7						
Karbala	3	6	1					
Wasit	4	5	2					
Baghdad	17	26	24		1			2
Anbar			11	1	2			
Salahaddin			8	2	2			
Diyala	3	1	8			1		
Nineveh	1		20	1	1	8		3
Kirkuk			6			6		1
Arbil						10	4	1
Dahuk						9	1	1
Sulaymaniyya						8	9	
Total + compensation (C)	68 + 2C	87 + 2C	89 + 2C	4	6	42 + 1C	14	8

will supposedly be done at the IHEC website and in Iraqi newspapers tomorrow. The identity of the winners of the seven compensation seats (two for each of the three big lists and one for the Kurdish list) will be withheld pending a query to the federal supreme court about the rules for their allocation to individuals.

Ayad Allawi and Iraqiyya now go strengthened into the coalition-forming process. By winning more seats than expected south of Baghdad and almost as many seats as Maliki in Baghdad, Allawi has proved that he is more than "the candidate of the Sunnis" (which was always implausible given his own Shiite background). However, the two parties that are closest to each other on many key constitutional issues (and maybe the most promising combination to get an oil law passed anytime soon), Iraqiyya and State of Law, remain at loggerheads with each other mainly due to differences at the personal level between their leaders. In this kind of situation, probably the most logical step for Iraqiyya would be to explore the possibility of a deal with the Kurds that balances some solid concessions to Arbil with preservation of Iraqi nationalist ideals as far as the structure of government south of Kurdistan is concerned. Additional support could come either from Shiite Islamists who share the view of Iraqiyya on the importance of a centralized state in the rest of Iraq (for example the Sadrists), or, alternatively, all the small blocs and independents in parliament joined together (166 seats with Iraqiyya and the Kurds, barely above the 163 absolute-majority mark). It is to be hoped that Iraqiyya will avoid the earlier-floated, ideologically contradictive scheme of a deal with ISCI (the pro-Iranian decentralist Shiite party with which Iraqiyya only shares certain ties at the personal level), since it would mean another oversized, ineffective government populated by parties with little in common. At any rate, ISCI now has diminishing clout within INA due to the strong showing of the Sadrists at the level of individual deputies.

Also, some extra uncertainty has been added to the mix due to a ruling by the federal supreme court yesterday which explicitly makes it clear that the key definition of "the largest bloc in parliament" (which is supposed to form the next government) can also apply to post-election coalition projects. This in turn breathes new life into the scenario preferred by Iran of the two Shiite-led blocs, INA and SLA, joining together to a single big entity, on the pattern of what happened in 2004/2005. Talk about this has come to the fore again over the last weeks as Maliki gradually realized that his ambition of going it alone, separate from the other Shiites, was not going to be fulfilled quite in the way he had foreseen. It would, however, require considerable recalibration within Shiite circles, since the Sadrists are likely to overshadow ISCI in the INA contingent, and they are not known to be keen on a second Maliki premiership. Nonetheless, the mere fact that this option is now being talked about at all signifies the big irony of these elections: Ali Faysal al-Lami, the de-Baathification director, both lost and won them to some extent. He got just a few hundred personal votes for INA in Baghdad, and will not win a seat in parliament. But through his witch hunt he forced Maliki into a more sectarian corner, thereby preventing him from winning much-needed support north of Baghdad.

Meanwhile, the next procedural step is of a simpler character: The results will have to be formally certified in the Iraqi legal system. Only then will the clock for government formation start ticking in a formal sense. Upon certification of the results, the current president, Jalal Talabani, must call on the new national assembly to convene within fifteen days. At that point, the council will have to elect a speaker with two deputies. In theory, that election is separate from the government formation, although it seems likely that whoever is forming the next government will want allies to fill those posts: With the control of the parliamentary agenda that comes with them, they are going to be more important during the next four years than the office of the president, which is scheduled to become a purely ceremonial position as the transition period defined from 2005 to 2010 is coming to an end. The new president, in turn, is to be elected within 30 days of the first parliamentary meeting. The constitution stipulates an aspiration of a two-thirds majority for the election of the president but allows for a simple-majority run-off in case that requirement should prove elusive: This in turn means that it is the 163 mark that needs to be met in order to secure the election of the president and thereby get the government-formation process on track in earnest, with a deadline of another fifteen days for the president to formally charge the nominee of the biggest parliamentary bloc to form a government within another thirty days. In other words, if certification takes place around 1 April, a meeting of the new parliament must be held within 15 April, a new president must be elected within 15 May, a PM nominee must be identified by 1 June, and a new cabinet must be presented for approval by parliament before 1 July. The psychological deadline is likely to be the start of Ramadan around 10 August and the scheduled completion of withdrawal of U.S. combat troops by 31 August.

The Sadrist Watershed Confirmed[2]
March 29, 2010

The allocation of seats to individuals released by IHEC today confirms the growing strength of the Sadrists within the mainly Shiite Iraqi National Alliance (INA), as shown in Table 7.2. The Sadrist position has in fact been consolidated in the final allocation (where the female quota has been taken into account), leaving it with 39 deputies which is 57% of the 68 INA deputies confirmed at the individual level. Additionally, depending on a decision by the federal supreme court, they may get two more seats since IHEC regulation 21 awards the compensation seats (two are due to INA) to those vote-getters with the highest number of votes that failed to achieve representation.

Table 7.2: Distribution of seats within the Iraqi National Alliance (INA) in the March 2010 election, by party and province					
Governorate	Sadr	Badr	ISCI	Jaafari	Fadila	Other
Basra	3	1			2	1
Maysan	3	1			1	1
Dhi Qar	4	2	1		2	
Muthanna	2	1				
Qadisiyya	2	1	2			
Babel	3	1	1			
Najaf	3	1				1
Karbala	2		1			
Wasit	3	1				
Baghdad	12		2	1	1	1
Diyala	2	1				
Nineveh			1			
Total	39	10	8	1	6	4

It is worth mentioning that the main competitor of the Sadrists within INA—ISCI and Badr, who now emerge weakened with no more than around 18 seats altogether—will be watching (and maybe pressing) the court on the issue of compensation seats, since it benefitted enormously from the old arrangement back in 2005, whereby it received no less than a third of its 30 parliamentary seats through "compensation seats" awarded by the party leadership without reference to the preferences of the electorate. In this way, many ISCI representatives in the previous parliament received their seats on the basis of no more than a few hundred votes in obscure locations (from a Shiite point of view) like Anbar. Other significant INA developments include the complete marginalization of Jaafari (only he himself won a seat), along with a slight improvement on the part of Fadila, helped mainly by the female quota.

Intra-list re-ordering of candidates as a result of the personal vote is somewhat less systematic with respect to other entities. It is however noteworthy that much of the attempt by Nuri al-Maliki to build bridges to Sunnis and secularists by welding together a diverse list has been reversed by the electorate in places like Baghdad. Many Westerners hailed Maliki for bringing Sunnis and secularists like Hajim al-Hasani, Abbad Mutlak al-Jibburi, Abd al-Qadir al-Ubaydi, Mahdi al-Hafiz and Izzat al-Shabandar into his camp; however with less than a thousand votes each, they have all been demoted to non-winning positions on the Baghdad list for State of Law.

Not Another Governing Council, Please![3]

April 6, 2010

Among the several scenarios for a new Iraqi government that are floating around, one stands out as particularly unattractive and potentially destructive for Iraq as a state: The vision of a grandiose coalition combining all the blocs that won large numbers of seats in the 7 March elections.

This idea is becoming increasingly recurrent in Iraqi discussions. Early on, it was only Adil Abd al-Mahdi of the pro-Iranian Islamic Supreme Council of Iraq (ISCI) that talked about it, referring to a potential combination of his own Iraqi National Alliance (INA), Maliki's State of Law (SLA), Iraqiyya and the main Kurdish alliance. More recently, however, also Ammar al-Hakim and other ISCI leaders have expressed interest in this kind of scenario, and no one in Iraqiyya has yet had the courage to rule it out. Predictably, decimated blocs (like Tawafuq) plus Unity of Iraq and the various minority representatives are calling for even bigger iterations of this scheme, including, unsurprisingly, themselves in ministerial roles.

Any government of this category would mean a sorry return to Iraq of 2003 and the "governing council" that was put in place by Paul Bremer back then. Its hallmarks will be indecision, incompetence and corruption—the inevitable characteristics of a government that has no single vision or unity of purpose, and basically has been thrown together with the aim of letting as many people as possible prey on the resources of the state in the hope that this will keep them from fighting with each other instead. Expect no progress on key legislation (since bills will never achieve consensus even inside the government), and no improvement of governance capacity (since ministers inevitably will be political appointees rather than technocrats). But above all, this will be a government defined first and foremost by its bigness, with an oversized cabinet and an additional number of ministers without portfolio.

Alas, this silly idea is likely to get an ecstatic reception in the international community. Few will be surprised that Iran likes it: Absent the creation of a purely Shiite or Shiite–Kurdish government, Tehran's next best option for Iraq is an oversized government incapable of making decisions (which in the case of an oil law would directly threaten the Iranian oil policy of low output, high price), with the sub-identities of the country's population forming an implicit or explicit role in the dynamics of government formation (meaning Shiite Islamists will continue to dominate). But beyond Iran, the label that is being used by the Iraqi proponents of this idea—*shiraka* or partnership—will likely be welcomed also by Western players whose fear of exclusions and the concomitant creation of "spoilers" is such that it leads them to uncritically embrace the logic of "the more, the merrier" (or "inclusiveness" as they euphemistically label it). In their view, the only thing that matters is to keep the surface calm around the time of the U.S. drawdown by the end of August, quite regardless of the potential for severe complications further down the road.

The big irony of this is of course that two of the prospective participants in such a government of national unity would in fact do a lot better if they formed a government alone. So why is it that Malik and Allawi cannot put aside personal differences and create a strong government (180 seats in parliament) that would have the potential to rule Iraq far more effectively? If the two men are to endure the discomfort of sitting in the same government anyway, why not ditch the two other and smaller partners—INA and the Kurds—whose sole contribution after all would be to create ideological contradictions along the centralism/decentralism axis and therefore a considerable potential for complete paralysis? With their common position on the virtues of pragmatism and a strong centralized state, such a two-party government would be able to push through legislation on the oil sector and revenue distribution faster than anyone else—which in turn would enable it to deal with more controversial issues in a less tense atmosphere later on. Crucially, with its strong popular basis from Basra to Mosul, this kind of government would have sufficient room for maneuver to offer generous concessions to the already autonomous Kurdistan without destroying the concept of centralized government in the rest of Iraq.

The problem is that because of personal differences, both SLA and Iraqiyya have avoided the logical step of moving closer together, and instead invented rather strained discourses of mutual antipathy to justify their turn to less logical alliance partners (SLA and the Kurds; Iraqiyya and INA). For example, Iraqiyya leaders criticize Maliki for concentrating power and for allowing Daawa to acquire strength in the public sector in undemocratic ways. True, these are valid and important points that need to be dealt with. But is the solution to add the Kurds and INA to the mix? With their ties to the Kurdish *asayish* secret police, the Badr brigades and the Iranian revolutionary guards, are these so much more democratic than the Daawa? Was it not after all INA that initiated the attack on Iraqiyya through the de-Baathification process? Similarly, Iraqiyya has failed to give Maliki due credit for some of the good things he did back in 2008, including turning against Shiite militias, highlighting the significance of revising the constitution, and attempting to move away from power-sharing towards more ideologically based political alliances. For their part, the Daawa has not been sufficiently responsive to some of the positive overtures from the Iraqiyya camp during 2009. Take for example the Hadba/Iraqiyyun/Nujayfi bloc from Mosul, which has repeatedly called for more troops from the central government to the northern parts of the Nineveh governorate. This act of profound recognition of the Shiite-led government by a mainly Sunni party with strong local backing represents an important step forwards towards national reconciliation that has so far not received the attention it deserves in SLA circles.

The Intra-List Power Balance in Iraqiyya and State of Law[4]
April 9, 2010

It is quite natural that discussions of internal stability within the four big coalitions that won the 7 March parliamentary elections should focus on the Shiite-led Iraqi National Alliance (INA). Not only does the internal fragmentation in INA seem most dramatic in terms of strong centrifugal forces; there is also a marked contradiction between a leadership heavily dominated by the weaker blocs (ISCI/Badr; Jaafari) and a numerically strong element that is poorly represented at the top (the Sadrists). Nonetheless, it may be worth taking a look at the internal politics of the two other big alliances, Iraqiyya and State of Law, which despite a stronger degree of internal coherence (or a greater lack of obvious foci for large-scale defections) both exhibit certain interesting trends as far as the use of the open-list system by voters is concerned, at least in some of the governorates.

An internal document from Iraqiyya provides an overview of the affiliations of its winning candidates that can be summarized in Table 7.3.

Several points are noteworthy regarding Table 7.3. The first concerns termi-

	INM (Wifaq)	INM (Hiwar)	Nujayfi	Karbuli	Hashemi	Eisawi	Yawir	TF*	Abtan
Basra	3								
Dhi Qar	1								
Qadisiyya	2								
Babel	3								
Karbala	1								
Wasit	2								
Baghdad	8	4	1	5	3	3			
Anbar		3		3	2	3			
Diyala	1	4	1	1		1			
Salahaddin	4	1		1	1	1			
Nineveh	2	2	7	1	1		6	1	
Kirkuk		2		1				2	1
TOTAL (89)	27	16	9	12	7	8	6	3	1

Table 7.3: Distribution of seats won in the March 2010 election by candidates of the Iraqiyya bloc, by affiliation and province

* TF: Turkmen Front

nology: Wifaq (the Ayad Allawi group) and Hiwar (the Salih al-Mutlak group) have been listed separately in the party document because that reflects their status at the time of the registration of political entities for the elections in the summer of 2009. However, the two merged to form an integrated political movement, the Iraqi National Movement, later in the autumn. In that sense, they are now formally more closely integrated than, say, the two Daawa branches or even ISCI and Badr (somewhat confusingly, Iraqiyya also sometimes uses INM as an acronym for the entire Iraqiyya coalition). With 43 seats altogether, the Iraqi National Movement will probably be the biggest coherent entity in the new parliament, slightly bigger than the Sadrist bloc. It will be the only group in parliament with representation from Basra in the south to Nineveh in the north.

Another notable feature is that if the premise of the institutional unity between the Allawi and Mutlak blocs is accepted, the potential challenges from competing centers of power are less pronounced than in the case of INA. This is so partly because of size (the biggest such bloc is that affiliated with Jamal Nasir al-Karbuli, president of the Iraqi Red Crescent, with 12 seats; Rafi al-Eisawi, sometimes referred to as an emerging player, has got only eight) and partly because of regional concentration/limitation (the Nujayfi and Yawir blocs are limited to Nineveh where they have almost all their seats). Moreover, since it is the Mutlak and Karbuli groups that have been targeted most intensely by the de-Baathification committee (including an attempt at banning them as entities), any post-election de-Baathification that promotes other candidates of the list is only likely to strengthen the position of Allawi. With respect to the use of the open-list system, Iraqiyya voters south of Baghdad have largely followed the preferences of the party leadership, but in the capital and areas north there are certain interesting promotions, including examples from Baghdad like Hasan Khudayr (a *sahwa* figure affiliated with Wifaq who jumped from 83rd to third position), Hamid Jassam (from the Karbuli camp, from 107th to eighth) and Talal Hussein al-Zawbai (Nujayfi group, from 129th to ninth). Some of these tendencies can also be seen in Nineveh, but on the whole the usage of the open-list system has a less dramatic and systematic impact on intra-list dynamics than in the case of Sadrists within INA. With the possible exceptions of the Karbuli bloc in Baghdad and the Yawir bloc in Mosul (Shammar tribe), the challenges "from below" are not particularly strong or concerted when it comes to Iraqiyya.

Many of the same tendencies can be seen with regard to State of Law, although the source material is less comprehensive here—limited to complete breakdowns for Basra and Wasit, a list of 40 candidates of the Tanzim al-Iraq branch of the Daawa (for all of Iraq), a list of the much smaller independent bloc affiliated with oil minister Hussein al-Shahristani (ditto), as well as complete lists from Baghdad and Najaf without entity affiliations but with some tribal names that make identification of individuals somewhat easier. Table 7.4, which summarizes the information about the distribution of seats in the SLA, includes around 18 deputies whose affiliation is unconfirmed at the time of writing; as such, it probably puts the main branch of the Daawa somewhat lower than what it should be since "unconfirmed" candidates are likely to include additional Daawa deputies.

Table 7.4: Distribution of seats won in the March 2010 election by candidates of the State of Law Alliance (SLA), by affiliation and province

	Daawa (Maliki)	Daawa (Tanzim)	Harakat al-Daawa	Shahristani	Other independent	Unconfirmed
Basra	5	3	1	2	3	
Maysan		3				1
Dhi Qar	2	4		1	1	
Muthanna	3				1	
Qadisiyya				1	1	2
Babel	2	1			2	3
Najaf	1				3	3
Karbala	1			1	2	2
Wasit	3				2	
Baghdad	6	2		1	10	7
Diyala	1					
TOTAL (87)	24+	13	1	6	25	18

SLA voting in Baghdad offers perhaps the best example of voters taking a passive (or, some would say, futile) approach to the open-list. On the one hand, there is the big "prime ministerial" vote for Maliki the person (622,000). Then, with the exception of Jaafar al-Sadr (29,000), there is a huge gap to the next vote-getters, with many winners in the 3,000 range. Moreover, these candidates tend to be from the Daawa or they are independents, and as such are unlikely to pose a big challenge to Maliki's leadership.

That same tendency applies across the governorates where SLA won seats. The only systematic exception is the performance of Tanzim al-Iraq, which is particularly strong in the far south. In Basra, this is counterbalanced by a healthy score for Daawa candidates, but in Maysan and Dhi Qar the ascendancy of this SLA element—often thought to be somewhat closer to Iran than the rest of the Daawa—seems significant. Elsewhere, though, the "independent" bloc of Oil Minister Hussein al-Shahristani has gained only a modest number of seats. Additionally, many of the "independent" individual candidates seem to reflect the successful recruitment by SLA of government officials, who may be particularly loyal to Maliki personally for that reason. Typically, they are director-generals or high-ranking officials in the service sector, including a high number of medical doctors. Notable "climbers" within the SLA include Adnan Rumayyid al-Shahmani (an ex-Sadrist who advanced from 93 to 10 in Baghdad) and Ibrahim al-Rikabi (a tribal shaykh of the Bani Rikab, from 76 to 19 also in Baghdad). Given the overall picture, though, these seem to represent successful cases of co-option rather than zones of insecurity for Maliki.

Maliki vs. Lami, Maliki/Lami vs. Allawi[5]
April 29, 2010

The prominent role of Tariq Harb, a legal counsel to Nuri al-Maliki, in communicating the decision of the electoral judicial panel to exclude 52 candidates and annul their votes retroactively has now been explained: A leaked letter from the panel indicates that the call for exclusion came from two different sides—the accountability and justice board headed by Ali al-Lami of the Iraqi National Alliance (INA) and, in a separate complaint, the State of Law alliance (SLA) led by Nuri al-Maliki.

Equally important is the essential three-way character of the struggle, with Lami and Maliki still attacking the secularists in Iraqiyya from two different sides, and sometimes striking against each other instead. This is best illustrated in the legal reasoning behind the complaint from SLA. Their argument is that since their own candidate in Najaf, Abbud al-Eisawi, was de-Baathified shortly before the election and deprived of his votes at one point during the counting process, the same logic should apply to the 52 recently banned, i.e., the entities should lose their votes entirely. Not to be overlooked, though—but conveniently ignored by State of Law—is the fact that towards the end of March, one assumes by way of

Iraqi magic, Eisawi was cleared by the special appeals court for de-Baathification and his votes were therefore counted in the normal fashion (he is a seat winner in Najaf and is recognized as such by IHEC). In other words, Maliki was first attacked by Lami and his competing Shiite faction who sought to exclude Eisawi; Maliki then got Eisawi reinstated by the appeals court but is using the dubious "Eisawi precedent" to exclude others who were not so lucky, and who happen to be mostly from Iraqiyya. In short, one senses that one arm of the Iraqi system, the de-Baathification board, is still largely an INA preserve, but that Maliki is increasingly able to get the decisions he wants from the de-Baathification appeals board and the electoral judicial panel (as seen in the decision on 19 April to do a manual recount in Baghdad). Tragically, of course, by choosing this approach Maliki is in practice perpetuating the de-Baathification issue whose revival in 2009 was designed by Iran as a two-pronged attack against himself and Ayad Allawi, the two most popular politicians in Iraq.

The Presidency Council Intervenes in the De-Baathification Debate[6]
May 4, 2010

The Iraqi presidency council, consisting of President Jalal Talabani, Vice-President Adil Abd al-Mahdi and Vice-President Tariq al-Hashemi, has today intervened in the de-Baathification debate in an interesting way: It expresses the view that regardless of the de-Baathification status of individual candidates, no votes shall be taken from lists. Also, in a move probably intended to highlight that demand and speed up the certification process, the council suggested that the Iraqi judicial authorities proceed with certification of all governorates and leave only Baghdad open, where the manual recount is expected to last for another week or two.

These measures are helpful in that they could serve to bring some kind of closure to the de-Baathification process, which has long ago run out of control and has become an arena for settling scores and advancing party interests. The move protects the right of the Iraqi voters, and might go some way towards focusing minds on the necessary negotiations ahead. Nonetheless, it cannot escape notice that two of the authors of today's decision, Talabani and Abd al-Mahdi, only a few months ago supported the first revival of the de-Baathification debate—directly through the presidency council and, in the case of Abd al-Mahdi, also indirectly in his newspaper *Al-Adala* and through the work of people in his own electoral alliance, INA. In this way, the rise and fall of the de-Baathification issue looks very much like a trap designed to ensnare Nuri al-Maliki, whose consolidation of power was disliked by all three members of the presidency council. And to some extent, this succeeded since Maliki eventually gave in to the temptations of using the de-Baathification card, whereas the parties that initiated the campaign are now switching to a softer tone and are making all the sounds Washington wants them to make. Maliki comes across in a worse light since he is now using the de-Baathification logic in an attempt to manipulate the result so that he himself, and not Ayad Allawi of Iraqiyya, will be heading the "biggest bloc" in parliament.

Of course, what the presidency council is doing here is somewhat messy in terms of its constitutionality. True, the presidency has a general task of safeguarding compliance with the constitution, but no specific powers or instruments to implement that task have been put in place except for the veto power of the presidency council. Indeed, when today's press release calls for non-interference in the work of the Iraqi judiciary it all smacks of self-contradiction: Interference is precisely what the presidency council is up to! Nonetheless, the point can probably be made that the Iraqi electoral process long ago strayed from the legalist path, and in today's situation any move that can serve to restore some credibility to the process should be welcome.

At Long Last, Tehran Gets Its Alliance
and the Clock Is Turned Back to 2005 in Iraq[7]
May 4, 2010

Ever since the provincial elections in January 2009, Iran has worked steadfastly to revive the then-defunct United Iraqi Alliance (UIA), the sectarian Shiite alliance that was created back in 2004 and that largely collapsed in 2007. After Ahmad Chalabi played an initial role in bringing the Sadrists and ISCI back together as the Iraqi National Alliance (INA) in the first half of 2009, the final reunification took place Tuesday night in Baghdad when the State of Law list headed by Prime Minister Nuri al-Maliki joined the other Shiites to form a single parliamentary bloc. The successful revival of the de-Baathification agenda was probably the key factor in destroying the promising tendencies of a more nationalist and less sectarian approach by Maliki in 2009.

Few details about the reunion have been published so far (and notably no PM candidate), but it is known that it was held at the house of Ibrahim al-Jaafari. Jaafari came out with the best result in the informal Sadrist "referendum" for the next prime minister that was held in early April.

It is expected that the new alliance (which so far does not appear to have a name or a bloc leader) will claim the right to form a government despite the fact that it was created after the elections and thus in disregard of the electorate (which was not told much about this prospect during the brief campaign). The all-Shiite bloc will likely turn to the Kurds next, but it is noteworthy that it is just four seats or so away from a parliamentary majority of its own so those smaller groups that dare will probably be handsomely rewarded if they opt to join and help the new alliance avoid painful compromises with Arbil. Of course, they also risk being labelled Sunni "stooges" of a sectarian Shiite government.

Under any circumstances, this seems to be a step backwards to Iraq and a return to the unhealthy sectarian climate that dominated much of the period between 2005 and 2007. However much they talk about "unity", the members of the new alliance have little in common except the fact that they are mostly Shiites. It is a far cry from the situation just half a year ago, when Maliki was talking about political majorities and ideologically consistent cabinets.

The Plot Thickens: State of Law Asked for the Cancellation of the Votes of Three Candidates[8]
May 27, 2010

The political dimension to the latest attempt at post-election candidate disqualification in the Iraqi parliamentary election has now been spelled out: In an interview, IHEC commissioner Amal al-Birqadar has made it clear that there is a specific request from Nuri al-Maliki's State of Law (SLA) for the votes of the three candidates, two from Iraqiyya (Najm al-Harbi in addition to Abdallah Hasan Rashid) and one from the mainly Shiite Iraqi National Alliance (INA), to be annulled, on the basis of two legal convictions and membership in the Iraqi armed forces respectively. If those votes are cancelled, preliminary calculations show that SLA could suddenly emerge as the biggest bloc in parliament, indicating the extent to which Maliki may still be seeking to emerge as the biggest winner in the final, certified result. That could make him the obvious candidate to form the next government without any need for a post-election super alliance with his fellow Shiites in INA.

As for the IHEC response, it has emerged that it has proceeded to replace Harbi and Rashid by others from Iraqiyya, whereas the INA candidate, Furat al-Sharaa from Basra, has apparently been successful in presenting evidence that he is no longer a member of the armed forces (the strict legal criterion on this should however relate not to today's situation but to the date of nomination, which was last autumn). Birqadar goes far in suggesting that IHEC considers there will be no annulment of votes (and hence no seat-allocation changes), but she also says the commission will make a decision within days.

Birqadar does not refer to a specific law or regulation but says IHEC's position has been made clear on this in public: If any candidate becomes non-eligible, the next person on the list will follow. This could be something that is buried in an IHEC regulation, but it might also simply refer to article 14 of the 2005 election law which still stands, and which says that "if a member [i.e., deputy] loses his seat for whatever reason, he shall be followed by the next person on the list".

Since this procedure has already been confirmed by IHEC as applicable to the current situation in Nineveh—where a recently-elected MP for Iraqiyya, Bashar al-Agaydi has been murdered—it should mean that it applies generally to the transitional period between the announcement of the uncertified result and the swearing in of the new parliament. As such it should also make all kinds of politically-motivated post-election exclusion attempts redundant (whether on de-Baathification or other grounds), since the seat allocation will remain unaffected regardless.

From the point of view of democratic theory this is a promising stance by IHEC, but it has to be noted that Birqadar is considered the IHEC commissioner that is closest to Iraqiyya, and it will be interesting to see what the others conclude. Faraj al-Haydari, the chief of the commission linked to the KDP, is however also on record as saying that annulled candidates should get their votes transferred to their lists. In general INA is thought to be more influential within IHEC than SLA, but lately SLA has increasingly managed to get what it wants from the Iraqi judiciary. Today there are reports that the court has asked IHEC for certain clarifications pertaining to the certification of the result, and it is also noteworthy that the votes of Ibrahim al-Mutlak—another casualty of post-election de-Baathification—appeared to have been subtracted from the Iraqiyya total when the results of the Baghdad recount were announced on 16 May.

A Certified Mess[9]
June 1, 2010

The Iraqi federal supreme court has today ratified the final result of the 7 March elections—sort of. The caveats relate to two of the 325 candidates that were not approved, Furat al-Sharaa of the Iraqi National Alliance (INA) in Basra, and Umar Abd al-Sattar al-Karbuli, a compensation seat appointee of Iraqiyya. The two men could be disqualified on the basis of membership of the armed forces and legal verdicts respectively, and their cases remain pending.

The main point in the result is that the seat distribution announced in late March remains the same and Nuri al-Maliki's numerous attempts at challenging the result (so that he and not Ayad Allawi would have the most seats) all failed in the end. The following minor discrepancies from the provisional final result released on 26 March can be noted from press reports pending publication of the revised list of seat winners by the Iraqi election commission (IHEC):

- Abdallah al-Jibburi and Najm al-Harbi of Iraqiyya in Diyala were apparently replaced by others from their lists before the result was sent to the court for certification, all with reference to past convictions (or in the case of Harbi, an arrest warrant).

- The 7 compensation seats have been allocated as per earlier reports to two candidates with Turkmen connections in State of Law; to Humam Hammudi (ISCI) and a Sadrist for INA; to Fuad Masum for the Kurds; and to Muhammad Allawi, a relation of Ayad Allawi for Iraqiyya. Iraqiyya has yet to fill the latest compensation seat after Karbuli was disqualified.
- IHEC has said the two latest disqualifications of Sharaa and Karbuli, if implemented, will lead to replacements by their own lists. This is good as far as democratic theory is concerned, but it creates a major inconsistency in the result: 52 of the earlier post-election exclusions reportedly resulted in votes being annulled (though no seats changed, but that was simply due to the low number of personal votes involved), whereas the rest of the more recent post-election disqualifications did not prompt a recalculation of the electoral divider.
- It is noteworthy that the exclusion of Sharaa from INA had been sought by the other major Shiite-led bloc, the State of Law alliance (SLA) with which it is supposedly on its way to a pan-Shiite merger. The fact that Sharaa of INA was in fact disqualified is an interesting testament to persistent friction between INA and SLA.
- In the election law all candidate requirements (de-Baathification, not being a member of the armed forces etc.) are placed on the same footing. Also there is no mention of post-election disqualification leading to annulment of votes. Both these principles have been sinned against in a politicized way during the process of certifying the result.
- In an apparent attempt by the federal supreme court to rectify some of this, Ibrahim al-Mutlak of Iraqiyya—who had been excluded in the revised list of winners that emerged after the Baghdad recount—has now been reinstated and his replacement loses his seat. This looks like a positive move and would go some way towards repairing the damage, even if only a restoration of all the votes of the 52 excluded candidates would create some consistency in the result and put a decisive end to the machinations of the de-Baathification committee (which singlehandedly invented the idea of penalizing entities rather than candidates).

The presidency council is now obliged to call parliament to convene within 15 days.

The Second Shiite Merger Attempt and the Unconstitutional Hakim Game Plan[10]

June 11, 2010

Yesterday's "merger" between the two main Shiite-led lists in Iraq, State of Law (SLA) and the Iraqi National Alliance (INA) was in itself not terribly interesting. After all, exactly the same thing took place some weeks ago, except that it did not quite work out and the parties continued to quarrel about key issues—most importantly the question of who should be the premier candidate of the resultant super-bloc. The only difference this time is that there is a new name: The National Alliance (Al-Tahaluf al-Watani).

More important is probably the small print. In particular, some of the ideas highlighted by ISCI leader Ammar al-Hakim after his meeting with the Grand Ayatollah Ali al-Sistani yesterday are of interest: Hakim said the new alliance was considering the possibility of entering parliament with "more than one premier candidate" and obtain the views of the rest of the parliament in order to decide the candidate of the alliance (probably hoping that the Kurds will find someone from INA less objectionable than Maliki). Some will perhaps think this sounds constructive, but it is in fact deeply unconstitutional. No matter what one thinks of the part of article 76 of the constitution that deals with specifying the biggest bloc (and where there is some real ambiguity), the requirement for "one candidate", in the singular, is 100% unequivocal. If the new Shiite alliance cannot agree on a single candidate then they cannot fulfill the constitutional requirement and hence cannot come into consideration as the biggest bloc, no matter how many deputies they are. A *kutla* (bloc) without a single premier candidate is not a *kutla* in the Iraqi definition of the right to form the government, period.

This latest move follows previous attempts by ISCI to circumvent article 76 altogether. Their reasons for doing so are obvious: With 70 seats—most of which are actually held by Sadrists—INA can never hope to be the biggest bloc alone, and although they have been pressing for the alliance with SLA to get round that problem, they seem to face chronic difficulties with getting rid of Nuri al-Maliki as the premier candidate for the new alliance. Their first strategy was to call for a "roundtable" to discuss the next government, where all the winning blocs would take part. This played well with the international community but it is of course a blatant attempt by a medium-sized bloc to dilute article 76 of the constitution which establishes priority for the biggest bloc. And now there is this second attempt which effectively involves dismantling article 76 even further, since the rest of the parliament is not supposed to have a say in the selection of the premier candidate at all.

Alas, this kind of unconstitutional move to circumvent one of the few majoritarian elements in the Iraqi constitution is likely to meet with an enthusiastic reception in the international community—including the UN agency in Baghdad

(UNAMI) and the Obama administration. During his recent visit to Washington, Ad Melkert of UNAMI in fact specifically encouraged this kind of approach, disregarding procedure and looking at the end goal instead. He even went as far as to openly suggest that agreeing on a political program was secondary to solving the puzzle of who should be in the government! But it is high time Iraqiyya realizes that through this move their "friends" and supposed "partners" in INA intend to deprive both Allawi and Maliki of the premiership and thereby reduce them to partners in a weak and oversized government where every party is invited to colonize a couple of ministries to serve their own narrow interests.

The Damascus Summit:
Crunch Time for the Dialogue between Iraqiyya and INA[11]
July 19, 2010

Today's meeting with Muqtada al-Sadr in Damascus means that for the second time within a week, Ayad Allawi, the leader of the secular Iraqiyya party, has had talks with leaders of the Shiite Islamist Iraqi National Alliance (INA) that are described as "fruitful".

Unfortunately, initial reports from the meeting have been short on details about areas of agreement and with vague talk about "program committees" dominating, but for Allawi the real answer should be utterly simple since there is only one outcome that can satisfy Iraqiyya in its dialogue with INA: That they declare the Shiite super-alliance between INA and State of Law (SLA) null and void, and accept the claim by Iraqiyya that they should form the government as the biggest bloc in parliament. Any other outcome would be worthless: If next Sunday, when another meeting of political leaders has been scheduled, INA is not prepared to sign up for the practical scheme reportedly proposed by Iraqiyya for implementing their preferred vision of an Allawi-led government—i.e., giving a second term as president for Jalal Talabani of the Kurdistan Alliance and the speakership of parliament to Humam Hammudi of ISCI within INA—Iraqiyya would be better off by returning to its negotiations with Nuri al-Maliki and his SLA. INA has been dithering in its attitude to the pan-Shiite alliance for weeks now, and if they cannot declare it dead then Iraqiyya is only deluding itself by continued talks.

Armistice and Governance in the Iraqi Government-Formation Process[12]

August 26, 2010

As the end of the U.S. combat mission in Iraq is drawing to a close on 31 August 2010, there are two basic approaches to the ongoing, stalemated process of government formation in Iraq.

The first approach assumes that Iraq's citizens are more interested in issues like security, health and services than in sectarian bickering and that it is possible to form a government based on common views on basic political issues instead of taking into consideration calculations relate to ethno-sectarian identities. Typically, this kind of government would be a "minimum-winning" one, i.e., just above the 163 mark needed to secure a parliamentary majority (and hence strong enough to pass whatever legislation it wishes to pass) but not much above that (in order to maximize the prospect for developing internal coherence and avoiding the multiplication of sinecures inside government). This kind of government would offer the best chances of maximizing the autonomy of the Iraqi government versus a hostile regional environment. It is also the approach that presents the best fit with the Iraqi constitution; by way of contrast the idea that all winning lists need to be represented or that all ethno-sectarian groups must be included in government has no constitutional basis as such.

The second, opposite approach, is focused on armistice rather than governance. It presupposes that no proper, issue-based government in Iraq is possible due to assumed insurmountable ethnic and religious tensions, and that the aim should therefore be to make sure as many players as possible are "inside the tent" where they would be less likely to create trouble. These ideas do not come from the constitution (where there are no guarantees for ethno-sectarian veto rights after the transitional period comes to an end in 2010); rather they are inspired by Western models of "consociational" democracy and power-sharing and point in the direction of an oversized cabinet with a weak prime minister. It is therefore important to point out that the case of Iraq fits badly with the standard criteria cited by theoreticians of consociational democracy as prerequisites for success—including a relatively low case-load on the political system as a whole; a public willingness to accept backroom politics (or the existence of alternative means of expressing the popular will when government becomes invisible, such as frequent referendums); and not least internal coherence in the sub-communities included in government through a formula of power-sharing. Typically in the Iraqi case it would be vitally important that the Sadrists be represented if this kind of "armistice" approach is followed, since the whole idea is to make a compact between what is believed to be the "main tribes" of the community instead of transcending tribal and ethnic loyalties altogether (as in the governance-focused approach). Needless to say, this kind of government is unlikely to develop any internal coherence and will often experience paralysis. It will, in other words, easily fall prey to the schemes of regional powers.

After some initial confusion as far as Washington's preferences are concerned it is now possible to situate U.S. policy within this dichotomy. Firstly, it seems clear that the idea of building an issue-based, progressive government is not seen as realistic by Washington: Ambassador Chris Hill recently repeated the view that the Kurds "had to be included", simply on an ethno-sectarian basis. Thus the U.S. proposal for Iraqiyya and State of Law to move closer together does not really seem to be based on a vision of them excluding the others; rather the idea seems to be that the two would take the most important positions and give the rest to the others in what would still be an oversized power-sharing formula.

Secondly, Washington has now introduced a specific suggestion for how to solve the tug-of-war between the leaders of the two biggest blocs, Nuri al-Maliki and Ayad Allawi, regarding the premiership. The proposed solution would involve giving one of the two men (i.e., the loser in the premiership contest) compensation in the shape of the presidency for the Iraqi national security council. Conceptually, then, this kind of proposal—described by American officials as a "way of increasing the number of chairs"—seems to be leaning towards the "power-sharing" end of the government-formation typology, since governance in Iraq today would mean reducing the number of chairs, not increasing them. This is especially so because the security council chosen as the key device for solving the problem (let's face it, the idea is to create two premierships and kick the problems further down the road), is conceptually related to other institutional innovations supported primarily by the Kurds in the post-2005 period with the aim of further reducing the prospect of a strong government in Baghdad. There are striking similarities between the membership composition of the national security council defined in 2006 and the oil and gas commission proposed in 2007 (unsurprisingly, the president of the Kurdistan region is supposed to sit on both), and the aim of having consensus decisions in these forums means that they are likely to remain ineffective and weak.

Whatever one may think of this U.S. strategy, the challenges and the uphill struggle it faces seem rather obvious. Firstly, at the procedural level, and judging from leaks from the talks held so far, it seems designed to fit a scenario in which Maliki would continue as premier and Allawi would get the newly revived post as head of the national security council. There are several problems here. In the first place, Allawi does not seem particularly interested, since he is still hoping for the premiership instead. Secondly, if Maliki is to continue as premier he also needs to be the candidate of the biggest bloc in parliament, meaning that unless he allies with Allawi in a bloc (in which case no further partners would be needed and a more governance-focused cabinet could be formed instead of a power-sharing one), a Maliki premiership, as per the apparent U.S. preference, is predicated on the survival of the Shiite alliance of both State of Law and the Iraqi National

Alliance, i.e., Iran's preferred scenario (otherwise Maliki would not have the seats to form the biggest bloc). Again, absent a bilateral deal with Iraqiyya, the sole legal path to a second Maliki premiership is a perpetuation of a Shiite alliance on the pattern of the United Iraqi Alliance in 2006, and even that would likely be disputed by Iraqiyya for being a much too flexible reading of the constitutional article 76 on the entitlement of the biggest bloc to form the government since it involves post-election bloc formation.

In other words, this outcome would be the exact opposite of what Joe Biden and other U.S. leaders have been telling Washington lately about a supposed decline in Iranian influence in Iraq. Not a big surprise, though: Ambassador Chris Hill informed a USIP audience in Washington last week that he expected the next Iraqi premier to be a Shiite—an assertion that completely lacks any basis in the Iraqi constitution and represents exactly the kind of sectarian paradigm of Iraqi politics that Iran prefers. One cannot fail to get the impression that either U.S. policy is grossly contradictive, or there is an unspoken underlying policy of détente with Iran in Iraq, at the expense of the governance of that country and its citizens. Had Washington truly put Iraqi interests first, it would instead have aimed to draw a wedge between the two Shiite-led alliances by having one inside government and the other on the outside, thereby allowing the one in government to develop a more lasting bond with the other main forces in Iraqi politics, without being susceptible to cheap tricks like the de-Baathification revival that so easily brought Iraqi politics to a standstill earlier this year.

Constitutionality—or rather the lack of constitutionality—is the second main issue with the U.S. proposal. The problem, of course, is that the national security council does not even exist in the constitution (although Hill seemed to think so at USIP last week); it was created in 2006 and has been dormant for most of the time since its inception. The pro-Iranian parties have already dismissed the scheme as unconstitutional and rightly so: In short, it would be a major risk for Iraqiyya to accept this kind of position in lieu of the premiership since it would require some instant constitutional fixes to get the whole process going. Rest assured that other ideas would come up, too, if the broader question of constitutional revision were reopened in the midst of the government-formation process.

As far as Iraqi perspectives on the process are concerned, there is unfortunately not much sign of rapprochement between State of Law (SLA) and Iraqiyya towards a governance-focused, two-party government. Some members of State of Law have increasingly began referring to sectarian governing formulas ("a Shiite must be prime minister"), and their talks have lately focused more on the idea of union with the other main Shiite list, the Iraqi National Alliance (INA), than on dialogue with Iraqiyya. Iraqiyya, for its part, is increasingly expressing exasperation in its talks with INA, perhaps realizing that this is probably all a game in which they are being exploited in the internal Shiite tug-of-war between SLA and INA for the premiership. They keep talking about a Sadrist miracle, with or without Syrian help, and of course if the Sadrists or indeed all of INA were truly prepared to give the premiership to Allawi then this would represent a meaningful step towards a restoration of Iraqi distinctiveness in the region and a clarification of the Byzantine Syrian role between Iran and the Arab world—even if the resultant government would look ideologically incoherent, to say the least. Right now, however, it is the scenario of INA and SLA trying to force their way to power via the putative all-Shiite alliance that seems to dominate, with the possibility of a showdown with the Kurds and their maximalist demands further down the road marking the main difference with the situation in 2006 (the Kurdish votes can be dispensed with this time because the two-thirds majority requirement for selecting the president is gone). Iran appears comfortable with this kind of end game, and the United States does not seem to be doing anything to stop it; in fact at times it seems to be pushing in exactly the same direction.

Muqtada al-Sadr Preparing His Supporters for the Dirty Game of Politics[13]
September 29, 2010

In an interesting official statement published by the Sadrists, Muqtada al-Sadr tackles the question of a second Maliki premiership head on. The document simulates the format of a "request for a fatwa" and the questioner asks how a second Maliki premiership can be acceptable given the past highhandedness of the Maliki government against Sadrists in numerous locations across Iraq (Karbala and Nasiriyya are highlighted).

Sadr's reply is interesting: He alludes to the "give and take" of politics and cites his father (as he always does in these quasi-fatwas) to the effect that politics is a heartless game. He then goes on to order his followers to support whatever position is taken by the Sadrist politburo!

This could, in other words, be another indication that the Sadrists are preparing to switch allegiance to Maliki, this time probably with Iranian support in order to achieve their basic aim of having a (mostly) unified Shiite front in the shape of the National Alliance (NA) that would combine the two Shiite alliances. It is interesting that the normally pro-Iranian Islamic Supreme Council of Iraq (ISCI)—which in early September nominated their own Adil Abd al-Mahdi to face off against Maliki in the internal NA contest—have lately gone quite far out on a limb in an attempt at challenging Maliki. The interesting question now is how big the INA defection from the NA will be if Maliki after all emerges as their premier candidate.

Maliki Nominated as the National Alliance Premier Candidate[14]
October 3, 2010

Gradually the dust is beginning to settle after Friday's somewhat abrupt nomination by the all-Shiite, theoretically 159-man National Alliance (NA) of Nuri al-Maliki as premier candidate for the next government. For months there had been discussion of consensus procedures, with intricate formulas involving 80% and then 65% agreement in a committee of so-called "wise men". In the end, Maliki was simply adopted by acclamation by the parties that were present at the final meeting—basically the three Daawa factions (including Jaafari), the Sadrists, the Iraqi National Congress (Ahmad Chalabi), and Hadi al-Amiri of the Badr brigades. The only NA factions that had no representatives present were the Islamic Supreme Council of Iraq (ISCI) and Fadila.

The exact position of ISCI/Badr (19 seats) remains unclear: ISCI is still publicly negative to Maliki, but some in Badr are showing a willingness to preserve the NA at any cost. Similar tendencies apply to Fadila (6 seats), which however today announced that it remains part of NA. The Kurds are obviously signaling great interest in developments: Due to the unexpected defections from NA they are now needed to form the government and thus finally achieve the kingmaker position they have been seeking from the start but which was always going to be secondary to the triangular struggle between the two Shiite blocs and Iraqiyya. Positive noises have also come from some in Tawafuq, whereas Unity of Iraq—which was once closer to Maliki—recently said they preferred his defeated rival, Adil Abd al-Mahdi of ISCI.

Most interesting, of course, is the reaction of Iraqiyya, which lately has promised to never take part in a government led by Nuri al-Maliki. At least one element of their response strategy is positive: It consists of building a parliamentary alternative to State of Law by reaching out to ISCI, Fadila, Unity of Iraq and possibly Tawafuq. Few other things than hatred of Maliki bring these groups together, but this kind of alliance would at least signify some kind of Iraqi reaction against developments where Iranian pressure on the Sadrists to accept Maliki as their new PM favorite seems to have been a key factor—and in the case of ISCI would also mean some kind of definitive Iraqization after a long period of close coordination with Iran. Together, these parties might be able to convince the Kurds that there could be advantages in keeping Iran at an arm's length in the coming period, although the Kurds are probably equally interested in concessions related to more local demands concerning Kirkuk and oil.

Let the Kurdish Drama Begin![15]
October 6, 2010

It is a strange sight: The two would-be saviors of the Iraqi nation, Ayad Allawi and Nuri al-Maliki, trying to outbid each other in an attempt at satisfying the author of one of the most separatist agendas for Iraq's political future, the Kurdish leader Masud Barzani. All because Allawi and Maliki cannot trust or even talk to each other.

But that is where we finally are, some seven months on from the 7 March elections. The nomination dynamics within the recently-reconstituted all-Shiite National Alliance (NA) played out in way that suited the Kurds more perfectly than they could have ever dreamt of: The size of the internal protest against Maliki—in the range of 10-20 NA deputies—was just big enough to make him totally reliant on the Kurds, instead of having the theoretical alternative of building ties to smaller parties like Tawafuq, Unity of Iraq and the independent minority representatives. It was also big enough to keep the scenario of an alternative Allawi-led government afloat, at least in a theoretical sense, thus finally turning the Kurds into real kingmakers.

Maysun al-Damluji of Iraqiyya yesterday said "Iraqiyya looks positively on the Kurdish list of demands". As for Maliki's approach, Muhammad Khalil of the Kurdish alliance said his initial response consisted of "positive signs". Let's not forget what the Kurdish list of demands is: It consists of 19 points aimed at deepening the emasculation of Baghdad that was begun with the constitution adopted in 2005. According to the Kurdish perspective, the constitution did not go quite far enough, so they included additional points about decentralizing the oil sector, settling territorial disputes within a new timeline and prolonging presidential veto powers based on ethno-sectarian formulas of power-sharing. Additionally, there are some striking new demands, including the idea that "the government is considered resigned if the Kurds consider it to be in violation of the constitution and withdraw from it".

The question is whether Maliki can satisfy the Kurds, who felt short-changed during the previous government, and this time are demanding firmer guarantees. He will probably have problems given the considerable but often under-estimated opposition to Kurdish demands from within his own ranks, where there are those who think of both oil and Kirkuk in centralistic terms and are generally quite critical of the Kurds. The recently-announced government decision to postpone the planned census a couple of months—against the wishes of the Kurds—is another indication of the limited room for maneuver available for Maliki. But the point is that neither Maliki nor Allawi seems able to do anything else at the moment—and the Iraqi electorate seems incapable of articulating the level of disgust that this ironic twist of events so clearly warrants. So maybe we should all lean back and watch the Kurdish drama unfold for some time?

Three Competing Paths to the Next Iraqi Government[16]
October 13, 2010

Today, there are apparently three races going on in the struggle to form the next Iraqi government.

Firstly, there is the Maliki project. This is based on his recent success—apparently with a little help from Iran and the Sadrists—in strong-arming parts of the Iraqi National Alliance (INA) to accepting him as the premier candidate for an all-Shiite National Alliance (NA) that also has the backing of Maliki's own list State of Law (SLA). Quantifying the exact level of support for Maliki among non-Sadrist INA deputies is an inexact science, but it is thought that he has got at least the 89 SLA deputies, the 40 Sadrists, plus Ibrahim al-Jaafari and Ahmad Chalabi on his side—which would bring the total number to a minimum of 131. On top of this, Maliki is obvious angling for the support of the Kurdish parties (58), which would easily bring him above the magical 163 mark required to have a majority in parliament. Additionally, it seems clear that Maliki is also hoping to lure a new coalition between Unity of Iraq and Tawafuq into his alliance (10 deputies altogether with vague promises of more), in order to serve a symbolic "Sunni representation". Importantly, even though Maliki is clearly trying to satisfy the Kurds when it comes to their long list of demands for supporting a government, he is not particularly positive to the idea of making constitutional changes (such as limiting the powers of the premier) as a basis for government formation. Still, it is noteworthy that the project involves two "regional" kingmakers: The Sadrists with Iranian support, and the Kurds and perhaps especially Jalal Talabani, again with an apparent nod from Iran. It is being talked about as a "political-majority" government, but it is a far cry from the issue-based alliance Maliki was discussing back in 2009. Instead it is based on an ethno-sectarian alliance full of ideological contradictions and reliant on Iranian support.

Second there is the Allawi project. This appears to consist of a competing path to hit the 163 mark: First building a coalition between Iraqiyya and as many INA breakaway elements from the NA as possible plus Tawafuq and Unity of Iraq; then convincing the Kurds that this kind of coalition would be favorable compared to a deal with Maliki. Again there is the problem of estimating exactly how many NA deputies can be trusted to join: ISCI including Badr plus "Hizbollah in Iraq" account for around 20 deputies, Fadila have six, and one Shaykhi deputy from Basra is reportedly leaning in this direction too. That would add up to around 27 on top of the 91 Iraqiyya deputies, thus 118 and still some way to go to catch up with Maliki—and there is the added insecurity about what the Badr representatives (and "Hizbollah in Iraq") would ultimately do if it came to a vote. All of the ISCI-affiliated parties were traditionally close to Iran, and whilst the current level of protest against what appears to be increasing Iranian support for Maliki is unprecedented, many commentators still believe that ultimately some of these elements will fall back into the NA fold. The latest twist relating to this project is the apparent willingness of Ayad Allawi to let Adil Abd al-Mahdi of INA/ISCI be the premier candidate in a move that could perhaps make this kind of alternative more attractive to the Kurds, and might also serve to compensate for the inability of Iraqiyya to meet Kurdish demands on oil and Kirkuk (which would bring them into trouble with their own electorate).

It is important to note that both these projects are competitive. Each of them pays lip service to the idea of all winning blocs eventually joining, but it seems likely that in reality the Maliki alternative will marginalize Iraqiyya and the Allawi alternative will marginalize State of Law: The "invitation" to their main opponent to join is mostly tongue in cheek. By way of contrast, the Americans still seem to be hoping that all the original four big winning blocs—Iraqiyya, SLA, INA and the Kurds—will somehow eventually get together in a single coalition to form the next government, preferably without the Sadrists in a too-dominant role. In this third approach to government formation, the Americans are actually raising the threshold in more than one way. Firstly, a four-way agreement is logically speaking more difficult to achieve than a three-way one. Secondly, and this has perhaps not received the attention it deserves, almost all American proposals on the subject of government formation seem to involve simultaneous measures of constitutional reform, since redefining the powers of the presidency—scheduled to become symbolic only with the end of the transitional period in 2010—now appears to be an aim after the initial failure to resuscitate the dormant Iraqi national security council as a way of appeasing Iraqiyya.

Constitutional reform, in turn, can be achieved in one of two ways in Iraq: Either under the transitional article 142 of the constitution, according to which a single batch of changes can be approved by an absolute majority of parliament (163) but then would need popular approval in a popular referendum where a two-thirds majority against the changes in any three governorates can torpedo the whole project. Alternatively the changes can be passed with a two-thirds majority in parliament (216), to be confirmed in a general referendum, this time with no special-majority requirements. The more general point is this: Any government-formation involving constitutional reform is risky and potentially time-consuming business. If the route to constitutional reform under article 142 is chosen one needs to remember that the Iraqis have been working on this package of reforms since 2007 without being able to agree on it. The other alternative, however, involves a special majority in parliament of 216. The question then is, even if Washington should succeed in pushing for a move that would strengthen the presidency to such an extent that it becomes attractive to Iraqiyya, is it not likely that Iran would seek to introduce counter-measures if it felt threatened? It would then need only 109 deputies on its side to derail the whole project and everything would be back to square one. Have we already forgotten what happened in Iraq in February and March this year, when almost the entire Iraqi system succumbed to the pressures from Iran and Ali al-Lami, the great de-Baathification leader? And then of course, there would be the long wait for confirmation in a referendum and the concomitant risk involved for the party that is banking on an empowered presidency: What if the referendum disapproves of the changes and the presidency remains in its current form, with symbolic powers only? Clearly, it would be unconstitutional and therefore quite impossible to "upgrade" the presidency before any such a move had been approved by the population in a general referendum.

The bottom line is that any government-formation process involving constitutional reform (i.e., the "broadly inclusive" policy of the Obama administration) is likely to take many months, with no realistic prospect for a referendum on the required changes until some time in 2011, at best. For this reason alone, the more straightforward but competitive attempts at acquiring absolute majorities of 163 in parliament seem more realistic in terms of timely government formation in Iraq.

Nujayfi, Talabani and Maliki—Plus Lots of Hot Air[17]
November 11, 2010

In a repeat of the procedure used in April 2006, the Iraqi parliament today met and elected not only its speaker (Usama al-Nujayfi of Iraqiyya) but also the president (Jalal Tabalani of the Kurdish alliance). Talabani went on to nominate Nuri al-Maliki as premier candidate of "the biggest bloc in parliament"—the National Alliance, consisting mainly of Maliki's own State of Law alliance (89 deputies) and the Sadrists (40 deputies). It is noteworthy that constitutionally speaking, parliament could have delayed the president's election until one month after the speaker had been elected and then the president in theory would have had 15 days to nominate the candidate for premier. For some ten minutes of the session, this appeared to be a real possibility as Iraqiyya deputies objected to persevering with the election before parliament had discussed the political deal by bloc leaders that brought about today's meeting, including the question of the de-Baathification status of some of its leaders. However, instead of using his newfound authority to throw the session into disarray, Nujayfi continued to chair the session for a while even as many of his fellow Iraqiyya deputies stormed out. Eventually Nujayfi himself temporarily withdrew, enabling his newly elected deputies, Qusay al-Suhayl (a Sadrist from Basra) and Arif Tayfur (of the Kurdish alliance and a deputy speaker also in the previous parliament) to go along with the vote on the president. Nujayfi returned to chair the final part of the session, and embraced Talabani as he entered the stage to make his acceptance speech.

Many will try to claim credit for the apparent "breakthrough" after more than 8 months of stalemate. For example, ISCI leader Ammar al-Hakim has suggested that the recent flurry of talks reflected his own desire for a "roundtable". The president of the Kurdistan Regional Government, Masud Barzani, has tried to acquire ownership of the process by referring to it as his own initiative and demanding that the last round of meetings be held partly in Arbil, the Kurdish capital, and partly in Barzani's private house in Baghdad. However, the truly significant developments took place on 1 October, when the Sadrists and State of Law with Iranian support agreed to nominate Nuri al-Maliki as candidate for premier, and on 24 October, when the federal supreme court went ahead with a decision to bring an end to the open session of the parliament. That decision seemed pegged to Maliki's calendar and the loud protests from Iraqiyya and others signified suspicion about political pressure on the court. The 24 October decision, in turn, put pressure on the Kurds to make up their mind, and the "Barzani initiative" ended up as an attempt to maximize Kurdish gains within the parameters of a future Maliki government. For the past weeks, Maliki's nomination as such has not appeared to be under realistic threat.

It may be useful to recap what the main players actually managed to achieve today. Iraqiyya has moved the furthest away from its original position of demanding the premiership and is making a big gamble. Indeed, it is unclear whether it will stay in the political process at all. True, it has ostensibly secured the powerful speakership of parliament, which is a more valuable asset than many seem to appreciate. But other than that, it has based its participation on the presidency of an institution that is not even in the constitution, and whose powers are ill-defined today: the so-called national council for strategic policies. That will supposedly go to Ayad Allawi, and parliament is supposed to adopt the relevant legislation later on. But the position does not enjoy any constitutional protection, and until the council is up and running with truly effective powers, it could potentially end up as the fraud of the century, with Allawi as a minister without a real portfolio.

Reportedly, Iraqiyya will also be shut out from all the security ministries, which makes it even more important to them that what is currently merely a fantasy institution will actually come into existence in the real world. Its voters may certainly want to reflect on how much better they could have come out in a bilateral deal with Maliki, and Iraqiyya leaders are already facing threats from the more militant elements of its electorate. Still, Iraqiyya has not formally withdrawn from the process. It is noteworthy in this context that Nujayfi, an Iraqi nationalist with a Sunni Arab background from Mosul who has faced frequent accusations about Baathist sympathies, eventually did return to the session to fulfill his duties as newly elected speaker and install a Kurdish president of Iraq. Nujayfi had managed to obtain 227 votes in the assembly for the speakership, in other words more than Talabani's 195 for the presidency. At the same time, he did not shy away from talking frankly about problems in the previous government and the need for constitutional reform during his acceptance speech.

The media will make a big point out of the fact that the Kurds got the presidency, but many will fail to notice that, firstly, in the moment Jalal Talabani was elected he lost the veto power he had as a member of the transitional presidency council (which expired in that second), and, secondly, that he also lost almost every other power when he some ten minutes later designated Nuri al-Maliki as the nominee for premier. Absent a failure on Maliki's part to put together a new government (in which case Talabani can designate whomever he pleases as a second candidate), Talabani henceforth will enjoy symbolic and ceremonial power only.

The big winner is of course Maliki, but it may be useful to see what the rest of the Shiite Islamist camp got from the deal. Relatively little attention has been accorded to the fact that the Sadrists look set to take over a number of governor positions (Maysan and Babel or Diwaniyya) in exchange for their participation. So much for decentralization in Iraq! There are also reports that Hadi al-Amiri is seeking to reconnect with the all-Shiite National Alliance to bring the Badr organization back into the fold, but right now the other INA defectors who rebelled against Maliki, especially ISCI, are looking a little lonely even though they say they intend to participate.

As for the regional and international players involved in this, the outcome is a mixed one. In one way, the United States managed to secure its goal of having all the players "inside the tent", if only just. But there are some major problems too. Recently, the Obama administration spent an awful lot of energy trying to convince the Kurds to give up the presidency to Iraqiyya. This in itself signaled diplomatic incompetence since the presidency is more or less worthless in its current shape and cannot be upgraded to something more powerful except through constitutional change with a special majority in parliament and a subsequent popular referendum. Additionally, the failure of Washington to sway the Kurds, even after direct phone calls from President Barack Obama, did not play well in the region in terms of prestige. If the U.S. president was unable to get what he wanted, he should have avoided such a humiliating sequence of events. Still, the most important problem lies in the fact that the United States has staked its policy on some kind of informal premiership for Ayad Allawi, with Vice-President Joe Biden's national security advisor Tony Blinken even going as far as trying to portray today's deal as an alliance of the Kurds and Iraqiyya *against* Maliki! That narrative rather distorts the fact on the ground as of today, where Maliki remains premier and commander in chief of the armed forces with his constitutional prerogatives in good order— and the support of the Sadrists, the Kurds and Iran.

CHAPTER NOTES

1   The original version of this text can be found at http://historiae.org/uncertified.
asp.

2   See http://gulfanalysis.wordpress.com/2010/03/29/the-sadrist-watershed-confirmed/.

3   See http://gulfanalysis.wordpress.com/2010/04/06/not-another-governing-council-please/.

4   See http://gulfanalysis.wordpress.com/2010/04/09/the-intra-list-power-balance-in-iraqiyya-and-state-of-law/.

5   See http://gulfanalysis.wordpress.com/2010/04/29/maliki-vs-lami-maliki-lami-vs-allawi/.

6   See http://gulfanalysis.wordpress.com/2010/05/04/the-presidency-council-intervenes-in-the-de-baathification-debate/.

7   See http://gulfanalysis.wordpress.com/2010/05/04/at-long-last-tehran-gets-its-alliance-and-the-clock-is-turned-back-to-2005-in-iraq/.

8   See http://gulfanalysis.wordpress.com/2010/05/27/the-plot-thickens-state-of-law-asked-for-the-cancellation-of-the-votes-of-three-candidates/.

9   See http://gulfanalysis.wordpress.com/2010/06/01/a-certified-mess/.

10 See http://gulfanalysis.wordpress.com/2010/06/11/the-second-shiite-merger-attempt-and-the-unconstitutional-hakim-game-plan/.

11 See http://gulfanalysis.wordpress.com/2010/07/19/crunch-time-for-the-dialogue-between-iraqiyya-and-ina/.

12 See http://historiae.org/governance.asp.

13 See http://gulfanalysis.wordpress.com/2010/09/29/muqtada-al-sadr-preparing-his-supporters-for-the-dirty-game-of-politics/.

14 See http://gulfanalysis.wordpress.com/2010/10/03/first-reactions-to-the-maliki-nomination/.

15 See http://gulfanalysis.wordpress.com/2010/10/06/let-the-kurdish-drama-begin/.

16 See http://gulfanalysis.wordpress.com/2010/10/13/three-competing-paths-to-the-next-iraqi-government/.

17 See http://gulfanalysis.wordpress.com/2010/11/11/nujayfi-talabani-and-maliki-plus-lots-of-hot-air/.

PART II

Selected Themes in Iraqi Politics

Chapter 8

Federalism in Iraq: Power-sharing, Oil, and Disputed Territories

The Latin term immaturus *(unripe) is most commonly used in botany, but it has also been employed in the university system of several countries to denote a failed academic exam. It may be the most suitable term there is for the system of federalism that was introduced in Iraq after 2003.*

One of the basic points in the texts in this chapter is that interest in the concept of federalism in Iraq south of Kurdistan is limited—and to the extent that it does exist it is mostly limited geographically to Basra and the far south. Even there, it is a relatively marginal phenomenon though it refuses to go away entirely (which is pretty much in line with what analogies to the 1920s would suggest.) After 2003, Basra was the first area south of Kurdistan to launch a bid for a separate region. In January 2009, that attempt failed miserably, but the general regionalist sentiment in the area was seen as sufficiently strong that in May 2009 Prime Minister Nuri al-Maliki—supposedly the great centralizer—acceded to the longstanding demand by local politicians that Baghdad grant a per-barrel fee to Basra for the oil exported from the governorate.

Other texts in this chapter deal with the federal system in Iraq in a more theoretical way and with the considerable contradictions within the constitution adopted in 2005 and the subsequent legislation on the implementation of federalism. One particularly fascinating subject has been the essentially boundless character of the Iraqi federal system, since the theoretical modalities for region-forming allow for countless scenarios of new federal regions (which need not even be territorially contiguous). Experts in the study of statistical permutations and combinations have stood aghast as they surveyed the range of potential options! Another intriguing theme has been that of the ongoing attempts at sorting out a basic contradiction in the constitution whereby, in one article, federal regions and governorates nor organized into a region have exactly the same residual powers (in all matters not explicitly allocated to the central government), whereas elsewhere in the charter extra powers for the federal regions—but not the governorates—are specifically listed, which of course should not be necessary if those powers were already held by the regions under the residuary clause of the constitution (article 115). In early

2007, this problem was seen in the draft oil law, in which oil-producing federal regions were given a more advantageous status than mere governorates. In 2008, yet another kind of contradiction was introduced in the law on the powers of the governorates, which granted local councils the right to sack some but not all government officials appointed by Baghdad (for example, judiciary, military and higher education officials were exempted from local control without reference to any constitutional provision). Rulings by the federal supreme court on these matters were inconsistent, ranging from radical support for the rights of the governorates in 2007 to a somewhat more centralistic position from 2008 onwards. In theory, though, one might still argue that the 2005 constitution turned Iraq into a federation of 16 states in everything but the name (Kurdistan plus 15 governorates).

The U.S. discussion about Iraqi federalism, too, has been rather immature. I am not talking here about "soft partition," which has a pathology of its own and is covered in greater detail in chapter 10. But even among government analysts in Washington, especially in 2006, there seemed to be an expectation that at some point a "Sunni interest in federalism" would miraculously awaken and thereby ensure "national reconciliation." As late as in 2009, I heard a person who had been a high-ranking U.S. advisor during the CPA era (2003–2004) complain that it "took so long for the Sunnis to realize their interests" in a federal system. The big problem, of course, was that the whole American desire for "Sunni federalism" was premised on the erroneous assumption that the Shiites were particularly pro-federal in the first place.

I can, however, vouch for a general absence of a British interest in federalism projects in southern Iraq. I had several meetings in London with members of the Foreign and Commonwealth Office in summer 2007: We discussed, among other things, the prospect of regionalism developing as a force in the Basra area, where the British forces were concentrated. In one of those discussions I rather carelessly referred to the crucial date of April 11, 2008, without explaining that this was the expiration date, as defined in the October 2006 law on region formation, of the moratorium on the forming of new federal regions. I thought the significance of the date needed no explanation, since I assumed everyone was up to date on the nitty-gritty of forming regions and aware that there was a real (if slight) possibility that Basra might emulate the example of Kurdistan come April 2008. However, after the meeting, one senior official quietly asked if I could explain what that key date of April 11, 2008, was all about, leading me to conclude that all the talk in the Arabic press about a British plot to dismember Iraq through the creation of new federal regions such as Basra was probably a little exaggerated.

Intimately linked to the question of federalism in Iraq are two other main issues that highlight the links between radical decentralization and opportunism in the pre-2003 era: oil and the status of Kirkuk. As far as oil is concerned, Western misperceptions of Iraqi realities are once more rife. Take the cliché that all the oil in Iraq is located "in the Shiite and the Kurdish areas." A recurrent point in my writ-

ings was the fact that most of the oil is actually located in Basra, period. In other words, many Shiite areas are just as deprived as the Sunni areas, whereas even the most optimistic estimates for the Kurdistan region are dwarfed by the figures of the Basra reserves, something that in turn highlights the relative significance of the limited pro-federal sentiment that seems to survive there. But again, it is important to stress that even among Basrawis, this profederal feeling is far from universal. At a conference on Iraq held in Como, Italy, in November 2006, I presented a detailed critique of the Iraqi federalism law only to learn afterward that one of the other participants, Safa al-Din al-Safi, a minister in the Maliki government, considered himself its author. We had a long discussion about the law, and it was interesting to hear how frequently Safi, who is himself from Basra, came back to the point that "the central state must be very, very strong." Federalism, in his words, was more like a "passport," an option that could be used, but whose use was by no means mandatory.

Oil is also the only aspect of Iraqi politics in which my home country, Norway, has been directly involved. Since 2004 a small private company, DNO, has been operating in Kurdistan under a controversial deal which has never been submitted to Baghdad for approval (on which more follows in chapter 10). Additionally, in recent years the only true Norwegian "big oil" company, Statoil, has been considering numerous options in southern and central Iraq, leading finally to a technical service contract in a Lukoil-led consortium for the West Qurna field north of Basra in late 2009. I consistently criticized both companies for their Iraq overtures in private meetings and in op-eds in the Norwegian press but with limited success. Only a planned deal between Statoil and the Kurdistan authorities in 2007 may have been influenced to some limited extent by the debate in the Norwegian media before it was finally aborted. Concerning DNO, my argument was that the deal it had concluded with Kurdistan authorities back in 2004 created evident complications in the ongoing attempts to revise the constitution and agree an oil law for Iraq. (The idea of Kurdish autonomy in the oil sector is, in fact, so novel that the Kurdish parties' own draft constitution for Iraq in 2003 had still defined oil affairs as the exclusive prerogative of the central government.) As for Statoil, after its initial Kurdistan adventures, it opted to support the Maliki government at a time when Maliki had yet to clarify his government's position on the key issues of national reconciliation. In that sense, it was equally problematic. On balance, though, the technical service contracts entered into by Statoil seem comparably favorable to Iraq, with a relatively low remuneration for the foreign companies involved. Conversely, the way DNO shareholders encouraged others to buy DNO shares for their grandchildren seemed indicative of a rather different profit-sharing model being involved in the Kurdistan contracts, with huge profits expected to leave Iraq altogether.

Finally when it comes to Kirkuk, to an historian, the way this issue has been discussed in the West has been emblematic of the degree to which ignorance has prevailed and thereby allowed opportunism to reign in the realities of post-2003 Iraq.

Before the 1960s, few had heard about Kurdish claims to the city of Kirkuk, where the largest segment of the population for centuries had been Turkmens with a close connection to Baghdad as the center of Ottoman administration. Nonetheless, the Kurdish claims to the city—actually based on post-1960 immigration, but construed as some kind of "Jerusalem" with reference to shadowy accounts of the situation before the Saljuqs came in the 11th century—are readily taken at face value in the West today, even among academics who claim to know the region. The inclusion of an article in the constitution in 2005 to the effect that the status of the city should be decided by referendum underlines the extent to which that constitution provided a recipe for dismembering the country despite its historical legacies. I have not seen many promising proposals for how to deal with the Kirkuk question. One proposal, suggested by the International Crisis Group, would create a stand-alone federal entity of Kirkuk and give the Kurds the right to administer their own oil sector, thereby effectively carving up Iraq even further and reducing Baghdad's power even more. Probably the best idea I have come across involved giving the Kurds, in return for rescinding their claims to Kirkuk, a bigger share of oil money redistributed via Baghdad than they would have deserved under a strict demographic formula; this would keep the centralized structure of the Iraqi state intact south of Kurdistan while giving the Kurds an incentive for staying in Iraq. Another good option has been described by a colleague of mine, Liam Anderson, and involves rewarding the Kurds with international recognition of their special autonomy within Iraq in return for moderation in disputed issues—on the pattern of the Åland Islands whose governance was settled in this way between Finland and Sweden after the First World War.

Basra and the Threat of Disintegration[1]
October 12, 2005

When the modern state of Iraq had just been formally established in the 1920s, a group of notables in Basra made a bid to establish the Gulf city as a separate merchant republic. They envisaged a pro-British enclave that could become an emporium for the entire Gulf region. Their second-best option was federation with Baghdad. In the end, all failed and Iraqi nationalism triumphed, sealing the fate of the Gulf city for the rest of the century.

After 2003, localist movements have once more emerged in Basra. Much of the political thinking bears a striking resemblance to that of the Basra notables in the 1920s, but the goals are different. Today, the threat to Iraq's territorial integrity comes from elsewhere.

The maxim of the early Basra separatists was that their area should not suffer by becoming embroiled in unpredictable Baghdad politics. To them commerce was more important than politics, and they feared that distant demagogues would exploit their wealth for grandiose nationalist projects. Substitute "oil" for trade, add the suffering of the south during the wars with Iran and Kuwait, and a clear picture emerges of bleak prophecies that have come true.

What would those separatists have made of the new Iraqi constitution? No doubt, they would have preferred it to the British-sponsored unitary state model of the 1920s. Its provisions for regional control of oil and security would have pleased them. Its protection of regional rights from constitutional amendment would have allayed their fears of a dominant Baghdad.

But freedom from Baghdad was not the separatists' sole concern. They also cherished stability. And so they would have wondered: Isn't the decentralization almost overdone? With so many regional checks on the federal government, there is the unavoidable impression of the center of politics in Iraq having been all but evacuated.

Then more caveats would have emerged. Just how are new federal entities to be established? By combining governorates into regions—but without any ceilings on the number of provinces, and without unequivocal mechanisms for holding referendums. And those Basra notables (a multi-sect coalition not particularly concerned with religious issues) would have started asking tough questions. Who is to be amalgamated with whom? Will Basra join with its immediate neighbors or get swallowed up into a larger Shiite principality? Calling a referendum requires only the support of a tenth of the electorate in the "affected" provinces, so the prospect of competing federal schemes is very real. Najaf may want to unite with Basra, but Basra may have other preferences.

This is where the old Basra separatists meet with today's situation. For the past two years, local movements in Basra have been working on a scheme for a federal "region of the south". This is a non-sectarian project, involving only the three southernmost Iraqi provinces and professing overall commitment to the idea of a unified Iraq. Many envision it as a resurrection of Basra's Gulf identity, with the United Arab Emirates as a model. This regionalism does not operate in tandem with the rest of Shiite-dominated Iraq. In Basra, even some of the Shiite Islamists complain over being sidelined in the national Shiite parties, and many are skeptical to a single Shiite canton as marketed by politicians from areas further north. Outside sponsorship, whether Western or Iranian, is not a priority either.

The new constitution is a challenge to the Basra regionalists. Two specific problems stand out: The lack of size limits for new federal entities and, ironically, the heavy bias toward securing regional rights—so intense that the overall stability of the new political system is threatened. Non-sectarian regionalist projects may face hard challenges from large-scale sectarian competitors, and the multicultural hub of Baghdad may become divested of real power. The constitution may lead to unbridgeable fissures in the Iraqi polity along sectarian fault lines, instead of controlled small-scale devolution.

After much soul-searching, the Basra separatists of the 1920s might well have voted Yes to the new Iraqi constitution. Their goal, after all, was an orderly, if not overly intimate, relationship with Baghdad, and they would have preferred dialogue to armed hostilities. But they would have stayed alert in the case of a Yes victory. To prevent their patria from once more becoming reduced to the play-ground of outside forces they would have jealously guarded the post-referendum proceedings for creating new regions. In negotiations over the blank spaces in the constitution they would have appealed to other Iraqis with similar views of stability as being more important than ideology. In that spirit, they would have worked to create a new Iraq based on a middle course: between the excessive centralism of the old regime and the boundless sectarian fragmentation latent in today's proposed constitution.

Building Federal Subunits by Way of Referendums: Special Challenges for Iraq[2]
June 9, 2006

There are indications that many international experts involved in UN work with Iraq consider Spain as an ideal model for Iraq. The UN Office for Constitutional Support as early as in June 2005 gave the Spanish constitution the place of honor on its website. In subsequent dialogues with the Iraqi constitutional committee, international experts hired in as consultants repeatedly emphasised the advantages of a constitutional system in which different regions could achieve federal status with different tempi—precisely one of the principal distinguishing characteristics of the Spanish charter adopted in the post-Franco era. Today, there are some conspicuous parallels between article 119 of the Iraqi constitution, on the forma-tion of federal regions, and article 143 of the Spanish constitution. Both stress the importance of local initiatives in the demarcation of the building blocks in a future federal system. Whereas a more traditional practice for federalizing states is to merely convert existing administrative units into federal entities, these innovative constitutional mechanisms have been designed to unlock administrative legacies of the past and to open for fresh configurations: in the case of Spain, it allowed the country's provinces to combine in new ways to form new regions (known as "autonomous communities"); in Iraq, the idea is that existing governorates can amalgamate into new entities in accordance with their own wishes.

By choosing this interesting and ultra-democratic path to a federal state model, Iraq has also exposed itself to special challenges and risks. In fact, in comparative perspective, it is highly unusual for federations to let their inhabitants have a say in the delineation of the subunits in the federal system. The majority of federations in the world are instead of an "evolutionary" type, which have materialized as unions of pre-existing political units (for instance Switzerland), or on the basis of imperial remnants from earlier ages (including such widely differing cases as Russia and Micronesia). A second group of federations are those that have been deliberately "designed", often after a period of political upheaval and regime breakdown. Examples of this include post-war Germany, South Africa after apartheid and Ethiopia in the democratic era. Here too, the popular input to the process has been highly limited; most often "experts" or elite politicians have drawn up the maps, with the role of the public at large often reduced to voting Yes or No to a complete constitutional package.

There are hybrids of these categories as well. Many Latin American federations, for instance, started on the basis of imperial remnants but witnessed shake-ups in their federal maps after periods of internal political upheaval (Venezuela) or because of special security arrangements implemented during times of war (Argentina, Brazil). There are also some "evolutionary" and "designed" federations that have incorporated certain more democratic features with regard to future administrative changes—as seen for instance in Brazil, Germany and Ethiopia. But in practice, the administrative changes that have been effected in accordance with these constitutional devices have been quite minimal. And finally, there is the interesting case of Russia, which since 2005 has embarked on a process of rationalizing its convoluted federal system, partly through special legislation, and theoretically with a considerable element of local initiative. But early reports suggest that in practice the democratic spirit of this process has been considerably tempered by the central government's tight control of local governors—with whom the initiative for federal mergers technically rests.

Even the Spanish parallel, on which international experts apparently pin their hopes as a model for Iraq, may not be as instructive as many think. Whereas theoretically, the Spanish people were to have a decisive influence in structuring their new federal world after the authoritarian rule of General Franco, there were important limits to the supposedly unshackled articulation of the popular will when the new federal system was established between 1978 and 1983. On paper, it all looked beautiful: a genuine grass-roots process, starting with the municipalities. But in fact, many features of the new federal Spain were rather abruptly agreed on by an elite of politicians in the spring and summer of 1981, after political crises had threatened to reverse the democratization of the country. And more importantly, in the end, the process was to a considerable extent influenced if not dictated by administrative divisions of the past. Surely, Spanish politicians quibble over some of the new subdivisions that have emerged after 1978 (and the "genuineness" of their historical roots), but there is no escaping the fact that a comparison of the "new Spain" with administrative maps of earlier times reveals some striking similarities and shows that the basic features of today's federal map, if not all the details, are older than is often thought—a majority of today's regions were in fact candidates for regional autonomy also in the 1930s, before the Spanish Civil War.

In other words, in delineating its federal structure, Spain was aided by history to a larger extent than the voluntarist and blank-slate spirit of its much-lauded constitutional clauses on regionalism would seem to suggest. Even some of the Spanish regions commonly dismissed as "artificial" have in fact quite substantial historical roots—as can be seen for instance in the case of Cantabria.

These two aspects of the Spanish experience—the impact of a modicum of elite consensus, and the considerable role played by historical legacies in shaping the current federal system—are of crucial significance to the current Iraqi debate. Achieving elite cooperation has been a problem in Iraq, so can the Iraqis at least expect to find a helping hand in history? The answer to this must be No. Iraq does not share Spain's degree of correspondence between past administrative structures and contemporary regionalist ambitions. True, for much of the twentieth century, there was in Iraq a relatively fixed system of 18 administrative provincial units (called *liwas* and later *muhafazat*, or "governorates"), but the idea of simply transforming those units into federal states has repeatedly been dismissed by the Iraqis themselves. And the earlier administrative legacy of the area that makes up Iraq similarly does not offer obvious blueprints that correspond to today's discussions about Iraqi federalism. To the extent that there was a degree of stability, it rested in the three Ottoman provinces of Basra, Baghdad and Mosul, although the two first ones (and sometimes all three) were often ruled as a single entity. But today, only a minority among Iraq's Shiites—principally those of the far south in the triangle of Basra, Nasiriyya and Amara—are interested in re-establishing the borders of the old Ottoman *vilayet* of Basra. Others are discussing a large-scale, sectarian unit extending from the Gulf to Baghdad (for which there is no historical precedence), whereas there are also many Shiites who see no need for federalism at all. In the north there is similar incongruence between the long-established Mosul province of the past and the ethnically defined Kurdish regional entity that has emerged since the 1990s. But in this case there is at least a certain degree of continuity with regard to the Kurdish demand for self-rule, which in one form or another dates back almost until the establishment of Iraq after the First World War. Thus, only the northern part of Iraq exhibits a relatively well-defined regionalism comparable to those localisms that form the backbone of today's Spain.

The lack of congruence between past and present regionalisms—as well as rivalry between competing contemporary federal visions—are likely to be brought into play during the implementation of federalism in Iraq with a force quite unlike anything experienced by Spain, simply because of the great differences with regard to historical regional stability. A key problem in this regard is the salient article 119 of the Iraqi constitution—which includes no mechanisms for dealing with a multitude of conflicting federal visions competing for the same areas. One tenth of the "concerned" population, or a third of governorate council members in the "concerned" governorates, may demand a referendum for achieving federal status for "their" areas. But this could create a chaotic situation in places like Basra, where there may well be disagreement on what exactly constitutes the "concerned area". A third of the governorate council may wish to transform their area into a single-governorate oil-rich region; another third may prefer amalgamation with neighboring Maysan and Dhi Qar in a slightly bigger entity; and the remaining members may favor a bigger single Shiite entity and unity with the Shiite spiritual heartland around Najaf and Karbala. On top of this, even if public opinion should crystallize around one particular vision, the current constitution does not contain any provisions that will prevent discontents for mounting new challenges, through new referendums.

The danger is that situations like these could create chaos and chronic administrative instability. They could play right into the hands of those who wish to derail the entire process of establishing a new democracy in Iraq. It should be remembered in this regard that it took Spain no less than five years to create its federal map between 1978 and 1983; this despite the stabilizing role of the monarchy, the relatively benign international climate, and not least a considerable degree of consensus on what the new map should look like. The Spanish debate on the relationship between the center and the various autonomous units—with their different statuses and ambitions—is still going on today. Can Iraq afford a similar and probably even more time-consuming process? Might not this come at the expense of basic security and public services?

One possible remedy is to try to make article 119 of the constitution more robust, so that it can deal with a greater number of eventualities. This should be of interest to all Iraqis, regardless of their preferences for any particular federal scheme, simply as a precautionary measure against the danger that federalization might create further political instability. Some help is in fact at hand in the Spanish constitution which Iraq has emulated in other areas. The Spanish charter establishes a five-year moratorium for any failed regionalist projects; this is a simple device which could provide at least a minimum of respite during the transitional period. Another feature of the Iraqi constitution worth looking at is the requirement for calling a referendum, especially the stipulation that a third of the members of a provincial council can make a referendum initiative. This seems rather overindulgent. In a political climate dominated by militias, a faction of that size is exceedingly easy to create. It will be open to manipulation, by Iraqi political parties from outside the region "concerned", or even by foreigners. Tighter rules in this area will be needed to achieve stability; again the Spanish precedent may offer possible alternatives. Here the initiative for creating regions is vested in the municipalities, which due to their sheer numbers may be more difficult to manipulate.

But beyond the ongoing federal puzzle-solving activity, there is also a second and more radical option—that of accepting the historical dissimilarities between Spain and Iraq. That would mean sealing off all entrances to the federal labyrinth south of the Kurdish highlands. This could be done permanently or at least temporarily; in any case the goal would be to make a determined effort to focus energies on what most Iraqis demand most: security, jobs and general stability. In the absence of those basics, many Iraqis will continue to consider federalism debates as an abstract elite pastime with minimal relevance to their own situation. They will see it as a paradoxical political game which merely serves to postpone the rehabilitation of a country that has the potential to be one of the richest in the Middle East—if its politicians could only move on from political squabbles to actually governing the country. And while some Shiites increasingly refer to security as an argument for federalism, there is also the fear that the federal process could easily drag on and thereby deliver the opposite result. Before implementation, there would have to be constitutional revisions, legislation for implementing federalism and referendums—if all went according to plan, that is. Probably there would be some kind of federation in the end, but perhaps, as the Iraqi saying puts it, only "after the destruction of Basra". Over the past year, Iraq's politicians have globetrotted and have been globetrotted extensively in search of the perfect federal model; it is to be hoped that after their next meeting in Madrid they will spare a few glances for their own history before putting the finishing touches to the planned revisions of the Iraqi constitution.

The Draft Law for the Formation of Regions: A Recipe for Permanent Instability in Iraq?[3]
September 27, 2006

The first reading of the new Iraqi draft law for the formation of federal regions took place in the Iraqi parliament on 26 September 2006. Several features of this legislative project give reasons to worry about the prospect for national reconciliation and political stability in Iraq.

It could have been much worse. Leading political parties eager to carve out their own fiefdoms could have been tempted into watering down the Iraqi constitution to the point where they themselves could dictate the exact demarcation of federal regions. Kurdish and Shiite lawmakers could have made an attempt at bypassing the Sunni Arabs altogether, by pressing ahead with the law and thereby create a federal system before the issue of federalism had been revisited through the one-off constitutional revision process stipulated in the Iraqi charter adopted in October 2005. None of this happened. The proposed law to a large extent preserves the unique features of the Iraqi constitution that give the electorate and regional politicians—not Baghdad elites—the initiative in the creation of new regional entities. And it was decided that before the law was read, the long-awaited committee to revise the constitution should be formed; this started on 25 September and was completed with the naming of its members on the next day. Additionally, in a backroom deal between leading Kurdish, Shiite and Sunni political leaders it has been agreed that the committee shall have one year to complete its work, and that any legislation passed on the formation of regions must wait 18 months before implementation.

Despite these limited but significant moves towards an atmosphere of reconciliation, several problems concerning the implementation of federalism in Iraq remain. The most hazardous aspects of the new law are those that relate to the overall stability of the new federal system. The law opens up for a system that can be changed in perpetuity: not only can new regions be formed on the basis of existing governorates, but regions can join with each other and governorates can be annexed to regions (article 1; the two latter points are options that were not explicitly specified in the October 2005 constitution, moreover they have been designed mainly as tools for political elites because it is the "regional" councils only—not the people—that can activate them, article 2.3–4). Crucially, in the case of a failed attempt at establishing a region (or super-region), the required lapse of time before another attempt can be made is alarmingly short: one year, and then a new referendum can be held (article 9; other countries with similar arrangements such as Spain have used five-year moratoriums as a stabilization element). These processes can apparently go on ad infinitum—the question of separatism from existing or newly formed entities is not explicitly dealt with. In its present form the law thus threatens to form a constant distraction from the process of establishing security and basic services, and with its acute need for political stability, it is remarkable that Iraq is not aiming for a more conservative and restrictive arrangement.

A key issue where the constitution had left a blank was the eventuality of competition between different federal schemes involving the same geographical area. Some in Najaf may want to form a separate region, some in Basra, Maysan and Dhi Qar may want to join together, and some Shiites may want all of the governorates south of Baghdad to become a single region. With the lax requirements for calling a referendum under the constitution, it is entirely conceivable that all three projects will be able to muster the required minimum level of support (through a tenth of the electorate or a third of the local council members). The new law stipulates the procedure for dealing with this kind of rivalry: Unless one of the projects enjoys a two-thirds majority in the local council, the local authorities are to carry out a "poll" (*istibyan*), and the project that receives the largest number of votes in this poll is the one that will be put to a referendum (article 4.2.b). The exact modalities for this exercise are not determined in the law; this represents another potential source of future controversy.

But the new law cannot be studied in complete isolation. It must be considered in conjunction with the formation of the committee charged with revising the constitution, as well as the political agreement on postponement of implementation of federalism until 18 months after the law has been adopted. During the revision, those who are skeptical about federalism may wish to revisit the very principle of federalism south of Kurdistan, and theoretically they could make the entire law on the implementation of federalism superfluous. Periodically, there have been signs that at least some Shiite politicians within the United Iraqi Alliance, primarily Sadrists but also some Fadila, Daawa and independent representatives, are prepared to compromise with the Sunnis in a nationalist project of restricting federalism (for instance by size limits for new regions) or limiting it to the Kurdish areas only.

Still, based on the composition of the pro-Shiite United Iraqi Alliance (UIA) contingent to the newly formed constitutional revision committee of 27 deputies, it seems unlikely that this forum will be transformed into an avenue for radical changes in the federalism question. The most coherent grouping among the 12 UIA members appointed to the committee is made up of individuals close to the Supreme Council for the Islamic Revolution in Iraq (SCIRI) and its sympathisers. They include prominent figures like Humam Hammudi and Jalal al-Din al-Saghir, in addition to Badr member Abd al-Karim al-Naqib from Babel province, and known SCIRI sympathisers like Abbas al-Bayati (a Turkmen)—all of whom can be expected to press for minimal interference with SCIRI's pet project of forming a nine-province Shiite federal entity south of Baghdad. Additionally, some non-SCIRI representatives who in the past have voiced skepticism towards federalism now seem more supportive of SCIRI on this issue (or at least on the idea of having detailed legislation on federalism); they include members of the "Tanzim al-Iraq" branch of the Daawa party. The latter, a splinter faction of the Daawa, is represented on the committee by Ali al-Allaq of Babel, who accompanied Nuri al-Maliki on his recent visit to Iran, and Abd al-Karim al-Anizi—who only some years ago spoke fervently against any application of federalism in Iraq.The only UIA committee member who in the recent debate has outspokenly challenged SCIRI's ideas about rapid passage of the federalism bill is Hasan al-Shammari of the Fadila party. The Sadrists are notably absent in the committee; ex-Daawa member Sami al-Askari is the only committee member who in the past has had ties with them and his current position is not entirely clear. The omission of Basra and Maysan representatives is noteworthy as well, especially given the existence in these areas of a Shiite-led small-scale federalist project that competes with that of SCIRI.

As for the new timeline agreed on for the work of the committee (and for the implementation of any law on federalism), it hardly seems helpful from a governance perspective. A delay of 18 months does not mean that the project of federal subdivisions within the Arab-majority areas is in any way shelved or forgotten. If the sectarian violence continues, the advocates of federalism are likely to prosper—whereas the alternative project of restoring a unitary form of government south of Kurdistan will not benefit from the breathing space that a longer moratorium on federalism could have allowed for, or the potential synergies of a re-emergence of Iraqi nationalist sentiment and an expedited withdrawal of foreign troops. In fact, the extension of the deadline for the work of the constitutional committee to 12 months represents a riddle in itself. This seems distinctly unconstitutional (the constitution specifies 4 months as the committee's mandated lifetime) and probably should have required a special majority for adoption as such. And it is unclear what Iraqi legislators are supposed to do with this vast amount of time. There is the danger that if they try to put everything under the sun into this package, it will founder simply due to overload: there is little use in a splendid parliamentary compromise in Baghdad if it gets struck down in a referendum in three Iraqi governorates.

The Final Version of the Federalism Bill[4]

October 12, 2006

Reports on the parliamentary process that led to the adoption of the federalism bill yesterday are still incredibly sketchy. But if newspaper quotes from the final text of the law can be taken at face value, there are at least some changes from the draft that was made public after the first reading of the bill. First and foremost it has been reported that article 6 now reads, "the referendum [on the formation of federal regions] is successful if passed by a simple majority in *each* of the governorates that wish to federate as a region provided that participation is not lower than 50% of registered voters [italics added]". This would be a significant change from the original text in that it offers somewhat improved protection of regional interests against annexation by larger neighboring provinces or regions, and it would better conform to the idea of bottom–up federalization as outlined in the Iraqi constitution. It may have mollified Shiite deputies from the far south who are interested in having a region of their own and who may have feared absorption into a greater Shiite federal entity, and it may have gone some way to alleviate the concerns of those who worried that the law would almost automatically generate a particular (i.e., sectarian) form of federalism. Also, the explicit mention of the possibility of regions combining to form super-regions (one *iqlim* uniting with another), present in the first draft, has been removed.

However, at least two other potentially destabilizing elements of the original text remain. The incredibly low threshold for calling a referendum is still in place (a third of provincial council members—a highly manipulatable segment), and apparently no safeguards against a perpetual cycle of referendums have been added (new plebiscites can be called once every year if a unification attempt should fail). Additionally, the manner in which the law was adopted may in itself create controversy: The quorum threshold (138) was almost missed, and there were loud protests about hesitant deputies being dragged into the assembly to fill the required number of seats. It could be disturbing news for Iraq's democracy that almost half of the deputies chose to boycott the proceedings instead of taking part in a process that could perhaps have yielded a compromise solution. As such the passage of the law is very reminiscent of the final stages of the constitutional negotiations in 2005 and strongly suggests the need for improved dialogue inside the Iraqi national assembly.

Iraq's Draft Oil Law: The Federal Dimension[5]
March 6, 2007

What seems to be an authentic version of the Iraqi draft oil and gas law is now publicly available. It is expected that the law will be presented to the Iraqi parliament shortly after the assembly reconvenes later in March.

As far as questions relating to federalism and Iraq's state structure are concerned, the final version of the law is broadly similar to the third draft that was leaked in January 2007. One of the key features of the law in this regard is the creation of a "federal oil and gas commission", a name that in some ways may seem a misnomer. Firstly, the commission is not an institution of the federal government as such, but rather a hybrid that combines representatives of the central and provincial levels of government. Secondly, its innocuous-sounding name rather masks the fact that it represents a further stage in the weakening of Iraq's machinery of central government, as it completely emasculates the existing oil ministry in some key areas of decision-making. The language says it all: the commission "approves", "decides", and "changes" such vital instruments as standard oil contracts; the ministry, on the other hand, merely "proposes" policy (or even "submits" it, to the commission), and generally is more concerned with routine "monitoring" and "planning". The commission is a creative and quite radical solution to the ambiguity of the 2005 Iraqi constitution, which stipulated a shared but undefined process of policy-making in the oil sector: the central government will devise strategy "with" (ma'a) the regions and the producing governorates.

The rules of representation in the new commission are of critical importance. From the central government, four ministries plus the premier will be included, alongside top officials from relevant government agencies (three are specified) and a further maximum three "oil experts" (whose criteria for appointment are not given). From the provincial level of government, each federal region will be represented by a minister, and each "producing governorate" not belonging to a region will have a representative of its own. The requirement to qualify as a "producing governorate" is an output of no less than 150,000 barrels of oil per day, hence, as of today, only Basra and Kirkuk (Tamim governorate) are entitled to seats on the commission in addition to Kurdistan (which is represented not by virtue of its production but due to its federal status.)

There has been some suggestion that the oil and gas commission will further tilt the balance in Iraqi politics, away from Baghdad and towards enhanced peripheral control. Whilst the enfeeblement of the oil ministry would clearly seem to support that kind of interpretation, the center–periphery balance of the commission itself should not be seen as a foregone conclusion. As of today, the center is far stronger than the provinces in terms of numbers of representatives on the commission. It will probably remain so for some time to come, because it may take some years before those existing governorates that are next in line (probably Maysan, Dhi Qar, Wasit and Nineveh) reach the required production targets. The scenario most likely to cause a shift towards provincial dominance in the oil and gas commission involves the creation of several uni-governorate or small-scale regions which will obtain representation regardless of oil production levels, but only after a lengthy process of federalization. Hence, suggestions that the new oil law automatically introduces caste-like divisions among Iraqi governorates (producing and non-producing areas) are not necessarily valid. Rather it is the weakening of the professional ministry vis-à-vis a largely political body (the energy commission) that appears to be the dominant feature.

The other important elements of the law affecting center–periphery relations include the signing of contracts for discovered but undeveloped fields (this is now explicitly delegated to the regional level of government, but apparently is not a prerogative of oil-producing governorates not organized in a region since the term *iqlimiyya* usually denotes a federal region as opposed to a governorate), and a provision for unspecified provincial representation on the board of the Iraqi National Oil Company (INOC). Earlier drafts of the law had established a ceiling of a maximum 50% ownership for producing governorates in INOC's operating subsidiaries; however, in the final draft, this entire issue has apparently been circumvented.

The discrepancies between media accounts of the law and what is actually in it (and how it was made) are quite remarkable. There has been much fanfare about a "decisive deal" on revenue sharing, in a "compromise between Shiites, Sunnis and Kurds". In actual fact, the law does very little with respect to revenue beyond reiterating the constitutional provisions for a "fair" (but undefined) sharing of revenue. That this "fairness" should mean "revenue-sharing among regions and provinces on the basis of population", as claimed in US Ambassador Zalmay Khalilzad's 3 March op-ed in *The Washington Post*, is in fact not reflected in the law itself, but rather something that is expected to be laid down in subsequent and separate legislative acts. Similarly, the claim that the law represents a "historical deal" between three Iraqi ethno-religious communities rather distorts the picture of the negotiations that have taken place over the past months. In reality, the whole process stalled for several months mainly due to Kurdish intransigence over who should have the right to sign contracts for discovered but undeveloped fields, with pretty much everyone else opposing them.

Another aspect of the strange reporting on the oil law is the Western tendency to view every single aspect of the entire process through sectarian lenses. The BBC, for example, reported on 27 February, "most of the oil-fields are in the Shiite-dominated south, while the best prospects for future drilling are in the Kurdish north". This account fails to mention the fact that more than 80% of the oil in the "Shiite-dominated south" is concentrated in one particular area—Basra—whose reserves in turn are many times larger than even the most speculative estimates of future "Kurdish" fields. In other words, none of the politically dominant factions inside the Iraqi government—the Kurds, and the Supreme Council for the Islamic Revolution in Iraq (SCIRI), one of the Shiite parties—actually possesses any significant amount of oil in their core territories (SCIRI being in the opposition in local government in Basra, and the Kirkuk fields lying outside the KRG area and under any circumstances are defined as "existing" fields controlled by Baghdad). As for the Sunnis, supposedly "much reassured" by the agreed (but still uncodified) agreement to share revenue, they have actually been quite marginal to the negotiating process. Symptomatically, in a recent *New York Times* article on how "new oil find in Iraq gives hope to Sunni areas", the interviewees marshalled to vouch for the new "hopefulness" were not Sunnis, but—predictably perhaps—American soldiers. It was another indication of the way in which sectarian caricatures are being imposed on the Iraq situation: Shiites and Kurds supposedly united internally and with each other in their "oil-rich" regions, with Sunnis desperately searching for ways of getting hold of the oil, as if that constituted their sole concern.

The draft raises numerous questions. Why, for instance, should non-producing governorates not be entitled to seats on the federal oil and gas commission? After all the oil is owned by the entire Iraqi people. On the other hand, is it really necessary to infect such existing institutions of the central government as the Iraqi National Oil Company with the pie logic in which everything is divided according to a quota system? Certainly some of the provincial concerns could be addressed through "softer" methods, such as the relocation of certain ministry operations out of Baghdad. And finally, why cannot the guarantee about a fair division of revenue according to population be inserted directly into the law? That sort of reassurance may be required if the law is to stand any chance of passing in the Iraqi parliament, where skepticism against the combination of decentralization, privatization and foreign investment is likely to run high.

The Powers of the Governorates Not Organized in a Federal Region[6]
February 11, 2008

The governorates law that is about to be adopted by the Iraqi parliament is of particular importance because it relates directly to the fundamental struggle between centralist and decentralist forces in Iraq—and, more generally, to the debate about the ideal structure of Iraq's future democracy. But at the same time it has the potential to become a particularly thorny piece of legislation, due to its intimate links to one of the most fundamental contradictions in the 2005 constitution. On the one hand, the constitution's article 115 unequivocally puts federal regions and governorates that have not opted for a federal status on a 100% equal footing: They have all the powers that have not specifically been given to the central government. Accordingly, any law that gives a governorate less power than a federal region could be challenged for being unconstitutional. The problem is, however, that the constitution itself goes quite far in the direction of violating precisely this principle. The whole idea of the concept of residual powers in a federal system is that only a single specification of powers is needed—either those of the central government, or those of the provincial entities. And in the case of Iraq, the dominant focus in the charter is clearly on specifying the (relatively few) powers of the central government. Anomalously, however, the document then enumerates a number of specified powers for federal regions and governorates not organized into a federal region, where certain privileges of the federal regions (in particular the right to organize internal security forces, as well as the specific mention of a legislative power) are not explicitly repeated with respect to the governorates (there is however mention of the concept of "laws issued by the non-federated governorates", which has to be seen as an implicit recognition of legislative authority). Despite considerable attempts in 2007 by UN staff to encourage a rethink on these issues during the process of constitutional revision, no measures to clear up the situation were included when the revision committee finished its report.

Early drafts of the law that is currently being considered by parliament began appearing in the summer of 2007. In general, the law does not endeavor to resolve the issues related to distribution of power that were left unanswered in the constitution. For example, whether the governorates are allowed to follow the example of the federal regions and establish their own security agencies simply remains unclear, as does the question of whether the local government can legislate in areas of shared competencies with the central authorities such as health and education (on this latter point the constitution actually accords precedence to local laws whereas the current governorate law draft in a somewhat incongruous fashion stipulates that no local law shall contradict the constitution *or federal laws*). Similarly, the question of the right to impose taxes is not answered in a definitive way: taxes and "revenue from border crossings" can form part of governorate financial resources "as long as this is in harmony with the constitution and federal laws"—a vague formula that was probably chosen because a modest strengthening of the central government's power to tax happens to be part of the proposed constitutional revision package that is currently stalled in the Iraqi parliament. Interestingly, there is a list of exceptions to the governor's inspection powers which does not seem to square 100% with the constitution: It includes some areas of shared competency (like education), but not all (for example, environmental agencies are not listed even though they are an area of shared power); this is paralleled in a concept of "senior positions" in the governorate to be under local control, defined as all higher officials with the exception of those working in the courts, the military and higher education.

Where available drafts of the law really do seem to offer some substance is on the subject of hiring and firing of local staff. Here, real power is bestowed on the governor (who nominates candidates for all leading administrative positions in the governorate, inclusive top security agencies with the exception of the army), and the governorate council (which selects three of them for the consideration of the relevant ministry). Historically, Baghdad's dominance with regard to appointment of local government officials has been disliked in many of Iraq's provinces, and if these new measures survive in the final version of the law they will no doubt go some way towards mollifying local discontent about the role of outsiders in local administration. However, at the same time, they could hamper the development of cohesive and professional state bureaucracies, if, as seems to be the case, also federal/central government agencies operating in the governorates are subject to these procedures of appointment.

Basra, the Failed Gulf State, Part II: Wail Abd al-Latif Concedes Defeat[7]
January 17, 2009

Wail Abd al-Latif, the chief protagonist of the campaign to transform Basra into a stand-alone federal region, has told Iraqi radio that his project has failed. While Abd al-Latif did not know the exact numbers of signatures collected since the legally fixed month-long campaign period started on 15 December 2008, this declaration by the principal advocate of the scheme seems to be a certain indication that the goal of mustering 140,000 signatures in favor of the project—the precondition for a referendum—is unachievable at present.

This failure shows two things. Firstly, to the extent that there is an interest in federalism in Iraq south of Baghdad, such sentiments are concentrated in Basra in the far south—and they focus on non-sectarian schemes for transforming Basra into a small federal region that would be defined by its geography and history, not by the Shiite religion of the majority of its inhabitants. Since 2005, there has been much fanfare about the grander designs of the Islamic Supreme Council of Iraq (ISCI) and their plans to create a nine-governorate federal region extending all the way from Basra to Baghdad (though lately more so in the Western media than in Iraq itself); it seems significant that the only scheme that so far has been translated into a degree of practical politics is the Basra project with its far more local outlook. Secondly, the Basra scheme itself, while clearly the preference of a group of local politicians that combines secularists and Islamists, is not immensely popular among the people of Basra at large. We now have a quantitative indicator of the true level of popular support: it is somewhere between the 2% of the electorate that turned in the first 30,000 plus signatures required to get the initiative going last autumn and the 10% of the electorate that the federalists were unable to mobilize between 15 December 2008 and 15 January 2009.

The fate of the Basra federalist initiative comes across as a fascinating replay of events that unfolded in Basra in the early 1920s. At the time, a small, cross-sectarian elite of merchants—including Najdi Sunnis, Christians, Jews and a few Shiites including some Persian merchants—launched a bid to transform Basra into a Gulf statelet under British protection, akin to Kuwait. However, the separatist leaders failed to attract London's interest, and, equally significant, did not manage to mobilize popular support among the rural Shiite Arab majority of Basra and the young intellectual elite of the city (which was multi-ethnic and multi-sectarian in composition). The federalism initiative of Abd al-Latif is of course different in that it does not envisage separation, but instead aims at achieving a special status for Basra within Iraq, similar to Kurdistan. But the reasons for failure seem very similar in the two cases. Firstly, neither the Basra separatists of the 1920s nor the Basra federalists that have emerged since 2003 managed to present an identity project that resonated with the local population and was able to compete with Iraqi nationalism. Indeed, these leaders' own desire to hang on to Iraqi nationalism is probably a limiting factor for their project overall. They criticize the Kurds for not flying the Iraqi flag, maintain that Baghdad should remain in control of the oil sector (though perhaps with some kind of special share of the income for Basra as Iraq's main producing governorate), and portray their scheme as a strategy for saving Iraq's unity by forestalling any moves by ISCI to create a nine-governorate federal region that would be loyal to Iran—all of which means focusing on Iraq as much as on Basra. Secondly, the failure of today's federalists to dominate the public space and the media with compelling arguments in favor of their scheme (in fact, much of the propaganda has been limited to the rather uninspiring vision of additional layers of local bureaucracy that could give more jobs to the area) is a striking echo of similar problems seen in the separatist efforts in the 1920s.

Instead, Wail Abd al-Latif and his supporters were on the defensive from day one of the initiative, criticizing the elections commission for not providing a sufficient number of polling stations across Basra and for a lack of adequate information about the initiative for the general public. In a sign of desperation, a committee that supports the project at one point undemocratically declared itself the sole legitimate point of contact regarding the federalism scheme. These hapless maneuvers are all the more remarkable in view of the fact that the party that controls the governor position in Basra—Fadila—has generally supported the bid, even if its leaders may have sensed the turn of the tide and have been less intimately associated with the campaign lately, the governor himself preferring to show up with the Iraqi national football team in Oman.

Few doubt the anti-Iranian agenda of Abd al-Latif and the Fadila branch in

Basra, but many Iraqi nationalists disagree with the tactics adopted by the Basra federalists in their attempt at stopping the steadily growing Iranian influences in Iraq—and also suspect a degree of involvement by a player that wants neither a strong Iran nor a strong Iraq: Kuwait. But while Basra popular opinion clearly has shown its disdain for federalism projects more generally, a potential problem with the current federalism legislation is that once new governorate councils are elected on 31 January, it becomes far easier to launch ever more federalism referendums on the basis of the consent of a mere third of the members of the affected governorate councils (councils formed before the constitution was adopted in 2005 are not allowed to make such federal initiatives). This opens the door for backdoor politics of the kind ISCI excels at, and while creating a nine-governorate region in one go may prove too complicated, the lax law on federalization that was adopted in October 2006 allows for a gradual process that could slowly change the administrative map of Iraq and weaken the concept of a unified state.

Maliki Makes a Concession to Basra Regionalism[8]
May 10, 2009

News reports from Basra suggest that Iraq's Prime Minister Nuri al-Maliki has made an interesting concession to regionalist sentiment in the southern oil-export city of Basra. According to a statement by the spokesman of the new governor in Basra (who is also a Maliki ally), one-half U.S. dollar will henceforth be deducted from every barrel of oil exported from Basra and placed in a special development fund for Basra.[9]

In some ways, the move could be seen as compatible with—and indeed inspired by—the 2005 constitution, where a general provision for the temporary positive discrimination of particularly deprived governorates through the use of oil revenue is found. Most statistical surveys single out Basra as the area of Iraq where living standards remain at the lowest level, in glaring contrast to the governorate's position as the major oil producer and exporter in Iraq.

However, while the relevant constitutional clauses focus on deprivation, the link to Basra's role as producer has other roots. The half-dollar deduction will meet a longstanding demand by Basra politicians that their area's role as the kingpin of Iraq's economy be reflected in some kind of special political privilege. Actually, back in December 2007, Basra politicians of the Fadila party proposed an arrangement which is remarkably similar to what is now being talked about as a governmental "decision": Basra should receive one dollar per barrel of oil exported from the south. The difference between Fadila in 2007 and Maliki in 2009 of half a dollar can reasonably be attributed to the general decline in oil prices and a bit of bazaar-style haggling between center and periphery.

While one incarnation of Basra regionalism was roundly rejected by the local citizens as they chose to ignore the federalism initiative headed by Wail Abd al-Latif in the winter of 2008/2009, the apparent decision of a centralist like Nuri al-Maliki to make concessions to local sentiment even after his particularly strong result in Basra in the January provincial elections testifies to its survival in other forms.

Disputed Territories in Iraq:
The Practical Argument against Self-Determination in Kirkuk[10]
May 25, 2009

If history should provide the guidelines, it would be relatively easy to prescribe a solution to what is frequently seen as one of the most "complicated" issues in current Iraqi politics: The status of the oil-rich city of Kirkuk. A variety of different historical sources prior to 1957 and dating back several centuries unequivocally describe Kirkuk as a town dominated demographically by Turkmens, who for their part were famous throughout the Iraqi region from Basra to Mosul for their leading role in the Ottoman and later Iraqi administrations. Traditionally, the Kurds in this area—whose relationships with the Ottomans and later the Iraqi government in Baghdad were far more tenuous—had their strongest presence in the rural hinterland outside Kirkuk. Accordingly, any attempt to sever the longstanding ties between Baghdad and the city of Kirkuk itself on the basis of two waves of Kurdish immigration to the city proper in the late 1960s and since 2003 would be ahistorical in the extreme, and not incomparable to, say, a Scottish bid to annex selected slices of Northumbria in the north of England.

However, today's Iraq presents a confusing situation, and many commentators reject the validity of any attempt to use history as a determinant for tomorrow's political maps. To them, what matters is the current situation on the ground. In particular, many advocate a solution based on "self-determination", mostly in the shape of some kind of decisive referendum—a solution which reportedly features in all four scenarios for Kirkuk presented in a recent report on Iraq's "disputed territories" by UNAMI, the primary ÙN political agency in Iraq. Despite considerable attempts by the Baathist regime to gerrymander the population balance in Kirkuk to the disadvantage of the Kurds towards the end of the twentieth century, it is expected that the mass influx of Kurdish migrants to the city of Kirkuk in the late 1960s and early 1970s plus additional immigration since 2003 (when Kurdish militias acquired control of the city and encouraged Kurds to settle there) mean that there might be vote in favor of annexation by the Kurdistan Regional Government (KRG) if a referendum were to be carried out under present circumstances.

But in addition to the historical argument against this kind of outcome, two very practical considerations also militate against any use of the self-determination principle in Kirkuk. The first has to do with lessons from the recent history from the 1960s and 1970s, and the way in which the very idea of using plebiscites or censuses for determining the borders of Kurdistan became the focus of attention of the autonomy negotiations between the Baathist regime and Mulla Mustafa Barzani, the main Kurdish leader at that time. Towards the end of those negotiations, Barzani introduced claims for the annexation of a host of territories (such as Kirkuk) where the Kurdish population element was thin or only recently established; the Baathists accordingly sought refuge in the principle of ethnic demography as a determinant for the allocation of territory. This formed the background to the 1970 peace agreement, where Baghdad confidently agreed to autonomy for all areas with a "Kurdish majority", believing it would be restricted to the governorates of Sulaymaniyya, Arbil and the newly-constituted Dahuk (which had been separated from Mosul as a concession to Kurdish demands).

But the recourse to demography also constituted the beginning of the end of the peace agreement. The promised census never materialized (first both sides agreed to a postponement; later Baghdad put it off unilaterally), and the Kurds refused to use the previous censuses of 1965 and 1957 as a basis (knowing they would show no Kurdish majority in Kirkuk). Then followed a dirty game in which both sides appear to have applied unscrupulous methods to secure an outcome in their own favor. The Kurds accused the Baathist regime of flooding Kirkuk and its neighboring areas with Arabs in order to neutralize growing Kurdish demographic weight; the central government suspected that Barzani and his allies were importing Iranian Kurds to settle them near Kirkuk. It seems likely that misdeeds were committed on both sides, and the regime's decision to expel tens of thousands of Fayli Kurds—indigenous to Iraq but many of their forefathers held Persian passports in Ottoman times in order to avoid conscription—represents a particularly brutal aspect of the developments.

All of this escalation and human suffering was the singular result of the promise that "demographic realities" would be used to demarcate the boundaries of Kurdistan. It does not require much fantasy to imagine that something similar could take place in the future if "self determination" were employed as the main criterion for settling the current dispute. In fact, to some extent, this has already happened. Since 2003, Kurdish authorities have been accused of bringing in huge numbers of Kurds in and around Kirkuk in order to bolster their own claim to the city. With tendencies of growing assertiveness by the Iraqi central government since 2008, a counter-campaign focused on beachheads among its potential allies—particularly the non-Kurdish population elements of Kirkuk such as the Turkmens, the Arabs and the Christians—seems perfectly possible. In other words, any promise of "self determination" along the lines of what UNAMI is now apparently considering would almost inevitably set off a violent tit for tat process which could easily surpass the 1970s and the immediate post-2003 period in intensity and violence. What the international community needs to realize today is that "self determination" in Kirkuk has become completely meaningless as an exercise of democracy because so much gerrymandering and dirty tricks have already been brought to bear on the situation. Essentially, in Kirkuk the slogan of "self-determination" is like a greasy old rag that will never become clean and dry again, no matter how many times it is washed.

There is also a second practical argument against any application of self determination in Kirkuk: The likely domino effect in the rest of Iraq. This represents a danger because the concept of "disputed territories" was never defined at the time of its fateful insertion in the Transitional Administrative Law (TAL) in March 2004, from where it was transplanted into the 2005 constitution. Hence, in theory, today, any politician anywhere in Iraq can invent a case of a "disputed area" for whatever piece of land he or she might wish to politicize. Thankfully, so far, few other than the Kurds have been keen to exploit this option, with most other Iraqi politicians seemingly holding on to the existing framework. But, for a considerable time, a small group of Iraqi Shiite politicians have been interested in importing the same concept of territorial conflict to certain governorates south of Baghdad. As early as in 2005, just weeks before the launch of the project by the Islamic Supreme Council of Iraq (ISCI) to create an all-Shiite federal region of nine governorates south of Baghdad, press reports suggested that Abd al-Aziz al-Hakim had voiced an interest in redrawing the boundaries of the Karbala governorate so that it would also comprise the desert area of Nukhayb, presently a part of Anbar. And since April this year, other Shiite-oriented politicians—ranging from the Maliki-supported new governor of Karbala to Ahmad Chalabi—have joined a growing chorus of leaders calling for changes to Karbala's border. Nukhayb is wanted by Karbala politicians not for its ties to Shiism—most of its tribes are Sunnis—but because of its strategic location on the road to Saudi Arabia, where many Iraqi pilgrims have been killed by terrorists in the past.

The case of Nukhayb illustrates the serious problems of employing the notion of "disputed territories" across Iraq. During the monarchy area, boundary delineation in the desert areas was approximate at best, and a 1957 map of Iraq, for example, shows lines in the sand extending from the river areas of the Euphrates towards the west, but stopping shortly after Bahr al-Milh and thus leaving the jurisdiction of the rest of the vast territory between Iraq and Saudi Arabia to the imagination. The exact subsequent development remains a matter of dispute, but certainly government maps from the late 1960s showed Nukhayb firmly within what was then called Ramadi province and today is Anbar. Importantly, at this stage, a number of other administrative changes—only some of which are currently considered as "disputed" by the proponents of the concept—had yet to be made. For example, there was no Dahuk province; that area was part of Mosul and was only detached to form a separate governorate after the peace treaty with the Kurds in 1970. Also, the governorates of Najaf and Muthanna did not exist: they were carved out from

Karbala and Diwaniyya/Nasiriyya later on. Hence, if the Baath era is to serve as basis for some kind of *status quo ante* logic, it will be exceedingly hard to pinpoint exactly when the "original sin" of the former regime took place. In other words, the consistency and the assumed objectivity of the whole process disintegrate entirely as soon as a pick and choose approach is applied.

A good solution for Kirkuk should seek to bring an end to the logic of "disputed territories" instead of proliferating it. Rather than pursuing a maximalist demand that is dangerous to Kirkuk as an urban community and to Iraq as a society of coexistence, Kurdish politicians should try to envisage the potential value of alternative incentives, of which quite a few have been proposed. In particular, Liam Anderson has suggested using as a model the case of the Åland Islands from the post–First World War settlement, where the autonomy of the Swedish-speaking archipelago west of Finland had its autonomy guaranteed by the international community in a robust "autonomy plus" arrangement that should be of interest to Kurds (whose main concern during the twentieth century, after all, has been distrust of Baghdad). Internationally guaranteed autonomy for the areas the Kurds currently control would offer them assurances of non-interference that are stronger than the 2005 constitution, and could be a good reason to reverse their maximalist approach to Kirkuk—after all such guarantees used to be very central to the Kurdish agenda in the pre-2003 period. As for the Kurds of Kirkuk, an emerging "Kirkuk first" attitude can already be found among some of them, and this could be promoted further. In an interesting development, Kurdish politicians in Kirkuk recently emulated Basra regionalists in calling for a "half dollar per barrel of exported oil" to be set aside in a local development fund—the kind of negotiable, "soft" federalism that would be relatively easy to integrate within a unitary state structure.

Finally, a territorial compromise at the elite level could be used to round off these negotiations. The best solution for Iraq would of course have been if the troublesome "disputed territories" concept had never entered the TAL in the first place in 2004—it would in fact have been perfectly possible to deal with the issues of forced resettlement during the Baathist era on a family by family, property by property basis, without any resort to the abstract and problematic concept of ethnicity that is implied in the "disputed territories" nomenclature. Nevertheless, expectations of some kind of territorial settlement are now very strong in the Kurdish camp, and could prove difficult to reverse. Equally important, to some extent it should be possible to achieve this without deviating very much from past attempts at compromise. In the 1970s, for example, the regime was prepared to cede Kurdish-dominated areas near Kirkuk such as Chamchamal and Kalar for the sake of peace. In general, from the point of view of history, the idea of the sacrosanctity of the territorial integrity of the Tamim governorate—reportedly another cornerstone of UNAMI's report—is less readily understandable than the principle that Kirkuk, the city with its multi-ethnic fabric, should stay within the unitary-state framework of Iraq under any circumstances. In that kind of perspective, it could make sense that certain rural parts of the Tamim governorate in the future should gravitate towards the autonomous KRG. At any rate, whatever course of action is chosen, a grand compromise for the north of Iraq should be done as an affair at the elite level. The inhabitants of the area have already suffered enough and should not have their lives destroyed by serving as pawns in a long-winded, fictitious process of "self determination".

The End of Transitional Rule in Iraq[11]
February 18, 2010

What has yet to receive serious attention in today's chaos in Iraq is that regardless of the outcome of the de-Baathification process, the fundamental rules of government formation in Iraq are scheduled to change in less than a month's time.

Back in 2006, the government headed by Prime Minister Nuri al-Maliki was formed on the basis of a Byzantine procedure involving special majorities and power-sharing between ethno-religious communities. There was a requirement that the president—who in turn invites the prime minister-designate to form a government—be elected with a two-thirds majority in parliament. The president was required to stand for office alongside two vice-presidential candidates, with a single two-thirds vote required to fill all three positions—and with an expectation among the dominant political parties that this triumvirate should represent the three main ethno-sectarian communities of Iraq, Shiite Arabs, Sunni Arabs and Kurds. As a consequence, the selection of the prime minister also required a pre-vote consensus among the two-thirds majority required to approve the president; it is no surprise, therefore, that almost five months passed between the December 2005 elections and the formation of Maliki's government.

These arrangements were only transitional, stipulated to last from 2005 to 2010 and reflecting the novelty of such highly formalized structures of power-sharing in Iraq. The three-man presidency council is set to expire after the 7 March elections and henceforth, according to the constitution, governments will be formed on the basis of a new set of rules. The president, now possessing symbolic powers only, is to be elected separately from his deputies, and if no candidate receives two-thirds of the vote then a simple majority will suffice. In theory, then, forming the next Iraqi government could be a lot easier than it was in 2006. Beyond the removal of the supermajority requirement, there is also no stipulation for consensus defined in ethno-sectarian terms between Kurds, Sunni Arabs and Shiite Arabs. The threshold required to assemble a winning coalition has been lowered substantially; regardless of the results of the vote, Iraq's next parliament will be governed by radically different political dynamics.

Evaluating the effects of this shift depends on how one understands Iraq as a state and a nation. For those who believe in a non-sectarian Iraq, the change appears to be a positive one. First and foremost, abandoning the requirement for a supermajority means diminishing the number of special interests that must be accommodated simply to form a cabinet. It should now be possible to construct a government that actually agrees on the details of a coherent political program—a stark contrast to the current coalition, in which the only truly common agenda is the need to hold on to power.

So there is optimism among nationalist and secularist Iraqis, who have criticized the present power-sharing arrangement for solidifying rather than dissipating ethno-sectarian rifts, and for placing party interests above those of the people as a whole. In their view, the way to eliminate corruption and make government more effective is to reduce the size of the cabinet: Nationalist Iraqis will typically say they would prefer a professional and effective government made up by 20 competent Christians to an oversized "government of national unity" based on a carefully calibrated attempt at accommodating the wishes of parties claiming to speak in the name of Sunni and Shiite interests. For a while, especially in the first part of 2009, Maliki himself began to suggest that too much power-sharing could create a paralyzed and ideologically incoherent cabinet—highlighting the extent to which Iraqi nationalist ideals exist to an equal degree among Sunnis and Shiites, if perhaps not among Kurds.

But the prospect of these new constitutional arrangements has aroused concern, particularly among established politicians and parties: majority rule will mean more power for those in government, but it poses the threat that the "losing" parties will be excluded altogether. Most of the dominant parties in the Maliki government prefer instead a permanent formula for power-sharing among the three big ethno-sectarian communities—and last year attempted to derail the scheduled change by inserting a clause in the draft revised constitution that would perpetuate the three-man presidency council. Ironically, however, bitter disagreements among these parties, including over governance of the oil sector, prevented them from bringing the revision to a vote.

Similarly, the knee-jerk reaction in international think-tank circles has been fear that the era of power-sharing is coming to an end. These analysts, like the exiled elites who returned to post-2003 Iraq, are largely accustomed to thinking of the country as a conglomerate consisting of three monolithic communities; today they are similarly alarmed at the prospect of a new government where the ratio of Kurds and Sunni Arabs may be different from their "true" share of the total population. The cure now being proposed is to encourage the Iraqis to preserve as much as possible of the current system and to ignore the stipulated change. Surely, it is said, nothing prevents Iraqis from forming a government of national unity if they wish.

Even if it would be hard to retain the powerful, veto-wielding three-person presidency council in its present form without first amending the constitution, there is in principle nothing to stop the formation of another grandiose cabinet with 30 portfolios representing every conceivable ethnic, sectarian and party interest. The question is whether this attempt to hold on to rules that were adopted by a narrow elite of Iraqis who returned from exile after 2003 would be of any benefit to the country and its people. The idea of ethno-sectarian quotas became the dominant principle of government in Iraq in 2003–2004 during the rule of Paul Bremer, who famously exemplified its underlying logic by referring to a gathering of seven Iraqis as "unrepresentative" because only one Sunni Arab was present (1.4 would have been the mathematically correct number). For its part, Tehran has repeatedly made it clear that it prefers the perpetuation of an identity-based system of government in Baghdad, under which it may more easily exploit its alliances with Iraqi Shiite Islamists. Conversely, the principal critics of power-sharing have been those Iraqis who did not go into exile, and not merely the secularists among them: In March 2004, even the Shiite Grand Ayatollah Ali al-Sistani described the idea of a tripartite presidency as a dangerous precedent that could lead to the partition of Iraq. The ultimate effects of the constitutional change will therefore be determined by the outcome of a larger debate over how Iraq chooses to define itself. The paradigm of an ethno-sectarian trinity has won a surprising number of adherents in the international community, but it has not delivered much to Iraqis in terms of security, governance and services.

The Akkaz Revolt: A Test Case for Iraq, and for Iraqiyya[12]
October 20, 2010

For the past couple of years an interesting energy revolt has been simmering in the mainly-Sunni governorate of Anbar: Local councillors are increasingly expressing a desire for a leading role for the local authorities in developing the Akkaz gas field. When the central government earlier this year included that field in a batch of contracts put up for auction to foreign companies, the local council protested and recently issued a threat about non-cooperation in case the deals went ahead.

Today, the Akkaz field was awarded to a South Korean consortium after an auction in Baghdad. It will be interesting to see not only how the governorate politicians in Anbar react, but also how the Iraqiyya coalition—which is strongly represented locally in Anbar— responds at the national level.

The constitutional facts of the matter are that the central government is supposed to be in the lead when it comes to "existing fields", albeit in some kind of unspecified cooperation with the local authorities. Back in 2007, when an attempt was made to agree on an oil and gas law, Akkaz—which was discovered in the

Saddam Hussein period before 2003—was listed in the annexes to the draft law in category 3 of "non-producing" fields in need of considerable investment. Of course the oil and gas law was never adopted (the Kurds also protested strongly at the way the annexes were drawn up), and the central government has since gone ahead with the award (or attempted award) of several category 3 fields in previous licensing rounds with foreign companies, including Badra, Gharraf, Kifl and a gas field in Diyala. It is thought that the degree of "coordination" with the local authorities in these mostly Shiite-majority governorates (that is, except Diyala) has been quite minimal, and whereas protests from the local governorates themselves have been limited—and possibly have been ameliorated by the generous fees given to oil and gas-producing governorates in the 2010 budget—a general challenge to the government's line has been mounted in the courts by Shadha al-Musawi, a former deputy of the old, all-Shiite United Iraqi Alliance, with respect to the contract signed with a British-Chinese consortium for the supergiant Rumaila field in the Basra area.

Thus, the question is whether the oil ministry needs to do anything more in terms of coordination with the Anbar authorities than they have done in places like Dhi Qar. It is interesting that so far, the vision of a dominant central government in these issues has been promoted by Hussein al-Shahristani, a close ally of Prime Minister Nuri al-Maliki. Conversely, the Kurds and forces close to another Shiite party, the Islamic Supreme Council of Iraq (ISCI) have been accused of abetting regionalist tendencies in Anbar, which used to have a nationalist orientation. Given the current rivalry between Maliki and Ayad Allawi to win over the Kurds in order to form the next government, it would be interesting to see where Allawi's Iraqiyya really stands on this important issue concerning the key question of whether Iraq should be centralized or decentralized.

CHAPTER NOTES

1 The original version of this text can be found at http://www.atimes.com/atimes/Middle_East/GJ12Ak03.html.

2 See http://historiae.org/Federalism.asp.

3 See http://historiae.org/Aqalim.asp.

4 See http://historiae.org/devolution.asp.

5 See http://www.historiae.org/oil-law.asp.

6 See http://historiae.org/governorates.asp.

7 See http://historiae.org/latif.asp.

8 See http://gulfanalysis.wordpress.com/2009/05/10/maliki-makes-a-concession-to-basra-regionalism/.

9 In the budget adopted in January 2010, the fee of $1 per barrel was eventually agreed for all oil-producing governorates.

10 See http://historiae.org/disputed.asp.

11 See http://www.thenational.ae/apps/pbcs.dll/article?AID=/20100218/REVIEW/702189992/1008/review.

12 See http://gulfanalysis.wordpress.com/2010/10/20/the-akkas-revolt-a-test-case-for-iraq-and-for-iraqiyya/.

Chapter 9

Aspects of Constitutional Law: De-Baathification, Government Formation, and Proportional Representation

One of the more lasting impressions from a conference of Iraqi parliamentarians I attended in Europe in 2006 was the striking image of one of the Kurdish delegates pulling his booklet of the Iraqi constitution from his inner pocket every now and then. He would look at it in silent contemplation, as if considering some kind of holy text.

Fast forward to 2010 and another Iraq conference, this time in New York City. Again, a Kurdish ex-minister expressed a constitutionalist approach: "We are with those who support the constitution." During the round-table discussion I pointed out that after the transitional regime involving the three-man presidency council lapsed in 2010, it would in fact be perfectly constitutional to have a government without any participation of the biggest Kurdish parties. The minister retorted that this was "unacceptable"; in the next session, to everyone's surprise, Peter Galbraith (on whom much more follows in chapter 10) appeared by her side to declare that it would be "impossible" to form a government without the Kurds.

This chapter looks at how Iraqi politicians have developed a habit of referring to the constitution to justify their own actions even in cases where there is no legal basis for doing so. One of the most recurrent phrases in Iraqi politics today—"that's unconstitutional"—has become something of a joke: It means simply, "I disagree with you." Another main theme in the chapter is how two of the Iraqi institutions often thought to be above the politicians' brawl—the federal supreme court and the elections commission (IHEC)—became seriously politicized during 2010.

Most of these articles, inevitably, relate to the question of de-Baathification. Politically, de-Baathification was a two-pronged attack by the pro-Iranian Iraqi National Alliance (INA) against its two main enemies, the State of Law Alliance headed by Nuri al-Maliki and the secular Iraqiyya. As such it was spectacular success, as described in greater detail in chapter 6. From the legal viewpoint, however, de-Baathification has been a horror story involving such savage attacks on the principles of due process and such creativeness when it comes to twisting the relevant legal frameworks that it is hard to comprehend that this madness was allowed to go on for several months in a country calling itself a democracy, even as the world was supposedly watching! The de-Baathification committee and its leaders, Ali al-Lami and Ahmad Chalabi, were clearly in the lead in this campaign; still, the complicity of the rest of the Iraqi political system—in particular, of all of the INA (including ISCI and the Sadrists), the Kurds, IHEC, and eventually even the federal supreme court—was equally striking and perhaps even more disturbing. After having first been a victim, the State of Law Alliance, too, jumped on the bandwagon and became one of the worst offenders, making a mockery of the reference to legalism in its name.

Another issue discussed in some of these texts is the role of the federal supreme court in interpreting the ground rules of Iraq's consociational democracy. The first of the contentious issues in this regard is the constitution's article 76, which defines which bloc has the right to nominate the premier candidate after parliamentary elections. Less attention has been accorded to some recent rulings by the court on matters relating to the Iraqi election law, such as the mechanics of the proportional representation system and the representation of minorities (the latter question is covered in chapter 11.) The court's rulings on these issues have been surprisingly radical in terms of the support they have given to a stronger form of proportionality and ethno-sectarian minority representation. The consequences of this, going forward to Iraq's next parliamentary elections, could be quite dramatic.

A final, important aspect of constitutional law hit the agenda in the summer of 2010, during the process of government-formation. Quite soon, it became evident that the United States—in tandem with the United Nations mission in Iraq, UNAMI—was doing its best to ensure that the next Iraqi government would be based on power-sharing between all the winning lists. This would be achieved, first, by including all the four big winning lists and, second, by implementing institutional changes that could make it attractive for both the two biggest winners—Nuri al-Maliki and Ayad Allawi—to join the same government. The first American move in this regard involved a convoluted scheme to reactivate the dormant Iraqi national security council, which was instituted in 2006 but is not even described in the constitution. The idea was to give the presidency for the council to Allawi in lieu of the premiership (which Washington at the time thought should go to Maliki), with the sole problem that Allawi did not find the idea particularly attractive, not least since the council was supposed to make its decisions by consensus and therefore would not provide a lot of power for its president. Later, the Americans gradually began realizing that much, and switched to supporting the idea of an empowered presidency to accommodate Allawi. But again, this was a hugely problematic proposition: The powerful three-man presidential council of the 2005 to

2010 period was a transitional arrangement only, and the "ordinary" presidency according to the Iraqi constitution is a purely ceremonial post. Any changes to this would demand first a vote in parliament and then a popular referendum before any government could be seated. I tried to warn about this problem in September during talks in Washington with the National Security Council and various intelligence analysts and State Department officials. One very prominent U.S. ambassador agreed with me, but most others made light of the problem. It was quite shocking to find that senior officials working with Iraq policy for the White House thought a quick-fix could be found in the shape of the partial constitutional-revision report from 2009, which did propose an extension of the current presidency council. What they apparently forgot was that the report would first have to be adopted by the Iraqi parliament in a special session and then put to a referendum in which it could be voted down by a two-thirds majority in any three governorates. Eventually, in the arrangement he agreed to in November 2010, Allawi did sign up to a variant of the national security council called the "national council for strategic policies." But without any basis in Iraq's laws or constitution it was still first and foremost a paper tiger, though one with the potential to disrupt or even explode the new power-sharing arrangements if it should fail to satisfy the aspirations of Iraqiyya.

Constitutional Disintegration[1]

November 19, 2009

Today's heated scenes in the Iraqi parliament are symptomatic of a more general tendency towards constitutional chaos in Iraq in the wake of the adoption of the elections law on 8 November and the subsequent veto of it—or parts of it—by Tariq al-Hashemi yesterday. At one point, the Sadrist head of the legal committee triumphantly announced that the federal supreme court had effectively vetoed the veto for being unconstitutional; on closer inspection it turned out matters were not so clear cut with the parliamentary speaker, Ayad al-Samarraie, saying there was no contradiction between the Hashemi veto and the opinion of the court.

The core of the problem here is the strong but not very detailed powers assigned to the temporary tripartite presidency council in the 2005 constitution. The presidency council reviews all legislation submitted by parliament; unless all its members agree to a bill it must be returned to parliament within ten days of receipt. This procedure can be repeated once more, but may then be trumped by a three-fifths majority of the parliament. Beyond the timelines and the general consensus requirement, no other specific procedural details are outlined in the constitution.

In terms of its constitutionality, then, the only possible problem of the constitutionality of the veto by Hashemi relates not to its content but to its form. This is an attempt at rejecting only a small portion of the amendment to the election law, relating mainly to voting procedures for Iraqis abroad. Through instructing the parliament to revisit only a limited section of the bill, Hashemi is entering unchartered constitutional territory that can easily become something of a quagmire unless there is a disciplined legal committee and strong-minded parliamentary presidency to do the navigation. Add to this the political context of all of this—and especially the fact that the Kurds are seeing an opportunity to press for a few more changes that would enhance their share of the pie, especially through larger minority quotas that could include pro-Kurdish representatives of the smaller minority communities in the north—and it is easy to be pessimistic about the prospect of an early resolution. If the outcome of all of this is a reversion to the closed list system of 2005 or no elections at all, then the net outcome of the veto will be a negative one for the nationalist forces Hashemi ostensibly is seeking to empower.

If the attempt by Hashemi to restrict the veto to a single article thus seems somewhat problematic, reactions to the veto by Iraqi parliamentarians have been even more worrying—and serve to reinforce the impression of constitutional frailty in today's Iraq. In a strongly worded letter, the second speaker of the parliament, Khalid al-Atiyya, a Maliki ally, today dismisses the veto for being unconstitutional "because it does not refer to a violation of a single clause of the constitution or to the by-law of the parliament". Atiyya then goes on and on with vague and abstract references to the "will of the Iraqi people" and threats to the Iraqi democracy. But where is the constitutionality of Atiyya's rejection of the veto? Where is the requirement that a veto be furnished with elaborate references to the constitution? After all, the presidency council is the ugly, omnipotent monster that the elites of 2005 created with the aim of guarding their own privileges; it vetoes but it does not necessarily have to speak its mind. In other words, the presidency council is not the constitutional court. At any rate, proving the constitutionality of Hashemi's demand for one deputy per 100,000 voters, living in Iraq or in exile, is exceedingly simple, since the requirement has been spelt out in the constitution itself (under the current system, the votes of the exiles count only towards the 7 compensation seats, alongside all other Iraqi voters, so they do not have a full vote). Nevertheless, almost all the members of the old Shiite Islamist alliance (UIA) have reacted with fury to the veto today, mostly without providing arguments that truly relate to constitutional aspects. One Maliki advisor even suggested that the veto was unconstitutional because it was not unanimous, which is to turn the whole logic of the presidency council upside down.

The whole situation inevitably brings up memories of the rather shameful attempt by KDP/PUK/ISCI to use the presidency council in March 2008 to veto the provincial powers law because it set a timeline for local elections (which those parties wanted to avoid). After first having voted in favor of other parts of the law, ISCI along with the Kurds tried to vote down the article that created an election timeline; ISCI subsequently presented a presidential veto that contained principled criticism of some of the articles on center–periphery relations they themselves had voted in favor of earlier! But it was the subsequent withdrawal of the veto that underlined the fragile constitutional situation in "the new Iraq". After an unannounced visit by U.S. Vice-President Dick Cheney the veto was promptly removed—despite the fact that there is no such "undo" option in the Iraqi constitution.

Constitutional Disintegration (Part II)[2]
November 22, 2009

It is a tall order for a non-Arab to challenge the Arabic reading skills of those who have practiced this complicated language for all their life. Nonetheless, that is precisely what will be attempted in the following analysis. Hopefully, this kind of audacious third-party intervention can at least serve to highlight the degree to which the whole political and constitutional process in Iraq is now worrying close to a complete collapse because of the ongoing dispute over the election law.

Only one day after the veto of the election law by Tariq al-Hashemi, Bahaa al-Aaraji (the Sadrist chairman of the legal committee in the Iraqi parliament) and Hadi al-Amiri (ISCI's head of the security and defence committee) made big headlines by revealing that a letter from Iraq's federal supreme court supposedly had declared the veto by Hashemi to be "unconstitutional" and therefore void. There were objections to this interpretation from both Sunnis and secular nationalists, but in many Iraqi media outlets the interpretation by Aaraji and Amiri went unchallenged. The next day, the Daawa party even organized popular demonstrations against the veto in places like Basra.

In the subsequent discussion about the veto, the fronts have hardened. Both sides claim the court supports their view. However, one highly important ingredient has been missing: The letter from the court itself.

The contents of this letter are now available and they are in fact exceedingly brief and simple. What follows after the introduction is the sense of the court, which is given as an "opinion" (*ray*) and not a decision (*qarar*). It refers to article 49 of the Iraqi constitution, and its provision that there should be one deputy for every 100,000 Iraqis, to be elected by secret ballot in a way that secures the representation of all elements of the Iraqi people. The court also cites the aspiration of a 25% female quota. It then goes on to say simply that "the Iraqi constitution does not distinguish between Iraqis at home and abroad; all it stipulates is that all components of the Iraqi population be represented and that the female share of seats should be no less than a quarter". It then adds, "It is for the Iraqi election commission (IHEC) to specify the [more detailed] electoral procedures".

And that is all. How can this possibly be construed as a hard and fast ruling about the unconstitutionality of Hashemi's veto? The foundation of his veto was precisely a worry that there would be discrimination between Iraqis at home and abroad, and if anything it is that sort of discrimination in the current law (and not the veto of it) which is implicitly denounced as "unconstitutional" in the opinion. Other than that, the letter seems to signal a desire of the court not to get too involved in the affair, since it refuses to engage with the veto itself in the decision—the veto is not even mentioned in the "opinion" part of the letter.

Nevertheless, a slightly more specific interpretation of the court's view will be attempted here. There is a focus on non-discrimination of Iraqis at home and abroad, and there is also a focus on the only quota-like criteria in the constitution—for women and population "elements". A proper election law and practical arrangements will need to take into account both aspects. One possible interpretation would therefore be that it is permissible to seek female and minority representation through quotas, whereas the right of exiles to be represented on par with Iraqis at home (whose inviolability in itself is highlighted) must be secured through other means. In other words, the opinion could be taken to signal "full representation for exiles, but (maybe) not by way of quotas".

This in turn relates to much of the current confusion concerning the "new election law" and exactly what it is—i.e., what consists of leftovers from the 2005 law, what is in the amendments, and what is left for IHEC to decide administratively. It is noteworthy that despite what the media says, there is no explicit "quota" of 5% for the out-of-country vote in the amendments. Instead, there is a 5% quota for "compensatory" seats (the total number of seats, in turn, is governed by statistics from the ministry of trade), and in a clause left over from the 2005 law it is specified that the exile vote will count at the "national" level (so far interpreted by IHEC as inclusion in the calculation of the compensatory seats). But under the current arrangements the compensatory seats do not in any way make up a fully fledged "nineteenth" electoral district because they also serve a number of other purposes. First, 8 minority seats are deducted, and then the remaining seats are distributed to the winning lists. Crucially, in this process the exiled vote is pooled with all the votes that have already been counted once in the governorates to calculate theoretical party shares in a truly proportional, single-constituency system. In this way, under the current arrangements, quite regardless of the percentage of "compensatory" seats, exiled voters will still be "second-class" citizen because their vote is counted only once. Conversely, the vote of the domestic voter is counted twice—first at the governorate level, and then at the national level. Only in the latter process is there true equality (and non-discrimination) under the current system.

Given parameters like these, one possible solution that would seem compatible with the view expressed by the federal supreme court would be to let exiled Iraqis vote according to their home governorates, whose quotas of seats in turn would need to be revised administratively to reflect the total of domestic plus exiled voters. This would however introduce the complicating practical factors of using governorate lists for hundreds of entities abroad as well as determining "governorate of origin" for millions of Iraqis abroad. A simpler solution which would also be more just than the current system would be a nineteenth electoral district proper for exiles.

Constitutional Disintegration (Part III): IHEC Is Making Up the Law[3]

January 15, 2010

One of the bewildering aspects of the recent decision to bar Salih al-Mutlak and some 500 other candidates from standing as candidates in the 7 March election is the apparent resolve of both the accountability and justice (de-Baathification) board as well as the Iraqi elections commission (IHEC) to enforce the ban also at the level of political entities, where some 15 parties are expected to be excluded. The rationale is the idea that an entire political entity should automatically meet the same fate as its political leader.

But where exactly is the legal basis for that approach? One would have thought that the source for such a momentous and far-reaching decision would be easily available. But it does not appear to be in the 2005 constitution. Nor is it included in what today remains of the 2005 elections law. It cannot be found in the series of amendments to that law that were adopted last autumn. Maybe it could be hidden in sections 6 and 7 of the provincial elections law from 2008, which were added to the parliamentary election law through a simple cross-reference in the amendments last autumn? No, it is not there either. Even a quick skimming of the various directives recently issued by IHEC in relation to the upcoming elections fails to return an obvious reference of relevance.

The fact is that the legal basis does not appear to exist. Rather, it has apparently been made up. The reason we can make such a sweeping claim is that IHEC itself revealed its uncertainty about the matter back in December last year, when it sent a query to the federal supreme court on the subject. Referring to article 7 of the constitution (which outlaws racist and terrorist parties etc., "and in particular the Baath party"), it asked precisely whether an entire political entity is automatically banned if its leader is affected by de-Baathification measures. The federal supreme court merely answered that this is outside its jurisdiction and is for IHEC to decide.

So it appears that in this vacuum, IHEC can make up the law as it pleases, and no force in the new Iraqi democracy apparently feels any obligation to intervene.

What is particularly remarkable in all of this is the timing. The request from IHEC to the federal supreme court is dated 16 December 2009, just a little more than a week after the legal framework for the elections had been finalized in the Iraqi parliament after a second presidential veto had been averted. On 7 January 2010, when the accountability and justice board announced its "bombshell" decision to bar certain candidates, it reproduced the exact language that had been used by IHEC in its query to the federal supreme court, i.e., "14 entities would be excluded because their leaders were affected by de-Baathification measures". Thus, the chronology of all of this suggests that there may have been close dialogue on the subject between IHEC and the accountability and justice board dating back at least to mid-December 2009, and that the decision by IHEC to go ahead with the exclusions may have been more carefully orchestrated than previously thought.

The Ruling of the Accountability and Justice Board[4]
January 19, 2010

IHEC had promised a list of the candidates recently disqualified by the account-ability and justice board; it then changed its mind and will now simply publish the candidate lists (i.e., those who qualified), fearing perhaps that the other approach would transform the excluded candidates into martyrs. And so while parliament today has been told about the 511 persons that are barred from standing in the 7 March elections, the detailed information is still not in the public domain and will probably filter through only gradually or in a media leak.

Meanwhile, while developments over the past weeks have demonstrated amply both the politicized nature of the de-Baathification bureaucracy as well as the legal impressionism of some of its decisions, it may be worthwhile to have another look at the general legal basis for the decision to exclude individual Iraqis from taking part in the next elections. What we do know from the parliamentary proceed-ings today is that altogether 511 candidates have been disqualified. 182 of them belonged to the secret and special security agencies of the old regime; 216 were members of the Baath; 105 were recipients of various medals of honour (including the "Mesopotamia" order); 5 had participated in repressing the 1991 *intifada*; 3 were "propagandists" in favor of the Baath.

The obvious question here is whether the de-Baathification body is operating beyond its remit in its eagerness to cleanse the Iraqi public sphere of any trace of Baathism. There is much to suggest that that is exactly what is going on. A key concept here is to be "subject to the de-Baathification rulings", which according to the 2005 constitution would bar Iraqis from various kinds of high office, including running for parliament. But what does it mean to be "subject to the de-Baathifica-tion rulings"? Clearly, this is not the same as being a member of the Baath party.

In that case, the following clause of the constitution (135/5) would be meaningless: "Merely being a member of the Baath party is not sufficient basis for transfer to the courts, and the Baath party member enjoys equality before the law and judicial protection, *unless he is subject to the de-Baathification rulings* [emphasis added]". In other words, the constitution clearly differentiates between the two.

A more reasonable place to start would be the procedures of the accountability and justice act of January 2008, which "de-Baathifies" the Iraqi bureaucracy by focusing on certain ranks of membership ("regional", "branch" or "section") or seniority in the bureaucracy (director-generals)—as well as on careers in the "repressive" components of the security forces (i.e., secret services and special forces). In this context—leaving for a moment aside the deeper questions about the legitimacy of the current accountability and justice board, which has not been seated in accordance with the law—one cannot help wondering whether its leaders may have gone too far. For example, apparently the board has disqualified people from running for office simply because of Baath membership, regardless of rank. Not only that, what about those who were recipients of medals? The fact that these are listed separately would seem to suggest that they were not party members at all, and after all some of these orders (the Rafidayn medal, for example) have apparently been issued since the days of the monarchy!

The separate group of those who participated in suppressing in the 1991 rebellion is particularly interesting, even if it is small. This probably relates to tribal leaders who were neither party members nor officers, but who opted to join the regime at the time of the 1991 uprising. As a matter of fact, by implication the 2005 constitution specifically *allows* such participants to become deputies, because it is a special criterion for becoming member of the presidency council of Iraq that one should satisfy "the same conditions as those required for becoming a deputy, *and also not have participated in repressing the 1991 uprising* [emphasis added]". In other words, the constitution specifically envisages the possibility that a person may lawfully become a parliamentary deputy—but not a member of the presidency council—even if he took part in anti-insurgency activities in 1991. In fact, exactly the same logic also applies to Baathist membership: A presidency council member also must not have been a Baathist member "for the last ten years prior to its fall"—leaving, by implication, a positive verdict that a Baathist member who quit after 1993 may well become a parliamentary deputy, as long as s/he does not try to become a member of the presidency council.

Finally, there is the ruling to exclude "Baathist propagandists". This is apparently an attempt by the accountability and justice board to evoke article 7 of the constitution, which outlaws Baathist revival attempts. The only problem is that according to the new accountability and justice legislation of 2008, this is not the business of the committee to deal with. There is no specific reference to article 7 of the constitution in that law (other than a brief mention of it in the glossary of terms) and this is in fact unsurprising since the special law called for under article 7 of the constitution has yet to be passed by the Iraqi parliament! All in all, then, even if these latter points affect just a handful of people, they serve to highlight the brazenness and totally arbitrary ways of a commission that does not even bother to create a semblance of legality for its decisions.

The Ghost of Paul Bremer Strikes Again:
Nine Entities Banned with Reference to CPA Order 97[5]

January 25, 2010

The Iraqi elections commission (IHEC) has earlier queried the federal supreme court about the relationship between excluded party leaders and the entities they represent. Last December it asked whether it would be constitutional to ban an entity if its leader were excluded; the court replied it did not want to issue an opinion on this and said the matter rested with IHEC. It was subsequently rumored that the accountability and justice board wanted to exclude between 10 and 15 entities, and it was thought that there might be an attempt at linking the banning of entity heads and their entire parties.

Today, IHEC has acted in a bolder fashion. Referring to section 5 of Coalition Provisional Authority (CPA) order 97 from 2004, it has cancelled the approval of 9 entities previously slated to take part in the elections. CPA order 97 is an unmistakable Paul Bremer creation. It pompously begins, "Pursuant to my authority as Administrator of the Coalition Provisional Authority. . . . " The relevant section simply runs as follows, "All further matters regarding the regulation and certification of political entities lie with the Commission exclusively". Very general and wide-ranging powers indeed. The document was signed on 7 June 2004; the "commission" referred to is what was then the "Independent Electoral Commission", which later became the "higher commission".

The entities affected include two sub-entities within Iraqiyya (most famously the Hiwar front of Salih al-Mutlak); two parties within Unity of Iraq; the party of Nehru Abd al-Karim; one party within State of Law, and the rest smaller lists and independents. The commission does not spell out what the banning of these parties will mean in practice. It says candidates cannot use the names and logos of these parties. That may possibly mean that the practical implications are limited— the case of Iraqiyya is in any case more convoluted because subsequent to their registration as separate electoral entities last autumn, Hiwar (now banned) technically merged with Wifaq to form a new movement or *haraka*, distinct from the coalition, and with Ayad Allawi as its joint leader.

What this whole issue shows is that once more IHEC is acting in concert with the accountability and justice board. The reversion to a carte-blanche article in a law authored by Paul Bremer—no specific coherent legal justification for the exclusion is offered, just a brutal attempt at asserting boundless power—serves to highlight the murkiness of the waters that we are headed for with this election.

Chalabi and Lami Also Control the "Independent" Elections Commission[6]

February 9, 2010

One of the many remarkable aspects of the continuing de-Baathification saga has been the apparent willingness of the Iraqi elections commission (IHEC) to more or less mechanically follow the recommendations of the accountability and justice board and its two leading figures, Ahmad Chalabi and Ali Faysal al-Lami, who are both candidates for the Shiite Islamist Iraqi National Alliance (INA). Nonetheless, until now IHEC has at least maintained a semblance of formal independence in its decision-making by providing its own "independent" consideration of the advice from the accountability and justice board before implementing it. This was the procedure that was followed for example in the recent exclusion of 511 candidates for the 7 March parliamentary elections.

However, with the release of the minutes from one of the latest meetings of IHEC, both the commission's independence as well as the distinction between the elections commission and the accountability and justice board are thrown into question in a serious way. Recently, on top of the ban of 500 plus candidates, IHEC also moved to cancel the approval of nine political entities. The logic that was followed was apparently that when an entity leader was subject to de-Baathification the entire list should have its approval annulled; however the sole legal justification offered was a reference to an order issued by Paul Bremer in 2004 (CPA order 97) which gave the predecessor of IHEC the right to basically cancel any political entity it wished to cancel—probably reflecting the absence of more plausible, precise and up-to-date legal justifications for establishing links between entity heads and their electoral lists in terms of de-Baathification. Importantly, when IHEC first issued its decision, one did get the sense that the elections commission had come up with the idea itself, which would have been the most natural procedure since the CPA order relates to the election law that was in use in 2004 and 2005 and since it is the commission itself that is empowered by the CPA law. But the newly released minutes reveal that the specific idea of reverting to a sweeping CPA edict in order to ban unwanted political entities came not from IHEC but directly from the accountability and justice board!

The brief summary of the relevant meeting on 18 January reveals in an unambiguous way the origin of the idea to use CPA order 97: "The assembly [of IHEC] discussed letter 231 from the accountability and justice board dated 18 January, entitled 'ban on participation' and referring to section five of law number 97 on elections and political parties from 2004, and accordingly decided. . . . " When this was later issued as a decision it looked like something that had been agreed by IHEC. In reality, it was the wording of the accountability and justice and its decision in everything but the name. In other words, the accountability and justice board is not merely influencing IHEC. Rather, at times the board is capable of acting as the guardian of the "independent" commission, thinking on its behalf and supplying the very arguments that are being marshalled to defend its supposedly autonomous position.

The Ban on Mutlak and Ani: Miscarriage of Justice in Iraq[7]
February 11, 2010

In his characteristic way, Ali al-Lami of the de-Baathification board late Thursday night, at the beginning of the Iraqi weekend, informed a small number of news agencies that two of the top Iraqiyya candidates, Salih al-Mutlak and Zafir al-Ani, have been barred from standing as candidates in the 7 March election after their appeals were rejected by the special appeals court for de-Baathification cases.

Few new details are known, but enough information about these cases is already in the public domain to label this act as a straightforward miscarriage of justice:

- The whole key to understanding what is going on is the realization that there is not a single law that governs the de-Baathification process. Instead, the framework that is being applied combines several elements, only some of which are regular laws adopted by the Iraqi parliament—and almost all of which contradict each other or are incongruous.
- The Iraqi constitution outlaws glorification of the "Saddamist Baath" party in article 7, but this clause also stipulates a ban on promoting racism and sectarian cleansing, all of which is to be combined in a special law. Such a law has never been issued by the Iraqi parliament, and it is fairly obvious that without it no "de-Baathification" can be carried out under this heading since one would then also need to investigate many other political parties who may be plausibly accused of racism or sectarian cleansing.
- The only relevant piece of extant de-Baathification legislation is the accountability and justice law of January 2008. Although this law makes brief references to several constitutional clauses (including article 7) it is clear that the only specific mandate created by it are those actions outlined in article 6, which stipulates that individuals that held certain ranks and positions in the former regime—not ex-members of the Baath generally—are subject to de-Baathification. Ali al-Lami has publicly admitted that the case of Salih al-

Mutlak does not fall under this category, and the same probably holds true for Zafir al-Ani.

- The appeals procedure in the accountability and justice act is stipulated in articles 15 to 17 and explicitly applies only to those subject to de-Baathification under article 6 of the accountability and justice law. This shows beyond doubt that the law was never intended to specifically implement article 7 of the constitution. It also means that this particular appeals procedure in fact does not apply to the case of Salih al-Mutlak and that Mutlak (and probably also Ani) should have the right to appeal to the federal supreme court and/or the court of cassation instead since their cases supposedly involve glorification of the Baath.

- The appeals procedure in article 15 to 17 involves an appeals deadline of 30 days and 60 days for considering the appeal, both of which have been violated in this case. The apparent explanation for this relates to the bastard character of the "legal" framework that is being applied: Here the accountability and justice act of January 2008 has been welded together with an IHEC regulation on "registration and approval of entities" that was never passed by parliament but simply enacted by the commission in 2009. That regulation has a three-days appeals procedure which apparently is being enforced in this case.

- The ambiguous and hybrid nature of this arrangement is further highlighted because the second appeals procedure (i.e., that of the IHEC regulation) says nothing about the special appeals court for de-Baathification cases at all, but instead refers to the "electoral judicial panel". But instead of following the regulation, IHEC has brought in the special appeals court for de-Baathification cases that was hastily created by the Iraqi parliament in January in an attempt at improving the legal facade of the de-Baathification process—this was seen as especially important since the current accountability and justice board was never seated according to the procedures stipulated in the accountability and justice act! In other words, IHEC in this case is neither faithful to the accountability and justice act nor in compliance with its own regulations. By cutting and pasting from the accountability and justice act and the regulations for approval of entities, IHEC has created a legal hybrid that is grossly incoherent and with an appeals process that is arbitrary in the extreme and vulnerable to political machinations.

- Mutlak has moreover had his whole list banned with reference to another document that was undemocratically adopted: CPA order 97 of 2004, which basically gives IHEC unrestricted right to ban any party it does not like. The recourse to this edict by Paul Bremer once more shows how the de-Baathification board has major problems with producing plausible legal justifications for its actions.

- The disintegration of the legal framework at the level of the judiciary and the electoral commission has set the stage for similar processes at the local level across Iraq, where vigilante de-Baathification is being reported in several governorates—often abetted by local leaders of State of Law and Iraqi National Alliance, the two main Shiite coalitions, who apparently compete in being toughest on de-Baathification. Legal justifications are being made up entirely, including a suggestion in Amara that "the constitution bars previous Baathists from having high positions in the state" (in fact the constitution only stipulates a special de-Baathification requirement for certain jobs including the presidency council), and the idea circulated in Babel that a member at the lowest level of the Baath party should be disqualified from the local administration (with the exception of the security sector, according to the law only members higher than the *firqa* level are to be de-Baathified.)

This all raises the question of whether yesterday's release of 6,172 candidate names was indeed intended as the final list. Other wire reports today say only 28 appeals were accepted, and a few reinstatements were in fact noted in the list that was published yesterday. In other words, we have seen an almost total reversal of the position of the special appeals court within less than one week, suggesting that considerable political pressure has been brought to bear on its members as they tried to navigate the utter legal chaos that is the Iraqi de-Baathification process.

The Secret Election Manifesto[8]

February 25, 2010

We are barely a week away from the 7 March parliamentary elections in Iraq, but the electoral campaign just does not seem to be going anywhere useful.

What has yet to receive attention, though, is that despite their current uncommunicativeness on specific political issues, many of the biggest Iraqi parties have in fact already issued a manifesto about where they want to take the country: The final report of the constitutional review committee, appointed in 2006, was put together last autumn with the support of many of the biggest parties. This report represents the minimum that at least the majority of the constitutional review committee could agree on. Back in 2007, the work of the committee had run into difficulties over Shiite–Kurdish disagreement about arrangements for the oil sector; what we currently have is therefore a watered-down version where most controversial issues have simply been left aside. For some time, there were even rumors that a vote on this package would be attempted before the 2010 elections, but with the prolonged debate on the election law that particular ambition seemed to gradually fade away.

The major new proposed addition to the constitution is the creation of a second chamber in parliament (starting with article 81). According to the draft, this new institution will consist of two members from each governorate (regardless of whether the governorate is organized in a federal region or not), except that Baghdad will have four representative—this should mean 38 senators altogether. The members will be elected at the same time as the parliament and the sessions of the two institutions will be concurrent; there will also be 5 additional members to be appointed jointly by the president and the premier on the basis of their "expertise" as well as considerations relating to the representation of the "elements" of the Iraqi people—in this context code for micro-minorities. The powers of the second chamber are not well specified, and appear to add further contradictions to the Iraqi constitutional framework. For example, in article 94 the senate is given the prerogative of initiating legislation that is specifically related to the governorates and the federal regions: This provision seems to be at odds with the basic idea in the existing constitution of residual powers for the governorates and federal regions in everything not specified as the exclusive competence of the central government or a shared area (where presumably the existing parliament legislates). More unequivocally, the senate will review laws passed by the parliament and can send them back for reconsideration within 15 days with a simple majority. However, the parliament can adopt the law as long as it first "considers" the grounds for rejection by the senate. In sum, the proposed second chamber is not a particularly strong body, although it certainly carries the potential for creating further hitches in the Iraqi legislative process.

Optimists had expected that the meatiest changes in the revision process would come in the definition of the powers of the central government, but it is noteworthy that in this draft hardly anything has changed from the exceedingly weak status accorded to Baghdad in 2005. Rather obvious areas like civil aviation are now formally a central-government prerogative, as are the environment and migration issues. But nothing has changed with respect to key questions concerning the administration of the oil sector. Instead, article 188 provides the clearest expression of the mindset of the drafters of the revised constitution. In it, the three-man, ethno-sectarian presidency council that will expire in a few weeks is given an extended period of life, stipulated to last until the first senate has been elected (although not more than one parliamentary cycle). In other words, under these arrangements, Iraqis would get at least four more years of formal *muhasasa* or ethno-sectarian power-sharing, with the concomitant potential of legislative deadlock caused by disagreement between the powerful members of the presidency council. It is perfectly conceivable that this kind of arrangement could lead to further postponement on key legislative projects like those related to the oil sector.

In sum, the parties behind this proposal wanted to keep Baghdad weak and perpetuate the Bremerian model of government of oversized governments of national unity and strong presidential vetoes at least until 2015. Today, when everyone talks about "unity" and being a "nationalist", the draft for a revised constitution may serve as a more faithful manifesto of where parties like the Kurdistan alliance, the Iraqi National Alliance and Tawafuq really want to go. The interesting thing is the position of two of the minority parties on the constitutional committee that are today considered among the strongest candidates for providing the next premier of Iraq: Daawa and Iraqiyya. In terms of getting the political debate back on track, perhaps issues like these could be a useful vantage point for Iraqiyya, which traditionally has had a firm nationalist position on constitutional issues. And what about the Daawa, whose centralism and resistance to power-sharing has sometimes put them at odds with fellow Shiite Islamists? Recent reports from Iraq say that the accountability and justice board is now attacking high-level security officials that have ties to Maliki, possibly with the aim of marginalizing him as a future premier; is this the point where Maliki might finally wake up and reverse his position on the de-Baathification disaster?

The Federal Supreme Court Goes Incommunicado[9]
April 1, 2010

It has emerged that one possible explanation for the recent decision by Iraqiyya to challenge the jurisdiction of the Iraqi federal supreme court could be sheer exasperation. After a period of long silence, and without much attention from the media, over the past few days the court has quietly issued a series of opinions that must have done little to inspire confidence in its ability to act as a neutral arbiter in Iraqi affairs.

The first is the much-anticipated and long-overdue response to a query from Salih al-Mutlak and Zafir al-Ani that was transferred by Ayad al-Samarraie, the parliamentary speaker, to the court on 28 February, i.e., more than one week ahead of the parliamentary elections. The two deputies were asking about the permissibility of their exclusion from the election based on a reference to article 7 of the constitution, which outlaws glorification of the Baath, racism and sectarian cleansing—but which also calls for a special law to implement those red lines in Iraqi politics. Mutlak and Ani asked whether one could be excluded with reference to this article at a point in time when the actual piece of legislation called for by the constitution has yet to be passed by parliament.

The court's decision is not particularly sophisticated. It simply says, the query does not call for an interpretation of article 7/1 of the constitution; accordingly it is outside the jurisdiction of the federal supreme court! And that's it. It is not unlikely that this striking move by the court (the query clearly *does* relate to constitutional interpretation) may have played a role in the recent breakdown of trust between Iraqiyya and the Iraqi legal system and the decision by the former to question the prerogatives of the court more broadly. The long period that lapsed from the initial query—and, obviously, the fact that the elections took place in the interim, without Mutlak and Ani—suggests that the court is now under so much political pressure that it cannot anymore be described as an independent broker in Iraqi politics.

It is interesting, too, in this regard, that the court refused to have anything to do with a query from the election commission, IHEC, about how to apportion compensation seats. In this case, one can perhaps to a greater extent understand the court's reluctance, since the issue at hand concerns the relationship between the electoral law and IHEC regulation 21 on the apportionment of the 7 compensation seats. Back in 2005, IHEC applied a fundamentally undemocratic procedure of simply allotting the compensation seats to party leaders who could do with them as they saw fit (i.e., remunerating loyal but not necessarily popular non-winning candidates within their lists). In that sense IHEC regulation 21 of 2009—which now gives the seats to the non-winning candidates with the most votes—was clearly a step in the right direction: IHEC objected to articles 17 and 18 of the old election law whereby party leaderships provide a list of nominees for the compensation seats, describing it as a remnant of the closed-list system. But today, powerful party elites want the old system back in order to reward their protégées with seats at the expense of candidates that did well among voters; hence the request to the federal supreme court.

Once more, the court says it has no jurisdiction in the matter—unable or unwilling to communicate, or perhaps a combination thereof.

What Does It Take To Be a *Kutla*?[10]
April 15, 2010

One issue that may postpone ongoing Shiite attempts at a post-election merger has to do with the criteria for achieving *kutla*-hood, i.e., satisfying the requirements for being identified as the "biggest bloc with in the parliament in numerical terms" and hence the rightful former of the next government. The much-cited federal supreme court ruling on this subject is disconcertingly short on detail, and only speaks more broadly of the need for the biggest bloc—whether it was formed prior to or after the elections—to have a "single-entity" form (*kiyan wahid*). However, Iraqi parliamentary tradition as it has developed since 2005 offers more specifics. In particular it is clear that every *kutla* needs to have a leader or *ra'is*. Such leaders are mentioned in the parliamentary bylaws of 2006, and, more importantly, in practice they have become quite significant because of a number of decisive meetings that have been held at the level of bloc leaders. In these meetings, the norm has been one leader per bloc, for example Fuad Masum for the Kurdistan Alliance, the late Abd al-Aziz al-Hakim for the United Iraqi Alliance (succeeded in 2009 by Jalal al-Din al-Saghir), Hassan al-Shammari for Fadila once they broke away from UIA, and so on.

Presumably, the need to agree on a bloc leader forms another complicating factor for the projected INA/SLA merger, since the Shiite parties will have to agree on a single person. They also need a name for the new alliance.

More Post-Election De-Baathification: Another Blow to the Idea of Democracy in Iraq[11]
April 26, 2010

Iraq's powerful de-Baathification committee has dealt another blow to the idea of democracy in Iraq: After many conflicting reports over the weekend, it is becoming increasingly clear that the board's attempt to de-Baathify 55 of the replacement candidates for other candidates that were themselves de-Baathified has been sustained by the electoral judicial panel, along with an acceptance of the proposal to annul the personal votes for these candidates instead of transferring those votes to the relevant lists.

With respect to the politics of this, the de-Baathification committee, of course, is largely controlled by the pro-Iranian Iraqi National Alliance, whereas the electoral judicial panel is seen as leaning towards Prime Minister Nuri al-Maliki after its recent decision to allow a Baghdad recount. The main victim of these decisions, Iraqiyya, has no significant influence in either body. The Kurdish chief of the elections commission IHEC, Faraj al-Haydari, had however previously expressed his distaste for the idea of annulling the votes altogether.

Because of the messy process in which candidates were struck from the ballots right until the last minute, it is still unclear exactly which individuals are subject to the new decision. Seat-winning candidates that could be in trouble include Ibrahim al-Mutlak, the replacement candidate for Salih al-Mutlak who got some 5,400 personal votes and a seat in Baghdad.

Crucially, the example of Mutlak shows that this is about more than candidates—it is also about voters. Here we have 5,400 Iraqis whose votes may simply be stolen from them according to procedures that are not based on any law or even any IHEC regulation. In particular, the decision to penalize voters for their active use of the open-list system (a passive list vote would not have been cancelled) risks putting the whole idea of democracy in disrepute in Iraq.

The de-Baathified candidates have been given one month to complain the decision—another ad hoc legal concoction by IHEC and something which firmly pushes certification of the results towards June, regardless of what happens to the Baghdad recount as well as further demands for recounts by the Kurds in some of the northern governorates (which apparently remain pending).

IHEC in Trouble Again[12]

May 28, 2010

New information keeps emerging about the attempts by State of Law (SLA) to have three parliamentary seat winners disqualified and their votes cancelled—two from Iraqiyya in Diyala and one from the Iraqi National Alliance (INA) in Basra. The likely net effect of such an action would be a gain for State of Law of one to two seats and a similar loss for Iraqiyya, putting the two on an equal footing or even making State of Law the biggest bloc in parliament.

The Sumaria television station is chasing these developments and keeps churning out useful information in its interviews with key players. Among them are Khalid al-Asadi of the Daawa, who has said that the rationale for seeking the cancellation of votes is that the 52 cases of post-election de-Baathification led to disqualifications as well as annulment of votes (as suspected earlier, this now seems confirmed in the Baghdad recount results and apparently includes such a prominent case as Ibrahim al-Mutlak). In Asadi's view, it is impossible to differentiate between the de-Baathifications and other cases of post-election exclusions, such as those now attempted with regard to the three seat winners. Abdallah al-Jibburi is sought excluded on the basis of a past conviction; Najm al-Harbi on the basis of an arrest warrant but not a conviction (this seems particularly dubious and is protested by Iraqiyya since the elections law is unequivocal in its requirement of a sentence having actually been passed—*mahkuman 'alayhi*). Furat al-Sharaa of INA has apparently been given the all clear from IHEC since he has produced evidence that he left the army before the relevant date.

That part of Asadi's argument, seen in isolation, is comprehensible in so far as the election law in its paragraph 6 on candidate requirements puts all these criteria—de-Baathification, membership in the armed forces and legal conviction—on exactly the same footing. In other words, slashing the votes of the de-Baathified ones without doing the same for other post-election exclusions would seem inconsistent, and the trouble is that IHEC has already accepted the exclusion of Harbi and Jibburi in principle (but without taking away their votes).

But that is where the logic of Asadi's arguments stops. He goes on to say, "the election law decrees that the votes of excluded candidates that don't meet the requirements for candidacy be slashed". Where exactly in the law is that? Or is it hidden in an IHEC regulation? All the election law appears to say is, in article 14 adopted in 2005, that if a member of parliament loses his or her seat "for whatever reason" then s/he should be replaced by the next person on that list, which would seem to support the idea of keeping the seat distribution between lists unaffected and hence not annul any votes at all. IHEC has already applied this to the case of the recently murdered Iraqiyya candidate in Nineveh, indicating it should apply generally also to the transitional period between the election date and the first meeting of parliament—otherwise the expression "for whatever reason" would be meaningless.

Rather, the idea of "cancelling" votes—*shatb* and *hadhf* are the Arabic terms that are being used interchangeably—seems to originate with the de-Baathification committee, which included this demand when it started its post-election attack back in March. What this all goes back to is the failure of IHEC and the international community to stand up decisively against the theft of votes implied in post-election disqualifications—and a concomitant domino effect of ever bolder attacks on political enemies. Before the elections IHEC and the international community failed to stem the wave of politically motivated de-Baathification. After the elections, the first batch of 52 exclusions may perhaps have looked innocuous since the seat allocation was not affected, and IHEC danced along with the demand from the accountability and justice board that these votes be annulled. The 9 additional and more recent de-Baathifications caused concern even at the presidential level since the personal votes in question were so many that the seat distribution might be upset, but instead of uprooting the problem of politically motivated attacks, the stop-gap measure of a reinstatement by the special appeals board for de-Baathification was used. All this established dangerous precedents and legal contradictions, and it is in this legal haze that the SLA and Maliki are now seeking a last-minute opening for winning the election in injury time.

Meanwhile, there are worrisome signs that the international community is not paying sufficient attention. A sometimes-erratic webcast from USIP yesterday seemed to convey a message from Ad Melkert of UNAMI (the UN agency in Baghdad) that "the good news is that everything is being done according to the books"! Which books, one wonders? *Rhapsodies on Islamic Democracy* by A. Chalabi, A. Lami et al.? *One Thousand and One Nights*? For the relationship between the certification process of the Iraqi elections and the relevant constitutional and legal frameworks is in fact now looking increasingly fictional and only a decisive message from the international community against post-election disqualifications can save the situation. With the results now having been sent to the court for certification, IHEC still retains a degree of leverage because the courts do not have the competence to recalculate the seats as per the SLA demand, and UNAMI and the international community have the opportunity to bring closure to this divisive issue by focusing on the idea of restoring votes to the relevant lists. Doing so for the 52 excluded cases would not change the seat distribution but would br_ng an end to the continuous wave of politically motivated attacks. As such it would be a far healthier solution than relying on the Iraqi courts, which risk becoming increasingly politicized over the coming week unless something is done to end this theater.

The Hammudi Files and Article 76[13]

June 10, 2010

On the eve of the first meeting of the Iraqi parliament (scheduled for next Monday) and amid frantic attempts by some Shiite leaders to unify their two blocs more effectively, the interpretation of article 76 of the constitution on the selection of the premier candidate has assumed renewed relevance. Basically, the biggest winner in the elections, Iraqiyya, is disputing a liberal interpretation of article 76 according to which electoral blocs would be allowed to form super-alliances after the elections, thereby gaining the right to form the next government by virtue of being the "biggest bloc" at the expense of Iraqiyya (which came first in terms of number of deputies returned in the elections themselves). Pieces of evidence relating to the constitutional drafting process in 2005 have recently been circulating in the shape of a video snip from the fourteenth meeting of the constitutional committee on 25 July 2005, and some of this material has been published by the television station Al-Sharqiya.

The brief video snip shows an altercation during a meeting in the constitutional committee mainly between Sami al-Askari (of Daawa) and Humam Hammudi (of ISCI, the committee chairman). There is also a third person involved mostly outside the view of the camera, possibly Nadim al-Jabiri (of Fadila) who appears at the very end of the snip. Most significantly with respect to the debate about the interpretation of article 76, there is reference to a report of a previous meeting which according to two of the three men states that the right to form the next government should be "according to the electoral achievements" (*hasab al-istihqaq al-intikhabi*), which would confirm the interpretation currently favored by Iraqiyya of disallowing post-election super-alliances of electoral blocs for the purpose of supplying the premier candidate. Hammudi protests, but not very effectively at first. He interjects and says, *hasab al-istihqaq al-intikhabi al-niyabi* or "according to the electoral parliamentary achievements". Seen in isolation this does not mean a big difference and would just refer to the distinction between percentages of the vote and the percentage of seats actually achieved, and as such also in conformity with the current Iraqiyya position. However, Hammudi muddles the situation by referring to the existence of "two views" on defining the right to form the government (alas, the Nokia tune corrupts his attempt at clarifying this!) and also mentions the term "parliamentary bloc" (*kutla niyabiyya*), which is indeed the language that ended up being used in the constitution and forms the basis of the more flexible interpretation allowing post-election bloc formation. The video ends without any conclusion to the debate.

The context in which this information emerged is in itself interesting. Sami al-Askari raised the question in relation to the scenario of a second premier candidate, in case of the failure of the first. There is discussion whether the second candidate should come from the same bloc that was given the first attempt, or from another one—obviously this is where the point about clarifying "electoral achievements" becomes particularly important. Again, though, the final version of the constitution in fact remains mute on this question and really places all power for selecting the second candidate with the president. The only requirement, actually, is that he should be a "different" candidate from the first, i.e., he could be any eligible Iraqi (same requirements as for president except a minimum age set at 35 years and a college degree etc.), and strictly speaking does not even have to belong to any of the parties in parliament. Nonetheless, some Iraqi politicians today still seem to believe that the right to be the second premier candidate belongs to the second biggest bloc in parliament.

On the whole, the video provides an important indication that these issues had been thought about in 2005, and that many Shiite Islamist members of the constitutional committee advocated the view that is now being promoted by Iraqiyya, to the point where this at one point was reflected in a written report. Clearly, it would be helpful if a copy of that report were put in the public domain too. On the other hand, though, it has to be remembered that many of the most catastrophic parts of the constitution were not really authored until the subsequent month of August (this was when the Kurds brought in people like Peter Galbraith to consult on matters relating to federalism). Against that backdrop, the video of the 25 July meeting is primarily a testament to an ongoing dispute at an early point of the constitutional drafting process rather than a definitive and unequivocal account of the true "intentions of the framers".

The Bloc-Formation Soap Opera Drags On[14]
June 20, 2010

Some of the chaos in today's government-formation process relates to the fact that bloc formation simply is not covered by any existing piece of legislation beyond the reference in article 76 of the constitution. In particular, its absence in the parliamentary bylaws adopted in 2006 is a striking omission: Here it is only mentioned en passant, although it is established that a bloc at least requires a leader or ra'is.

In fact, all we have to go by with respect to blocs is past practice in the period 2006–2010. So, just to recap, the original line-up of the Iraqi parliament as it convened in March 2006 consisted of 12 electoral lists that all transformed themselves into parliamentary blocs: UIA (128), KA (53), Tawafuq (44), Iraqiyya (25), Hiwar (11), Islamic Kurdistan (5), Musalaha wa-Hiwar (3), Risaliyun (2), Mithal Alusi (1), Turkmen Front (1), Rafidayn (1) and Yazidis (1). When the parliamentary term expired four years later in February 2010, the map of blocs had changed considerably, with the total number now increased to 16: UIA (85), KA (53), Tawafuq

(40), Sadrists (28), Iraqiyya (19), Fadila (15), Hiwar (9), Arab Independent Bloc (8), Islamic Kurdistan (5), Independents (4), Risaliyun (2), ICP (2), Alusi (1), Turkmen Front (1), Yazidis (1), Rafidayn (1).

The key point with regard to bloc formation precedents is that this process of disintegration (which has been the more common) and agglutination (seen more infrequently, for example, in the case of the Arab Independent Bloc) has taken place without any reference to any law or authorizing bodies whatsoever. So, when Iraqiyya leaders like Aliya Nusayf claim that in view of the latest communications from the federal supreme court and IHEC the door has now been "closed" for the Shiite coalition in legal terms, that is really besides the point. There is no legal mechanism for "certifying" the biggest bloc, period. At the end of the day, this is a question of interpretation and the only way to win the debate is for a bloc to obtain parliamentary support for a presidential candidate willing to declare it the biggest. With that president will ultimately rest the greater responsibility to the Iraqi electorate in terms of interpreting the result of the 7 March elections in a manner that does justice to the concept of democracy in Iraq.

A Remarkable Case of Judicial Activism, in Iraq![15]
June 17, 2010

The recent decision by the Iraqi federal supreme court to declare unconstitutional an amendment to the 2005 election law that was passed last autumn is clearly something of a surprise and a departure from a previous practice of only reluctantly departing from the letter of the constitution. Details of the decision still remain somewhat sketchy—what follows is largely based on press reports.

The decision concerns the distribution in the amendment passed last autumn of the so-called "surplus" seats: The seats that remain in each governorate after the initial allocation based on the electoral divider (typically 2 to 4 seats in a medium-sized governorate; not to be confused with the 7 compensation seats distributed nationally at the end of the seat allocation). In the new version of the law, these are simply distributed proportionally to winning lists only, so that they may win extra seats even if they have less surplus votes than a party that failed to win any seats under the initial allocation. And whereas the previous iteration of the election law comprised a mechanism whereby parties that failed to win governorate seats could be eligible for national compensation seats—thereby potentially aiding the cause of small parties with a nationwide following—no such mechanism exists in the 2009 version of the law (where the "compensation" seats are simply allotted to the winning parties, thereby further reducing proportionality instead of enhancing it). Unsurprisingly, the small Communist party was a leading force behind the complaint to the court, since it is a typical representative of an entity that loses out because the system is biased in favor of the biggest lists.

Many will probably conclude that the decision by the court to attack the clause that reduces proportionality is a good move towards a more fair distribution of seats in the Iraqi parliamentary system. However, the wider implications of the ruling could create a quandary for the court. Reportedly, the verdict of "unconstitutionality" was reached with reference to clauses in the constitution that no law should contradict "democratic principles" and the principle that all Iraqis are equal before the law. But to move from those very general principles towards striking down a particular electoral system is in many ways a far stretch. In practice the court seems to have settled for "proportional representation" as the most "just" and "democratic" electoral system available, but in that case, how can the court prevent a reversion to the old system of a single, nationwide constituency that was in use in January 2005 (instead of 18 governorate-based ones), which arguably is "more just" since it would better approximate the principle of one person, one vote? Of course, the 2005 system was abandoned because perfect proportionality has its disadvantages in terms of distance between voters and representatives, but once the 2009 amendment has been declared unconstitutional, it is difficult to see how the court can resist future challenges to the principle of governorate constituencies.

The court has added that the decision will not have any retroactive effect and so there is no suggestion that the seats in the new parliament be redistributed according to a principle of greater proportionality. This is in fact a similar approach to what was adopted when the previous iteration of the elections law was declared unconstitutional for using registered voters rather than total population as basis for seat distribution. The more profound implications of the ruling is that the court has now decided to touch on one element of the dual veto in the constitution— no laws can contradict the basic tenets of Islam or the principles of democracy—and potentially could be prompted to rule on similar issues in the future, including the question of the Islamic nature of laws passed. This in turn, inevitably, will bring focus on the fact that the current court is a relic of the CPA era and was not formed according to the constitution with the required mix of secular and Islamic judges. After a period in which the court seemed intimidated and almost silenced by political pressures during the de-Baathification process, this latest move, while bold, might potentially insert the court into ever greater controversy over the coming period.

The Empowered Presidency: Some Constitutional Hurdles[16]
October 18, 2010

The first major problem in the list of 19 Kurdish demands for taking part in the next Iraqi government is number four, the establishment of a senate within the first year of the parliament, and the extension of the veto powers of the presidency council until the senate is up and running. It is for the Iraqi parliament, not the government, to draw up the rules of the next senate, with a two-thirds majority! An attempt has been made at this through the work of the constitutional revision committee, but after three years of work the committee has only produced a partial report: Although it does outline the provisions for a senate, it has left many other questions unanswered and cannot be voted on in its present shape. Even more importantly, the current powers of the presidency council expire automatically as soon as a new president is elected. The presidency council was a transitional arrangement for 2005–2010 only (as per article 138) and therefore it was also given strong powers; by way of contrast the next Iraqi president will have no real power, as defined in article 73 of the constitution. To change this, one would need to change the constitution which can only be done in one of two ways: Either with a special two-thirds majority in parliament followed by a referendum (article 126), or as part of the broader constitutional revision with an absolute majority in parliament and a referendum in which any three governorates can vote the changes down by a two-thirds majority in their constituencies (article 142). Again, it is not possible to seat a government based on eventualities relating to parliamentary dynamics and forthcoming referendums. What if the proposal to expand the powers of the presidency council is rejected by the people?

Similar problems apply to the tenth Kurdish demand, acceptance by parliament of the latest oil and gas draft law (of 2007) "and its acceptance means recognition of the oil industry activities going on in Kurdistan and gives Kurdistan the rights to explore and export". Again, the government cannot do anything other than introducing the oil law to parliament, which it failed to do last time due to Shiite–Kurdish disagreement. Whether the parliament agrees or not is a different issue altogether. It is worth noting that the current draft oil and gas law appears to be unconstitutional in many ways, for example by treating producing governorates and regions on a different basis, apparently giving contracting rights to regions only (and not governorates). If a right to anyone outside Baghdad to sign contracts is indeed recognized by the Iraqi parliament—and that is a big if, since it would seem to violate article 112 which stipulates shared power in strategic energy policy—then it should apply to regions and governorates alike, otherwise it would be against article 115 of the constitution that puts regions and governorates on an equal footing in terms of residual powers. Of course, the Iraqi parliament would think twice before giving contracting rights to Basra, Maysan and Dhi Qar. Similarly, no Iraqi government can really promise to "implement" the parts of article 140 that relate to referendums on disputed territories, since special legislation on those referendums would first have to be passed by the Iraqi parliament.

One may agree or disagree with the Iraqi constitution of 2005, but in areas where it is clear it should be respected—if not, one might as well abandon all the nice talk about democracy altogether, and instead stage a military coup proper.

CHAPTER NOTES

1 The original version of this text can be found at http://gulfanalysis.wordpress.com/2009/11/19/constitutional-disintegration/.

2 See http://gulfanalysis.wordpress.com/2009/11/22/constitutional-disintegration-part-ii/.

3 See http://gulfanalysis.wordpress.com/2010/01/15/constitutional-disintegration-3-the-ihec-is-making-up-the-law/.

4 See http://gulfanalysis.wordpress.com/2010/01/19/the-ruling-of-the-accountability-and-justice-board/.

5 See http://gulfanalysis.wordpress.com/2010/01/25/the-ghost-of-paul-bremer-strikes-again-nine-entities-banned-with-reference-to-cpa-order-97/.

6 See http://gulfanalysis.wordpress.com/2010/02/09/chalabi-and-lami-also-control-the-independent-elections-commission/.

7 See http://gulfanalysis.wordpress.com/2010/02/11/mutlak-and-ani-are-banned-miscarriage-of-justice-in-iraq/.

8 See http://gulfanalysis.wordpress.com/2010/02/25/the-secret-election-manifesto/.

9 See http://gulfanalysis.wordpress.com/2010/04/01/the-federal-supreme-court-goes-incommunicado-over-de-baathification-compensation-seats/.

10 See http://gulfanalysis.wordpress.com/2010/04/15/what-does-it-take-to-be-a-kutla/.

11 See http://gulfanalysis.wordpress.com/2010/04/26/more-post-election-de-baathification-another-blow-to-the-idea-of-democracy-in-iraq/.

12 See http://gulfanalysis.wordpress.com/2010/05/28/ihec-in-trouble-again-and-melkerts-fairytale-from-baghdad/.

13 See http://gulfanalysis.wordpress.com/2010/06/10/the-hamudi-files-and-article-76/.

14 See http://gulfanalysis.wordpress.com/2010/06/20/the-bloc-formation-soap-opera-drags-on/.

15 See http://gulfanalysis.wordpress.com/2010/06/17/a-remarkable-case-of-judicial-activism-in-iraq/.

16 See http://gulfanalysis.wordpress.com/2010/10/18/the-kurdish-demands-some-legal-and-constitutional-problems/.

Chapter 10

Soft Partition

"Soft partition" can mean many different things in the Iraqi context. But almost invariably, it involves schemes designed by foreigners to restructure the administrative map of the country with the aim of making the subunits more "natural" and hence easy to govern. These schemes are also one of the easiest subjects in Iraqi politics to write about and criticize because the assumptions of their authors are so profoundly wrong and unempirical. What they all have in common is that they start from a false premise: That there is a problem with the territorial structure of the Iraqi state and that it somehow needs fixing. It doesn't.

Most of my writings on this subject are from 2006 and 2007, before there were any signs of political progress in Iraq and while opponents of the Bush administration were exploring ideas that could constitute some kind of counter-proposal in terms of Iraq policy. In particular, the discussion got heated during autumn 2007, when then-Senator Joe Biden emerged as the most forceful proponent of proactively using radical devolution and federalism to bring progress to Iraq. Many of my articles deal with the various incarnations of the "Biden Plan"—what it was, and what it wasn't. Biden was frequently misrepresented by his opponents (just as he himself grossly misrepresented Iraq and the Iraqis, it has to be added.) But even in it most stripped-down version, it was perfectly clear that everything Biden was proposing involved a gross violation of the Iraqi constitution. Many now say that those schemes are bygone. But in order to appreciate the problematic nature of policy making by U.S. Democrats in the Obama administration, it is important to investigate its epistemological roots as they emerged during the soft partition debate from 2006 to 2008.

Part and parcel of the soft partition saga are also the revelations about the former U.S. diplomat (and Democratic Party intellectual) Peter Galbraith that came to the fore in autumn 2009 and linked him to previous commercial interests in a relatively small Norwegian oil company, DNO, which operates in the Kurdistan region. Galbraith had not only been one of the most vocal advocates of an American embrace of the soft partition idea; he had actually served as a consultant to the Kurds and drafted many principles regarding the management of oil resources that eventually found its way into the Iraqi constitution in 2005. Crucially, Galbraith continued to take part in meetings relating to the constitutional process as late as August 2005, after he had already acquired an economic interest in DNO's Kurdistan operations.

In October 2010, an arbitration court in London awarded Galbraith a sum equivalent to some $35 million for the money he lost when he was forced out of his deal with DNO in 2008, indicating the kind of money that had been at stake in his combined roles as investor, advisor, and U.S. pundit on Iraqi affairs. As for the U.S. Democrats more broadly, they appeared eager to forget their erstwhile propaganda in favor of some kind of radical federal solution for Iraq. However, the marked absence of any strong Democratic reactions to the Galbraith revelations showed that there was still little readiness to make any kind of public break with him—quite possibly because the ontological foundation of Iraq as an ethno-sectarian union from which the whole concept of soft partition has been derived is still very much alive in the Obama administration. Tragically, when the news story about Galbraith and DNO broke in October 2009, many Democrats reacted by suggesting that this was all down to some kind of Norwegian conspiracy as revenge for Galbraith's criticism of a Norwegian diplomat working in Afghanistan, Karl Eide! First, one has to ask, even if such a plot by wicked Norwegians did indeed exist, would that absolve Galbraith from his complicity in shaping the Iraqi constitution in a particular direction back in 2005 when he himself had undisclosed business interests in Kurdistan? What is the problem, the messenger or the message? For my part, I tried to calm readers by noting that I had been criticizing Galbraith since 2006. I also made the point that technically speaking I am no more Norwegian than Galbraith himself is because I carry a Dutch passport (and for that reason cannot work for the Norwegian foreign ministry, as the conspiracy theorists alleged).

Maybe because most of my essays on the soft partition idea were very critical of its proponents I have not had the pleasure of meeting many of these people in the flesh. Still, in December 2007, at the height of the "soft partition" furor, an Iraqi friend in Washington managed to sneak me into a confrontation with Joe Biden's very young staff member Perry Cammack (who now works for Senator John Kerry) somewhere in the Senate offices on Capitol Hill. I found the meeting interesting. Cammack did seem genuinely interested in hearing about ways in which the "Biden Plan" for Iraq was in fact at variance with the Iraqi constitution. But at the end of the day, the only point he seemed to care about was to establish what he called "a compelling narrative" on Iraq. I readily conceded that: The soft partition scheme and the lore of division that surrounds it is indeed captivating—like a fairytale.

Iraq's Partition Fantasy[1]

May 18, 2006

A feature of political discussion of Iraq in recent weeks has been another flurry of propaganda by United States politicians in favor of dividing Iraq into three statelets or semi-independent federal entities. "Soft partition", "controlled division" or an "extension of the federal idea to the Sunni community" are but a few of the euphemisms that have been marshalled in support of this sort of exercise. The schemes are strikingly similar, and their proponents indefatigable: Iraq is dismissed as an "artificial entity"; its "proper" and "natural" constituent components are instead identified as three ethno-religious communities—Shiite Arabs, Sunni Arabs and Kurds.

In fact, Iraqi history fails to support such ideas—and particularly the notion that it should be necessary to enforce barriers between the Sunni and Shiite Arabs. Quite the contrary, if the pundits who urge partition had bothered to check what actually happened when centrifugal forces were pushed to the maximum in the south of Iraq in the 1920s, they would have seen that regionalism, not sectarianism, has historically been the main competitor to Iraqi nationalism south of Baghdad—and a feeble one at that. The idea of tripartite break-up, on the other hand finds little resonance in Iraqi history. In testimony to their sublime artificiality, contemporary partitionist misnomers like "Shiistan" and "Sunnistan" are altogether absent from the historical record; like much of the pro-partition advocacy they exist solely in the minds of outsiders who base their entire argument on far-fetched parallels to European political experiences.

In the early 1920s, for the first and so far the only time in Iraqi history, an actual attempt at separating the south from Baghdad was launched. This came soon after Britain had initiated a mandate administration to prepare the former Ottoman provinces of Basra, Baghdad and Mosul for nationhood as a unitary state. But the composition of the southern separatist elite of the 1920s—and the geographical scope of their project—should give today's partitionists pause for thought. For this was not a clergy-driven attempt at establishing some sort of Shiite state. Instead, it was a scheme to create a small merchant republic on the banks of the Shatt al-Arab, a pro-British enclave that would cover Basra and the strategic coastal strip between the Gulf and the delta of the great Mesopotamian rivers north to Qurna only. Moreover, it was an emphatically cosmopolitan enterprise: Arabs, Persians, Indians and Jews came together in pursuit of the Basra separatist movement. Sunni Arab emigrants from Najd were the moving spirits. Apart from a few pro-separation figures based in the immediate vicinity of the city of Basra, the Shiite Arabs remained totally aloof from the secessionist bid.

Even though it constituted the most concerted domestic "southern" challenge to the territorial integrity of Iraq in 20th-century history, the Basra separation movement ended in fiasco. The separatists were the richest men of Basra—owners of enormous tracts of fertile date gardens and successful businessmen with networks extending into other parts of the world—and yet, they were unable to muster popular support for their daring enterprise. Who was their enemy? An authoritarian regime in Baghdad with the military means to drive home its own megalomaniac ideas about Iraqi nationalism? A British colonial machine with a singularity of purpose so entrenched as to make impossible any challenges to London's preferred vision of a unified Iraq? Far from it. The Iraqi government apparatus of the 1920s was decidedly flimsy, and throughout the period of the mandate, the British would periodically contemplate scuttling "back to Basra". Both these forces would have had trouble in stemming the separatist project if it had in fact enjoyed universal local support.

No, it was the young men of Basra—impecunious and landless as they may have been—who defeated the separatist project, by presenting a competing and very different vision for the future. Many of them had been employed as civil servants in late Ottoman times, and had colleagues from the areas further north. Among themselves—and Ottoman documents prove this beyond doubt—they had referred to the territory between Basra and Mosul as "Iraq" long before 1914, quite contrary to the baseless but now widespread idea that there had been no sense of connection between Basra and Baghdad before the British. Armed with this "Iraq" concept, the young intelligentsia converted the south to Iraqi national-ism at an early stage, with schools, newspapers and voluntary associations—not extortion or the use of force—as their principal instruments. The process was more universal in the south than in the north of Iraq, but even in the Kurdish areas there have been considerable regional variations with regard to relations with Baghdad, and in historical perspective only Sulaymaniyya has an unbroken record of antipa-thy to the Iraqi capital.

This dualism—tentative regionalisms and quite robust Iraqi nationalism—is reflected in today's situation. Once more, if enthusiastic armchair partitionists in the West had cared to investigate the specific policy proposals of their would-be "Shiite autonomists", they would have discovered yet another misfit between their own map and the landscapes of Iraqi reality. For, contrary to what Westerners commonly think, the most longstanding post-2003 southern challenge to the para-digm of a unitary Iraqi state structure has been of a regionalist rather than a sectar-ian character. Ever since summer 2004, local politicians in the oil-rich triangle of Basra, Amara and Nasiriyya have advocated the establishment of a small-scale fed-eral entity limited to these three southernmost provinces of Iraq—in other words, a subdivision of the Shiite territories, by Shiites who say they have had enough of domination by other, "northern" Shiites. The idea of a single Shiite canton from Baghdad to the Gulf, on the other hand, is a more recent phenomenon, dating back only to summer 2005, when a caucus of Shiite politicians from central Iraq, mostly returned exiles, began promoting it.

While Western observers soon became enthralled by the project, ordinary Iraqi

Shiites have proven more difficult to convince, and grassroots activity in support of this sectarian scheme has remained limited. Moreover, just as in the 1920s, the alternative to decentralization—Iraqi nationalism—remains flourishing. Even today, in a climate of growing sectarian terrorism calculated to obliterate the idea of coexistence, many Iraqis stubbornly refuse to reveal their ethno-religious identity when interrogated by Western journalists. Many simply say they are "Iraqis"—an answer that tends to cause consternation among interviewers who expect more specific answers. Among several key Iraqi leaders who never went into exile abroad, the situation is much the same. "Federalism" appears not to exist in the vocabulary of the Grand Ayatollah Ali al-Sistani—who consistently emphasizes national "unity" in his official pronouncements—and Muqtada al-Sadr's radical Islamism comes with a strong Iraqi nationalist component that foreigners often overlook.

In sum, then, the process of regionalization in Iraq is far more tentative and open-ended than the orderly caricature maps currently bandied about in Western think-tanks would indicate. But those partition schemes are more than a distortion of Iraqi history and today's realities. They also demonstrate flagrant contempt for the fragile democratic process which is underway in Iraq. This is rather ironic, given that many of those who advocate partition take pride in describing themselves as staunch opponents of "neo-imperialisms" of all kinds.

But where many British colonial administrators at least had the tact to confine their worst excesses of impromptu line-drawing to sparsely populated desert areas, today's hobby-artists do not shy away from using even complex urban landscapes as canvas for their reckless activities. They simply do not seem to grasp the fundamentally anti-democratic nature of their demand that the Iraqis be divided into three mutually exclusive identity-categories. The crude maps that accompany the break-up propaganda are an affront to the complex historical experiences they claim to represent, and encapsulate a continuous and highly disturbing trend towards the complete expropriation of the Iraqi transition process.

There Is No Biden Plan[2]
October 26, 2006

To an outsider with no particular affection for the foreign policies of either U.S. political party, the chief interest of the November, 2006 mid-term elections lies in their ramifications for the rest of the world. One of the most striking features of current Iraq discussion in the United States is that much of what is being said is based on the false premise that there exists a radical "third way" territorial solution to the Iraq crisis: a tripartite division of the country.

This option, often referred to as the "plan" of Senator Joseph Biden, would involve active American policy steps to bring about a three-way separation of Iraq's ethno-religious communities—a Kurdish north, a Sunni Arab west, and a Shiite Arab center–south. These entities would form part of a loose confederation, with sharing of oil revenues as the glue that binds the system together. The senator has repeatedly stressed the supposed "constitutionality" of his plan.

The published accounts of this "Biden Plan" reveal, however, that it violates the Iraqi constitution in two significant ways. Back in May, Sen. Biden boldly declared that he wanted the establishment of "one Iraq with three regions". The problem here is that whereas the Iraqi constitution does establish federalism as a general principle of government for Iraq, it leaves the demarcation of any new federal units outside Kurdistan to the Iraqi people—who are empowered to create federal entities "from below", through referendums. This means that no outsider can dictate any particular future Iraqi state structure—it might be two federal entities, five, or fifteen, or for that matter a unitary rump Iraq federated with a decentralized Kurdistan, all depending on the choice of the Iraqi people.

More recently, Biden seems to have realized this deficiency in his plan, and last month he admitted that "the exact number [of federal states] should be left to the constitution". Still, he offered the "guess" that there would be three entities. But subtract the guesswork, and the bottom falls out of the plan.

Biden's second policy point, oil distribution, is based on his first: he wants to see an agreement on sharing of oil revenues between his three imagined Iraqi sub-communities; presumably this would be inserted in the constitution through the planned revision process. But again, this is in dissonance with the Iraqi legal framework. The revision of the constitution is to be completed before October 2007, whereas no federalization is supposed to take place before April 2008. Hence, the only oil revenue settlement that would be politically neutral and could avoid pre-empting any subsequent popular initiatives on federal entities would be one based on the existing 18 governorates.

The remaining points in Biden's plan are of less interest, either because they already enjoy cross-party support in the United States, or because they will be of limited significance to achieving political stability. "More Aid, But Tied to the Protection of Minority and Women Rights" is all fine, but frankly this is not something that will make or break the Iraqi reconciliation process. "Engage Iraq's Neighbors" is a good point, but one that already enjoys increasing support among realist Republicans and, reportedly, in the State Department. That leaves us with the final item on Biden's agenda—withdrawal of U.S. forces—which in turn means that we are back to where we started: If Biden wishes to adhere to the Iraqi constitution, then he simply does not have a policy alternative that is truly distinctive from the general debate on the U.S. presence in Iraq. It considerably weakens the whole American debate on Iraq—and that of the Democratic Party in particular—if an illusory and spurious policy proposal like Biden's is allowed to remain dominant.

Despite these contradictions, Biden continues his campaign, perhaps believing he can goad the Iraqis into adopting his own ideas. That too is problematic. In today's Iraq, there exists far more diversity than the simplistic three-community model would suggest, but through his black-and-white discourse Biden bulldozes this pluralism and chases the Iraqis further into the mental prisons of sectarianism. For instance, within the Shiite community singled out by Biden for separate treatment, some voices in fact completely reject the idea of federal subdivisions among the Arabs of Iraq, whereas others are calling for several non-sectarian sub-entities among the Shiites instead of a single unit. (Does the senator know that a single governorate—Basra—holds more than 80% of what he describes as "Shiite" oil reserves?) Why are these groups not to be given a democratic hearing in the new Iraq? Why should they be forced to accepting an ethno-religious formula that could easily produce ethno-religious dictatorships if internal tensions within the federal units (say, Sadrists versus SCIRI) are ignored? It is alarming that on questions like these, people like Sen. Biden should be allowed to muddle Democratic Party discourse (and the U.S. debate in general) by adopting an approach that was fashionable in the times immediately after the First World War but in recent years has been the preserve of neo-conservative fringe writers.

And sometimes there is an even more assertive Biden, one that does not restrict himself to "guessing" the outcome of the Iraqi federalization process. A few days ago, an angry voice could be heard on television: "Like heck we can't tell the Iraqis what to do". This was Joseph Biden, the Democratic senator! Yes, it is probably true that, if the United States seriously wishes to enforce a division of Iraq—by circumventing the Iraqi constitution—it has the military capability to do so. But it would be a tragic outcome of the supposed democratization of Iraq if Washington should choose to exit by neo-imperialistically imposing a particular state structure on the country. It would alienate huge sections of the Iraqi population. It would be a gross provocation to most of Iraq's neighbors, who view a tripartite federation as a particularly brittle state structure and a powder keg in terms of potential regional instability. And it would be the ultimate gift to al-Qaida—who would finally get the manifest evidence they have been craving in order to back up their conspiracy theory of the U.S. as a pro-Zionist force bent on subdividing the Middle East into weak and sectarian statelets. Senator Biden would do well to consider the long-term damage to American interests that would follow from such reactions before he annexes Basra to the Middle Euphrates, merges Diyala and Kut, and rips the heart out of Mosul.

Another Bout of Partitionism[3]
August 19, 2007

For a long time, the idea of an externally imposed ethno-sectarian partition of Iraq was the preserve of a few relatively isolated but loud U.S. politicians and pundits, including figures like Joseph Biden, Leslie Gelb and Peter Galbraith. More recently, however, certain academics have added their voice to the partitionist propaganda. These studies warrant close scrutiny, because their academic style and, in some cases, elaborate footnotes, make it very likely that they will achieve status as "serious pieces of research" among those who advocate partition.

In one sense, Edward P. Joseph and Michael E. O'Hanlon are refreshing in that they at least explain upfront what they want: to challenge the Iraqi constitution. In contrast to other "soft partitionists", what these two writers refer to as a "plan" is in fact a plan. But what a plan! In "The Case for Soft Partition in Iraq" Joseph and O'Hanlon plunge into the modalities of bringing about "the organized movement of two to five million Iraqis", no less, in order to create a decentralized state based on three ethnic communities. There is no question about the number—it has to be three. In fact, the authors are deeply worried that the Iraqi constitution with its protection of Baghdad as a separate entity (constitutionally, the Iraqi capital is not allowed to become part of larger federal regions) may create problems with regard to the consistent implementation of their own ethnic logic; they therefore demand that the capital region be partitioned too—with the Tigris river recommended as the most suitable partition line. The absence of popular support among Iraqis (they themselves acknowledge that "Sunni and Shiite Arabs have traditionally opposed partition, hard or soft") does not seem to deter them at all; instead they choose to focus on the "comparable" example of Bosnia-Herzegovina, "where one of us worked extensively".

On pp. 9 to 11, Joseph and O'Hanlon (who in 2006 complained loudly in the U.S. press after having been marginalized in the sessions of the Iraq Study Group) enumerate in greater detail the supporters of their plan. They appear to be, Joseph, O'Hanlon, most Kurds, and Abd al-Aziz al-Hakim, a Shiite politician. The authors are too modest: They could have added al-Qaida, which would welcome this kind of federation as a permanent scar on Iraq that would prove to the whole world how "Western crusaders are intent on dividing the Muslims", as well as Iran—which consulted closely with Hakim before he launched his campaign for a Shiite federal entity in the summer of 2005 and prior to the intensification of it in August 2006, and which would rival Saudi Arabia as holder of the world's largest oil reserves if it were able to exercise control over the Basra fields. At any rate, to their credit, the authors readily admit that only a minority among the Shiites of Iraq are in favor of federalism based on ethnicity. In fact, these days, even long-time defenders of the idea of a Shiite federal entity such as the Hakim family seem to speak with different voices on federalism, with Ammar al-Hakim now apparently more enthusiastic than his father Abd al-Aziz and other close associates.

But Joseph and O'Hanlon cannot entirely resist the temptation to construe the Iraqis as closet partitionists. In so doing they also reiterate several common misconceptions about Iraqi politics. First and foremost, this relates to the interpretation of sectarian voting in the parliamentary elections of 2005 as votes "for separation" (p. 1, repeated on p. 8). That is simply disingenuous, because no Shiite or Sunni political parties in those campaigns had any agenda of territorially dividing the Iraqis according to sect and ethnicity. To struggle for primacy within an existing unitary polity and to advocate the territorial devolution of that polity on a separative basis are two very different things. Similarly, Joseph and O'Hanlon elsewhere (p. ix) talk of "an Iraq ruled from Baghdad" as a possible future "symbolic threat to Shiite Arabs"—a colossal denial of the continued centrality of Baghdad to Shiite ambitions, which often simply consist of a desire to maintain the existing state framework but without the sectarian discrimination of the past. And on p. 9, where the two authors refer to the six-month deadline in the 2005 constitution for creating federalization procedures, they demonstrate their level of detachment from current Iraqi political debate more generally. Why do they not instead focus on the actual procedures for implementing federalism that were adopted in October 2006, which fulfilled the constitutional provision, and which made it superfluous?

What then follows in the section on "Implementing Soft Partition" should have come with some kind of warning to the reader. Here, using cool academic language, the authors review the nuts and bolts of relocating somewhere between 2 and 5 million Iraqis in order to create new ethnic federal entities. Snippets from this part of the report probably speak best for themselves: "We advocate where possible dividing major cities along natural boundaries" (p. 16); "on the actual day of the relocation operation, Iraqi and U.S.-led coalition forces would deploy in sufficient numbers to look for snipers, cover the flanks of the civilian convoys, inspect suspicious vehicles for explosives and conduct similar tasks" (p. 17); and finally, on p. 24, "this [internal border] control system would place some burdens on Iraq's internal trade and other aspects of its economy. It would complicate the efforts of individuals to cross from one region to another to visit family and friends. For the most part these burdens would be bearable. For individuals or businesses that need to make frequent crossings across Iraq's new internal borders, or those willing to pay for the privilege, an EZ pass system [sic] might be developed to expedite movements for those with important and regular business to conduct".

Perhaps none of this should come as a surprise in a report in which the 1947 partition of India is criticized not for the principle of division as such but for its poor technical execution (p. 19). But even those who may choose to accept the authors' ideas about the "inevitability" of an Iraqi partition will find it hard to be persuaded by some of the subsequent details considering implementation.

For example, the Arab League (probably one of the strongest opponents of Iraqi partition in the world) is identified as a possible candidate for a "lead role" in the partition process (p. 16). And on p. 28 Joseph and O'Hanlon present their scenario of how regional players supposedly would join in to support the new decentralized polity: "Sunni-majority states such as Morocco and Jordan and Saudi Arabia providing help for the Sunni Arab region, the United States helping the Kurds", and, wait for it, "a combined international mission working with the Shiites". Or could it just possibly happen that a certain neighbor to the east might wish to try to exercise a degree of influence in the Shiistan defined by O'Hanlon and Joseph?

What these writers overlook is the survival of Iraq as a territorial concept and as a frame of reference for aspirations of national unity. Those analysts who emphasize the continued existence of Iraqi nationalism among the population at large are often criticized because these ideals are not reflected at the elite level anymore. But that is just a testament to the growing gap between politicians and masses in Iraq, perhaps greater now than ever after the recent further narrowing of the Maliki governing coalition to include just two Shiite Islamist parties in addition to the Kurds. For example, the celebration of Iraq's recent football victory in the Asia Cup proved the continued strength of Iraqi unity as a widespread ideal among ordinary Iraqis and constitutes a formidable anomaly to those sharing the analytical lenses of O'Hanlon and Joseph.

But in general, this popular dimension is only rarely reflected in media reports from Iraq, which instead tend to focus on propaganda by sectarian political parties that have good communications skills and are able to spin small gatherings of their diehard supporters as "massive demonstrations". The problem is highlighted by these authors themselves: Joseph and O'Hanlon assert (p. 8) that there is "strong evidence" that "violence is steadily eroding national unity"—with a footnote to a short article by American journalist Sabrina Tavernise! Instead of engaging in this kind of contrived referencing they and other partitionists should take a long look at their own arguments, deal honestly with their most glaring denials of Iraqi facts, and then ask whether there is anything left at all. The U.S. invasion of Iraq was based on lies; it would do irreparable damage to the entire Middle East as well as American interests in the region if also the mechanics of withdrawal should be informed by fabricated evidence.

The U.S. Senate Votes to Partition Iraq. Softly.[4]

September 27, 2007

On 26 September 2007 the United States Senate voted 75–23 in favor of an amendment to the defense spending bill for 2008 that authorizes the U.S. government to "encourage" Iraqis to find a "federal" solution to the internal conflicts in their country.

At least two different interpretations of the bill are possible. First, one may choose to highlight its comparatively insignificant character: an amendment to the original text stressed that any political settlement should be "consistent with the wishes of the Iraqi people and their elected leaders". If this is taken literally, the amendment is meaningless since the Iraqis already have a constitution according to which those areas of the country that desire a federal status may seek one through specific mechanisms; accordingly there is nothing the United States needs to do to achieve a state structure that is consonant with the "wishes of the Iraqi people". In that sort of interpretation, it does not make sense to speak about a new "plan" because the proposed course of action would demand no policy adjustments on the part of Washington whatsoever.

However, Joe Biden, the bill's sponsor, presumably thinks that he does indeed have a "plan for Iraq"—that is at least what he says when he promotes his presidential bid for 2008. It is therefore more logical to focus on the parts of his rhetoric that involve pushing the Iraqis in a particular direction. The keywords in this regard are "conference" and the idea of some kind of comprehensive federalism settlement involving international assistance. This severely distorts the Iraqi constitution's provisions for federalism. Biden does not understand, or does not want to understand, that there is no imperative in the Iraqi constitution for every part of the country to seek a federal status. Federalism is but one of two options: governorates may also elect to retain their current status.

This is actually a feature of the 2005 constitution that is consonant with Iraqi political history. The drafters realized that the country has a long unitary tradition with widespread skepticism towards federalism among the population; in appreciating these political tensions they abandoned any idea of imposing federalism "from above". In fact, leading Iraqi politicians who drafted the 2006 law on implementing federalism have suggested that possibly no more than one or two governorates (like for instance Basra in the far south) will seek a status similar to Kurdistan when the federalism option formally becomes available in April 2008. Similarly, scattered evidence from Iraq's political process and from public opinion polls suggests that this anti-federal skepticism persists. Since the constitution was adopted in 2005 there have been several suggestions for constitutional amendment by Iraqi parties—both Shiite and Sunni—to limit federalism to ensure that no purely sectarian federal regions are allowed to develop. The latest poll numbers south of Kurdistan are not particularly supportive of Biden's plan either, with for instance 56% of Shiites expressing the wish to abandon federalism altogether (almost all Sunnis agree with them on this), and with the remainder divided between different federal projects—only a small portion of which would correspond to Biden's vision.

Again, this is all in conflict with Biden's idea of comprehensive, total federalization. The senator should be more honest about these problems and should follow in the footsteps of his fellow pro-partitionist Michael O'Hanlon, who openly asserts that only a minority of Iraqis support any idea of soft partitioning or federalism based on ethnic groups. And more fundamentally, Biden must understand the logical defect of his current argument: He cannot claim authorship of a distinctive "plan" and at the same time maintain that he does not propose to impose anything on the Iraqi people. In fact the contradictions in this area are even worse in the final version of the amendment than in early drafts, since the text now stipulates that the proposed international conference on Iraqi federalism should be based on the 2006 law for implementing federalism. This in itself is contradictory in the extreme because the key point of the 2006 legislation is that federalism shall never be imposed from the outside or from above in a single conference, but instead emerge gradually, only in those parts of the country that wish to adopt a federal model of government. Furthermore, who is to decide which Iraqis will take part in the projected conference? The Maliki government? This effectively brings back the question of how to nominate conference invitees and, more fundamentally, the basis (ethnic versus non-ethnic) on which to define representativeness in any grand "federal settlement" of the kind envisioned by Biden.

At the heart of this contradictory piece of legislation lie several more fundamental misunderstandings about Iraq among the many Biden plan supporters whose panegyrics adorn the senator's website. Consider for example Sam Brownback's recent exegesis of Ottoman history, delivered in the Senate during the adoption of the Biden amendment, and reproduced here with critical annotations in brackets:

> I show my colleagues a map that I think is kind of interesting. It is a map of Iraq under the Ottoman Empire. It is prior to the World War I divisions in Iraq. I think we ought to study history to keep from repeating past mistakes. I think we are repeating history now because we have not studied it sufficiently. So here is a map from 1914. This is fascinating. You have the north Ottoman *[sic]*, which were called *vilayets*. This is in the State of Mosul, the Kurdish north [it was actually mixed, Kurdish, Sunni Arab, Christian, Turkmen, Yazidi]. You had the *vilayet* of Baghdad, the Sunni area in Iraq [it was mixed and contained all the Shiite holy cities]. You had the *vilayet* of Basra, the Shia State [it had fewer Shiites than Baghdad, and was politically dominated by Sunnis]. Baghdad was the federal city—a very effective city at that particular time [this is pure nonsense: there was no federalism in these parts of the Ottoman Empire; Baghdad did however have some supervisory functions for all the three Iraqi *vilayets* for instance in customs, military affairs and justice]. . . . Again, here is a three-state solution that the Ottoman Empire put in place as a way of managing these different groups who do not agree with each other, who do not get along [again, this suggests that Brownback fully believes that Basra was somehow "more Shiite" and "less Sunni" than Baghdad, whereas

in fact all the *vilayet*s of the Ottoman Empire in this region were Sunni-dominated, politically speaking].

All in all the Biden amendment is an alarming but useful numerical indication of the level of support for an "ethnic" approach to Iraqi politics in the U.S. Senate (the supporters included presidential candidate Hillary Clinton), as well as a reminder of the remarkable unfamiliarity among even elite U.S. politicians with the finer points of Iraqi legislation on federalism. It does not bode well for the future that the potential successors to President Bush seem to converge on a scheme that would be even more unpalatable to the Muslim world than Washington's current policy. True, Bush invaded Iraq, and Paul Bremer weakened the country severely. There are worrying signs that some in the State Department, like Ryan Crocker, are already indistinguishable from Biden by tirelessly "encouraging" Sunnis to think in terms of federalism. But if his partition plans were implemented, Joe Biden would be remembered by Muslims and Arabs around the world in an altogether different way. He would be considered alongside other historical personalities who routinely are being accused by Middle Easterners for having destroyed their region completely: Arthur Balfour, Mark Sykes and Francois Georges-Picot.

Logical Breakdown of Biden's Iraq Plan[5]
October 10, 2007

Despite attempts by Sen. Joe Biden (D-Del.) to explain his plan for Iraq in greater detail ("Biden rebuts criticism of Iraq decentralization plan", 2 October 2007), some obvious flaws in his scheme remain. The main problem is purely logical: If Biden is to be given credit for a distinctive "Iraq plan", then this plan must either make the Iraqis do something they will not do of their own free will, or it must enable them to do something that they want to do but which the Bush administration is currently preventing them from doing. Biden denies that it is the former, so his challenge is to prove that the Bush administration is suppressing a genuine Iraqi desire to do something about federalism that corresponds to Biden's ideas. The problem with that is that if one asks Iraqis, they will refer to the full-fledged Iraqi legal framework for federalization that already exists and which requires no outside intervention whatsoever. The procedures for implementing federalism in Iraq, consisting of the Iraqi constitution and the detailed legislation adopted in October 2006, unequivocally assert that (1) no federalization can start before April 1, 2008; (2) any new federal regions should come as the result of popular grassroots initiatives in the existing governorates; and (3) there is no imperative for every governorate in Iraq to opt for a federal status (theoretically, the number of new federal regions may be anywhere from zero to 15).

Biden's plan either violates all three of these aspects of the Iraqi legal framework or it has no meaning it all.

Nonsense of Congress on Federalism in Iraq[6]
December 13, 2007

A bill is on its way to President George W. Bush with an enclosure that encapsulates the atmosphere of a disoriented U.S. Congress. Euphemistically titled "Sense of Congress on Federalism in Iraq" and attached to the 2008 defense authorization bill that was passed in the House of Representatives yesterday, this latest Iraq-related opus to emerge from Capitol Hill is so riddled with inconsistencies that it is the opponents of the idea of U.S. interference in internal Iraqi affairs that emerge as the clear victors in this strange, little affair.

It may be useful to briefly recapitulate the flaws of the precursor to the text which is now being turned into law. Contrary to accounts in the U.S. press, the Senate's "Biden amendment" of September 2007 did not specifically seek to divide Iraq into any particular number of federal states, nor did it advocate full partition. It did however violate the Iraqi constitution in two major ways. Firstly, by introducing the idea of a "conference settlement" of Iraq's federal question, it sought to circumvent the democratic procedures for creating federal regions "from below" through grassroots initiatives as outlined in the Iraqi constitution. Secondly, by anticipating an Iraq that would be wholly divided into federal regions it usurped, by implication, the constitutional rights of individual Iraqi governorates to retain their unitary state status if that should be the wish of their populations. In short, the "Biden amendment" ignored Iraq's status as a unique specimen within the world's family of federations, namely, an asymmetrical federation where the demarcation of federal entities is gradual and where the right to create new federal entities is vested exclusively in the local populations of the existing governorates. This is a dual system combining federal and unitary-state elements, and even though existing governorates (for example Basra or Najaf) can try to opt for a federal status in the future, the federalization process may well stop where it is today, with one federal region only (Kurdistan). To those searching for comparisons, the United States is entirely irrelevant; it is to Spain and Russia (and, arguably, the United Kingdom) one should look for cases with certain parallels to the asymmetric division of power between center and regions in force in today's Iraq.

The "Biden amendment" of last September also highlighted the logical flaws of the U.S. senators' approach as they seek to apply the concept of federalism to create an alternative Iraq policy. Their problem is that Iraqi parliamentarians and the

Bush administration happen to speak with one voice on this particular issue. They follow the 2005 constitution and the law on implementing federalism of October 2006, which together provide detailed principles, procedures and timelines for creating federal regions in those parts of the country where there is a genuine desire for such federalization. These procedures are finite and clearly defined: unless one intends to break the law, there is no need for additional "conferences" or "international assistance" of any kind. Accordingly, if U.S. senators wish to produce something that is somehow "more federal" than this, they will have to violate the Iraqi constitution—which is just what they did through their September resolution.

Unsurprisingly, Senator Joseph Biden and his allies flatly deny that they are transgressing the Iraqi constitution. But their handling of this in the final Congress conference version of the bill has been particularly awkward. The two elements of the original amendment that are clearly in breach of the Iraq constitution are still there—the "conference for Iraqis", and the idea of a "comprehensive", one-off settlement where, by implication, the entire country is to be subjected to federalization. Instead of resolving this, the U.S. congressional conferees have simply littered their text with caveats that invite the Iraqis to break their own constitution if that is seen to be the popular will! The key clause is now rendered as follows: "*if the Iraqi people support a political settlement in Iraq* based on the final provisions of the constitution of Iraq that create a federal system of government and allow for the creation of federal regions, consistent with the wishes of the Iraqi people and their elected leaders, the United States should actively support such a political settlement in Iraq [emphasis added]", followed by the suggested ingredients for this kind of settlement—including action by the international community to "support" a federalism deal, as well as the previously mentioned federalism conference, neither of which, of course, is actually mentioned anywhere in the 2005 Iraqi constitution.

This is disingenuous in two ways. First, the Iraqi federal system as outlined in the 2005 constitution is simply not of the "settlement" sort (i.e., one big, convenient conference of "major" factions, of the kind that would seem palatable and perhaps manageable to U.S. senators) but instead is based on gradual evolution through bottom–up processes. The reason for this is that the concept of federalism is so contested in Iraq that, for fear of popular resistance, even the elites who wrote the 2005 constitution did not dare impose any particular federal formula on the country beyond recognizing Kurdistan as a federal region. Basically, the arrangement is supposed to guard against any federal entities being imposed on parts of Iraq where there is no popular demand for federalism. Second, how could the existence of "popular support" for such a "settlement" be ascertained prior to the proceedings themselves? Through a popular referendum? In that case, the question to be put to the Iraqi voters would have to be framed in a very inventive way, because the real question would be: "Do you support the idea of temporarily dispensing with the 2005 constitution and the 2006 law for implementing federalism, so that Iraq instead can have a (U.S.-designed) process including international 'support' and a 'conference for Iraqis' to divide their country into federal regions?"

The irony is that during this work the senators were actually quite close to the key to an alternative Iraq policy. They even touched on it when they inserted the words "final provisions of" before "the Iraqi constitution" in the conference version of the bill—presumably a reference to the fact that the Iraqi constitution itself is an evolving project, with an ongoing process of revision by committee. Where the senators made their big mistake was in focusing on federalism instead of constitutional revision. This is where there is room for the "grand settlement" (including features related to federalism) which the senators so clearly want. This is also where such "settlement" can be sought without violating the Iraqi constitution, because the process of revision itself is constitutionally mandated. But the direction of change likely to meet with Iraqi approval would again be the opposite of the general thrust in the latest U.S. Congress bill. Instead of asking for more federalism (or a more rapid path towards federalism), many Iraqis seem to favor delays for implementing federalism, stricter criteria for forming federal regions, or guarantees against a federal arrangement where new demarcation lines would correspond to ethnic and sectarian divisions—in short, they maintain the general skepticism towards federalism that has been reflected in successive opinion polls among Shiites and Sunnis alike. But because the committee charged with revising the Iraqi constitution is clearly not responding to these signals from below, this may constitute an area where Iraqi nationalists might actually appreciate some kind of input or support from the international community—perhaps even from the U.S. Congress.

The "Biden amendment" of September 2007 was provocative in its flagrant violation of the Iraqi constitution. Thanks to the efforts of Iraqis who protested the bill, Congress has now been sufficiently shaken to present yet another version, this time with so many additional contradictions that the new text is best characterized as illegible. All in all, it is quite hard to see why the language on federalism was included at all.

While He Was Influencing the Shape of the Iraqi Constitution, Peter Galbraith Held Stakes in an Oilfield in Dahuk[7]

October 10, 2009

It is widely known that the former U.S. diplomat Peter Galbraith has been one of the most prominent figures in shaping the state structure of Iraq in the period after 2003, especially with his vocal advocacy of various forms of radical decentralization and/or partition solutions for Iraq's political problems—all reflected in his books and numerous articles in the *New York Review of Books*, especially in the period from 2004 to 2008. Until now, though, it has generally been assumed that Galbraith's fervent pro-partition propaganda was rooted in an ideological belief in national self-determination and a principled view of radical federalism as the best option for Iraq's Kurds. Many have highlighted Galbraith's experience as a former U.S. diplomat (especially in the Balkans in the 1990s) as key elements of his academic and policy-making credentials.

Today, however, it has emerged that the realities were probably rather different. For some time, Norway's most respected financial newspaper, *Dagens Næringsliv* (DN), has been focusing on the operations in Kurdistan of DNO, a small Norwegian private oil company, especially reporting on unclear aspects concerning share ownership and its contractual partnerships related to the Tawke field in the Dahuk governorate. One particular goal has been to establish the identity of a hitherto unknown "third party" which participated with DNO in the initial production sharing agreement (PSA) for Tawke between 2004 and 2008, but was squeezed out when this deal was converted to a new contract in early 2008, prompting a huge financial claim of around 500 million U.S. dollars against DNO which has yet to be settled. Today, DN claims to present proof that one of the two major "mystery stake-holders" involved in the claim was none other than Peter Galbraith, who allegedly held a 5% share in the PSA for Tawke from June 2004 until 2008 through his Delaware-based company Porcupine. Galbraith's partner was the Yemenite multi-millionaire Shahir Abd al-Haqq, whose identity was revealed by the same newspaper earlier this month. DN has published documents from Porcupine showing Galbraith's personal signature, and today's reports are complete with paparazzi photographs of Galbraith literally running away from reporters as they confront him in Bergen, where he is currently staying with his Norwegian wife. He refused to give any comment citing potential legal complications.

If proven correct, the implications of this revelation are so enormous that the story is almost unbelievable. As is well known, DNO has been criticized for the way its operations in the Kurdistan region interfere with Iraq's constitutional process. To their credit, though, DNO are at the very least perfectly forthright about their mission in the area: They are a commercial enterprise set up to make a maximum profit in a high-risk area currently transitioning from conditions of war. Galbraith, however, was almost universally seen as "Ambassador Galbraith", the statesmanlike former diplomat whose outspoken ideas about post-2003 Iraq were always believed to be rooted in idealism and never in anything else. Instead, it now emerges, he apparently wore several hats at the same time, and mixed his roles in ways that seem entirely incompatible with the capacity of an independent advisor on constitutional affairs.

It can be useful to briefly recapitulate the extent of Galbraith's involvement in creating the institutions of government in the "new Iraq". In fact, the best guide to this subject is Galbraith himself, who recounted his own role in the book *The*

End of Iraq, published in 2006. It seems clear he got involved on the Kurdish side early on in 2003: "Two weeks after Saddam's fall, I began discussions with the Kurdish leaders on the future of Kurdistan and *what they could achieve* in the new Iraqi constitution [italics added, p.159]". Supposedly, according to a later book by Galbraith, he was at this point a consultant for ABC News! Later, he appears to have been a regular consultant for the Kurds. While his various books only make vague acknowledgement as far as payment is concerned ("for a few months at the end of 2003 and the beginning of 2004 I did some compensated work for Kurdish clients", plus later a reference to "corporate clients with several of which I have an ongoing business relationship"), it seems pretty clear from the narrative in the book that at least some of this refers to consultancy work for the Kurdish political leaders in the period leading up to the drafting of the Transitional Administrative Law (TAL) which was adopted in March 2004.

It is Galbraith's description of the period between 2003 and 2005 that provides the fullest account of his influence on Iraq's current system of government. Two key principles of the 2005 constitution—the idea that residual powers belong to the provinces and not to the central government, as well as the supremacy accorded to local law over federal law—stand out in particular. In many central-ized states (and indeed even in certain federations), powers not explicitly granted to the regions belong to the center. In Iraq's constitution of 2005 it is the other way around, and the list of central government powers is hilariously short when compared to other federations of the world. This, it seems, comes directly from Galbraith and his influences on the Kurdish leadership back in 2003 and 2004. According to Galbraith,

> [A]fter I left Iraq in May 2003, I realized that the Kurdish leaders had a conceptual prob-
> lem in planning for a federal Iraq. They were thinking in terms of devolution of power—
> meaning that Baghdad grants them rights. I urged that the equation be reversed. In a
> memo I sent Barham [Salih] and Nechirvan [Barzani] in August, I drew a distinction
> between the previous autonomy proposals and federalism: "Federalism is a 'bottom-
> up' system. The basic organizing unit of the country is the province or state. The state
> or province is constituted first and then delegates certain powers (of its choice) to the
> central government. . . . In a federal system residual power lies with the federal unit (i.e.,
> state or province); under an autonomy system it rests with the central government. The
> central government has no ability to revoke a federal status or power" . . . . Finally I
> wrote . . . "any conflict between laws of Kurdistan and the laws or constitution of Iraq
> shall be decided in favor of the former" (pp. 160–161).

Later, Galbraith urged the Kurds to be maximalist about their demands: "The Bush administration might not like the Kurds insisting on their rights, I said, but it would respect them for doing so" (p. 163). Then, leading up to the TAL negotia-tions in the winter of 2004, Galbraith worked specifically for the Kurds in framing their demands. It is very easy to see how the Kurdish gains in the TAL and not least in the 2005 constitution are based on this contribution from Galbraith. Galbraith writes,

> On February 10 [2004], Nechirvan [Barzani] convened a meeting at the Kurdistan national assembly of the top leaders of the PUK and KDP. I presented a draft of a "Kurdistan chapter" to be included in the interim constitution [i.e., the TAL]. . . . Except for a few matters assigned to the federal government (notably foreign affairs), laws passed by the Kurdistan national assembly would be supreme within the region. The Kurdistan Regional Government could establish an armed force. . . . The Kurdistan Region would own its land, water, minerals and oil. Kurdistan would manage future oilfields (and keep revenues) but the federal government in Baghdad would continue to manage all oilfields currently in commercial production. Because there were no commercial oilfields within Kurdistan as defined by the March 18, 2003 boundaries, this proposal had the effect of giving Kurdistan full control over its own oil. . . . The permanent constitution of Iraq would apply in Kurdistan only if it were approved by a majority of Kurdistan's voters (pp. 166–167).

Subsequent achievements noted by Galbraith as personal successes include staging the informal 2005 referendum on Kurdish independence (p. 171).

The influence of Galbraith can be discerned already in the 2004 Transitional Administrative Law (where the principle of residual powers for the provincial entities was put in place), even if Galbraith was dissatisfied with the relatively long list of powers accorded to Baghdad and blamed the "centralizing" policies of Paul Bremer and the Bush administration generally for this "defect". But his hand is even more evident in the 2005 constitution, which combines residual powers for the regions with the supremacy of local law (albeit not if it contradicts the constitution, a "shortcoming" Galbraith later tried to gloss over), and which also specifically mentions the regional right to local armed forces. The narrative in Galbraith's book turns somewhat weaker in this period, and it is less clear exactly how he continued to exercise influence—apparently less directly now, and more through the general advice on federalism given to the Kurds earlier. But at one revealing point in the book, he clearly cannot resist the urge to reveal just how influential he was until the very last minute of the constitutional process in 2005. On p. 199, in a footnote, he writes,

> A British treasury official serving as an advisor to his country's embassy nearly derailed the constitution two hours before the final deadline. He was reading an English translation being made as drafts of the Arabic text became available, and realized the federal government had no tax power. He was about to charge into a meeting of Iraq's political leaders when a quick-thinking Kurdish constitutional advisor grabbed an available Westerner—me—to explain the situation. The omission, I told him, was no mistake and

he might want to consult with his ambassador before reopening an issue that could bring down Iraq's delicate compromise.

Almost drunk with success, it seems, and probably truly convinced that Iraq was heading for breakup, Galbraith could not disguise his satisfaction. Indeed, with the new information about his supposed economic interests, the way he engaged on specific issues relating to oil in the U.S. public debate at this fateful point of transition seems positively reckless. In August 2005, during the final negotiations, while he appeared to be satisfied with the way the new constitution developed as far as decentralization was concerned, he did voice skepticism to growing Islamic influences in the new document and at one point considered the alternative of an overhaul of the TAL to make the regions stronger in that charter instead. He wrote again in the *New York Review of Books*, this time stressing how "the Kurdish leaders would accept its [i.e. the TAL's] continuation *provided the text was clarified to assure Kurdistan's ownership of petroleum in the region* and if the status of the disputed region of Kirkuk were resolved [italics added]". He also expressed hope that "oil contracts made by the Kurdistan government" could be exempted from general federal control through separate bilateral agreements between Baghdad and Arbil (one of the few at that time was of course Tawke, to which Galbraith now has been linked through the PSA).

As for the ramifications of these revelations, when they become known in Baghdad, it is really hard to predict. There has been a myriad of conspiracy theories concerning secret schemes to partition Iraq; while most of them are probably exaggerated the Tawke saga seems to be the most explicit intersection yet of international capitalism and advocacy of a divided Iraq, embodied in Peter Galbraith through his dual role as an alleged stake-holder in the Tawke oilfield and intellectual advocate of Kurdish secession from Iraq. While he was advising the Kurds on the principles of federalism and trying to persuade an American Democratic audience about the virtues of partition as an alternative to the Bush administration policies in Iraq, Galbraith supposedly held a 5% stake in an oilfield whose profit potential was directly governed by both the Iraqi constitutional as well as the U.S. policy decisions Galbraith was seeking to influence (his suggestions also included the idea of a permanent U.S. airbase in Kurdistan). Under any circumstances, this new development is likely to strengthen the tendency among Iraqis to be more critical about the details of the 2005 constitution and not least the historical context in which it was conceived—a criticism that even Prime Minister Nuri al-Maliki articulated during the run-up to the last local elections in January.

Another problem related to this issue is the close association in the past between Galbraith and the apparent Iraq tsar of the current Obama administration, Vice-President Joe Biden. The two often supported each other loyally, even as late as in the autumn of 2008, when Galbraith described Biden's candidacy for vice-president as "very encouraging" because he "has been the prime proponent of a decentralized Iraq". Of course, Biden's own initiatives to move towards a soft partition of Iraq, though not as radical as Galbraith's ones, were the dominant feature of "alternative" Iraq proposals in the U.S. debate in the period between 2005 and 2008, although they are not believed to be favored by President Obama. At one point in the summer of 2008, other Democratic senators including Chuck Schumer weighed in on this issue with specific reference to oil, warning Baghdad not to enter into any agreements with foreign companies to ramp up production until there had been an agreement with the Kurds, thereby also perpetuating the anti-centralization oil policy to which Galbraith had contributed so amply at a time when he is believed to have been a stake-holder in the Tawke field. David Brooks, an influential *New York Times* columnist, declared him "the smartest and most devastating of the critics" of the Iraq policies of George W. Bush.

It is of course somewhat ironic that these revelations should come at a time when Galbraith seems to possess the high moral ground in another controversy also involving Norwegians and Middle Eastern conflicts: The ongoing dispute with UN diplomat Kai Eide over Afghanistan's elections result. In that case one can get the impression that Galbraith is standing up in the name of transparency, while Eide is taking a line so pragmatic that it may ultimately serve to divert attention from widespread electoral fraud.

Galbraith Was Paid by DNO When He Sat In on Sensitive Constitutional Drafting Sessions in 2005[8]

November 12, 2009

In many ways, today's story in *The New York Times* on Tawke-gate serves to corroborate the account of events already conveyed earlier by Norway's *Dagens Næringsliv* (DN). In particular, the impression that it was the Norwegian oil company DNO (rather than the KRG) that awarded a stake in the Tawke oilfield to Peter Galbraith back in 2004 is strengthened in the article, and there are interesting remarks by Abd al-Hadi al-Hassani—one of the few officials close to the Maliki administration who has had the courage to comment publicly on the affair so far. Also, it is refreshing that the NYT, which in the past has given ample space to Americans advocating a soft partition of Iraq, has chosen to publish this kind of critical perspective on one of the leading intellectuals of the soft partition crowd.

Perhaps the single most significant piece of new information in the story is the confirmation that Peter Galbraith, whose consultancy work for DNO in 2004 has previously been revealed by DN, also received payment from DNO in 2005, "throughout the constitutional negotiations in 2005 and later". On this aspect, Iraq's former ambassador to the UN, Feisal Amin al-Istrabadi comments to *The New York Times* as follows: "The idea that an oil company was participating in the drafting of the Iraqi Constitution leaves me speechless". Istrabadi emphasizes that DNO in practice had "a representative in the room, drafting".

It is often not realized how secretive and closed those final negotiations of the Iraqi constitution in August 2005 really were. A good description has been offered by Jonathan Morrow of the U.S. Institute of Peace in a paper entitled "Iraq's Constitutional Process (II)":

> After August 8, constitutional negotiations took place in a series of private, ad hoc meetings between Kurdish and Shiite party leaders—the "Leadership Council", as it was termed by the international press, or more informally by Committee members, "the kitchen" (*matbakh*). In its basic form, the Leadership Council consisted of SCIRI leader Abdul Aziz al-Hakim, Shiite Dawa party leader Prime Minister Jaafari, Kurdish PUK party leader President Jalal Talabani, and Kurdish KDP party leader Masoud Barzani. These meetings took place at irregular intervals at a number of private residences and compounds in the International Zone. These were meetings at which the Sunni Committee members had no right of attendance, to which they frequently requested attendance, but were not often invited. The expectation was quite clear: the Shiite and Kurdish parties would agree to a constitutional text, which would then be presented as a fait accompli to the Sunni Arabs, who would be asked to take it or leave it.

Someone who was admitted to these meetings, however, was Peter Galbraith, the paid DNO consultant and stake-holder in the Tawke oilfield. Again, according to Morrow, "the Kurdish parties were able to invite into the ad hoc meetings experienced non-Iraqi international negotiators and constitutional lawyers, including former U.S. diplomat Peter Galbraith and University of Maryland Professor Karol Soltan, to advance the Kurdish case".

It seems Galbraith was doing more than just "advancing the Kurdish case": The Iraqi constitution adopted in October 2005 for the first time establishes a regional role in administering the country's oil sector, more or less on the lines advocated by Galbraith in a policy paper from early 2004. It is noteworthy that the KDP draft constitution for Iraq from 2003, by way of contrast, accorded exclusive sovereignty to Baghdad in administering the oil sector. Today's revelation that Galbraith also received payment from DNO, a foreign oil company, when he was sitting in on those sensitive Iraqi constitutional meetings in August 2005 where the regional role in the oil sector was established, takes the whole Tawke-gate affair to unprecedented levels of scandalousness.

Weak Attempt at Rebuttal:
Galbraith (2009) Is Contradicted by Galbraith (2006)[9]
November 16, 2009

"Innuendo". "Absurd". "Offensive". Those are the words employed by Peter Galbraith over the weekend in an attempt to dismiss the charge that he had an impact on the shape of Kurdish demands in Iraq's constitutional negotiations back in 2005. After a front-page, above-the-fold story in *The New York Times* last week, the Tawke-gate saga has for the first time attracted the attention of U.S. mainstream media in a big way and Galbraith is gradually becoming more talkative.

Galbraith now maintains that his role for the Kurds back in 2004 and 2005 was that of a mere facilitator who had no impact on the formulation of Kurdish goals and ambitions as such—which in his view means that it was also unproblematic for him to simultaneously have a consultancy contract with the Norwegian oil company DNO that began operating in the Kurdish areas of Iraq at the time. He has added that the fact that his "business arrangements" were known to the Kurdish leadership meant it was unproblematic for him to sit in on key meetings related to the constitutional process in the summer of 2005. Galbraith stresses that he "did no drafting".

The fundamental problem for Peter Galbraith is that there exists a detailed published account that tells a very different story. Moreover, this source is authored by someone who was extremely close to those events back in 2004 and 2005 and probably knew a lot about what was going on—Peter Galbraith himself. In his book *The End of Iraq*, published in 2006, Galbraith recounts in considerable detail how he not only made an impact through shaping Kurdish demands, but also how almost all of his suggestions were verbatim inserted in the Kurdish negotiating proposal of February 2004 that was later to have such a great impact on the Iraqi constitution that was eventually adopted in 2005.

On p. 160 of his book, Galbraith describes his own arrival on the scene in 2003 as follows: "While they had secured support from the Iraqi opposition for federalism, the Kurds had yet to think through some practical issues. What powers would belong to Kurdistan and what to the central government in Baghdad. . . . Who would control the police and security forces? And there was the all-important issue, who would own the oil of Kurdistan"?

Galbraith then goes on to bemoan the "conceptual problems" of the Kurdish leaders before he describes the liberating effect of memos written by himself from the summer of 2003 onwards. His choice of verbs tells the whole story: "I urged" . . . "Kurdistan should" . . . "I argued". Among his demands was the following: "Kurdistan should, I argued, own and manage its own oil resources". Summing up his contribution, Galbraith remarks on p. 161: "These ideas [referring to his own proposals] eventually became the basis of Kurdistan's proposal for an Iraqi constitution". The reader clearly gets the impression that Galbraith's role was a decisive and even a transformative one—an interpretation that makes sense also on the basis of a comparison with the previous and much less radical constitutional proposal by the Kurdish leadership from 2003 (where in article 59.4 Baghdad was given control of "all kinds of armed forces", and in article 59.11 the oil sector was similarly described as the prerogative of the central government).

Later, on pp. 166–167 of his book from 2006, Galbraith describes how his own more detailed proposal in early 2004 was more or less copied wholesale by the Kurds to form their negotiating position as defined in February 2004. He summarizes his paper Special Provisions for the Kurdistan Region of Iraq which is also reproduced *in toto* in an appendix to the book on pp. 225–229. These proposals—which included the key distinction between existing and future oilfields that would later enable stronger regional influence over new oilfields in the 2005 constitution and which forms the basis for the current dispute between Baghdad and the Kurds over oil—were "accepted" by the Kurdish leadership, and then forwarded to the CPA, "as a submission by the Kurdistan National Assembly"! According to Galbraith, his own proposals became the Kurdish proposal in all its details save for one extremely minor "amendment": "Kosrat Rasul . . . wanted to clarify that deployment of the Iraqi Kurdistan National Guard should not only be approved by the Kurdistan National Assembly, but should only occur a the request of the federal government in Baghdad". All the rest had been penned by Galbraith.

As to the direct influence of this "proposal" on the constitution of 2005, Galbraith is once more an excellent source. On p. 168 of *The End of Iraq*, he explains, "Masud Barzani took the initiative to organize a Kurdish delegation and negotiating position that would achieve each objective outlined in their February 11 proposal [which Galbraith had formulated in its entirety] and then some". Galbraith's book is also informative when it comes to his own role in radicalizing the Kurdish position during late 2004 and 2005, especially on p. 171:

> In September 2004, the Referendum Movement organizers [who campaigned for a referendum for Kurdish independence] asked me to meet with them. . . . As we sipped Turkish coffee, we discussed how other independence movements had promoted their own causes. I recalled that at least one independence movement conducted an unofficial referendum on the same day as the country's general election, setting up informal polling places near the official ones. The Referendum Movement leaders thought this was an interesting precedent but doubted that the Kurdish authorities would allow it. I explained that in a democracy the authorities could not prevent such expression of free speech as long as the organizers did not interfere in the official voting". As is well known, the referendum was indeed held along the lines suggested by Galbraith. Not bad for an "advisor?

In a key paragraph of his book on p. 169, Galbraith summarizes the way in which multiple elements of the "Kurdish" proposal of 11 February 2004 actually found their way into Iraq's 2005 constitution. For example, he writes, "as the Kurds proposed in February 2004 the regional governments have exclusive control over future oilfields". Note, however, how different this sentence looks if we insert in brackets additional information provided by Galbraith elsewhere: "As the Kurds proposed in February 2004 [entirely on the basis of my own proposal] the regional governments have exclusive control over future oilfields [in one of which I hold a business interest through DNO]". But even though all the information in the brackets above has been confirmed by Galbraith personally on separate occasions (elsewhere in his 2006 book and in newspaper interviews in 2009 respectively), he today dismisses the juxtaposition of the facts as "innuendo" and instead tries to describe exactly the same relationship using very different words: Three days, ago, on 13 November, he told *The Brattleboro Reformer* (a local newspaper in Vermont) that "I gave them advice and the end result *that they achieved* was identical to what was already proposed in February 2004 [emphasis added]". What Peter Galbraith does not admit in 2009 is what he boasted of in 2006, namely that 99% of the February 2004 proposal was his own work and not that of any Kurdish leader.

In retrospect, it may seem odd that Galbraith should have chosen to publish a book in 2006 that would implicate him so clearly in an unacceptable mixing of roles in business (DNO), constitutional consultancy (for the Kurds) and Iraq policy advocacy (at home in the United States, including before the U.S. Senate). However, the book from 2006 was a reflection of its time. Iraq seemed to be heading downhill back then, and Galbraith was probably convinced the country would break apart (as per his suggestion). Accordingly, he was not only extremely forthcoming with information concerning his own role; he actually appeared to be glowing with the pride of a would-be Kurdish T.E. Lawrence. What he failed to realize was that Iraq was a little more resilient than the pessimistic title of his book suggested.

In other respects, there is not much that is new in Galbraith's latest attempts at rebutting *The New York Times* article. He still has the audacity to suggest that the fact that he informed "Kurdish leaders" somehow exonerated him from any possible conflict of interest! What about the rest of the Iraqis who participated in the negotiations, did they know everything as well? And what about those in the drafting committee who did not belong to KDP/PUK and SCIRI/Daawa and were excluded from the "leadership meetings" in early August 2005, where key decisions were made, and where Galbraith himself participated repeatedly? Iraq's former ambassador to the UN, Feisal Amin al-Istrabadi has said it best: "You don't let Firestone draft the constitution of Liberia. You don't let Shell draft the constitution of Nigeria. We shouldn't have had an oil company [i.e., Norway's DNO] drafting the Iraqi constitution".

Finally, in a welcome development, the editorial board of *The New York Times* has ruled that Galbraith did indeed have a conflict of interest which should have been disclosed when he wrote op-eds in the paper in favor of the soft partition policy in Iraq. This should make it clear once and for all that there is more to this case than the primitive Norwegian "conspiracy" alleged by some Vermont newspapers, according to which the whole affair has been fabricated by all-powerful Norwegian trolls bent on revenge for the Eide/Galbraith dispute in Afghanistan.

CHAPTER NOTES

1 The original version of this text can be found at http://www.opendemocracy.net/conflict-iraq/partition_3565.jsp, where many of the relevant sources are linked.

2 See http://justworldnews.org/archives/002196.html.

3 See http://historiae.org/partition.asp.

4 See http://www.historiae.org/biden.asp.

5 Letter to the editor published in *The Hill* (Washington, D.C.)

6 See http://historiae.org/congress.asp.

7 See http://historiae.org/galbraith.asp.

8 See http://gulfanalysis.wordpress.com/2009/11/12/galbraith-was-paid-by-dno-when-he-sat-in-on-sensitive-constitutional-drafting-sessions-in-2005/.

9 See http://gulfanalysis.wordpress.com/2009/11/16/a-weak-attempt-at-rebuttal-galbraith-2009-is-contradicted-by-galbraith-2006/.

Chapter 11

What Can the Outside World Do for Iraq?

I downgraded my expectations with respect to what good the international com-munity could do for Iraq quite a long time ago. Already by 1996, when I was just beginning to get acquainted with Iraqi history, it was easy to see how U.S. policy toward the country was often contradictory and verged on the ridiculous. The big-gest episode that stood out then, during the Clinton administration, was the U.S. response to the civil war inside the Kurdish areas. In summer 1996, one of the two main Kurdish factions, the PUK, entered into an alliance with Iran whose forces crossed the Iraqi border in an attempt to wipe out the PUK's main competitor, the KDP. The KDP, in turn, made a deal with the Iraqi regime in Baghdad and with its military assistance (in the shape of ground forces) managed to win back control of Arbil. In other words, Baghdad had intervened to help one of the Kurdish fac-tions against the other and sided with the one that was fighting against Iran at the time. Now, the interesting part, as ever, was the U.S. response. On this occasion it consisted of condemning the Iraqi "intervention" (in Iraq), expressing concern about "repression" of the population (presumably the pro-Iranian PUK militia), and—wait for it!—extending its unilaterally imposed no-fly-zone in the south of Iraq from the 32nd to the 33rd parallel (i.e., into the mainly Shiite-populated areas south of Baghdad). The brazen Iranian incursion in Iraq, on the other hand, did not meet with any response by either the United States or the UN Security Council.

After I began blogging in 2005, I thought the first great paradox in the Bush administration's Iraq policy was the unwillingness to use leverage to achieve political ends. I had no problem with the idea of a troop surge in early 2007 since I thought the damage had already been done when the war was started and one might as well try to repair some of that damage. Or, as I used to put it, in many medical conditions there is a choice between conservative approaches and radical surgery; what should never be done, however, is to start surgery using high-tech equipment and then leave the patient halfway through the procedure, decamp and hand over the user manuals to confused relatives and neighbors. Still, the absence of any kind of conditionality in the Bush administration strategy at the time was striking: U.S. forces built up the Iraqi military, in return for which the Iraqi government did absolutely nothing in terms of progress towards national reconciliation. "The surge" without a credible political component was always going to be singularly unproductive.

Another subject that I kept bringing up in this period was the lack of a southern "surge" in 2007. This was the result, chiefly, of Washington's reluctance to challenge its dear partner SCIRI/ISCI, which was the most pro-Iranian of the Shiite Iraqi parties. (For more on its relations with Washington, see chapter 2.) As a result, no anti-Iranian movement on the pattern of the turn against Al-Qaida that occurred in the Sunni areas—with considerable U.S. support—ever materialized in the majority-Shiite areas. Eventually, and perhaps inevitably given the lack of U.S. interest, some of the would-be nationalists of the south drifted into a more sectarian and pro-Iranian direction.

More generally, throughout the tenure of Ambassador Ryan Crocker, there appeared to be a systematic failure on the part of Washington to understand the driving forces behind the positive turn toward greater Iraqi nationalism during 2008. Crocker continued to back the Kurds and ISCI (and sometimes the Iraqi Islamic Party as a "Sunni ornament") as the assumed "moderates" of Iraqi politics. It is interesting, though, that on this issue there appeared to exist counterforces in U.S. policymaking circles that ultimately lost out. For example, The Washington Post reported on October 22, 2007, that "some U.S. diplomats disagree with military officials who think the U.S. should exert more influence to weed out Iraqi government and security force officials who follow sectarian agendas in how they distribute resources and whim they target. Petraeus has a notebook in which he keeps the names of sectarian officers and officials". Crocker, on the other hand, must have had a notebook with separate sections for Shiites, Sunnis, and Kurds!

Since I had already engaged in pretty robust criticism of Joe Biden's thinking on Iraq, I was not particularly optimistic when the Obama administration took charge in 2009. In addition to being Obama's vice-president, Biden was also explicitly named as the administration's chief decision maker and coordinator on Iraq. Thankfully, the most objectionable parts of his earlier "plans for Iraq" were quietly shelved—including not only the federalism bit but also the call for some kind of "grand settlement" more generally. However, many of the central assumptions behind those plans lingered and were to create further inconsistencies in U.S. policy. This was seen above all in the process whereby, on the one hand, Iraq's shift away from sectarian tensions toward a more issue-based form of politics was celebrated by Washington while on the other hand, U.S. diplomats continued to support and encourage those very sectarian and ethnic forces that this development was supposed to leave behind. Key examples include the overt embrace of the Kurdish position with respect to joint patrols in disputed territories in the north and the general support that Washington continued to voice for the inclusion of Kurds in the next government no matter how extreme their demands might be. As *the government formation process got heated in summer 2010, Ambassador Chris Hill even expressed support for the totally unconstitutional idea that the next premier should come from a particular sectarian community—the Shiites!*

Related to this was the tendency of prioritizing the withdrawal timeline above any other consideration and dressing up the facts on the ground to this end if necessary. Thus we saw the Obama administration first failing to do anything about the gross miscarriage of justice that was the de-Baathification process before the elections of March 7, 2010, and then later in the summer seeming to have no qualms about the prospect of a government being formed by a premier candidate from the pan-Shiite sectarian front brought about by the de-Baathification antics—as long as this government could be put in place swiftly. This tendency of bending over backward to the forces of the regional environment and Iran in particular seemed to me to resonate with the worldview upon which the whole "soft-partition" trend had been founded: A fundamental skepticism toward—and even distrust of—Iraqi nationalism that generally seemed to be more pronounced among Democrats than Republicans in the United States. The net result is not exactly the secret deal (safqa) between Iran and the United States that is so prominent in the conspiracy theories of the pan-Arab press; rather, it seems to be some kind of informal American–Iranian détente, with the poor population of Iraq serving as pawns in a bigger regional reconciliation process. This process started with the Bush administration carelessly bolstering Iran's clients in Iraq, apparently basing its approach on the premise of an imminent war with Iran that never materialized (and thankfully so.) It ended with the Obama administration apparently seeing no other choice than to leave the carcass it inherited as fast as possible and to hand it over politely to regional forces while covering the whole charade as best as possible for the American public. To a mostly pacific Scandinavian historian, it all looked rather Chamberlainian.

Not to be forgotten under this heading are the forces of the "international community" that at least in theory are more independent from Washington and its biases. Unfortunately, however, there were numerous instances in the period from 2005 to 2010 in which these players, too, unconsciously or otherwise, would often support the forces that flamed ethno-religious tensions in Iraq instead of combating them. I have included some examples from recent years regarding the UN assistance mission in Iraq (UNAMI) and the International Crisis Group. Much more could be said about episodes that occurred between 2003 and summer 2005 and that antedate the scope of this book. For example, back in 2004, the UN reportedly had a key role in pushing for a single electoral constituency in the first election for a constituent assembly on January 31, 2005. That approach, which maximized the potential for an ethno-sectarian vote (there were no cross-cutting cleavages in the shape of governorate boundaries) was allegedly chosen for "technical" reasons. Similarly, in 2005, the UN helped to enshrine the sectarian paradigm for Iraqi politics when it insisted that the head of the independent electoral committee be a Shiite.

My greatest shock of all regarding the role of the United Nations came when I found a document on federalism apparently authored by the chief advisor on constitutional affairs to the UN mission in Iraq, Nicholas Haysom, in August 2005, just weeks before the final version of the constitution was prepared. In a scheme clearly influenced by the Spanish post-Franco constitution, and dated August 10 (i.e., shortly before SCIRI had formally introduced the idea of a Shiite region) the UN proposed modalities for making the principle of federalism applicable to any part of Iraq (i.e., not just Kurdistan). The previously unpublished document, entitled "A Framework for Decentralized Government in Iraq," also contained the following proposal on the precedence of regional legislation, apparently inspired by Peter Galbraith:

In case of a contradiction between regional and national legislation in respect of a concurrent competency, the regional law shall override the national legislation. The only occasion in which national legislation shall be considered pre-eminent over regional legislation in respect of the concurrent competencies, will be where, [subject to a high threshold of approval by the Council of Governorates], national legislation is necessary in respect of a matter that a single governorate / region cannot deal with effectively (e.g., interstate waters, international air traffic, contagious animal diseases).

This UN-endorsed formulation eventually found its way into the constitution in a revised form and hence is responsible for many of the problems between centripetal and centrifugal forces in Iraq today.

Cases like this, in which perfectly neutral international diplomats and academics who may have the very best intentions toward Iraq and its people nonetheless contribute to destroying the country, ultimately convinced me that much of the talk about an elaborate partition conspiracy against Iraq—often attributed to U.S. or Israeli machinations—tends to miss the point. The conspiracy exists, but it is much wider and less sophisticated than many pan-Arab newspapers claim. True, Israeli, Iranian, and pro-Kurdish academics also sometimes make unhelpful and uninformed noise about the alleged non-existence of Iraqi nationalism at Iraq conferences worldwide. The real conspiracy, though, is that perpetuated by all those Western intellectuals without any obvious agenda who are forced to present an educated opinion about Iraq without having the requisite knowledge of the country's history for doing so.

A Timetabled, Conditional Surge[1]

December 29, 2006

As President George W. Bush contemplates policy alternatives for Iraq, input from experts in Washington has become polarized. Opponents of the Iraq War consider any increase in troop numbers a non-starter and prefer to focus on the modalities for withdrawal. Supporters of the Bush administration seem incapable of framing their latest idea—that of a temporary surge of U.S. troops—as anything other than a repeat of the same old policy, perhaps with some added manpower and resources.

Either approach has its problems. Withdrawal of U.S. military forces from Iraq within one or two years seems a natural goal, but right now may be the worst time since 2003 for such an operation. The simple reason is that Iraqi politics has deteriorated dramatically: Today, sectarian militia activity has been maximized to levels never before witnessed in Iraqi history. At the moment, Iraq does need help from the outside, because its elected politicians are incapable of transcending their own narrow party interests in a bid for national unity. And whereas the Iraq Study Group may have offered some sound advice about enhanced regional diplomacy, on the whole their report seems more like a containment strategy than a plan that can pro-actively induce rapid political realignment inside Iraq.

A troop increase could be equally problematic. Even if more U.S. firepower should succeed in temporarily stemming the violence, there is nothing in the prevalent neo-conservative expositions of the "surge plan" that would address the fundamental problem of national reconciliation in Iraq. There simply is no new substance compared with what was being said back in 2003 and 2004; neo-conservatives still seem convinced that as soon as there is calm on the streets of Baghdad, a Mesopotamian zest for democracy will miraculously rise from the ashes. Within the Bush administration, the only vision about a parallel process at the political level is that of a "new coalition government"—involving a few cosmetic changes in the line-up of Iraqi elite politicians currently engaged in a game of musical chairs inside the Green Zone.

What is required in Iraq today is not cosmetic change, but heavy lifting. The colossal irony of the current situation is that a large majority of Iraqis actually agree with the declared aims of the Bush administration—national reconciliation followed by a withdrawal of U.S. troops—but their "representatives" in the Iraqi parliament (many of them newly returned exiles with limited insight into the situation of the ordinary people) are locked in petty shouting matches instead of working for national unity. It is the open-ended U.S. military commitment that enables them to go on with this: Certain Shiite politicians infuriate Sunni politicians with newly concocted demands for federalism; Sunni leaders, in turn, hesitate in condemning even the most grotesque atrocities committed by al-Qaida-linked terrorists. Forgotten in all of this are the ordinary Iraqis. The Shiite masses have so far expressed only limited interest in "Shiite federalism", and the average Sunni is quite prepared to denounce al-Qaida as long as a minimum of security can be guaranteed.

A troop surge offers a unique opportunity for resolving this paradoxical situation. If implemented in an innovative way, it could enable the United States to circumvent the bellicose Iraqi elite politicians and appeal directly to Iraqi nationalism. But success would require that the troop surge be offered as a package, with obligations for both sides. The United States should commit forces and economic aid to create the necessary momentum for a dramatic security improvement, but at the same time should realign itself with Iraqi nationalism by presenting a timetable for a withdrawal after the surge. Iraqi politicians, for their part, should undertake to make immediate constitutional revisions that could bring the Sunnis and secularists back in and achieve national reconciliation. While Washington should not seek to micro-manage this, it must be made perfectly clear that the forces that have so far dominated the constitutional process in Iraq (the two biggest Kurdish parties as well as SCIRI, one of the Shiite groups) will need to make general concessions in the areas of federalism and de-Baathification before any troop surge can be offered.

By making the surge conditional, Washington would for the first time create pressure on Iraqi politicians, through their own electorates. If presented with a credible plan for national reconciliation and the eventual withdrawal of U.S. troops, Iraqi politicians would find it hard to persist in their current squabbling. This would enable the United States to tap into a most remarkable factor in Iraqi politics: the seemingly unshakeable belief in the concept of "national unity" that has persisted among ordinary Iraqis, even in today's violent climate.

The Surge, the Shiites and Nation Building in Iraq[2]
September 13, 2007

For some time, analysts have been suggesting that the Bush administration's "surge" strategy may have achieved a measure of success in certain parts of Iraq. Many highlight the tendency on the part of local tribes in the Sunni-dominated areas to stand up against al-Qaida, in that way emphasizing their own "Iraqiness" as well as their unwillingness to join in an all-out war against Western civilization. The number of attacks against U.S. forces has declined in many of these areas, and there are signs that al-Qaida has been forced to relocate to new areas and to choose new targets.

Perhaps the most convincing indicator of a degree of "surge" success is one that has gone largely unnoticed. Reports out of Baghdad suggest that the Sunni politicians who for the past two years or so have worked with the Americans through participating in government and parliament are now becoming increasingly nervous about internal Sunni competition from the newly emerged anti-jihadist tribal leaders of their "own" community, for example in places like the Anbar governorate. In terms of Iraqi nation-building, this is a healthy sign. There was always a degree of doubt with regard to the true representativeness of the Sunni parties that emerged as "winners" in their fields in the heavily boycotted 2005 parliamentary elections. The fact that these parties are now worried about internal competition means that more Sunnis are interested in participating in the system, and that a group of politicians firmly attached to the vision of a unified Iraq but also enjoying solid popular backing in their core constituencies may be on the way up, assisted by the "surge". At the same time, foreign-sponsored groups, such as al-Qaida, and office seekers whose popular legitimacy is in doubt (for instance, some members of the Tawafuq bloc) are coming under pressure or are even being weeded out.

South of Baghdad, the logical corollary to this kind of "surge" policy would have been to build local alliances with those Shiite groups that have a historical record of firm opposition to Iran and are unequivocal in their condemnation of Iranian interference in Iraq. The principal aim would be to create a counter-balance to the most pro-Iranian factions inside the system, such as the Islamic Supreme Council of Iraq (ISCI, formerly the Supreme Council for the Islamic Revolution in Iraq, SCIRI) and their Badr brigades—organizations that since 2003 have been successful in obtaining a disproportionate degree of formal political power in the Iraqi political system and are currently profiting from their role in the Nuri al-Maliki government to consolidate their position further. In the south, there is a vast array of groupings with a long record of hostility to Iran, including factions like Fadila and at least some of the "mainline" followers of Muqtada al-Sadr (some of whom have even served jail sentences in Iranian prisons in the past), plus independent Shiite tribal groups that are fiercely proud of their Arab heritage.

Actual U.S. policy south of Baghdad is the exact opposite of this. Pro-Iranian ISCI and its friends in the Badr organization (now powerful in the Iraqi security forces) are being supported by the United States in their efforts to bulldoze all kinds of internal Shiite opposition, as seen for instance in the large-scale battle against an alleged cultist movement at Najaf in January 2007, as well as in the ongoing operations against the Sadrist Mahdi Army and its splinter factions. Indiscriminate mass arrests have often accompanied these incidents, with the Maliki government's wholesale designation of its enemies as "terrorists" apparently being taken at face value by U.S. forces, and with the persistent complaints from those arrested about "Iranian intrigue" being ignored. Today, apart from isolated rural enclaves, the sole remaining bastions of solid Shiite resistance to ISCI outside Baghdad are Maysan and Basra (which happen to be located outside direct U.S. control, in the British zone in the far south), but here too change may be underway: ISCI has worked for more than one year to unseat the Fadila governor of oil-rich Basra (he remained in office by early September 2007 despite an order by Maliki to have him replaced), and the Badr brigades are reportedly influential within the security forces in Maysan. Ironically, long-standing enemies of Iran like the Fadila party are now feeling so isolated that they see no other recourse than to upgrade contacts with their erstwhile foes in Tehran, if only tentatively. The apparent U.S. rationale for letting all this happen is the idea that the Sadrist Mahdi Army constitutes America's worst opponent in Iraq, and that some Mahdi Army factions are even being supplied with arms from Tehran.

An alternative reading is that Iran could be deliberately feeding weaponry to marginal (or splinter) elements of the Sadrists precisely in order to weaken the Sadrist movement as a whole, and to make sure that Sadrist energy is combusted in clashes with U.S. forces. Right now, from Tehran's point of view, the implementation of the "surge" south of Baghdad could not have been more perfect. Today, U.S. forces are working around the clock to weaken Tehran's traditional arch-enemy in Iraq's Shiite heartland—the Sadrists—while Iran's preferred and privileged partner since the 1980s, SCIRI/ISCI, keeps strengthening its influence everywhere. Back in the United States, think tanks concentrate their risk analyses on the ties between Sadrists and Iran and consistently overlook those factions that have truly close and long-standing ties to Tehran, whereas the recently released National Intelligence Estimate was devoid of initiatives to bring the Shiites into a more reconciliatory mode—suggesting that few ideas exist in Washington about alternative Shiite policies.

The great irony in this is that, from the historical perspective, the neo-conservative working assumption that Iraqi Shiites can be trusted to resist Iranian domination is generally sound—with the sole exception of the particular faction on which Washington has fixed its eyes as its special partner in the country. In the 1980s, SCIRI was designed by Iran to maximize Tehran's control of the unruly Iraqi opposition. Throughout its history, it has stressed the importance of subservience to Iran's leaders, first Khomeini and later Khamenei. In the mid-1990s, its leader Muhammad Baqir al-Hakim became one of the first Shiite intellectuals to produce an elaborate plan for the political unification of the Shiites from Iran to Lebanon in a federal system under the leadership of Tehran, and as late as 1999 one of SCIRI's key figures, Sadr al-Din al-Qabbanji, angrily attacked the Sadrists for daring to suggest that the Iraqi Shiite opposition could operate independently of Khamenei. Close scrutiny of SCIRI's highly publicized name change and supposed "ideological makeover" in May 2007 shows that none of this heritage has been annulled in a convincing manner: The new and much trumpeted "pledge" to Grand Ayatollah Ali al-Sistani is in reality nothing more than a non-committal expression of general praise, and there is no renunciation of a decades-long policy of subordination to Khamenei. It is suspicious that ISCI and Iran still hold virtually synchronized views on the sacrosanctity of the Maliki government and the 2005 constitution. Both tend to describe the idea of challenging Maliki as "subversive coup activity", and they are unified in rejecting challenges to the constitution by what they describe as neo-Baathists.

The problem is that Washington's "surge" is framed as a straightforward counter-insurgency operation in which the nation-building component is in the far background. "The enemy" is defined on the basis of a myopic interpretation of who is directly hostile to U.S. forces while the historical dimension of alliance patterns between Iran and Iraqi Shiite factions is overlooked. This prevents Washington from fully understanding who is friend and foe in Iraq. It is conceivable that ISCI may assist Washington in temporarily reducing the amount of noise out of Iraq, and this may well be what the Bush administration is looking for right now. Yet, even if its members are more genteel and well-behaved than the Sadrists, it is highly unclear what kind of "moderation" ISCI is really capable of delivering in Iraq, especially in terms of a political system based on true reconciliation between Shiites and Sunnis.

Washington Formally Embraces the Minority View in the Kirkuk Question[3]

August 21, 2008

Yesterday, U.S. Ambassador Ryan Crocker explicitly extended his support to a UN proposal of delaying the provincial council vote in Kirkuk without making any substantial changes to the province's current political line-up, while allowing the provincial elections to go ahead in the rest of Iraq's governorates. It is noteworthy that this is the exact approach that was earlier rejected by a majority of Iraqi parliamentarians, who in their historic vote on 22 July 2008 passed an elections law featuring transitional power-sharing arrangements in Kirkuk. In early August, after the presidential council had vetoed the first iteration of the elections bill, the pro-Kurdish government parties attempted to push through the version that is now being embraced also by Crocker—only to fail due to a lack of parliamentary support.

The upside of the UN approach to Kirkuk is that it is part of a grand strategy of diluting territorial issues in northern Iraq by tackling them piecemeal, starting with the easiest ones. This is a good approach because there are certain "disputed" areas that are not really disputed and which many Iraqis, regardless of ethnic origin, would be quite happy to assign to the Kurdish federal region. This approach would also confine the application of the concept of "disputed territories" to the north— an important factor with regard to political stability given that ISCI in particular has shown a proclivity for thinking in similar terms in Shiite-dominated areas south of Baghdad, for example in possible border adjustments between Karbala and Anbar. Theoretically this could form the basis for a grand compromise on territorial changes in the north that could bring closure to the Iraqi federalism debate and a renewed focus on development issues more broadly.

What is less clear is why this process should require a perpetuation of the status quo in the provincial government of Kirkuk. If instead steps towards a modicum of power-sharing were implemented, there are greater chances that any grand "final status" deal would enjoy credibility in the eyes of the majority of Iraqis. The proposal of the majority of the Iraqi parliament needs not be the perfect approach, but there is a clearly expressed desire not to carry on with existing arrangements, which are seen as too strongly supportive of the Kurdish position. This stance represents a challenge to the forces that see the 2005 constitution and the political set-up it created as a viable way forward, and for Washington to persevere in ignoring the majority of the Iraqi parliament on this issue seems like an almost self-destructive strategy. If anything, the forces that find it difficult to consider Kirkuk as anything other than "Iraqi"—and which therefore are reluctant to acquiesce in what is seen as undemocratic arrangements for the area—are probably even stronger outside parliament than inside it.

Maliki's Northern Headache, and How General Odierno Is Compounding It[4]
September 9, 2009

While fellow Shiite Islamists are creating plenty of trouble for Iraq's premier Nuri al-Maliki in Basra these days, the U.S. military in Iraq is doing its part in the north of the country. It was only this week that Western media broke the silence about one of the key issues that have been simmering for some weeks in Iraq now: The proposed patrols whereby forces from the U.S. military, the Iraqi central government, and the Kurdistan federal government would jointly deploy in what the Kurds refer to as "disputed territories" in northern Iraq.

Western commentary on the opposition to the scheme has focused on Hawija in Tamim, often described as a "Baathist stronghold". But this portrayal of the resistance to Odierno's scheme as retrograde mutterings from isolated pockets of Baathist loyalists is clearly inadequate. On 23 August, the Nineveh provincial council headed by the electorally successful Hadba front condemned the scheme. Members of the council have instead called for more central government troops, possibly strengthened by local recruits. On 1 September, Arab and Turkmen members of the local council in Kirkuk similarly rejected the Odierno plan, focusing on its contravention of the broad principles of the SOFA agreement as well as its implicit recognition of the Kurdish view of what constitutes disputed territories (to most non-Kurdish Iraqis, large swathes of the Tamim governorate are not "disputed lands" but rather Iraqi central government territory, period). Yet another

Mosul politician with ties to wider Iraqi nationalist circles, Nur al-Din al-Hayali, has criticized the Odierno scheme as a prelude to a Bosnia-like, enclave-based, partition of northern Iraq.

What Maliki and the rest of the Iraqi government think about the proposed scheme is not yet clear. It does come at a time when Kurdish reactions to the recently-announced one-year postponement of the general census—a move presided over by Ali Baban, the Kurdish, ex-Tawafuq minister of planning from Mosul—have been comparatively subdued, and one cannot help wondering whether some kind of bargain could be in the making. What is certain is that any approval of the Odierno scheme by Maliki is likely to cost the Iraqi premier dearly. For one thing, some of his centralist Shiite supporters (such as the editors of the hardline *Al-Bayyina al-Jadida* newspaper) have staked much of their Iraqi nationalist credentials on a rather rabid form of anti-Kurdish propaganda. Perhaps more significantly—in terms of the upcoming parliamentary elections especially— almost all the constituencies in northern Iraq that Maliki may want to target if he is to run separately from the new Shiite-dominated alliance, including the Hadba list in Mosul and the anti-Kurdish opposition in Kirkuk, are against the scheme.

Back in March this year, it seemed as if Maliki was sincere about reaching out to these forces, cooperating in several governorates north of Baghdad with groups like Hiwar and Iraqiyya (whose electorate is often Sunni, but whose ideology is Iraqi nationalist), but closing the door to Tawafuq and its key component, the Iraqi Islamic Party (these also appeal to many Sunnis, but often in an overtly sectarian way). That potential still remains: The recent sacking of the Tawafuq governor by the Iraqiyya-led governorate council in Salahaddin is a case in point, making the situation there more similar to Diyala (where Maliki's supporters are also allied on a nationalist basis in opposition to the ethno-sectarian alliance of Tawafuq and the Kurds). But if Maliki instead is once more navigating towards compromise with the two big Kurdish parties then in the end the next parliamentary elections may well turn out to be very similar to those held in 2005.

Joint Patrols and Power-sharing in Mosul:
Unbalanced Proposals from the International Crisis Group[5]
October 5, 2009

In the one corner, a steadily increasing group of Iraqi politicians of all sectarian backgrounds who reject the idea of joint patrols between the forces of the Iraqi central government, the Kurdish federal authorities and the United States in what the Kurds refer to as "disputed territories" in northern Iraq, including Nineveh. The latest addition to this camp is Abbas al-Bayati, a key ally of Prime Minister Nuri al-Maliki in his revamped State of Law coalition. In a statement to the press on 1 October, the day of the re-launch of the Maliki alliance, Bayati made his position on this crystal clear: The governorates of Kirkuk and Nineveh fall within the exclusive sovereignty of the central government, whose responsibility it is to protect the population of these areas with its security forces. In principle, according to Bayati, the forces of the Kurdistan Regional Government (KRG) have no legitimate role; any exception to this rule must meet with the full consent of both the central government and the governorate authorities concerned.

In the other corner, there are, of course, the two biggest Kurdish parties, KDP and PUK. Less easy to explain in rational terms but perfectly predictable is the presence of Washington, represented through its commander in Iraq, Ray Odierno, who has apparently invested a degree of personal prestige in the idea of joint patrols and whose army is increasingly in search of some kind of mission that can define its raison d'être in Iraq. And then, something of a surprise: the International Crisis Group (ICG). In its latest report on Iraq, "Iraq's New Battlefront: The Struggle over Ninewa", the ICG furnishes the most elaborate justification to date for the project of establishing joint patrols in the Nineveh governorate. Singling out the province as one of the potentially most dangerous in Iraq, the Crisis Group also makes recommendations for power-sharing in local government.

To find the ICG in this position is surprising because it has in the past produced a vast number of exceptionally well-researched, empirically based reports in Iraq, often with interesting policy proposals. Indeed, most of the analytical aspects of the most recent report seem to conform with the high standards of past ICG publications on Iraq. But some of the policy recommendations are troubling and distinctly less balanced than previous proposals by the group.

The first of these concerns the idea of joint patrols in what the Kurds refer to as "disputed territories" in northern Iraq. The ICG recommends the implementation of this mechanism, despite the fact that it is something that is supported by the Kurds whilst rejected by most other Iraqi politicians. Not only that, the ICG goes on to portray such patrols as somehow constituting a "compromise" position. This is where the logic becomes particularly hard to follow. The keystone of the argument reads as follows: "While Ninewa's Arab leaders accuse the KRG of expansionist ambitions, one reason the Kurds rushed across the Green Line in 2003 was to protect Kurds displaced under Arabization and to facilitate their return to their original homes and lands; the effort to incorporate these areas into the Kurdistan region came later (especially via Article 140 of the 2005 constitution)". The report then goes on to make an analytical distinction between Kurdish expansionism (allegedly this "came later") and the supposedly more humanitarian and basic agenda of "protecting" Kurds living in Nineveh. The ICG separates "protection" from "territorial ambition", and voilà, Barzani is a great philanthropist!

Frankly, in this case, to assume that one aspect of the Kurdish presence can be excised with surgical precision from the other is a way of reasoning that cannot survive for long in the real world. Indeed, the ICG itself has produced a far more level-headed assessment of this particular problem in one of its earlier reports, writing as recently as last July (in "Iraq and the Kurds: Trouble Along the Trigger Line") that "the Kurds also claim these areas as majority-Kurdish and historically part of Kurdistan, and in reality their presence should be seen as a bid to reclaim them by establishing facts on the ground in advance of a law-based resolution of their status". In other words, the distinction between "protection" and "expansionism" that forms the basis for the designation of the joint patrols as a "compromise" is in itself entirely artificial, and the ICG knows it. Just a quick glance at Kurdish maps issued long before 2003 should eliminate any doubt about this—they often include an extra "ethnic" line indicating areas claimed as belonging historically to Kurdistan.

In order to understand why Iraqis react so strongly to the joint patrols, it can be useful to revisit the legal basis for the controversy. In particular it is important to take note of how the singling out of areas as "disputed" ones so far has been an entirely unilateral process, controlled by the Kurds and sometimes with the support of the Americans, but never in any systematic dialogue with Baghdad. Thus, the only post-2003 definition of the geographical extent of Kurdistan as an area of administration is that of the Transitional Administrative Law (TAL) of March 2004 which was also confirmed in the October 2005 constitution, where the federal region is defined as those areas that were administered by the Kurds "on 19 March 2003 in the governorates of Dahuk, Arbil, Sulaymaniya, Kirkuk, Diyala and Nineveh", often identified with reference to the so-called green line that separated the *de facto* autonomous Kurdish region of the Baathist era from the central government. And guess what, there is of course an unspoken, logical corollary implicit in the TAL: Every square inch of land south of the Green Line is the exclusive sovereignty of Baghdad until progress has been made on the settlement of those "disputed territories" that are alluded to (but never defined) later in the document. True, Kurdish militias stormed over the Green Line in 2003, but their expansionism into these areas was coordinated only with the Americans and their continued presence there does not enjoy any legitimacy within the Iraqi constitutional framework.

In other words, any neutral and balanced international arbitration effort should use the Green Line as its point of departure. Like its namesake in the Israel/Palestine conflict, the Green Line is beautiful simply by virtue of its utter meaninglessness: In the murky world of ethno-nationalism it will prompt nothing but a "syntax error" response. It has no relationship at all to racially based claims and counter-claims, it is just where Iraqi and Kurdish forces happened to stand in March 2003. But whereas in the case of Israel/Palestine the international community has prudently accepted the 1967 lines as a point of departure for negotiations and has generally ignored Israeli maximalism of the "Judea and Samaria" type, in the case of northern Iraq both the ICG and the U.S. government choose to extend recognition to unilateral ethno-national expansionism by the Kurds. In fact, when the Iraqi government asserts control of areas that belong to it according to the TAL, Washington sees this as a "reckless" challenge to the Kurds, apparently ignoring the fact that Baghdad has judiciously abstained from what would be a logical counter-measure to the Kurdish policy: identifying "disputed territories" inside the KRG-controlled area (where there are many Arab and Turkmen minorities who historically have closer ties to Baghdad than to the Kurds, with some even seeing Arbil as a "disputed territory") and sending government forces to "protect" those groups against Kurdish highhandedness.

The second problem in the ICG report concerns the idea of power-sharing in Nineveh. Once more, the empirical basis for the proposed ICG solution is uncharacteristically weak and partial, and appears to have been lifted almost verbatim from an interview with a Kurdish parliamentarian without any critical discussion. Worse, the quoted matter is in itself so full of factual errors that it remains a mystery that the ICG should choose to take it at face value. It goes as follows:

Abd al-Mohsen al-Saadoun, a Kurdish parliamentarian, articulated the Ninewa Brotherhood List's perspective as follows: "In this last election, both lists won, the Brotherhood List and al-Hadbaa List. What I mean is that governance in all of Iraq is based on *muhasasa* [ethnosectarian quotas]. The presidency council is decided this way and so are the parliament speaker and his deputies, as well as cabinet ministers, and it also happens in the provinces—except Ninewa. In Ninewa, al-Hadbaa has gone with the idea of absolute-majority rule. This is not in the constitution. By not accepting the Brotherhood in local government, al-Hadbaa carried out a coup against democracy and national consensus". Moreover, he suggested, a double standard was being applied: "It's funny that everyone is demanding that the Kurds share power with the Arabs in Kirkuk but fail to make that same demand in Ninewa". As part of a power-sharing deal in Ninewa, the Brotherhood List, as runner-up in the elections, says it is entitled to the posts of council president and deputy governor, senior positions in the security apparatus and about a third of the "key" appointments in local government.

Also, added in a footnote: "Al-Saadoun said: 'Since they got the governor post, we should have the deputy position. When we say we want the council president post, we say they can have the vice-president position'. . . . " Later on in the report follow the recommendations by the ICG, which are in fact strikingly similar: "A Brotherhood presence in the top echelons of government, for example as deputy governor and/or council president, would give the Kurds the assurance they seek".

Let's deal with these contentions seriatim. The Kurdish representative alleges that local government in all of Iraq is based on *muhasasa* and that this principle has a constitutional basis. That is simply untrue. There just is no specific reference to the composition of local governments in the constitution, only a reference to future legislation. The only law that has materialized so far is the provincial powers law of February 2008, which failed to make any special provisions for power-sharing. Indeed, some of Iraq's governorates are ruled by simple, minimum-winning majorities (notably Basra), and there appears to be no *muhasasa* for example for Sunni minorities in Babel or the Shiites of Salahaddin. As for "double standards" regarding Kirkuk, it should be noted that local Arab and Turkmen groups there are not calling for power-sharing necessarily as an end goal but primarily as an instrument for creating a more level field, especially to address post-2003 changes to the demographic structure of the city pending final status negotiations.

Finally, at a more general level, the appeal to "constitutionalism" seems particularly hollow in this case. The constitutional approach for "disputed territories" was outlined in article 140, whose implementation was delayed beyond the original December 2007 deadline thanks not least to the inability of the Kurds to make compromise in other questions. The court of first instance here must now be the ongoing constitutional revision process. Hence, when local officials loyal to the KRG make unilateral declarations about "secession" from Nineveh and demand inclusion in the Kurdistan federal region, then frankly that is their problem: They are behaving in an unconstitutional way and are engaged in illegal forms of land-grabbing. At some point, the Kurdish authorities in Arbil will have to understand that they cannot claim the high moral ground of constitutionalism and state-building while simultaneously destroying the Iraqi state at the local level—although it is a big worry that both the ICG and Washington still seem to acquiesce in this kind of nonsense as if it represented acts of great statesmanship. Indeed, there are reports that U.S. military officials recently took part in functions inside Nineveh where the Kurdish flag was hoisted by the *peshmerga* forces.

Just for the record, back in 1919, Iraqi officers in Damascus including many from Mosul handed the British authorities a demand for the establishment of an independent Iraq within its "historical borders" from the Gulf to Dayr al-Zur on the Euphrates (in present-day Syria) and Diyarbakir on the Tigris (today in Turkey, historically considered the northernmost area of Arabic-speaking minorities). In more recent history, Iraqis in Nineveh wisely settled for a more pragmatic approach, abandoning their claims to Diyarbakir and ceding Dahuk to the Kurdish autonomous region that was created in the early 1970s. Today they are focusing on the territorial integrity of the rump Nineveh governorate. But sadly, on this issue, the Kurds, General Odierno, and the International Crisis Group all appear to be stuck in 1919 and its ethno-nationalist way of thinking.

What Exactly Is UNAMI Up to in the Iraqi Parliament?[6]
October 28, 2009

One of the remarkable aspects about yesterday's developments regarding the election law in parliament is that the UN's agency in Iraq, UNAMI, appears to have played a key role in derailing a deal that was in the making. In the early hours of the morning, a press statement was released by the Iraqi government to the effect that the "tri-lateral meeting of the presidents" (this time referring not to the presidency council but the three "presidents", i.e., Maliki for the council of ministers, Talabani for the presidency, and Samarraie for the parliament) had agreed on a "limited" draft of the election law. But around midday the parliamentary proceedings began, featuring among other things a meeting where UNAMI and representatives of the elections commission were present. And whereas this external presence has totally drowned in Western news reports on the developments (where the Iraqis are invariably blamed for the failure), remarks by some Iraqi politicians make it perfectly clear that UNAMI had indeed tried to shoot down at least two and possibly all the three alternatives for Kirkuk that had emerged earlier in the week during the meeting of the political assembly for national security. Referring to "technical problems", UNAMI rejected one of the more innovative proposals on the table, which apparently originated from ISCI's Adil Abd al-Mahdi and therefore also constituted something that should stand a greater chance of being accepted by the Kurds: The idea of subdividing the city into two constituencies, not on the basis of sect or ethnicity but instead with reference to residency status. This seems like an elegant proposal that would differentiate between long-established residents of Kirkuk on the one hand and recent arrivals and more fictitious "residents" on the other, thereby creating space for Kirkuk identity without tying it to any specific and wider ethnicity other than "Iraqi". Instead, UNAMI reportedly objected on technical grounds and advocated the adoption of the solution that is only favored by the two Kurdish parties, i.e. relying on the 2009 registers of voters, perhaps with some kind of extra scrutiny across the country, but without any special treatment for Kirkuk. Similarly, the second constructive alternative that has been circulating—that of reverting to the voter rolls compiled in 2004, before many of the demographic changes to which Arabs and Turkmens object had been reflected in the registers—has apparently also been rejected by UNAMI and its friends in the Iraqi elections commission.[7]

This is what it looks like at the surface. There may well be other explanations, but as long as UNAMI remains so uncommunicative about its activities in Iraq, it is really difficult to tell. And, in fact, the few UNAMI press releases that exist on this topic seem to suggest that the UN sometimes fails to appreciate the extent to which politics in Iraq has changed since the current constitution was adopted under chaotic circumstances back in October 2005. For example, in a statement to the press on 21 October, Ad Melkert, the new boss of UNAMI (who arrived in Baghdad only this summer), commented on the elections law as follows: "It is equally important that Iraqi parliamentarians recognize that the focus should remain on the national process and overcome any narrow considerations that could be the source of the current stalemate". The reference to "narrow considerations" in that context seems pretty clear: It refers to the demand by a large number of Iraqi parliamentarians for special treatment of Kirkuk. This is a perfectly logical demand for a more level playing field, given that Kirkuk is the only Iraqi governorate to have experienced large-scale demographic changes in the post-2003 period with the specific aim of changing its political status (and annexing it to Kurdistan). Moreover it is emphatically a national issue, and not something that can be plausibly reduced to "narrow considerations" and the "obstinate" demands of Arabs and Turkmens native to Kirkuk, as UNAMI (and some Iraqi politicians) like to think.

To many Iraqis, Kirkuk, with its multi-ethnic nature, is the real heart of Iraq, and to dismiss the issue as a local problem, as UNAMI seems to do, is simply an insult to Iraqi national sentiment. In fact, whereas the political council for national security produced three options that all studiously avoided the concept of ethnosectarian quotas (which would only reify ethnic divisions), UNAMI's only known proposal that even considered special arrangements in Kirkuk reportedly followed precisely that kind of narrow quota logic—apparently oblivious to the fact that the Iraqi federal supreme court many months ago rejected this approach as unconstitutional. Does UNAMI really believe Kirkuk is a perfectly ordinary Iraqi governorate and that all that has happened there after 2003 is irrelevant? On the whole, whereas pre-2003 injustices are amply covered in the TAL of 2004 and the constitution, problems in Kirkuk in the post-2003 period are inadequately addressed and this should not be glossed over by the international community.

Ambassador Hill and the Decision by Iraqiyya[8]
February 21, 2010

It is easy to understand the dilemma for Iraqiyya leaders who gathered in Baghdad over the weekend to decide on the question of participation in the 7 March elections. The outcome was not unequivocal: While they will resume campaigning, Iraqiyya still has complaints concerning the procedure and will continue to monitor the situation, including the fate of a query to the higher judicial supreme council by the speaker of parliament, Ayad al-Samarraie, regarding the legality of exclusions under article 7 of the constitution. Several candidates who were previously affiliated with the Hiwar front that was led by Salih al-Mutlak before it merged with Wifaq—some reports say as many as 75 individuals—still talk openly about a boycott. This all comes against the backdrop of the latest "elections campaigning" trend: Increasing ad hoc and vigilante de-Baathification in the Iraqi governorates, with stricter criteria coming into effect by the day. If this tendency continues, Iraqis will eventually need to have lived most of their lives in foreign capitals in order to be considered sufficiently "clean" for public service in Iraq!

Before they met in Baghdad, Iraqiyya had been hoping that there would be some kind of reaction by the international community against the almost boundless highhandedness by the de-Baathification board, which has taken the lead in excluding candidates that were seen as enemies of the slate of two of the board's dominant personalities, Ali al-Lami and Ahmad Chalabi (both are candidates of the all-Shiite Iraqi National Alliance). That kind of international response, it was hoped, could in turn both stimulate turnout and make it easier for the secularists and nationalists to return to the political process as a unified front. However, after the visit to Washington by Ambassador Chris Hill last week it increasingly became clear that this kind of warning from the United States is unlikely to be forthcoming. In fact, as shown by the excerpts below from Hill's press briefing on 17 February (critical comments have been added in italics), Washington is going surprisingly far in the direction of actually ascribing legitimacy to the recent de-Baathification antics, and this absence of a clearer American counter-position at least goes some way towards explaining the continued ambivalence among some Iraqiyya members with regard to participation in the upcoming elections:

AMBASSADOR HILL: . . . I think anyone who follows Iraq knows that there are twists and turns to any destination in Iraq. Certainly, de-Baathification was a major issue and a very tough issue, a very emotional issue, but I think we've gotten through that issue. The campaign has really started in earnest. There are campaign placards all over every surface in the country, it seems, right now. There are some 6,172 candidates. There are 18.9 million registered voters. There are 300,000 poll station workers. There are 50,000 polling stations spread over 9,000 polling centers. . . .

So the problem has been solved already? Really? Hill's focus on placards and statistics reveals a dangerous preference for making the facade tidy instead of taking a critical approach to the real democratic content of the process.

AMBASSADOR HILL: I think everyone is aware of the complexity of putting together coalition governments. At the end of the day, I think we will be looking at a government that has a Shiite representation, that it does indeed have Sunni representation, and will also have Kurdish representation. Now, what particular configuration, which parties those three identities will be represented, well, that will be up to the Iraqi voters on March 7th.

Saddam also had Sunnis and Shiites and Kurds represented. Sectarianism in Iraq is a little more subtle than this and Hill just gets it wrong if he thinks this a puzzle where can he check three boxes and then relax. By the way this whole "Sunnis and Shiites" paradigm reached a higher stage of ridiculousness yesterday as AP declared Hiwar as the "Sunni wing" of Iraqiyya, with Ayad Allawi's Wifaq as its "Shiite wing"!

AMBASSADOR HILL: I would be cautious about comparing these elections to those in 2005. You'll recall in 2005 we had a Sunni boycott. There are no signs whatsoever of a boycott by any of the communities at this time. In fact, all of the communities have been urging their voters to—their members to get out and vote.

So it is sufficient to the United States to see some "Sunnis" show up for a vote? What about the question of turnout among secular Iraqis?

AMBASSADOR HILL: But we don't see that this issue of excluding Baathist candidates is one that is leading to violence. Frankly, they were able to come together and work out a solution, and I think it's a solution that most people are living with.

So as long as there is no outright violence the United States will be happy with the elections no matter what?

AMBASSADOR HILL: I think it's important to understand that there are candidates who are unhappy at having been on the list, but there was a process by which they were able to appeal, there was a sequestered panel of judges from the cassation court that looked at these cases. In some cases, they ruled that the people should be able to stand for office; in others, they ruled against it.

Well, two weeks ago that court postponed all the cases and wanted to ask critical questions about the legitimacy of the accountability and justice board; one week later it dismissed all the appeals save 26. Not terribly reassuring as far as the question of political interference with the work of the judiciary is concerned?

QUESTION: Good to see you in person. Yesterday, General Odierno accused two Iraqi officials—let me read the names—Ali Faisal al-Lami and Ahmed Chalabi, who were both key members of the Accountability and Justice Commission, of being clearly influenced by Iran. I'm wondering if you agree with General Odierno's comments, and are you concerned with Iran's influence over this process concerning the candidates and the election in general?

AMBASSADOR HILL: Yeah, I absolutely agree with General Odierno on this. And absolutely, these gentlemen are affected by—are certainly under the influence of Iran. These were people, or in the case of Chalabi, he was named by the CPA administrator, Ambassador Bremer, back in '03 as the head of the de-Baathification Committee. It was a committee that went out of existence two years ago, replaced by the Accountability and Justice Committee. Everyone else understood that they—that that would—that their terms expired with the expiration of the committee, except for Mr. Chalabi, who assumed by himself the role of maintaining his—a position in a new committee to which he was never named.

There are two problems with the way Odierno and Hill address the Lami/Chalabi dimension. Firstly, they tend to isolate these two persons from the wider political alliance in which they take part—the Iraqi National Alliance, which was constructed in Iran in May 2009 with Chalabi as a key mediator between the Sadrists and ISCI, and which includes other old friends of Washington like Adil Abd al-Mahdi and Ammar al-Hakim. Hence to reduce the Iranian influence in Iraq to two individuals involves a severe underestimation. Secondly, the comments by Odierno and Hill merely express frustration of the most impotent kind; they are not using the dubious activities of Lami/Chalabi to create leverage with respect to the democratic quality of the upcoming elections by outlining what will follow if the elections are fraudulent.

The issue of de-Baathification was—came up in the context of the actual election process being underway. It became a very emotionally charged issue. I think Americans need to understand that if you're an Iraqi, very few people are indifferent to the issue of de-Baathification. After all Baathists pretty much destroyed that country, destroyed many families, destroyed many hopes in Iraq. So understandably, people are very concerned about ensuring that there is—that Article 7 of the constitution is lived up to and that there is action against Baathists.

In this paragraph, Hill actually goes as far as embracing the jurisprudence of Ahmad Chalabi. The idea of using article 7 of the constitution to exclude candidates from the elections is flawed—primarily because the law supposed to implement it has never been passed and secondarily because the article also covers sectarianism and racism which, if made applicable, would raise the question of a host of possible exclusions including key Shiite Islamist and Kurdish parties. A query by Ayad al-Samarraie to the higher judicial council concerning the legality of article 7 exclusions is still pending; hopefully someone will follow through on this since there is no way the de-Baathification board can get around this issue if an attempt is made to address it in a purely legal way.

I met with the sheikhs in Anbar who are, by and large, Sunni sheikhs. I met with other sheikhs in—tribal sheikhs in Baghdad. I had them over to my home for lunch. And the Sunni tribal sheikhs all said that they are very much in a get-out-the-vote mood. So we do not have a problem as of now in terms of Sunni nonparticipation.

And Vice-President Joe Biden once met with "Sunni sheikhs" who believed in a Sunni federal region "in their hearts" but dared not say so publicly…

AMBASSADOR HILL: Well, I think there are political reconciliation issues across the board. I mean, it is—I think it's something that we try to be helpful with the Iraqis. But I think increasingly we're seeing the Iraqis try to deal with these issues. And to see how the— some of the Shiite parties reached out to the Sunni during the election law issue, where we had Shiite and Sunni in the same room working on the law—in fact, working off the same piece of paper and trying to make adjustments on that piece of paper, showed that the election process, difficult as it is, is making people work together. So I think that—I think elections, if they're well done, can be a source of political reconciliation.

You had Sunnis (Tawafuq) working with the Shiites in 2005 as well. The problem is, as long as they work within the confines of narrow sectarian frameworks this will be theater by figureheads instead of sustainable national reconciliation.

More generally speaking, the remarks by Ambassador Hill seem to indicate refusal by Washington to challenge Chalabi and Lami in a meaningful way beyond a little public bluster. That kind of attitude will lead many Iraqis to once more revert to the widespread conspiracy theory to the effect that the U.S. is using their country as a giant dangling carrot in its dealings with Iran, searching for a great bargain or *safqa* instead of having Iraqi reconciliation issues as a number one priority. Depressing as that scenario is, it might at least help Iraqiyya make a decision on participation: More than ever before it seems clear that no support from the international community is likely to materialize; only a massive voter turnout on 7 March can now reverse the negative trend in Iraq and prevent the country from falling prey to rapacious regional forces.

The UN Security Council, UNAMI and the Yazidi Paradigm in Iraq[9]
August 4, 2010

Some serious problems are buried in the small print of today's report by the UNAMI special representative of the secretary-general in Iraq to the UN Security Council. The main part of the report is unremarkable: In predictable fashion it glosses over several of the shortcomings of the 7 March elections and ends up recommending an "inclusive and broadly participatory" government-formation process. But the section on "human rights" has flagged some interesting items that should serve as an indication to the Iraqis about what sort of assistance they can really hope to get from the international community. This part of the report contains several striking items, among them a congratulation to the Kurdish regional authorities for establishing an "independent board of human rights" coupled with a failure to elaborate on why the local elections in that region that were supposed to take place in 2009 have just been postponed until 2011. But by far the most remarkable entry is the following one: "In a further positive development, on 14 June the Iraqi Federal Court passed a ruling increasing the number of seats in the Council of Representatives for the Yezidi minority group in proportion to their population in accordance with the figures from the last national census".

Many Iraqis will fail to see the positive aspect of this much-overlooked ruling by the federal supreme council. For one thing, it is the latest in a string of partially contradictive rulings by the court on the use of minority quotas in the Iraqi political system. First, in a ruling on 20 July 2009 the court (wisely) struck down a proposal to subdivide the electoral constituency of Kirkuk into purely ethnic districts (Arab, Turkmen, Kurds) on the grounds that it would constitute racism and that the constitutional requirement of 1 parliamentary representative for 100,000 Iraqis was geographically based and had nothing to do with ethno-sectarian subdivisions. But the latest ruling made on 14 June—the "milestone" flagged by UNAMI— features instructions to the Iraqi parliament to adjust upwards the number of seats for the minority of Yazidis ahead of the 2014 elections with a reference to population data that show some 200,000 Yazidis already back at the time of the previous census (1997).

This will play well in the international community, where typically the situation of minorities attracts headlines far more easily than less dramatic bread and butter issues. But what are the consequences for Iraq? As is well known, the demarcation of ethno-sectarian groups in northern Iraq is a messy business, with the groups themselves often disagreeing on the criteria for self-definition. For example, some Christians believe they are a religious minority whereas other think they are "ethnic Assyrians"; similarly the Kurds try to convince Yazidis and Shabak that they are Kurds whereas many members of these groups virulently oppose Kurdish overlordship, partly on the basis of religious tenets (the Yazidis have their own religion and the Shabak are Shiites), and partly with reference to language. Ironically, because of the Kurdish attempts to dominate these groups indirectly by installing pro-Kurdish leaders among them, it is the Kurds and their clients that have spearheaded the quest for more "minority seats" in order to populate them with pro-Kurdish placemen—the very demand to which the federal supreme court has now yielded, and which UNAMI applauds before the Security Council. (It deserves mention that UNAMI and the Kurds and ISCI tried the same trick during the revision of the election law in 2008 but were trumped by what was then known as the 22 July group of Iraqi nationalist parties.)

So the question is what will follow next. By linking the criteria of numerical representation (1 to 100,000) to the level of minority groups for the first time (previously minority representation had a less mathematical, negotiated basis), the federal court, with the support of UNAMI, could be opening a can of worms where a far greater number of Iraqis may feel tempted to seek recognition according to ethno-religious criteria. If the Yazidis can, why not the Turkmens or the Kurds?

This, in other words, is what the UN Security Council has in store for the Iraqis: More Paul Bremer logics, where the Iraqi population is carefully calculated according to ethno-sectarian criteria and then given their proper share. It is the perfect way of legitimizing and perpetuating a neo-imperial approach: The Iraqis are seen as a primitive people forever locked in ancient communitarian hatreds above which they can rise only with the benevolent assistance of Western diplomats. It is a kind of epistemology that went out of fashion in academia somewhere in the early twentieth century, but in the UN Security Council it is apparently still taken seriously. Tomorrow, after the ongoing consultations, UNAMI is likely to have its mandate renewed for another year. That will probably not lead to a "salvation government", as some Iraqi newspapers had speculated, but the Yazidi paradigm will remain, almost unnoticed.

CHAPTER NOTES

1 The original version of this text can be found at http://historiae.org/surge.asp.

2 See http://www.jamestown.org/single/?no_cache=1&tx_ttnews[tt_news]=4396.

3 See http://gulfanalysis.wordpress.com/2008/08/21/the-usg-formally-embraces-the-minority-view-in-the-kirkuk-question/.

4 See http://gulfanalysis.wordpress.com/2009/09/09/malikis-northern-headache-and-how-general-odierno-is-compounding-it/.

5 See http://gulfanalysis.wordpress.com/2009/10/05/joint-patrols-and-power-sharing-in-mosul-unbalanced-proposals-from-the-international-crisis-group/.

6 http://gulfanalysis.wordpress.com/2009/10/28/what-exactly-is-unami-up-to-in-baghdad/.

7 On 29 October 2009, IHEC suddenly announced that the registers for 2004 had been "lost".

8 See http://gulfanalysis.wordpress.com/2010/02/21/ambassador-hill-and-the-decision-by-iraqiyya/.

9 See http://gulfanalysis.wordpress.com/2010/08/04/the-un-security-council-unami-and-the-yazidi-paradigm-in-iraq/.

Glossary and Acronyms

Glossary

amir: A prince, also occasionally used about very noble tribal chiefs.

Badr, or **Badr brigades:** Paramilitary forces loyal to ISCI/SCIRI.

fatwa: A legal ruling in Islam.

iqlim: A federal region.

intifada: An uprising.

kutla: A bloc in parliament.

marja or **marja al-taqlid:** "Source of emulation." In Shiism, a living cleric used as point of reference by the believers.

marjaiyya: The interpretive authority and spiritual leadership associated with a *marja*; also sometimes used for *marja*s (*maraji* in Arabic) as a collectivity.

muhafaza: A "governorate" or province, the former being the standard English translation in Iraq since the days of the monarchy.

muhasasa: Quota sharing in a spoils system, often on an ethnic or sectarian basis.

mujtahid: A Shiite cleric with the authority to issue *fatwas*.

Peshmerga: Kurdish militia forces.

Sahwa: "Awakening." Name given to the generally anti–al-Qaida paramilitary forces that arose in Iraq (mainly, northern Iraq) from 2006 on, with much financial help from the United States.

sayyid: A descendant of the Prophet, venerated by Shiites but without any religious authority as such.

ulama: The Islamic clergy.

vilayet: A province in the Ottoman Empire.

wilayat al-faqih: "The rule of the jurisprudent." The system of government implemented in Iran after the Islamic revolution.

Acronyms

CPA: Coalition Provisional Authority, U.S. administration in charge of Iraq, 2003–2004.

DN: *Dagens Næringsliv*, a Norwegian financial newspaper.

DNO: Det norske oljeselskap, a Norwegian oil company.

ICG: International Crisis Group.

IED: Improvised explosive device.

IHEC: Independent Higher Election Commission in Iraq.

IIP: Iraqi Islamic Party, a Sunni Islamist party.

INA: Iraqi National Alliance, an all-Shiite alliance.

INM: The Iraqi National Movement, the nucleus of the secular Iraqiyya list.

INC: Iraqi National Congress, an anti-Baathist movement founded in the 1990s and associated with Ahmad Chalabi.

ISCI: The Islamic Supreme Council of Iraq, a Shiite Islamist movement previously known as SCIRI. ISCI is the official abbreviation; "SIIC" is sometimes used but is rejected by ISCI itself.

KA: Kurdistan Alliance, an electoral alliance between the KDP and the PUK.

KDP: The Kurdistan Democratic Party, long associated with the Barzani family.

KRG: The Kurdistan Regional Government.

PUK: Patriotic Union of Kurdistan, long associated with the Talabani family.

SCIRI: The Supreme Council for the Islamic Revolution in Iraq, an all-Shiite party formed in Iran in 1982. It changed its name to ISCI in May 2007.

SLA: State of Law Alliance, the electoral list of Prime Minister Nuri al-Maliki.

SOC: South Oil Company.

SOFA: Status of Forces Agreement.

TAL: Transitional Administrative Law. The TAL was proposed and promulgated in early 2004 by the Coalition Provisional Authority and given a rubber stamp by a group of Iraqi politicians.

UIA: United Iraqi Alliance, an all-Shiite coalition formed in 2004.

UNAMI: United Nations Assistance Mission in Iraq.

USIP: United States Institute of Peace.

Bibliography of Relevant Academic Works by the Author

Books

Basra, the Failed Gulf State: Separatism and Nationalism in Southern Iraq. Berlin: Lit Verlag, 2005/New Brunswick: Transaction, 2006.

An Iraq of Its Regions: Cornerstones of a Federal Democracy? Edited with Gareth Stansfield. London: Hurst, New York: Columbia University Press, 2007.

Shi'at al-'iraq: judhur al-haraka al-fidiraliyya [The Shiites of Iraq: Roots of the Federalist Movement]. Baghdad/Beirut/Arbil: Ma'had al-Dirasat al-Istratijiyya, 2007.

Al-basra wa hulm al-jumhuriyya al-khalijiyya. Hudud al-infisaliyya al-janubiyya wa-manabi' al-wataniyya al-'iraqiyya [Basra and the Dream of a Gulf Republic: Limits to Southern Separatism and the Roots of Iraqi Nationalism], Berlin/Beirut: Al-Jamal, 2007.

Chapters in books

"Shi'i Perspectives on a Federal Iraq: Territory, Community and Ideology in Conceptions of a New Polity", in Daniel Heradstveit and Helge Hveem, *Oil in the Gulf: Obstacles to Democracy and Development.* Aldershot: Ashgate, 2004.

"The Surge, the Leap, and the Great Fall: Sectarianism and Nationalism during the Al-Maliki Government, 2006–2010", in *Volatile Landscape: Iraq and Its Insurgent Movements.* Washington D.C.: Jamestown Foundation, 2010.

Journal articles

"Basra, the Reluctant Seat of Shiastan", *Middle East Report* no. 242 (spring 2007).

"The Surge, the Shiites and Nation Building in Iraq", *Terrorism Monitor* vol. 5, no. 17 (September 2007).

"Ethnicity, Federalism and the Idea of Sectarian Citizenship in Iraq", *International Review of the Red Cross* 89, no. 868 (2007): 809–822.

"Historical Myths of a Divided Iraq", *Survival* 50, no. 2 (2008): 95–106.

"The Western Imposition of Sectarianism on Iraqi Politics", *Arab Studies Journal* 16, no. 1, (2008): 83–99.

"Taming the Hegemonic Power: SCIRI and the Evolution of US Policy in Iraq", *International Journal of Contemporary Iraqi Studies* 2, no. 1 (2008): 31–51.

"New Non-State Players and Implications for Regional Security: The Case of the Shiite Religious Establishment of Iraq", *SAIS Review* (autumn 2009).

"Proto-Political Conceptions of 'Iraq' in Late Ottoman Times", *International Journal of Contemporary Iraqi Studies* (autumn 2009).

"The Kurdish Issue in Iraq: A View from Baghdad at the Close of the Maliki Premiership", *The Fletcher Forum of World Affairs* 34, no. 1 (2010).

"Iraq Moves Backwards", *Middle East Report* no. 255 (summer 2010).

"Tribalism in Iraq: Resurgent Force or Anachronism?" *Contemporary Arab Affairs,* vol. 3 no. 4, 2010.

Reports and working papers

"Shi'i Separatism in Iraq: Internet Reverie or Real Constitutional Challenge?" *NUPI Paper* no. 686, August 2005, www.historiae.org/shiseparatism.asp.

"Sistani, The United States and Politics in Iraq: From Quietism to Machiavellianism?" *NUPI Paper* no. 700, March 2006, www.historiae.org/sistani.asp.

"Basra Crude: The Great Game of Iraq's 'Southern' Oil", *NUPI Paper* no. 723, 2007, www.historiae.org/oil.asp.

"Iran's Role in Post-Occupation Iraq: Enemy, Good Neighbor or Overlord?" *Century Foundation Report*, March 2009, http://www.tcf.org/publications/internationalaffairs/Visser.pdf.

"More than Shiites and Sunnis: Post-Sectarian Strategies for Iraq" (with Hassan al-Bazzaz et al.), NUPI, March 2009.

Academic conference papers

"Melting Pot of the Gulf? Cosmopolitanism and Its Limits in the Experience of Basra's British Community, 1890–1940", paper presented to the Global Gulf Conference, University of Exeter, July 2006.

"Federalism From Below in Iraq: Some Historical Reflections", paper presented to an international workshop on "Iraq after the New Government", Como, Italy, November 2006.

"A Rigid Conception of Britishness: Imperialism, Local Regionalism and Transnational Links among the British of Basra and Abadan, 1890–1940, paper presented to the British World Conference, Bristol, July 2007.

"Suffering, Oil, and Ideals of Coexistence: Non-Sectarian Federal Trends in the Far South of Iraq", MESA, Montreal, November 2007.

"The Sadrists Between Mahdism, Neo-Akhbarism and Usuli Orthodoxy: Examples from Southern Iraq", University of Glasgow, 25 April 2008.

"Social Complexity and National Identity in Hanna Batatu's Scholarship on Iraq", Georgetown University, Washington, D.C., 28 October 2008.

"The Sectarian Master Narrative in Iraqi Historiography: New Challenges since 2003", IHEID, Geneva, 6 November 2008.

"The Tribes of Southern Iraq: Resurgent Force or Anachronism in the Modern State? The Case of the Banu Malik", MESA 2008, Washington, D.C., 21 November 2008.

"Towards a 'Shiite Crescent' Incorporating Iraq? A Re-Examination of the Historical Evidence", ISA 2009, New York, 16 February 2009.

"Sectarian Coexistence in Iraq: The Experiences of Shiites in Areas North of Baghdad", Center for Islamic Shi'a Studies, London, 19 February 2009.

"The Shiite–Sunni Divide and the Question of State Structure in Iraq since 2003", Brussels, Palace of the Academies, October 2009.

"From Sharifian Officers to Bremerian Councillors: Political Elites and the Introduction of Federalism and Power-Sharing in Iraq since 2003", Bloomington, Ind., 13 November 2009.

"On the Margins of the Hawza: The Shaykhis and the Akhbaris of Basra and Their Relationships with the Shiite Centres of Learning", Royal Holloway College, London, 30 March 2010.

Acknowledgments

It is a special pleasure to publish this work with Just World Books, founded by Helena Cobban, to whom I owe a lot. I met Helena in 2005, on the internet of course. Back then, I had just created a website devoted to the politics of southern Iraq and was desperately trying to attract the attention of more readers to share my unorthodox views on Shiite politics—including my diehard, if somewhat lonely contention that despite what the U.S. media said, Abd al-Aziz al-Hakim was *not* the most powerful politician in Iraq. After I had posted a link to one of my own posts in the comments section on Helena's lively Just World News blog just before Christmas that year, she responded in the generous way that is characteristic of many bloggers: Within 24 hours, she had published a separate post analyzing and linking to my article! This generated a stream of new readers and subscribers to my website and gradually, my "complexity" argument on the Shiites of Iraq began winning more adherents, eventually even among some of those mainstream media journalists in Baghdad whose work I had been criticizing.

Obviously, to a large extent, it is the technology of the internet that helps empower counter-narratives of this kind in a way that was never possible in the age of the print media. On the internet, ideas move a million times faster than they used to, making it easier than ever before to challenge established paradigms and stale categories of analysis. But without fellow bloggers, commentators, and readers, none of this would have been possible. I am grateful to all my website subscribers during the past five years, starting with my dad (who was the first) and ending with number 3,000, who just recently signed up. I feel a particular sense of gratitude to readers who use the internet interactively and take time to share their own insights in discussions online. But over and above all, I would like to thank the Iraqis who read my work and comment on it. No compliment has meant more to me during these years than the fact of having an Iraqi readership.

Collecting and curating five years' worth of blogging for the Just World Books series has been a challenge but also a lot of fun. In addition to Helena, I would like to thank Jane Sickon and the rest of the staff at Just World Books for an impressive turnaround. Even though this is hard-copy publication and not cyberspace, it's not lagging much behind!